For the Glory

THE LIFE OF ERIC LIDDELL

www.**transworldbooks**.co.uk

For the Glory

The Life of Eric Liddell

Duncan Hamilton

Doubleday

LONDON · TORONTO · SYDNEY · AUCKLAND · JOHANNESBURG

TRANSWORLD PUBLISHERS
61–63 Uxbridge Road, London W5 5SA
www.transworldbooks.co.uk

Transworld is part of the Penguin Random House group of companies
whose addresses can be found at global.penguinrandomhouse.com

Penguin
Random House
UK

First published in Great Britain in 2016 by Doubleday
an imprint of Transworld Publishers

A CIP catalogue record for this book
is available from the British Library.

ISBNs 9780857522597 (cased)
9780857522603 (tpb)

Typeset in 11¼/14pt Minion Pro by Falcon Oast Graphic Art Ltd.
Printed and bound by Clays Ltd, Bungay, Suffolk.

Penguin Random House is committed to a sustainable
future for our business, our readers and our planet. This book
is made from Forest Stewardship Council® certified paper.

MIX
Paper from
responsible sources
FSC® C018179

1 3 5 7 9 10 8 6 4 2

In memory of Florence Liddell.
Some wife. Some mother. Some woman.

Contents

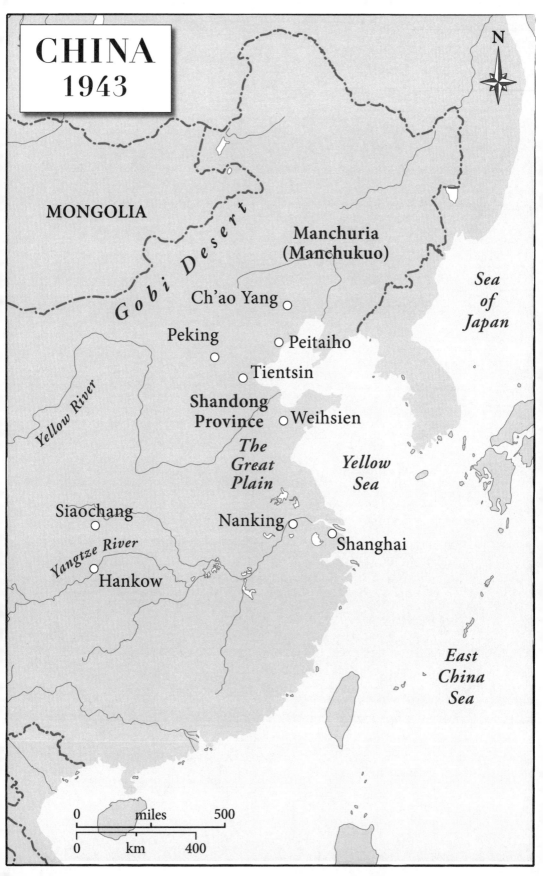

N

CHINA
1943

MONGOLIA

Gobi Desert

Manchuria
(Manchukuo)

Ch'ao Yang ○

Peking
○

○ Peitaiho

○ Tientsin

Shandong
Province

○ Weihsien

*The
Great
Plain*

*Yellow
River*

*Yellow
Sea*

Siaochang
○

Nanking ○

○ Shanghai

Yangtze River

Hankow
○

Sea
of
Japan

East
China
Sea

0   miles   500

0   km   400

The Last Race of the Champion

Weihsien, Shandong Province, China

1944

HE IS CROUCHING ON the start line, which has been scratched out with a stick across the parched earth. His upper body is thrust slightly forward and his arms are bent at the elbow. His left leg is planted ahead of the right, the heels of both raised slightly in preparation for a springy launch.

Exactly two decades earlier he had won his Olympic title in the hot, shallow bowl of Paris's Colombes Stadium. Afterwards, the crowd in the yellow-painted grandstands gave him the longest and loudest ovation of those Games. What inspired them was not only his roaring performance, but also the element of sacrificial romance wound into his personal story, which unfolded in front of them like the plot of some thunderous novel.

Now, trapped in a Japanese prisoner of war camp, the internees have teemed out of the low dormitories and the camp's bell tower to line the route of the makeshift course to see Eric Liddell again. Even the guards in the watchtowers peer down eagerly at the scene.

In Paris, Liddell ran on a track of crimson cinder. In Weihsien, he will compete along dusty pathways which the prisoners have named to remind them nostalgically of faraway home: Main Street, Sunset Boulevard, Tin Pan Alley.

Liddell claimed his gold medal in a snow-white singlet, his country's flag across his chest. Here he wears a shirt cut from patterned kitchen curtains, baggy khaki shorts, which are grubby and drop to the knee, and a pair of grey canvas 'spikes', almost identical to those he'd used during the Olympics.

As surreal as it may seem, 'Sports Days' such as this one are an established feature of the camp. For the internees, it is a way of forgetting – for a few hours at least – the reality of incarceration; one prisoner wistfully calls each of these days 'a speck of glitter amid the dull monotony'.

Even though he is over forty years old, practically bald and pitifully thin, Liddell is the marquee attraction. Those who don't run want to watch him. Those who do want to beat him.

Though spread over 60,000 square miles, the coastal province of Shandong, tucked into the eastern edge of China's north plain, looks minuscule on maps of that immense country. Weihsien is barely a pencil dot within Shandong. And the camp itself is merely a speck within that – a roll of land of approximately 3 acres, roughly the size of two football pitches. Caught in both the vastness of China and also the grim mechanism of the Second World War, which seems without respite let alone end, the internees had begun to think of themselves as forsaken.

Until the Red Cross at last got food parcels to them in July, there were those who feared the slow, slow death of starvation. Weight fell off everyone. Some lost 15lb or more, including Liddell. He dropped from 160lb to around 130. Others, noticeably corpulent on entering Weihsien, shed over 80lb and looked like lost souls in worn clothes. Morale sagged, a black depression ringing the camp as high as its walls.

Those parcels meant life. While hunger stalked the camp, no one had the fuel or the inclination to run. This race is a celebration, allowing the internees to express their relief at finally being fed.

Liddell shouldn't be running in it.

Ever since late spring cum early summer he's felt weary and strangely disconnected. His walk has slowed. His speech has slowed too. He's begun to do things ponderously and is sleeping only fitfully, the tiredness burrowing into his bones. He is stoop-shouldered. Mild dizzy spells cloud some of his days. Sometimes his vision is blurred. Though desperately sick, he casually dismisses his symptoms as 'nothing to worry about', blaming them on overwork.

Throughout the eighteen months he's already spent in Weihsien, Liddell has been a reassuring presence, always representing hope. He has toiled as if attempting to prove that perpetual motion is actually possible. He rises before dawn and labours until curfew at 10 p.m. Liddell is always doing something; and always doing it for others rather than for himself. He scrabbles for coal, which he carries in metal pails. He chops wood and totes bulky flour sacks. He cooks in the kitchens. He cleans and sweeps. He repairs whatever needs fixing. He teaches science to the children and teenagers of the camp and coaches them in sport too. He counsels and consoles the adults, who bring him their worries. Every Sunday he preaches in the church. Even when he works the hardest, Liddell still apologizes for not working hard enough.

The internees are so accustomed to his industriousness that no one pays much attention to it any more; familiarity has allowed the camp to take both it and him a little for granted.

Since Liddell first became public property – always walking in the arc-light of fame – wherever he has gone and whatever he has done has been brightly illuminated. The son of Scots missionaries born, shortly after the twentieth century began, in the port of Tientsin. The sprinter whose locomotive speed inspired newspapers to call him 'The Flying Scotsman'. The devout Christian who preached in congregational churches and meeting halls about scripture, temperance, morality and Sunday obser-vance. The Olympic champion who abandoned the track for the sake of his religious calling in China. The husband who booked boat passages for his pregnant wife and two infant daughters to enable them to escape the torment he was enduring in Weihsien. The father who had never met his third child, born without him at her bedside. The friend and col-league, so humbly modest, who treated everyone equally.

The internees assume nothing will harm such a good man, especially someone who is giving so much to them. And none of them has regis-tered his deteriorating physical condition because he and everyone else around him look too much alike to make his illness conspicuous.

Anyone else would find an excuse not to race. Liddell, however, doesn't have it in him to back out. He is too conscientious. The camp expects him to compete, and he won't let them down, however much the effort drains him and however shaky his legs feel. He is playing along with his role as Weihsien's breezy optimist, a front concealing his distress. Every few weeks he merely slits a new notch-hole into the leather of his black belt and then pulls it tightly around his ever-shrinking waistline.

Liddell makes only one concession. Previously he has been scrupulously fair about levelling the field. He's always started several yards behind the other runners, giving them an outside chance of beating him. This time there is no such handicap for him. That alone should alert everyone to the fact that he is ailing.

Liddell says nothing about it. Instead, he takes his place, without pause or protest, in a pack of a dozen other runners, his eyes fixed on nothing but the narrow strip of land that constitutes the front straight.

The starter climbs on to an upturned packing crate, holding a white handkerchief aloft in his right hand. And then he barks out the three words Liddell has heard countless times in countless places.

'Ready . . . set . . . go!'

Weifang, Shandong Province, China

Present Day

He is waiting for me at the main gate on Guang-Wen Street.

He is dressed smartly and formally: white shirt, dark tie and an even darker suit, the lapels wide and well cut. He looks like someone about to make a speech or take a business meeting.

His blond hair is impeccably combed back, revealing high widow's peaks. There's the beginning of a smile on his slender lips, as if he knows a secret the rest of us don't and is about to share it. Barely a wrinkle or a crease blemishes his pale skin, and his eyes are brightly alert. He is a handsome, eager fellow, still blazing with life.

On this warm spring morning, I am looking directly into Eric Liddell's face.

He's preserved in his absolute pomp, his photograph pressed on to a big square of metal. It is attached to an iron pole as tall as a lamp post. This is Communist homage to a Christian, a man China regards with paternal pride as its first Olympic champion. In Chinese eyes, he is a true son of their country; he belongs to no one else.

A study in concentration. Eric Liddell's studio portrait taken during the mid-1920s.

More than seventy years have passed since Liddell came here. He's never gone home. He's never grown old.

The place he knew as Weihsien is now called Weifang, the landscape unimaginably different. Liddell arrived on a flat-bed truck. He saw nothing but a huge chequerboard of field-crops stretching to the black line of the horizon. Narrow dirt roads, along which horse-drawn carts rattled on wooden wheels, linked one flyspeck village to another. Each was primitively rural.

I arrived on the sleek-nosed G-train from Beijing, a distance of 300 miles covered in three rushing hours. What I saw were power stations with soot-lipped cooling towers, acres of coal spread around them like an oil slick, and the blackened, belching chimneys of factories. The city that needs this industrial muscle is the epitome of skyscraper modernity, a gleaming example of the new China built out of concrete and glass, steel and neon. Skeletal cranes are everywhere, always creating something taller than before. These structures climb into a sky smothered in smog, the sun glimpsed only as a shadowed shape behind it.

Guang-Wen Street is the bridge between this era and Liddell's.

When he arrived in 1943, the locals, living as though Time had stopped a century before, parked hand-held barrows on whichever pitch suited them and bartered over home-grown vegetables, bolts of cloth and tin pots and plates. Today's traders, setting up canvas stalls, sell iron-mongery and replica sports shirts, framed watercolours and tapestries, electrical gadgetry and a miscellany of ornamental kitsch. There's a pudgy, middle-aged man with tobacco-stained teeth who tips pocket cameras and mobile phones from a black bin liner. Next to him another man, balding and gut-heavy, is peddling blood-red Manchester United shirts, Chicago Bulls vests and an unsteady stack of New York Yankees peaked caps. There's also a stooped-shouldered woman with pitted skin who looks ancient enough to remember the Boxer Rebellion. She drapes bolts of coloured silk across outstretched arms, bowing her head at each polite refusal to inspect them. Her neighbour offers the most surreal sight of all. Wearing tangerine-coloured training shoes and a sleeveless black cocktail dress, like a semi-stylish Holly Golightly, she holds aloft pendants and chain-link bracelets. Her fingers, the false scarlet nails tapered into talons, are decorated with broad gold rings.

At one end of Guang-Wen Street is an office high-rise with tinted windows. At the other is the People's Hospital, its facade whiter than a doctor's house coat.

What counts, however, is the plot of biscuit-brown land between them. Number Two Middle School is a motley assortment of low, dull structures which look anachronistic and architecturally out of kilter with everything nearby.

The camp once stood here.

The buildings familiar to Liddell were bulldozed long ago. Gone is the whitewashed church. Gone is the bell tower and the rows of dormitories. Gone also are the watchtowers with arrow-slit windows and conical tops, like a Chinese peasant's hat.

The Japanese called it a 'Civilian Assembly Centre', a euphemism offering the flimsiest camouflage to the harsh truth. A United Nations of men, women and children were prisoners alongside Liddell rather than comfy guests of the Emperor Hirohito. There were Americans and Australians, South Americans and South Africans, Russians and Greeks,

Dutch and Belgians and British, Scandinavians and Swiss and Filipinos. Among the nationalities were disparate strata of society: merchant bankers, entrepreneurs, boardroom businessmen, solicitors, architects, teachers and government officials. There were also drug addicts, alcoholics, prostitutes and thieves, who co-existed beside monks and nuns and missionaries, such as Liddell.

Weihsien housed more than 2,100 internees during a period of two and a half years. At its terrible zenith, between 1,600 and 1,800 were shut into it at once.

The place already had a past. It had previously been an American Presbyterian mission. Born there was the Nobel laureate Pearl S. Buck, who wrote the Pulitzer Prize-winning novel *The Good Earth*, which made China less mysterious to the millions who read it in the 1930s. Henry Luce, founder of *Time* and father of its subsequent empire, lived within the compound as a boy. The Chinese had christened it Le Dao Yuan – Courtyard of the Happy Way. The Japanese left the phrase chiselled across the lintel of the grand entrance, as though mocking those forced to pass beneath it. Awaiting them to deter disobedience or escape were armed guards, some with German Shepherd dogs on chain leads, and an electric fence. A trench, dug 6 feet deep, came next.

A man's labour can become his identity; Liddell testifies to that. Before internment, he worked in perilous outposts in China, dodging bullets and shells and always wary of the knife-blade. After it, he dedicated himself to everyone around him, as though it were his responsibility alone to imbue the hardships and degradations there with a proper purpose and make the long days bearable.

The short history of the camp emphasizes the impossibility of Liddell's task. In the beginning it was filthy and insanitary, the pathways strewn with debris and the living quarters squalid. The claustrophobic conditions brought predictable consequences. There were verbal squabbles, sometimes flaring into physical fights, over the meagre portions at mealtimes and also the question of who was in front of whom in the queue to receive them. There were disagreements, also frequently violent, over privacy and personal habits and hygiene as well as perceived idleness, selfishness and pilfering.

Liddell was different. He overlooked the imperfections of character that beset even the best of us, doing so with a gentlemanly charm.

With infinite patience, he also gave special attention to the young, who affectionately called him 'Uncle Eric'. He played chess with them. He built model boats for them. He fizzed with ideas, also arranging entertainments and sport, particularly softball and baseball which were staged on a miniature diamond bare of grass.

Sceptical questions are always going to be asked when someone is portrayed without apparent faults and also as the possessor of standards that appear so idealized and far-fetched to the rest of us. Liddell can sound too virtuous and too honourable to be true, as if those who knew him were either misremembering or consciously mythologizing. Not so. The evidence is too overwhelming to be dismissed as easily as that. Amid the myriad moral dilemmas in Weihsien, Liddell's forbearance was remarkable. No one could recall a solitary act of envy, pettiness, hubris or self-aggrandizement from him. He bad-mouthed nobody. He didn't bicker. He lived daily by the most unselfish credo, which was to help others practically and emotionally.

Liddell became the camp's conscience without ever being pious, sanctimonious or judgemental. He forced his religion on no one. He didn't expect others to share his beliefs, let alone live up to them. In his church sermons, and also during weekly scripture classes, Liddell didn't preach grandiloquently. He did so conversationally, as if chatting over a picket fence, and those who heard him thought this gave his messages a solemn power that the louder, look-at-me sermonizers could never achieve. 'You came away from his meetings as if you'd been given a dose of goodness,' said one member of the camp congregation. 'Everyone regarded him as a friend,' said another, giving voice to that unanimous verdict. Someone else saw an enigmatic side to him amid all this subjugation of the self. Aware of how ably he disguised his own feelings, she thought him 'elusive'. She pondered what Liddell was really 'thinking about when he wasn't speaking', which implies how much anguish he bottled up and hid away to serve everyone else's needs.

One internee spoke about Liddell as though Chaucer's selfless and chivalrous 'verray parfit gentil knight' had been made flesh. 'You knew you were in the presence of someone so thoroughly pure,' he explained. A second put it better, saying simply, as if Liddell were only a step or two from beatification: 'It is rare indeed when a person has the good fortune to meet a saint. He came as close to it as anyone I have ever known.'

In his own way, Liddell proved that heroism in war exists beyond churned-up battlefields. His heroism was to be utterly forgiving in the most unforgiving of circumstances.

Of course, most of the world sees a different Eric Liddell. It frames him running across a screen, the composer Vangelis's synthesized soundtrack accompanying every stride. The images, the music, the man and what he achieved in the Olympics in 1924 are familiar to us because cinema made them so.

We know that Liddell, then a twenty-two-year-old Edinburgh University student and already one of the fastest sprinters in the world, believed so strongly in the sanctity of the Sabbath that he sacrificed his chance to win the 100 metres. We know the early heats of that event were staged on a Sunday. We know that Liddell refused to run in them, leaving a gap that his British contemporary Harold Abrahams exploited. We know that Liddell resisted intense pressure – from the public, from his fellow Olympians and from the British Olympic Association – to betray his conscience and change his mind about Sunday competition. We know that he entered the 400 metres, a distance he'd competed in only ten times before. And we know that, against formidable odds and despite the predictions of gloomy naysayers, he won it with glorious ease.

We know all this because the film *Chariots of Fire* told us so and took four Oscars as a consequence in 1982, including Best Picture.

In it, Liddell claims gold in super-slow-motion; he's then chaired off in front of a raucous crowd. The story has its perfect full stop – tidy and neat and also clinching evidence that cinema does what it must to fulfil its principal purpose, which is to entertain. To achieve it, the first casualty is always historical fact. Fictional contrivances shape anew what actually happened to create a compelling drama. Most of us are smart enough to realize that film-makers who pick history as their subject tinker with the veracity of it. But our perception of an event or of a person still becomes inextricably bound to the image presented to us. So it is with *Chariots of Fire*. So it is with Liddell. We've ceased to see him. We see instead the actor Ian Charleson, who played him so compassionately.

I regard myself as possessing dual nationality. My birthplace was England, not far from where Hadrian built his wall. My other country is Scotland. My father was born there in a village only 2 miles from the site where Robert the Bruce won the Battle of Bannockburn in 1314.

The significance of that date constituted my first history lesson.

In contests between Scotland and England our household always wore tartan. I was brought up on seminal Scots. From architects such as Mackintosh to poets such as Burns and also the writers Scott and Stevenson. From Smith the economist to Hume the philosopher. From the inventors Baird and Bell to the philanthropist Carnegie and the multi-faceted Dr Livingstone.

And then came Liddell too.

I saw *Chariots of Fire* twice in the week of its release from the cheap seats of the local cinema, where the curling blue-veins of others' cigarette smoke and showers of casually flicked ash blurred my view of the film-makers' recreation of 1920s Paris. After Oscar success initiated periodic re-releases, I watched it a third and then a fourth time, never caring then or now about the intentional inaccuracies. On each occasion the price of the ticket reaffirmed one piece of knowledge: the best portrayals of sport are never about the sport itself, but rather the human condition in pursuit of its glories, which is why you can excuse *Chariots of Fire* its intentional inaccuracies. It captures the inherent decency of Liddell. He is much more fascinating and likeable than the relentlessly driven Abrahams, presented as his implacably bitter rival to ratchet up the drama.

Liddell was never fixated on anyone else's form the way Abrahams became fixated about his. Losing in Paris would have mortified Abrahams, probably destructively, because he believed his status was dependent on his running. Liddell was no less competitive. But he saw Abrahams as an adversary rather than as the enemy; and he considered athletics as an addendum to his life rather than his sole reason for living it.

Indeed, there are countless anecdotes of his sportsmanship towards fellow competitors that sound a bit like the brightest boy in class allowing everyone else to copy his homework. In competition he'd lend his trowel, used to dig starting holes, to other runners who lacked one. He once offered to give up the precious inside lane on the track, swapping it with the runner drawn unfavourably on the outside. On a horribly cold afternoon he donated his royal blue university blazer to a rival, freezing in only a singlet and shorts – even though it meant shivering himself. On another occasion he noticed the growing discomfort of an Indian student, utterly ignored before an event. He interrupted his own preparations to seek him out; their conversation went on until the starter

*Harold Abrahams, whom the French newspapers called the
'Cambridge Cannonball'.*

called them both to the line. This was typical of Liddell. He'd engage
anyone he thought was nervous or uncertain, and listen whenever the
inexperienced sought advice on a technical aspect of sprinting. He'd
share what he knew before the bang of the pistol pitted them against
each other. In the dash to the tape, however, Liddell suspended friendship. He was fearsomely focused, the empathy he instinctively felt for
others never slackening his desire to beat them.

    He toiled to become the fastest, testing himself in all sorts of ways.
Through hilly Edinburgh he'd audaciously race against corporation buses
to spice up his training, challenging the driver from the pavement. If a
bus beat him to a traffic light, Liddell would reproach himself for coming
second.

Obscure one moment and a feared title contender the next, he lit up athletics like a flash of sheet-lightning, and did it despite the fact that he was so stylistically unconventional as to be a freak.

We prefer our sporting heroes to possess aesthetic as well as athletic prowess. We want to see poetry and hear the song of the body in their movements, the impeccable coordination of mind and eye and limb that enables the fan in the stand to make this specific claim: that watching sport is akin to watching one of the fine arts. The obvious allusion is to dance, usually ballet. That comparison has been made so often, consequently becoming a cliché. But it never invalidates the legitimacy of the argument – even if those unappreciative of sport struggle to understand the idea. The best dancers are performing athletes and vice versa. And what always stirs us, viscerally, is the beauty that exists within them. Think of Roger Federer whipping a crosscourt backhand past a bewildered opponent. Think of George Best on one of those slalom runs from halfway line to penalty box, the defenders sometimes beaten twice. Think of Viv Richards holding his pose, eyes following the arc and drop of the ball after another six has cracked off his bat. Think of Muhammad Ali doing his shuffle.

Sometimes, though, the ugly duckling wins.

Liddell didn't look like a sprinter before a race started. He was only 5 feet 9 inches, which was considered slightly too short for the distances he ran. In an 11-stone frame, his bull-chest was heavy and his legs were short and thin.

He looked even less like a sprinter when a race got underway.

There was an ungainly frenzy about him. Liddell swayed, rocking like an overloaded express train, and he threw his head well back, as if studying the sky rather than the track. In Scottish colloquialism, this 'heid back' approach became his signature flourish. His arms pumped away furiously and his knee-lift was extravagantly high, like a pantomime horse. The New York Times thought Liddell 'seemed to do everything wrong'. In one cartoon the Daily Mail's celebrated caricaturist Tom Webster sketched Liddell as if he were a rubber contortionist. His body is shaped into a capital S, his head tilted so far backwards that it is almost touching his waist and he can see only where he's been and not where he's going. The caption reads: 'Mr Liddell wins his race by several yards. He could never win by a head because he holds it back too far.' In another cartoon Webster nonetheless highlighted that means, however peculiar, could always be justified by a triumphant end. Liddell, he said, ran a furlong at Stamford Bridge in what seemed to be 'three or four seconds' and 'created a draught that was felt at Wimbledon'. That draught would have swept all the way through the decade and into another Olympics – if he had decided to carry on running.

Liddell broke away from athletics at the peak of his flight. Sportsmen who reach the summit of their sport usually try to cling on there until their fingernails bleed. Well in advance of the Olympics, Liddell had talked of his intention to abdicate gracefully because his real calling was elsewhere. For most of us that would be an easy vow to make before we became somebody – and an even easier one to break after the blandishments and the fancy trimmings of fame seduced us. Liddell never let it happen to him. He had promises to keep. That he kept them then and also subsequently is testament to exceptionally rare qualities in an exceptionally rare individual. Overnight, Liddell could have become one of the richest of 'amateur' sportsmen. But he wouldn't accept offers to write newspaper columns or make public speeches for cash. He wouldn't say yes to prestigious teaching sinecures, refusing the benefits of a smart address and a high salary. He wouldn't endorse products. He wouldn't be flattered into business or banking either. He made only trivial concessions to his celebrity. He allowed his portrait to be painted. He let a gardener name a gladiolus in his honour at the Royal Horticultural Show. In everything else Liddell followed his conscience, choosing to do what was right because to do anything else, he felt, would sully the gift God had given him to run fast.

Chariots of Fire didn't have the room to explain any of this. Nor could it expand on what came afterwards for him. So his final two decades were concertinaed into two sentences – white lettering on a black background. Reading it, rather than having it spoken to you, somehow makes the message more powerful still. It is as bleak as the inscription on a tombstone.

ERIC LIDDELL, MISSIONARY, DIED IN OCCUPIED CHINA AT
THE END OF WORLD WAR II. ALL OF SCOTLAND MOURNED.

That such a gentle man died such an ungentle death here hardly seems possible. At least not today. Spring has dressed everything in blush pink and peach blossom, the flame-red of early hibiscus and also wisteria, which is a swell of livid lake-purple. Sprays of dense bloom waterfall from the branches of trees, run across gables and guttering, fences and trellising. Alive with greenery, lightly drowning the pale paths in leaf shadow, the bigger trees remind me that I am walking exactly where others, including Eric Liddell, walked decades before. With smaller trunks and spindlier branches, these trees bore mute witness to Weihsien's woes.

The Chinese, wanting no one to forget them, have created a museum. The exhibits, preserved in a sepulchral half-light, are mostly enlarged black and white photographs, watercolours and pencil drawings fastened behind glass. Liddell has a commemorative corner to himself. I see him winning a race shortly before the Olympics, his head back as always and his eyes half-closed. I see him on his wedding day, super-smart in morning coat and winged collar. I see the short wooden cross carved for his grave, obscured by overgrown foliage.

The earth that held him during the war holds him still; though no one has known precisely where for more than half a century because the graveyard, located in the Japanese quarters, was cleared and then built over during the period when Shandong Province became more difficult to reach for the non-Chinese. No one can identify the date when his cross was removed and the clearance began either. So, instead of a grave, Liddell now has a monument – an enormous slab of rose granite shipped from the Isle of Mull in the Hebrides.

Standing in front of that monument, I am aware of what no photograph of it can ever convey: its hulking size – 7 feet high and 2½ feet across; how age has weathered it; how the heat of the day warms the granite; how its edge, left deliberately rough and uneven, feels against my hand.

One of my favourite stories about Liddell is also the first ever told about him. He was supposed to have been christened Henry Eric until a family friend stopped his father on the way to register the birth and asked what 'the wee man' was going to be called. The friend gently pointed out that the initials – H. E. L. – were scarcely appropriate for a missionary's offspring, which is why his Christian names were reversed. This comes back to me as I stare at his name. The sun, at last burning a hole through the smog, appears with impeccable timing and makes the gold lettering glow.

The accompanying inscriptions include the quotation from Isaiah, chapter 40, verse 31, that *Chariots of Fire* slipped into its script to cap a pivotal scene: 'They shall run, and not be weary.' A few, scant lines of biography cover the cardinal points of his forty-three years and thirty-seven days: his birth, his Olympic success, his death. The phrase 'fraternal virtues' acknowledges his missionary service.

'Fraternal virtues' isn't the half of it. Everything you need to know about the heart Liddell had – and what he did with it – is contained in one fact.

Every morning in Weihsien, while the camp still slept, he lit a peanut oil lamp in the darkness and prayed for an hour. Every night, after studying the Bible, he prayed again. He did not discriminate. He prayed for everyone, even for his Japanese guards.

How do you pay proper respect to a man as humane as that; a man, moreover, who strove every day for perfection in thought, as well as deed, and whose death engulfed those who knew him in a sadness almost too deep for words? I do the best I can. I place a cellophane-wrapped spray of flowers – gold tiger lilies, white carnations, orange gerbera – on the wide plinth of this grand tower of granite.

When I turn towards the noise and colour of Guang-Wen Street again, I am convinced of one thing above all others. Whoever comes to this corner of China will always leave knowing the full measure of the man who is to be found here.

The place where his faith never broke under the immense weight it bore.

The place where his memory is imperishable.

The place where, even on the edge of death, the champion ran his last race.

Part One

Faster

CHAPTER ONE

How to Become a Great Athlete

THERE WAS AN IMPISH look about him. He was slight and lightly built, barely 5 feet 4 inches tall. The flattish features of his face were disturbed only by the shallow rise of his cheekbones and an upturned chin, leaving a hard crease. His nose was a long blade. His mouth appeared to be nothing more than a slit. His eyes had bags beneath them. In profile he had a blankly stony look, like the countenance of an Easter Island carving.

To strangers Tom McKerchar appeared sternly unapproachable, as if any enquiry might produce a grunt in reply. To those who knew him, however, McKerchar was the opposite – a pleasant and helpful gent who'd pass on his expertise to whoever asked for it politely.

In early 1921 McKerchar was forty-four years old, the father of twelve children. He worked for a printing firm in Edinburgh, where the ink from the commercial presses stuck to the hand the way coal dust clung to the skin of every miner. He began there as a paper ruler and then became a lithographer. Away from the drudgery of clocking on and off, the mainstay of his life was sport. He advised the professional footballers of Heart of Midlothian – once multiple winners of the Scottish League Championship and Scottish FA Cup – and trained amateur athletes in Scotland, including those of the Edinburgh University Athletic Club. The students were expected to take physical excellence as seriously as book-knowledge. In 1887 the university's elders placed the gilt figure of an athlete carrying the Torch of Learning on top of the dome that rose above its Old Quad – a reminder that improvement of the mind shouldn't neglect improvement of the body too.

McKerchar, though never an academic scholar, proved to be the perfect coach for the students. Like most of his working-class generation, raised during the final quarter of Queen Victoria's reign, he'd said goodbye to school at thirteen to bolster the household budget: he'd delivered groceries for pennies. Midnight oil came later for him. From books, and also through empirical testing on the track, McKerchar studied the physiology and psychology of the games-player and the training necessary to make him better. When he began dedicating himself to it, the subject was seldom treated scientifically. To some sportsmen, climbing into an enamel bath swimming in blocks of ice provided the answer to every question about achieving and maintaining fitness and health. The freezing water was supposed to energize the heart and pump the circulation, harden the soles of the feet and tone the muscles. Advocates of this and nothing else were like those doctors from the Middle Ages who slavishly prescribed leeches for every ailment presented to them. Other Victorian and Edwardian theories for sharpening performance seem now like the ravings of cranks, quacks and charlatans. Some believed smoking cleared the lungs and improved breathing capacity. A couple of pints of beer were considered perfectly acceptable too; the bitter hops were reckoned to be strength-giving. Various potions and so-called pick-me-ups also swirled around the market. Among them were Mrs Winslow's Soothing Syrup, which included morphine, a French tonic wine called Vin Mariani, which included cocaine, and Anti-Stiff, a kind of rub-on-all-over embrocation, which included petrolatum. McKerchar was nobody's fool. He didn't fall for these advertisements, never believing the wondrous promises made on the packets.

Athletics meetings during McKerchar's early days pulled in crowds able to gamble openly. Only the Streets Betting Act of 1909 evicted the bookmakers, making considerably poorer some of those who regularly made a cash-killing either by winning or by deliberately losing. Immediately after the Great War, the carnival and social atmosphere of these meetings continued nonetheless because the organizers became more eager than ever to create it. The country was desolate, discontented and in debt. Those who didn't come back from the fighting were later described by the historian A. J. P. Taylor as 'the men of promise born during the eighteen-nineties whose promise was not fulfilled'. Those who did were initially seduced by the catchy, alliterative slogan of 'Homes for Heroes', a glib pledge stirring expectations no government could ever meet. There was anger and a sense of futility when conditions after the war were found to be no better – and often far worse – than those before it. Spectator sport offered escape from all this. So even brass bands blared away to accompany both track and field events to provide more razzmatazz. Sometimes this dissolved into farce. One Edinburgh high jumper, unable to concentrate, had to ask for a particularly brisk, jazzy tune called 'The Hitchy Koo' to stop before attempting to clear the bar. When another band began playing at the very start of a one-mile race, the competitors found it impossible to run because the rhythm of their stride was incompatible with the rhythm of the over-loud military two-step thumping around them; only a 'frantic waving of arms' silenced the music.

The athletes themselves were a sober-looking lot. Shorts were never above the knee. Spikes were always black. T-shirts rather than vests were worn. Instead of today's Lycra, Spandex or shiny, luminous-coloured tracksuits with fancy piping and sponsors' names, the runners draped a double-breasted overcoat over their shoulders like a heavy cape. To combat the north-easterly winds of Edinburgh, woollen gloves and extra-long scarves were vital too. The scarves were wound like cladding and then knotted tightly. Ex-servicemen were conspicuous: each wore a military greatcoat with brass buttons that caught the light like the eyes of a cat.

In the thick of everything, McKerchar was known among the university athletes as a coach who didn't take short-cuts; who didn't tolerate time-wasters, late-comers or shirkers; and who didn't waste sentences for the sake of them, as if wanting to prove that Shakespeare was right to say 'men of few words are the best men'. He also liked to get as close as possible to the action, frequently appearing as a starter for races in which his athletes competed.

He put his faith in proper preparation. It wasn't common for runners to 'limber up' in advance of an event; McKerchar, though, insisted on the procedure. He saw the relationship between himself and the athlete as an equal collaboration of talent and, like the good teacher nursing the promising pupil, he cared about general welfare.

What also set him apart from the pack was an innovative spirit.

Pupil and master. A particularly slim and youthful-looking
Liddell and the dapperly dressed Tom McKerchar.

In the early 1920s, there were coaches who believed the size of the heart and the capacity of the lungs wouldn't allow a human to run a mile in under four minutes. Reaching that mark was as unthinkable to them as the prospect of rocketing to the moon. But McKerchar knew his athletics history. He was not only aware of how athletic performance had evolved, but also appreciated that the athlete of tomorrow – through better nutrition, better sports science, better equipment and technology – would always be fitter and faster than his predecessors. He embraced the future. When massage and physiotherapy were dismissed as crass fads, McKerchar championed them. When the mechanics of coordination could be inspected through sequential photography and slow-motion film – after the photographer Eadweard James Muybridge pioneered them – McKerchar benefited from it, spotting weaknesses in a stride pattern or deficiencies in arm and upper body movement. When new training methods were introduced elsewhere, particularly in Europe, McKerchar adopted them rather than wailing – as a platoon of insular coaches did – that importing them was unnecessary because nothing could possibly trump the superiority of British thinking.

This attitude and approach matched those of two of his contemporaries. The first was the quixotic Sam Mussabini. The second was Alec Nelson. Mussabini was an eccentric, his mind sparking a dozen ideas between breakfast and lunch and then another dozen before supper. Nelson was a different personality, less boisterous and more methodical. He'd been a professional half- and three-quarter-miler before becoming coach at Cambridge University, orchestrating Varsity dominance over Oxford. He had an especially dry humour. His instruction to one less than promising high jumper was the laconic 'Throw your leg over the bar . . . and follow it as soon as possible'.

McKerchar was an 'amateur', sandwiched between these two 'professionals', only insofar as he took no payment. He nonetheless punched equal weight alongside them, and the triumvirate respected one another unequivocally. Tips and gossip were amicably traded and one coach was freely able to offer advice to another's athlete without generating friction.

Eric Liddell always saw them as a trio. 'What these three trainers don't know about getting their charges fit, and telling them how to run their races, isn't worth knowing,' he said. He was convinced nonetheless that timing and geography had serendipitously given him the best of these sages. He called McKerchar 'my friend'. In return McKerchar would call him his 'wonderful boy'.

The admiration began in June 1921.

McKerchar could be found almost every weekday evening at one of Edinburgh's two stadiums, Craiglockhart or Powderhall, where he observed training discreetly and then gave his impressions at the end of the session. Craiglockhart was a spacious expanse of grass, a throwback to the pre-cinder era. The track was lime-marked. The focal point of the arena was a mock Tudor pavilion with twin gables, a central white-faced clock and a shallow tier of black wooden seating. Powderhall was the pros' domain, the dark grey cinder making it so. There was a rickety low grandstand and a banked ridge surround. Edinburgh's castle and the out-line of the Old Town were a single dark shape in the distance. Scotland was searching for another Wyndham Halswelle, winner of the 1908 Olympic gold in the 400 metres. Halswelle, while born in London, was an adopted Caledonian. He'd trained in Edinburgh, where Powderhall became his natural habitat. Halswelle won his title in a walk-over. The final had to be controversially re-staged after an American rival was dis-qualified for elbowing him in the ribs during the closing stages. The two other Americans in the race, peeved at the decision, refused to run again in a display of solidarity. Halswelle, who'd broken the Olympic record during qualification, consequently had the track to himself. The Americans complained the team had been 'rooked, bilked, cheated, swindled and robbed'; Scotland merely saluted its champion and expressed contempt for the cheat. A sniper's bullet during the battle of Neuve Chapelle in France killed Halswelle in 1915. He was only thirty-two.

McKerchar made it his business to know every runner who came to either Craiglockhart or Powderhall, for the next new face might be the next Halswelle.

It didn't take him long to pick out the choice candidate.

Eric Liddell was Edinburgh University's reluctant athlete.

He had been seen running occasionally – purely to stay fit – and looked impressively fast. A friend approached him at the rump end of his second term. Would he compete in the Annual Sports at Craiglockhart? There were only six weeks to train for it, and Liddell initially said he was too 'busy' to swap bookwork for track-work. There was 'no time for that sort of thing', he added. Within twenty-four hours, however, he realized his mistake and chastised himself for it. For someone who prided himself on filling every one of Rudyard Kipling's unforgiving minutes with sixty seconds' worth of effort, his original answer began to strike him as a feeble and fatuous excuse; and to hide behind it had made him appear idle as well. 'The very words I used seemed to startle me,' he remembered. 'Busy? Work? These two words were new to me. They seemed to be strangers trying to settle down in a home that wasn't their own. They were soon dislodged.'

The young athlete. Eric Liddell (extreme right) is part of the Edinburgh University team.

Liddell tore into his training. But, at nineteen, without a coach and ignorant of how to approach a race, he committed a dumb error. 'I was only a novice then,' he admitted. Less than a month beforehand, Liddell set off on a six-day cycling holiday to Ben Nevis – a round trip of nearly 350 miles and a climb of almost 4,500 feet to the mountain's summit. He expected to see the sun rise spectacularly across the landscape. What he saw instead were banks of unbreakable clouds. 'One of those days in which the sun did not rise,' he remarked. Liddell also expected to come back from his break far fitter than before. It never occurred to him that the combination of a hard saddle, repetitive pedalling and a bone-shaking bike on winding, unmade roads would leave him feeling as tender as a piece of pulverized butcher's meat. Nor did he understand that the pull on his leg muscles – especially strenuous on Ben Nevis's steep gradients

– was incompatible with sprinting. 'I went to see if I would be able to run,' he said after returning home. 'I was stiff.' As well as the soreness, Liddell said he lost his 'spring' as a result of his rashness. That he managed to regain it so soon was a pointer to his potential. He would never be so blithely cavalier about his physical condition again.

Dressed in white vest and longish black pants, Liddell won the Annual Sports' 100 yards in 10.4 seconds, half a yard ahead of the field. He came second in the 220 yards, losing so narrowly that only inches denied him a double. A fellow competitor described him as 'just a slip of a man' who on that late May afternoon established himself in only two races as a 'new power in Scottish athletics'. Tom McKerchar recognized it too. Liddell had beaten seasoned runners on a grassy surface that didn't flatter the gift of speed and necessitated a standing, rather than a crouched, start.

Preparation at Powderhall came next for him. 'It was the first time in my life I had ever seen a cinder track,' said Liddell, making the sight of it sound like one of the undiscovered Wonders of the World. Dropped into an unfamiliar environment, he felt awkwardly self-conscious and looked askance at the pros, who trained alongside – and were scornful of – amateurs such as himself. Liddell said he watched them dancing on their toes 'as if stepping on hot bricks', and digging 'big holes' like trenches to practise starts. He didn't want to make 'a fool' of himself like that, he explained, before adding: 'At first I felt that every eye was turned on me when, as a matter of fact, there was nobody watching me at all.' Tentatively, he began to dance as well and also to work his shoulders and then copy whatever else was happening around him, such as back-bends and running on the spot, stretching and sharp 10-yard dashes. 'The exercises seemed unimportant at first,' confessed the callow Liddell, convinced that he could run without them.

To survive, let alone progress, Liddell was aware he needed a coach. McKerchar's civilian attire was a three-piece suit and a trilby. His working clothes at Powderhall were flannel trousers, a sweater or a towel tucked into the neck and a bobble hat or flat cap. Sometimes he puffed hard on short-butt cigars. In a crowd, he was easy to find. He also lived less than a mile from the track, which allowed him to wander in and out. Liddell summoned the courage to introduce himself, as though McKerchar couldn't possibly have seen him in the Annual Sports and had no notion of what he'd achieved during it.

In an attempt to coach himself, Liddell had read a book called *How to Become a Great Athlete*.

The book, published in 1911, was written by the Austrian-born naturalized German Max Sick, who made his living from his physique. He was a 5-foot-4-inch-tall strongman, a weightlifter, a gymnast and also a side-show, circus-like entertainer who liked to study nature and quote the writings of poets, philosophers and scientists. He drew crowds to variety halls after learning to make his muscles twitch in synchronization with music played from the orchestra pit. He adopted the stage name Maxick. As a child, he grew up puny and undernourished. As an adult, he made even Charles Atlas look weedy. *How to Become a Great Athlete* dealt with the science of athleticism in relation to muscular power. An athlete without strength, said Sick, was 'useless'. He illustrated the manual with photographs of his own body, which he boastfully said made him 'the most wonderfully developed and strongest man of my weight'. What impressed Liddell was Sick's desire for constant self-improvement. Certain that strength came from muscle control, Sick insisted readers of the book should know thyself. 'There must be knowledge of the sets of muscles which are to be used in any particular effort.' These, he continued, 'should become the object of your mind'. Sick was adamant that any athlete needed to research his sport 'deeply', should 'only pay attention to the advice of those who do things', and ought to 'leave those who theorise severely alone'. Sick's number one rule was: 'Practise with your superiors – never with your inferiors. If you can't practise with better men, watch them.'

Liddell took note.

Sick claimed to be 'mentally possessed of so strong a will' that he could live frugally. He argued that those who aspired to be top athletes should never over-eat and that 'tea, coffee, alcohol and tobacco' should be labelled as 'poisons'. An 'occasional sip of Bovril', he declared, was perfectly permissible, as if advertising the brand. Liddell agreed with other Sick suggestions, such as the need to 'keep warm', and also his haughty contempt for the 'Spartan like treatment to which many physical cultural enthusiasts subject themselves'. Sick waved them aside as being 'little short of madness'. He made one recommendation in particular that Liddell repeatedly followed: 'If your sport requires speed, avoid weight-lifting as you would the devil.' He thought too much bulky muscle was like trying to run with a sackful of coal lashed to each leg. Where Liddell and Sick differed was in the matter of massage. Sick was generally in favour of it, though emphatically not in the days immediately before an event. Liddell believed massage was 'essential' in the hours before competition. McKerchar thought so too.

Looking back on those initial attempts to prove himself as an athlete, Liddell said that he went to McKerchar with pre-conceived theories of how to run and also how to prepare for running. McKerchar threw a lot of them out, like unfashionable clothes from a wardrobe, before dressing Liddell anew. 'He taught me where I was going wrong,' he said, which was a polite way of putting it because the account of their first meeting scarcely seems like a cosy togetherness of matched hearts and minds. McKerchar comes across as spiky and irritable. Liddell comes across as thoroughly ticked off. The exchange between them seems more like scolding than instruction. 'He told me that my muscles were all too hard. They needed to be softened by massage,' said Liddell. Without it, McKerchar cautioned that 'one day' one of his muscles would 'snap' on the starting line. The coach got to work. 'He pounded me around like a piece of putty, pushed this muscle this way and that muscle the other way in order to get me into shape,' said Liddell. McKerchar ordered him to complete a short run. At the end of it Liddell pulled up suddenly, as if colliding with an invisible wall. 'I asked him what he thought of it,' he remembered. McKerchar's utter horror at what he'd just witnessed sounds in the telling as though Liddell received a shock akin to the angry crackle of electric current. 'He answered that if I wanted a breakdown I was going about it in the best possible manner . . . one must never stop abruptly on reaching the tape.'

There are winces of pain in Liddell's recollection of how dispirited he became afterwards. He said he'd been 'thoroughly humiliated'; that his 'reputation had been dragged through the mud'; and that his 'self-respect was . . . wallowing in the mire'. He worried that every muscle in his body was about to 'give way', and that he'd 'remain a physical wreck until the end of my days'. But he also conceded that McKerchar had begun putting him into 'a fit mental condition to start an athletic career'.

These were baby steps, and the greatness of McKerchar as a coach is evidenced in them. Liddell was an athletics dunce. He didn't know how to start from the holes. He didn't know how to dip at the tape. He didn't know how to train either, and he'd relied on a book by a vaudeville performer to hone his body. He also had that terrible arm-jerky, head-back style – the worst in living memory; so bad it seemed sometimes as though the top half of his body didn't belong to the bottom half. Most coaches – despite the explosive boom of that raw, ravishing speed – would have made an excuse and left Liddell to it, thinking his component problems were so dire that no whole solution could ever be found to conquer them. But McKerchar was a man of mettle, and perseverance was always prevalent in his approach. However much criticism he fired at him, Liddell was never a lost cause; he put him through the wringer only because he believed his talent was worth the bother.

Having learned that personality was reflected in performance, McKerchar made it his business to explore his athlete's past and family history. He only had to scrape the topsoil off Liddell's to conclude there was a solid base beneath. The teenager in front of him knew all about loyalty, service, self-sufficiency and self-reliance and also commitment. He'd been brought up not to let anyone down. That is why McKerchar agreed to coach him.

Only another three years, two months and 146 races would separate the two of them from Olympic triumph in Paris.

There was no sporting streak in Eric Liddell's genealogy. His father, James Dunlop Liddell, went to Mongolia in 1898 to make certain another corner of a foreign field remained under the flag of the London Missionary Society. As a probationary, his specific corner was Ch'ao Yang, an inauspicious spot 250 miles north-east of Peking. He was twenty-seven years old, a former draper ordained in the ministry. The Reverend Liddell came from the central belt of Scotland. His village, Drymen, minuscule but picturesque, was at the western end of the Campsie Fields, close to Loch Lomond. His fiancée was a qualified nurse, Mary Reddin, who arrived in China twelve months after him. Her home was Paxton, an equally tiny map-dot near Berwick-upon-Tweed. The North Sea coastline lay only 5 miles away.

Mr Liddell and Miss Reddin had met in Stirling and married in Shanghai after a six-year engagement. Their timing was terrible. The wedding in October 1899 coincided almost exactly with the bloody birth of the Boxer Rebellion. Married life began under the threat of the sword and the bullet.

James Liddell had announced before going to China that he'd willingly

Proud parents: James and Mary Liddell,
when Eric was ordained into the ministry in
Edinburgh.

endure 'duties pertaining to a real pioneer experience'. In his wedding photograph he still looks more like a senior bank clerk or a bookkeeper than a rough and ready son of the elements. Entirely in keeping with the picture protocol of that era, he and Mary wear expressions solemnly reminiscent of a funeral service rather than a matrimonial breakfast. The husband folds his hands in front of him. His mouth is almost completely hidden beneath a moustache, which probably took longer to grow than a hothouse plant, and confirms that a Victorian chap wasn't considered to be properly attired without one. His wife loops a white-gloved hand into his left arm. Her hat is a small hill of lace and taffeta and its spacious, flat brim casts her forehead and eyes in thin shadow.

A missionary and his wife. James and Mary Liddell were married in 1899.

The couple had barely said 'I do' to each other before finding themselves in the midst of turmoil.

Ch'ao Yang was a hard row to hoe for a new missionary. Robbery, rape and banditry were common. Kidnap and ransom were routine. A family believed to have money often found a body-part in a box at the front door and a note demanding cash from them. Were it not forthcoming, other pieces of hacked-off flesh would follow. Non-payment would lead to public immolation for the dismembered victim. What remained of him or her was smothered in oil or cooking fat before being set alight.

The Boxer Rebellion was more terrible still.

The originally clandestine peasant movement the Society of Righteous and Harmonious Fists sought to violently eradicate all foreign participation and influence in China. It despised Christianity. It despised the missionaries, such as the Liddells, who preached it. And it despised the subservience of the 1860 Treaty of Tientsin that had sanctioned the teaching of the Bible with impunity.

From the early disturbances in the autumn of 1899 through to the autumn of 1900, the total of deaths in the conflict was calculated in high numbers: more than 250 missionaries – Catholic and Protestant – and over thirty thousand Chinese Christians. As many as seventy-five were burned alive at the American mission in Tung-chau. In Pau-tong-fu six British missionaries, most known to that community for more than twenty-five years, were knifed to death. One atrocity followed another, the use of the machete, the halberd and the club frequent. Lootings and sexual assaults on women were commonplace. The diplomatic compound in Peking was even under siege for fifty-five days. In one of the most horrendous incidents the governor of Shanxi invited Christians to his provincial capital under the pretext of offering sanctuary and then had forty-four of them killed, including women and children. Westerners referred to the Society as the Boxers, essentially because its members practised martial arts. The Boxers chanted for the blessings of Taoist and Buddhist spirits and believed a ghost army of others like them would descend from the sky as reinforcements against their enemies. The Society also believed diet and incantation would allow its soldiers to fly and make them immune from the blast and slash of weaponry. It took the Eight Nation Alliance – a super-fighting force comprising fifty-four warships and almost forty-nine thousand troops from Britain, the United States, France, Germany, Italy, Japan, Russia and Austria-Hungary – to disabuse them of both fantasies.

After the Boxers were finally defeated, the Chinese signed the Boxer Protocol, a punitive document ordering executions and reparations. Like the Treaty of Tientsin, four decades earlier, it was a fuse waiting for a lit match. The Protocol stored up grievances, grudges and angers that would explode soon enough, and more violently than before.

The fighting had become so bad in the early summer of 1900 that James and Mary Liddell were forced out of Ch'ao Yang. Mary, already seven months pregnant, left the village in a sedan chair that six Chinese Christians risked death to carry. She gave birth to her first son, Robert, in Shanghai, where she and James had fled to safety. The faint-hearted, especially those beginning a family, could have made an excuse and packed for home despite the restriction of a missionary contract. James Liddell was different. Father, mother and baby went instead to Tientsin.

Father and son. James Liddell beside Eric, his second child, in Turkey in 1903.

James settled them in and then headed back to Mongolia in 1901 on a mission of reconnaissance and repair. For four months Mary heard nothing from him.

Tientsin had been at the centre of the Boxer Rebellion. The city had been locked down for four weeks only three and a half months before the Liddells got there. More than 1,500 soldiers of the Eight Nation Alliance died or were wounded. Among those dodging artillery during the siege of such a strategically important point was a twenty-six-year-old mining consultant who saved children in the crossfire. His name was Herbert Hoover, the future American President.

This is where Eric Liddell was born on 16 January 1902.

The Liddells weren't allowed to linger in Tientsin. Near the year's end the London Missionary Society dispatched them almost 700 miles to Siaochang on the Great Plain. The last, long furlongs of that journey were completed on a wooden mule-drawn cart that rattled in the ruts left by thousands upon thousands of other carts before it. A contemporary eyewitness estimated there were ten thousand villages spread over the Great Plain's 159,000 acres. The ten million villagers inside them sowed and reaped harvests of millet and wheat and lived primitively on the brown flat earth where almost nothing broke the horizon except for low shacks or reed huts, each resembling the other. Siaochang was no better and no bigger than most of them. The gated, mud-walled compound comprised four large houses in a row, each with verandas upstairs and downstairs on two sides. A stone church and a school lay behind these properties.

James Liddell tended to his flock across an expanse of land alien to him. Agriculture was blighted. The crops repeatedly perished because of droughts, flooding or locusts. Gangs of bandits roamed indiscriminately. The peasant population was illiterate and the elders in the farming communities regarded reading as a distraction from labour. There was no concept of the world beyond the nearest trading town or city. During the torments of the rebellion there, the Boxers wrecked nearly a hundred churches and approximately five hundred Chinese Christians died. Rebuilding and restoration were now extra duties for the missionaries. James Liddell was on a treadmill of constant work, and Mary strained to cope with his absences.

The Liddells on parade: (from the left) Eric, Jenny and Rob.

To steel herself for the daily adversities of being a missionary wife, Mary had moved to the Hebridean Isle of Lewis in the months immediately before her wedding. The remoteness of its crofts was her preparation for the rural bleakness and isolation of China. But she was a fragile thing, weighing less than 8½ stone, and Siaochang was a demoralizing place because of the climate, the insects and the loneliness. Always tired and frequently ailing, Mary nearly died after her third pregnancy. A daughter – christened Janet but always called Jenny – was born in 1903. Less than seventy-two hours afterwards Mary, frail and worn down, was diagnosed with peritonitis. She was at 'death's door', said Jenny later. The doctor even said he 'expected' her to die. James prayed beside her bed. Somehow she survived, her recovery to full health taking almost a year.

Everyone who knew him as a child remembered three standout things about Eric Liddell. The family had its own servants, including an amah called Chi-nai-nai. Her feet were bound, so when Liddell misbehaved or ran away she couldn't catch him. Since Chinese words seldom begin with vowel sounds, she was also unable to get her tongue nimbly around the name Eric. She called him 'Yellie', the closest pronunciation she could manage. Yellie always cried salty tears over the hymn 'Ninety and Nine', the song-story of the shepherd searching for the one sheep lost on the hills. And, aged four, he fell desperately ill with dysentery. There was no doctor and his mother had to nurse him as adequately as she could, pouring out tablespoons of Valentine's Meat Juice, a concoction of pressed liquid that came from torn, raw beef. The legacy of that illness was numbness in his legs. He walked so awkwardly during his recovery that a neighbour swore he would 'never be able to run again', and pitied him for it.

In the cocoon of childhood, protected within the walls of the compound, Liddell saw himself as Chinese. In winter, like his siblings, he wore a padded coat and a wide crowned hat against the below-zero temperatures. In summer he went to the seaside resort of Peitaiho, where the LMS owned wooden beach bungalows, the breeze and the water there cooling the family in temperatures that climbed as high as 110 degrees. He ate like the locals and tried to speak their language. He uttered his first Chinese phrase after friends adopted a family of kittens. Unable to capture them on his unsteady legs, Liddell learned to scream 'Hsieo mao pao la', which meant 'Little cat has run away'. He knew nothing of customs or environments elsewhere. Everything for the family revolved around the LMS. When she caught him banging a nail into the wall of the house, his mother scolded, 'Don't do that. It belongs to the mission.' Liddell stopped, then asked her whether *he* 'belonged to the mission' too? It felt as though he did.

His sister, Jenny, said her brother 'remembered much': walking through dust storms, sitting on the veranda, the tenderness of his amah, the spread of the land and the sight of those who lived on it and from it. Nothing, though, enforced Liddell's idea of China as being the beating heart of him more than the family's leaving of it on furlough in 1907. Liddell was told he was 'going home' to Scotland; but that country, which seemed so far away, wasn't 'home' to a boy who had never seen it. China was 'home' to him, and he was glad of that fact; he didn't want to uproot himself from it.

Like Tweedledum and Tweedledee: Rob (left) and Eric in their Eltham College uniforms.

The Liddells first went to Drymen, renting rooms in a house there and sending Eric and Rob to the local school. This was a preparatory step, acclimatizing them to both the greenery of their new surroundings and formal education. James had a bigger duty to perform before Siaochang called him again. He enrolled his boys in the 'School for the Sons of Missionaries' in Blackheath in south-east London. It subsequently outgrew that site and moved to the more spacious former Naval School at Mottingham, where it became known as Eltham College. The mellow stone of the college, and its fine facade of pediment and columns and roof balustrades, soared like the buildings described in *Tom Brown's Schooldays*. But however fine its architecture, and despite the manicured acreage of its sports fields, Eltham wasn't exactly a warm hearth and a soft bed. For the cherubically innocent-looking Liddell, being wrenched

The all-round sportsman: Eric Liddell in cricket whites at Eltham College.

away from his parents was like being orphaned. On the day she sailed back to China his mother unobtrusively watched him, oblivious to her imminent departure, play cricket. That night Liddell, aged six, wept himself into a fitful sleep.

Eltham became Liddell's substitute family for the next decade. This forced adoption forged a strong character. Even at eight years old, Liddell was dissuading older boys from bullying younger ones. When the headmaster broke his own rule about not bicycling through the quadrangle, the voice he heard in rebuke – 'Hey, no cycling there' – was Liddell's. The headmaster punished Liddell rather than himself. He was sent to his room without supper, which wasn't necessarily purgatorial. The kitchen at Eltham soaked food in inedible fat; Liddell regularly spat it into a wastepaper basket.

As the elder, Rob, whether he liked it or not, was pressed into becoming father and mother, counsellor and comforter to his brother. In an early photograph of them at the college he and Eric look like Tweedledee and Tweedledum. The brothers are of the same height and stature and their hair is the same shade of mousey blond. The uniform each wears seems comic to us now – an Eton collar with a thin bow tie

The avuncular A. P. Cullen:
teacher, friend and part-
mentor to Eric Liddell.

and knickerbockers, the jet black socks turned 6 inches above a pair of ankle-laced boots. What sets them apart is Rob's deadly seriousness beside the smirk that is beginning to spread across Eric's face.

In the college Rob was Liddell Number One and Eric was Liddell Number Two. The personality differences between them were soon apparent. Rob was an extrovert, an orator with the Literary and Debating Society. Eric was reticence personified. In a production of *Alice in Wonderland*, he played the Dormouse successfully because he hid meekly behind the costume and became the character. Away from the stage and the classroom, he deferred to Rob. Among his favourite teachers was the classics master, Augustus Pountney Cullen, who curled his lip at those highfalutin Christian names and preferred to be known as plain 'AP'. He was a Cambridge graduate – sporty, pipe-smoking and tweedy – who spoke to his dog in Latin. Once the dust of academe had settled on him at Eltham, Cullen looked more mature than someone in his early twenties. As well as classics, he covered lessons in science, English and history. Science was Liddell's subject. Experiments entranced him, and Cullen brought each alive through quirky demonstrations and dramatic readings of dense textbooks.

Sport offered solace to Liddell too. That role of the Dormouse briefly brought him the obvious nickname of 'Mouse'. But in any game, this Mouse roared, which was a substitute for speech. As a rugby wing-three-quarter, he couldn't be caught. As a sprinter, he usually didn't get caught either – unless his brother did the catching. The crowning glory for them as a pair was the 1918 school championships – otherwise known as the Liddell Games. Eric won the 100 yards in 10.8 seconds, edging out Rob. He then took the 440 yards and the long jump too. Rob claimed the sprint hurdles, the high jump and the cross-country titles. If only their parents could have seen them . . .

Separation is the cruellest hardship for the children of missionaries. Between 1908 and 1920 Liddell's parents returned just once – shortly before the outbreak of the First World War – and then only because Mary required surgery to remove gallstones. Their new baby, Ernest, born in 1912, came with them. The family was split up again in March 1915. Jenny was spared the trauma of that parting. She was supposed to board permanently at Walthamstow on the other side of London. Her mother, learning she was wretched there, took her back to China instead. As adolescents and teenagers Eric and Rob got to know their parents primarily through letters, written twice weekly on thin paper and always delivering news several weeks old.

The Eltham motto was *Gloria Filiorum Patres*: The Fathers Are the Glory of the Sons. His own father's absence didn't dissuade Liddell from wanting to be exactly like him. Indeed, rather than resenting it, the gap his father ought to have filled in his upbringing accentuated Liddell's desire to become a teacher-missionary and live up to his ideals. Liddell later told a friend that he'd decided to become a missionary in China at 'eight or nine'. He went to Bible class and read the scriptures daily. At fifteen he was confirmed in the Scottish Congregational Church. As the war crawled towards an armistice, he then volunteered to work in a medical mission.

What was once said about James Liddell would be later said of his second son too. He was the 'ideal of Christian brotherliness'. He possessed 'such a big heart'. There was 'no shadow of meanness or narrowness' in him. And he gained true satisfaction only 'when doing something for others'.

Tom McKerchar was among the first to discover that after Liddell gained a place at Edinburgh University.

The dreary commonplace of practice is necessary for any athlete. Eric Liddell initially found the rigour of it too testing for him. It was 'not the easiest thing to do', he said, because the 'continual repetition of certain exercises' was unutterably boring. He disliked practising his start. 'Time after time you go to your holes, rise to get the "get set" position and wait for the pistol to go. Someone tries to go off before the pistol and so we all have to get up and start from the beginning again.'

Tom McKerchar allowed Liddell the leeway to ease himself into becoming professional about his running rather than moonlighting at it. McKerchar knew that Rob Liddell was taking his medical qualifications in Edinburgh. He knew that his new recruit relied on his brother – and vice versa – for stability and comradeship. He knew Eric Liddell had only got into university after obtaining his entrance certificate, which meant becoming competent in a language; and that he'd paid for a French tutor through farm labouring to achieve it. He also knew that Liddell was a committed teetotaller as well as a committed Christian, and that his church was Morningside Congregational, which sat on what the locals called 'Holy Corner' because of the cluster of other churches gathered around it. With the red-yellow glow of its Burne-Jones window, Morningside was conspicuous in its support of the London Missionary Society through its original minister, who had worn a monocle, and a walrus moustache so splendidly wide that it resembled a pair of wings. The church had sent its first missionary to China in 1896. Liddell frequently arrived late at Powderhall because he was attending services, taking care of the needy or administering Bible classes at Morningside. McKerchar let it pass.

Such patience is one of the greatest debts Liddell owed him. The other – again highlighting McKerchar's calibre as a coach – is that he tried only fleetingly to alter Liddell's running style. Liddell was frequently asked to explain his ungainliness, as if those who saw him regarded it as a high mystery and couldn't believe how something so awful could produce something so successful. He was compared to a 'startled deer', a 'windmill', the sails off kilter, a 'terrified ghost' and someone whose joints had never been oiled. It was said sophisticated experts were reduced to 'ribald laughter' watching him. Liddell relied on humour to avoid questions about it. He'd say that his distant ancestors had lived on the Scottish–English borders. From there, commando-like raids to rustle cattle and filch provisions were launched beneath the cover of starless nights. 'They had to hurry back,' explained Liddell, emphasizing with a cheeky grin that 'one did not look for correct action when one was returning from such raids'.

McKerchar did attempt to improve Liddell's arm-action and tried to stop him from hurling his head back, like someone trying to swallow a big pill with a gulp of water. He soon abandoned it, realizing it was not only pointless but also counter-productive. For why fix what only looked broken?

To force him into change would have thrown the mechanics of his running hopelessly out of sync. McKerchar focused on the basics instead, allowing Liddell's speed to do the rest. He did hone him out of the holes. He made sure Liddell's front foot was about 4 inches behind the line and he insisted on a 14- or 16-inch gap between each foot. The fingers of his hand rested exactly on the start line. 'At the words "get set" my balance was such that almost all the weight of my body rested on the front leg and the hands,' said Liddell. 'The first step taken was a short one – just a foot or perhaps 18 inches.' McKerchar told him not to go off too quickly. 'The first 10 yards or so should be spent gradually rising,' added Liddell. In training he always completed three or four 50-yard dashes and then a 220-yard run. According to Liddell, 'The first 100 yards was not "all out". The last 120 was as fast as I could do it.'

He wrote down what he called his 'athletics experiences' in a notebook, listing the races in black fountain pen and sometimes adding remarks about the other runners he either competed against or observed. Liddell also quoted little homilies, which could easily have been framed posters on a wall. 'Failure comes when you fail to keep mind and body at the point of perfection . . . Look after your body . . . A rub down before and after running is essential . . . a simple diet all through the season is much better than trying to cut out this and that'.

However simple that diet, it would make the modern athlete cringe. On race days he'd feast on roast beef or steak and chips. Liddell avoided only pastries and anything 'stodgy', he said, which would be 'heavy passengers' on the track; though once he ate a plum pudding before a race and still won easily.

During the remainder of his first season he was bettered only once over 100 yards – and that came in a handicap. In only his tenth race he won the Scottish AAA title at Hampden Park in 10.4 seconds. His 220 yards time was more revelatory still – a new championship record of 22.6 seconds. He admitted to feeling 'various emotional tremors that vibrated through my system' that day. Nervous energy made him throw up his food. 'It makes you ask yourself: Is it all worth it?' he said.

Thankfully, he decided it was.

The prizes piled up. As well as a ribboned medal or a cup, the winner of races was always given a gift so as not to compromise his amateur status with the mucky handover of money. This gift was usually a gold watch or household goods: a tea service, a clock, cutlery in a teak box, a figurine or a decorative ornament, a silver tray or a coffee pot. Soon Liddell had more silver than he could polish. And he had enough cabinet china to set up his own department store. He gave most of it away as presents.

No one who had waved Liddell goodbye from Eltham recognized him as a future star. He never won the school's most cherished honour, the Bayard Prize, which was given to the pupil who had most influenced his contemporaries. Rob, however, *was* a Bayard recipient. An accolade of a different kind was given to Eric. Assessing his first phenomenal summer of running, the *Glasgow Herald* published a summary that now reads like a piece of crystal ball clairvoyance. It forecast that Liddell would become a 'British Champion' and 'might even blossom into an Olympic hero'. The newspaper also said that Liddell's emergence from nobody to somebody in just sixteen weeks was 'one of the romances of the amateur path'.

Not everything went so smoothly for him.

Liddell once raced in Greenock and rode home in the carrier of a motorbike. When a nut was shaken loose on the way, he fell hard on his behind. The motorbike travelled on for another hundred yards before the driver discovered that his passenger was missing. The carrier was patched up with a ball of twine and Liddell, expecting to be bumped off again, clung on desperately. McKerchar was unimpressed, imagining his number one sprinter incapacitated for months.

The athlete and the coach made an odd couple. When each got to know the other well, hardly a word passed between them during training or after it. McKerchar even massaged Liddell's muscles in near silence. Liddell understood what McKerchar expected of him; and McKerchar understood that Liddell didn't have to be prodded to get a performance out of him. His pride made that superfluous.

McKerchar also became aware of something else that went unspoken between them. Liddell's commitment to athletics was secondary to his commitment to the Church.

CHAPTER TWO

Just a Drop of Strong Tea

Eric Liddell could identify precisely when his life changed. It was 6 April 1923. The time was shortly after 9 p.m.

A week earlier he'd received an unexpected visitor at George Square, the digs he shared with friends and fellow students near Edinburgh University. The Union Free Church evangelist David Patrick Thomson – always known as DP – had been deputized to recruit Liddell to the interdenominational Glasgow Students Evangelical Union. The idea was to ask Liddell to speak in Armadale, a town almost 25 miles west of Edinburgh.

Armadale was not the sort of place to attract the postcard photographers. Coal and brick dust clung to it. A forest of headstocks and factory chimneys dominated the landscape; one resident counted forty-four of them in the 1920s. There were clay pits and ironworks too, and the hard-palmed, cloth-capped men who toiled in these dirty industries were condemned to the drudgery of shift work, the reward for which was low pay and lung and chest infections that caused a shortness of breath and a hacking cough. The workers washed afterwards in tin baths placed in front of the hearth at home. But, no matter how much soap accompanied the hot water, a thin film of grime accumulated on the skin and could never be scrubbed off altogether, leaving them with a blue-greyish pallor. The population of Armadale – almost five thousand in total – chiefly gathered around four long, rough-tracked roads, the reek of industry hanging in the damp air. The GSEU, including Thomson as organizing

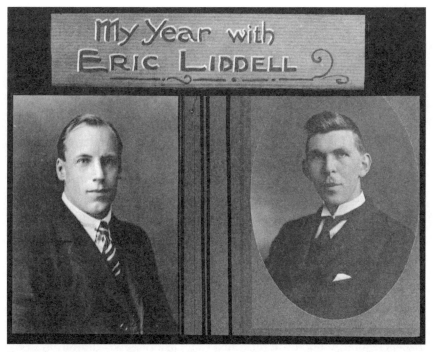

D. P. Thomson gave an illustrated talk on his religious campaigns alongside Eric Liddell. This is the opening slide.

secretary, had been zealously preaching among the community, mostly persuading women to come to meetings. As Thomson conceded, as tactfully as possible, 'the men of the non-churchgoing class proved very difficult to reach'.

Another of Thomson's duties was his secretaryship of C. T. Studd's Heart of Africa Mission. It gave him an insight into the importance of a figurehead. Studd, then sixty-two, had broad appeal as a former England, Middlesex and Cambridge University cricketer.

He'd made his England debut in 1882 against Australia at The Oval. That Test match was historic. It led to the creation of the Ashes after a comic conclusion in which Studd was unwittingly pivotal. He'd found himself in a last-wicket partnership with Ted Peate, an oafish and corpulent Yorkshire slow bowler. With no pedigree as a batsman, Peate unilaterally decided that he – rather than Studd – would swish the bat and attempt to score the measly ten runs that England needed to win. He was clean-bowled. Loss of supremacy to Australia – the colonialists were patronized as social and cricketing subservients to Queen Victoria's gentlemen – killed one spectator in his seat, the poor chap dying of shock because of the result. Asked afterwards why he'd been so incompetently cavalier, Peate replied, 'I couldn't trust Mr Studd.' Everyone else, however, did trust him. Studd was respected for his philanthropy and his charitable countenance – even towards Peate, who he refused to criticize afterwards.

Studd had found religion at his public school, Eton, and went to China to work for the poor. On the death of his father he gifted his £30,000 inheritance to religious causes. And, despite his cricketing success, Studd always asked: 'What is all the fame and flattery worth?' He was able to build up his own mission because those who wouldn't necessarily be attracted to the Church were drawn to hearing him speak as an ex-sportsman. He filled Edinburgh's Free Assembly Hall on the basis that anyone who came could shake hands with him afterwards. Thomson imagined Liddell fitting into Studd's mould.

The men of Armadale weren't well educated. Newspapers, rather than books, were read in their terrace cottages. Since Liddell appeared in the papers regularly, Thomson reckoned that curiosity and admiration would draw them to listen to an athlete rather than another earnest clergyman. Thomson could have telephoned Liddell to make his pitch. The number of his digs – 4211 – was in the book. But he thought it was imperative to see him face to face. Thomson, who often travelled as a hitch-hiker to save a penny or half-penny fare, thumbed a lift to Edinburgh on the back of a potato truck. He already knew Rob Liddell well, and thought it tactically sensible to approach him first. Would his brother agree to go to Armadale? 'He really couldn't tell. I would have to see him myself and put it to him,' said Thomson. Liddell was called into the dining room, and Thomson remembered putting the question to him as 'directly and as forcibly as I could'. Liddell dropped his head, as if in prayer; he hadn't spoken in public before and the prospect daunted him. Thomson never forgot the 'moment's silence' as he waited for his answer and then the firmness of the promise Liddell made to him. 'All right,' he said in a friendly tone, 'I'll come.' The assurance was as binding as a legal contract. 'I felt then a sense of immense relief,' Thomson recalled.

What Thomson described as 'a special mass meeting for men' was held in an unprepossessing town hall which resembled a large house with a high pitched roof. Another pitched roof marked the entrance, which had been tacked on long after the construction of the main building. Outside there was a low wall topped with black metal railings and a 25-yard path to the main door.

No one counted the attendance; Thomson estimated it as '60 to 80'. This was a decent number in the circumstances. There hadn't been much time to advertise Liddell, so Thomson relied on word of mouth. It was also a Friday night. Every worker in Armadale had collected his wages in a brown envelope that afternoon. The temptation to fritter them away on a boozy session in the pub was the counter-attraction. No one noted down a verbatim transcript of what was said either. Thomson remembered only that Liddell talked about 'what his own faith meant to him' and also how he reconciled his religion with his athletics.

This is how it began: Liddell had become a public speaker for God.

Sometimes it can be difficult to grasp a sense of something when it is actually happening; comprehension often comes only when it is over. But, sitting alongside Liddell afterwards and listening to his easy dialogue with the congregation over cups of tea, Thomson instantly understood the impact of the moment. He also assessed the consequences correctly. Not everyone had known Liddell was a committed Christian. Until Armadale, he'd been 'a secret disciple', explained Thomson. 'It was not what happened in Armadale that mattered most,' he added. 'It was the fact that every newspaper in Scotland carried the news the following morning. After that, there could be no turning back and there would be no want of an audience wherever he was billed to speak.'

A mural of the town's motto, May Their Work Flourish, was displayed in Latin inside the hall. The sentence was appropriate for Liddell. His own work flourished from there. What Armadale started was 'a life of dedicated service that only death could end', said Thomson.

Liddell would say the brief exchange with Thomson in George Square counted as the 'turning point' for him. He thought preparing his address for that hard-as-flint workforce in Armadale, and then rising to deliver it, amounted to the 'bravest thing' he had ever done. From then onwards he and Thomson became inseparable, almost as close as brothers. The friendship, said Thomson, 'meant everything to me'.

Before Armadale neither Liddell nor Thomson was aware of how much each had needed the other. After it, both of them – but Liddell in particular – believed that no earthly coincidence had brought them together. For the morning after accepting Thomson's invitation, Liddell slit open a letter from his sister Jenny, who was living in Tientsin. Included in it was a passage from Isaiah 41.10. 'Fear not, for I am with thee; do not dismay, for I will guide thee.' No one posting a letter from China to Britain could know when it might turn up on the mat. Mail could take up to a month or more to complete its passage. Reading and re-reading the quotation convinced Liddell that its arrival that day, over rough lands and rougher seas, was much more than chance. It had come into his hands when he most needed reassurance. For Liddell, the timing was further proof that divine inspiration was shaping his path. He believed God had spoken to him, describing it like this: 'I was brought up in a Christian home where the stories of the Bible were often told and became familiar to me. The time came when the appeal of Christ became more personal and I began to realise it was going to affect my life.'

Somewhat shamefacedly, Liddell conceded that prior to Armadale 'his whole life had been one of keeping out of public duties'. But, even as he spoke there, he sensed he was 'being called to do a piece of work'.

That work was as a preacher and a mentor; though Liddell confessed that he felt 'absolutely unqualified' to be either. He nonetheless pressed on, thinking that 'If He called me to do it, then He would have to supply the necessary power.'

For Thomson, the influence of divine inspiration had come much earlier.

D. P. Thomson had been born into a prosperous family from Dundee. He was raised in the company of servants – cooks, cleaners, nurses and nannies. His father was a noted lawyer and treasurer of the Home Mission Union. Their house – one of the best in the town – regularly hosted missionaries and evangelists for Sunday worship in the drawing room, where in his early teens Thomson gave Bible readings and preached. In his youth he had a long face and sticky-out ears, a high wave of dark hair and the sort of toothbrush moustache that Charlie Chaplin had already made popular and Hitler eventually made infamous.

Of the generation who trekked to the Great War – longing to believe the propaganda promise of a Christmas 1914 end – those, like Thomson, born in the first half of 1896 had no real chance to experience adult life before death became their neighbour. At just eighteen years old, Thomson abandoned an apprenticeship, as a junior clerk in a jute factory, to enlist as a private in the 4th Seaforth Highlanders. He was quickly schooled as an officer in the Army Service Corps, the training for which protected him from the front line in France. He got no further than Le Havre, where his duties in the field bakeries were cushy; the most arduous task was censoring other soldiers' letters. Shipped to Salonica in Greece, Thomson contracted dysentery and began to suffer from a dilated heart and gastric complaints, which led to his medical discharge in the autumn of 1917. After a cardiac examination, the doctors gave him the gloomiest prognosis: he would either die within six months or become a semi-invalid during a foreshortened life.

War changed the lives of those it did not consume. After it, Thomson asked himself the same questions as every other survivor. How – and why – had he managed to come through that filth and gore and still be breathing? His elder brother, James, had died at the Somme in 1916, aged twenty-six. Five of his cousins had perished too. Thomson thought it tragically ironic that he, the weakling and the war casualty, came home. He dwelt guiltily on his brother's death. 'I have had all the time to live and work that was denied him,' he said. Thomson concluded he'd been 'saved' to become an evangelist. A student of Glasgow's Bible Training Institute, Thomson was an active preacher, an ebullient, bustling organizer and a can-do promoter of tireless campaigns. He was a bibliophile who never stopped working except to read. His friends said the true meaning of his initials was 'Dynamic Personality'.

Thomson seemed this way to Eric Liddell, fooled like everyone else by his new friend's confident approach, which hid doubt and insecurity behind it.

Liddell had no notion that Thomson was wrestling with the black dog of depression. A profound personal crisis of faith and belief had engulfed him for disparate reasons. He was lonely after two friendships with women had recently collapsed. He was physically ailing, a terrible hangover from his condition in 1917. Then, without prior warning, his father announced that the family firm was on the lip of bankruptcy, the business facing imminent foreclosure. Thomson was attempting to combine his studies and his preaching with the creation of a small-print publishing house. He saw no solution to either his father's or his own financial hardships. He waded through all this darkly, brooding about what else might go wrong for him and questioning whether his training for the ministry was worthwhile. There seemed to be an element of sour self-loathing lurking in Thomson too. As well as being a book collector, he was a compulsive diary writer, putting his thoughts on to paper in a crabby, hard-to-read hand. In one entry, after the worst of his depression had passed, Thomson revealed his most mournful thoughts and what he regarded as his duplicity. He chastised himself as an 'arrant hypocrite'. The self-flagellation continued: 'My life has been a living lie these many months. Prayer has died down in my heart . . . the cankerworm has been eating at my heart . . . pride has been full blooded and full-blown . . . impurity has had its way'.

Two things dragged him out of this pit in the early and mid-1920s. The first factor was a book called *Life Changers*. Written by Harold Begbie – best known as the ghost-writer of polar explorer Ernest Shackleton – it explored the teachings of the American Frank Buchman, the founder of what would later become known as the Oxford Group. Buchman, a Lutheran evangelist, said that the 'only sane people in an insane world were those controlled by God'. The second factor in Thomson's rehabilitation was Liddell. As Thomson's biographer, Frank Bardgett, astutely said: 'It may not be too much to say that . . . Liddell saved Thomson for the Church's ordained ministry.'

Liddell's liveliness not only inspired his new mentor, but also made him feel less frail and vulnerable than before. His purpose in the Church renewed, Thomson liked to stride around the stage and his bass voice needed no artificial amplification. He could be heard a street away from the podium. But there was a refreshing boldness about Liddell, who didn't need to be as sonorous or theatrical. Watching him meet and greet parishioners after services, Thomson admired his skills in finding a common conversational thread that bound him and them together without the awkwardness that normally occurs when strangers meet.

Accusation and indignation were the worn tools of the firebrand orators who, swelling themselves into a fake frenzy, built towards the direst warnings of damnation. This sort of act soon blew itself out because the script was so predictable. Liddell approached the task from a different angle. He made individuals in the congregation believe he was talking directly to them. His assuredness at Armadale convinced Thomson that he possessed something rare as a speaker. This became clear as he and Thomson set off on weekly tours to convert the non-churchgoing class of manual labourers in the Scottish heartlands.

The front pages of a lot of newspapers were still reserved for lucrative advertising rather than news, and Thomson regularly booked block ads directly below the masthead to give Liddell the highest possible pre-publicity. He was billed as 'The Great Eric Liddell'. Until he lived in Scotland, Liddell had no hint of the local brogue in his voice. At Eltham, he'd sounded like a middle-class Englishman. But those who heard him now remarked on the light lilt of Scots that had infiltrated his accent. He peppered his vocabulary with colloquialisms too. He became known for the slowness of his delivery, the clarity of his diction, the certainty of his beliefs and his egalitarianism. 'Sometimes,' said one observer, alive to his 'quiet earnestness', Liddell spoke 'in scarcely more than a whisper' that was nevertheless 'distinctly audible'. His sincerity endeared him to blue-collar audiences. There are speakers who begin each sentence with a trumpet and seem to be saying 'applause, please'. Liddell wasn't like this. There was no affectation of power or arrogant superiority when he addressed them. He didn't conceitedly strut, like a dandy dressed in his Sunday suit, in front of those who'd come to see him. Nor did he ever give the impression of being better than them. He often rose on his tip-toes to make a point and his approach was gently persuasive.

As one correspondent wrote in *The Scotsman* – making it apparent that Liddell didn't fall into the same category – 'there are many who think that being a Christian means being a milksop or a prig'. Liddell knew those who were both prigs and milksops and, believing such an attitude deterred would-be worshippers, he separated himself from them. He said he disliked the 'pious' and the 'preachy' whom, he thought, 'many will know from their own churches'. He went on: 'One finds many people about whom it is rightly said: if that is a typical example of a Christian, I am jolly glad I am not one.'

One sermon presented the quintessential Liddell. He gave a tutorial on the etymology of the word 'sincere', which derives from the Latin *sine ceres* – 'without wax'. 'Some sculptors in ancient Rome used wax to disguise a chip on a statue,' he'd say, conjuring an image of a craftsman hastily attempting to hide a mistake after a slip of his chisel. 'No one would see the flaw until the heat of the sun melted the wax or bad weather eroded it.' The sculptor was indulging in a deception, said Liddell; he was passing off an imperfect work as a perfect one. 'In this way he wasn't being truly sincere.' The audience waited expectantly for the punchline, which Liddell provided after a pause. 'If we allow cracks and blemishes to appear in our faith, and then ignore them or attempt to cover them up, we aren't being truly sincere either. We must strive to make our faith the perfect work. We are then sincere to ourselves and sincere to God.'

Time and again Liddell returned to the term 'be perfect'.

What he described as 'the stature of the perfect man' comprised nine credentials: patience, kindness, generosity, humility, courtesy, unselfishness, good temper, gentleness and sincerity. The imperative on that list was sincerity. He called it 'the basis of faith, mutual trust and co-operation'. And he regarded a lack of it as negating the other eight qualities, rendering them near worthless. Striving for perfection and an abhorrence of duplicity became paramount to Liddell. He expressed it through his liking for the power of plain words and short sentences.

The way he said all this was as important as what he said. Liddell liked the power of plain words and short sentences. The messages he delivered were uncomplicated. His methodology in preparing sermons never changed. While hours were spent thinking about the content of them, Liddell didn't write out rigid compositions. Having sat through countless formal sermons, he realized that prepared speeches could be stultifyingly dull for listener and reader alike. He preferred to make bullet-point notes in black ink and then speak extemporaneously. If a flare of fresh thought suddenly occurred as he spoke, Liddell could then incorporate it naturally into the text without disrupting his overall flow. He kept a profusion of fountain pens and mechanical propelling pencils in the top pocket of his jacket and the notes he made with them were composed in small, tight handwriting. The speed of pen over paper made it look as if one word was threatening to spill into the next. The upward and downward strokes of his letters were narrowly looped, and capital I's looked like upside down, lower case g's. To come across the notes, which he'd fold diagonally before slipping them into his Bible, would not necessarily have meant understanding them. One typical, but undated, entry was marked 'Faith' and plots his pattern of thought. It read:

A young man of 21. Pale face, tall lithe, serious
A solitary walk – on the edge of a precipice
Introspective – irritated
On the verge of the greatest discovery of his life

The description might refer to Liddell himself. He liked to weave his sermons around everyday happenings, his own experiences, or an item he'd seen in a newspaper, an overheard conversation or a scene he'd witnessed in a street. This, he believed, was always more relevant to people's lives than quoting the good book to them from the start. It was like stitching together a contemporary fable, the moral of which was always close to home. However circuitous his route to the crux of it, Liddell got there with a biblical passage.

Even as a seasoned speaker, Liddell claimed to lack the attributes to hold an audience, comparing himself to a beached fish. 'If I take a fish and ruthlessly cast it on to the heated sand, then ask it to breathe, I am asking it to do the impossible. If you take an athlete away from his proper sphere, his thin clothing and his fresh air, give him a stiff shirt and a collar that catches his neck [and] then on top of all that ask him to speak, you are asking him to break what I call the law of environment. He cannot speak. He can only gasp.'

He was being playfully bashful. Within two months of Armadale, now unafraid of crowds, he was in full song rather than gasping. Thomson said he was speaking 'better than I have ever heard him'. As the summer passed, Thomson noticed the difference in Liddell, commenting on the 'great strides' he was making: 'You would hardly know he was the same man as six months ago,' he wrote in his diary. 'We are getting on very, very happily together. I have never known a finer character in all my various experience . . . There has never been a hitch or a shadow in our friendship, and it is due to him almost entirely. He is pure gold through and through.' Liddell even wrote what Thomson called a 'very cheering' letter to him. In it Liddell said he was 'a changed man' after being asked to speak publicly. He explained that 'a new joy' had come into his life because of it. He regarded Armadale as a door that had suddenly materialized before him in a previously blank wall. In saying yes to Thomson, he had stepped through it.

The Paris Olympic Games were only fourteen and a half months away and Liddell's experiences as a preacher, moving from village to town and then on to city, fashioned his implacable response to them.

When a Scotsman does well, the English tend to call him British to associate themselves with the triumph. When a Scotsman does badly, the English usually refer to him as a Scot. At the beginning of the

1923 athletics season, Liddell was seen south of the border as a Scot.

Yes, he'd won six Scottish AAA titles, and another three were about to follow. Yes, he'd competed in, and won, the 100 yards in a Triangular International in Belfast. But his times didn't make poets of the news-paper reporters writing about him or send the Olympic selectors into rapture. To all concerned, he'd merely been running in minor events in minor places, such as West Kilbride, Saltcoats and Greenock, that had to be searched for on a map. His other meetings had been held under the banner of either football clubs, in Glasgow and Edinburgh, or the Scottish varsities. The competition against him was perceived as weak. What happened at Craiglockhart or Powderhall had almost no currency in London. Liddell agreed with his critics, saying that his times were 'not first class' and he was 'never up against the strength of the opposition' he'd later encounter elsewhere.

Apart from that boat trip across the Irish Sea, Liddell hadn't run any-where except Scotland. The Olympic selectors didn't think of him as a future champion. Liddell knew it. He thought the Amateur Athletic Association regarded it as a 'waste of £5' to send him to London for the British Championships at Stamford Bridge in July. 'The week before I had put up a miserable performance and the sporting writers were rightly pessimistic about the outcome of my trip,' he said. Liddell was treated as another Scottish athlete who would make up the numbers and catch the train home again afterwards.

The British 100 yards record stood at 9.8 seconds. In May Liddell had clocked only 10.6 seconds in the 100 yards at Craiglockhart. In June he'd improved, registering 10.1 – a Scottish record – and then won the Scottish AAA race in 10.4 seconds. The hyper-critical thought it revealed incon-sistency. Absent from that assessment was Liddell's time in a handicap 100 yards at Hampden Park, sandwiched between the first two races. Because of that handicap, he came second. His time, however, was 10 seconds flat.

Liddell said he was often asked why championship times in Scotland were 'so much slower than in England'. He was certain the rain and the chills of its unreliable summers and the frosts and snows of its winters were the cause. 'I am inclined to think it is mostly that. In our cold northern climate training is not nearly as interesting a business,' he said, suggesting that in the bleakest months – from November to the end of February – athletes had to chip away ice and shovel snow drifts simply to accomplish an outdoor stretching exercise. He also thought his home track, Powderhall, was 'meant to be a slow one', which adversely distorted results there.

On his way to Stamford Bridge, Liddell was aware of one thing above all others. These championships were 'the thing', he said, because 'there was never any doubt about the calibre of men I was drawn against'.

In *Chariots of Fire*, Liddell's duellist is Harold Abrahams. The two of them are portrayed as if locked in the athletic equivalent of an irresolvable Montague and Capulet-like feud – the roots of it lodged in Abrahams' shaking fear of losing to his rival. *Chariots of Fire* has Abrahams travelling to Edinburgh to spy on Liddell. He is seen in suit and straw boater discreetly taking his seat in the wooden stand. Liddell runs, and wins convincingly, on a grass track that resembles a suburban lawn gone to seed. Abrahams reacts to Liddell's speed as if someone has shot him, and his brain has been slow to tell the rest of his body about the bullet. His eyes widen. His teeth clench. He begins to scrunch up the event programme, wringing it in his hands as if rinsing out a dishcloth. 'He runs like a wild animal,' says Abrahams. 'He unnerves me.'

In fact, he had never seen Liddell run before Stamford Bridge.

Abrahams was twenty-three, gaunt and dark-haired, the hairline razor-straight across his forehead. As a Jew, the anti-Semitism he repeatedly encountered both at his public school, Repton, and his university, Cambridge, was appalling. Abrahams insisted one boarding house at Repton turned him down because of his religion. Some of the bigotry was sly and insidious, such as a stray remark or a social snub veiled as though neglect or an oversight, rather than prejudice, had caused it. Abrahams, though a Repton prefect, wasn't permitted to read the lesson during assemblies. As his faith didn't recognize Jesus as God's son, he was deemed unsuitable to say the line 'through Jesus Christ our Lord, Amen'. Abrahams offered a compromise to the headmaster. He'd say instead 'through Jesus Christ *your* Lord, Amen'. The headmaster refused. These were nasty bites, which left marks ever after. Abrahams admitted to having 'a chip' on his shoulder because of them. The slights he suffered propelled him towards 'something where I could score off people' and 'justify myself', he said. That 'something' was athletics.

Edinburgh University's magazine, the *Student*, said of Liddell that 'everyone is fond of him'. The same was never said of Abrahams at Cambridge. He found it impossible to be modest about his prowess. His entry in the *Dictionary of National Biography* explained curtly: 'If the road to popularity at university lies in never inculcating a sense of inferiority into one's contemporaries, Abrahams stood little chance of being popular.'

Cambridge, under the track tutorials of Alec Nelson, produced the *crème de la crème* after the war. As well as Abrahams, there were the middle-distance runners Henry Stallard, twenty-two, and Douglas Lowe, twenty-one, and the twenty-four-year-old Guy Butler, who had won the 440 yards AAA title as a whippy young fellow in 1919. He had a reputation for being a bit of a scatter-brain. One story – surely apocryphal – has a starter asking him whether he is ready to race. 'Of course,' he replied, 'why do you ask?' The starter looked at him quizzically and then said, 'Because you haven't tied up your laces.' Once he was said to have gone on to the track without his glasses, which he'd left in a jacket pocket. The race was delayed while he went to retrieve them.

Each of these athletes, like Abrahams, was a certainty to go to Paris. The difference between them was personality. Stallard, Lowe and Butler were convivial and clubbable and well liked. Abrahams was abrasive. When *The Times* asked him to write anonymously for them – a piece headlined 'Sports at Cambridge' – he committed the ungentlemanly error of saluting himself in the article. 'H. M. Abrahams did well to win the Hundred Yards race in 10.2 seconds against [the] wind and his winning leap in the Long Jump was a good effort,' he said. This counted against him when the Hawks Club, the elite union of Cambridge's sportsmen, debated his membership. He was black-balled.

Abrahams' focus on winning Olympic gold in the 100 metres was monomaniacal and he believed no one in Britain could match him, including Liddell. His opinion changed only when he watched Liddell run in the 220 yards during the AAA Championships. He'd later describe what he'd witnessed as 'the most misplaced direction of energy I had ever imagined possible . . . as a runner he had about every conceivable fault of form except the irresistible will to win'. He christened Liddell 'The Human Spider', a nickname meant to be derogatory because he considered him to be a 'complete model of everything that should not be done'. Liddell nonetheless won his opening heat in 22.4 seconds. This was deeply troubling to Abrahams, who had been the playground bully as far as British sprinting was concerned. Now he cringed at the prospect of being bullied himself. In the semi-finals – recording 21.6 seconds – Liddell demoralized Abrahams, 4 yards behind him at the tape. 'I realised his power to the full when I had a back view of him,' said Abrahams, who still had a chance of facing Liddell again because his own time – 22 seconds – qualified him for a run-off against another fastest loser. Abrahams bottled it. Not wanting Liddell to embarrass him again, he made his excuses and pulled out. The following morning he withdrew from the 100 yards as well, citing a 'bad throat' – an ailment that, somewhat curiously, reoccurred whenever the possibility of losing loomed ahead of him. The psychosomatic nature of it was confirmed later that same day when Abrahams arose improbably from his sick bed to win the long jump. The side-on photograph of the leap captures someone who looks to be the fittest human being on God's earth.

Abrahams liked to swallow a teaspoon of Easton's Syrup, the advertisements for which trumpeted it as an innocent, universal pick-me-up. This was no equivalent of the modern glucose drink. Easton's was a sinister and foul-tasting concoction containing a drop of strychnine (a banned substance for today's Olympians), which was liable to corrode the gullet and the stomach wall. Abrahams took it to pep himself up directly before a race. It was just as well he didn't take on Liddell over 100 yards; an industrial quantity of Easton's would have been needed to get close to him. The three timekeepers logged him at 9.67 seconds, 9.65 seconds and 9.65 seconds. This was officially levelled off to 9.7 seconds – a new British record. He then won the final of the 220 yards as well – his sixth sprint in less than twenty-four hours – in 21.6 seconds.

As usual Liddell was restrained about his success. He made it sound as though the weather had done the hard graft for him. The heat, filling Stamford Bridge, meant that Tom McKerchar didn't have to massage Liddell's legs to loosen his muscles. 'It was a grilling, hot day . . . perfect for short-distance running,' he said, as though reluctant to take credit for the quality of his performances.

The AAA Championships was an education for both Liddell and Abrahams. It taught Abrahams about his deficiencies. From somewhere – his start, his stride, his finish – he needed to extract an extra yard to make him competitive in Paris. It taught Liddell that he was a serious contender for the Olympics. 'I surprised even myself,' he said of his winner's medals. These pushed him into a decision that McKerchar had always said would need to be made eventually: Liddell would have to sacrifice his winter sport, which was rugby union.

Head up, chest forward, Eric Liddell wins the 220 yards at the AAA Championships at Stamford Bridge in 1923.

At the end of 1921, after appearances for Edinburgh University, Scotland had selected him for a trial on the wing and then picked him a few months later for an international in France, his pace securing him a place. Liddell was also considered to have fast hands as well as fast legs and to be a dogged defender. 'When he smother-tackled you, [then] you stayed smothered,' said one correspondent.

In a supreme coincidence, as if Fate was allowing him a dress rehearsal there, Liddell made his debut in the Colombes Stadium. The French and the Scots drew 3–3 in front of a crowd of thirty-seven thousand. Afterwards, as the rest of the team went to a Parisian show, Liddell walked to the top of the Arc de Triomphe. Another six appearances followed in two years, including Scotland's first win – 11–8 – at Wales's Cardiff Arms Park since 1890. There was another Eltham old boy in that XV. Called the 'vital, living force of the three quarter line', A. L. Gracie, awarded the Military Cross in 1915, proved a mercurial partner to his former schoolmate. Even the Welsh supporters chaired both of them off the field.

But rugby was a hazardous pursuit, the body unprotected. McKerchar worried whenever he thought of what might happen during a game. Should Liddell be caught up in a ruck or a maul, or get badly charged and fall awkwardly, he could break a leg or tear a cruciate ligament; then his career would only ever be talked about in the past tense. 'Rugby', said Liddell, was both 'a blessing and a small curse' to him. If he didn't play, he could build up his athletic strength. If he did play, he knew his stamina would improve. By eventually deciding it was more curse than blessing, Liddell pleased his coach. As much as he 'loved rugger', he explained, athletics held the 'strongest appeal' for him.

D. P. Thomson pointed out that Eric Liddell's participation in evangelism caused a few to say – and a lot more to fear – that his running was bound to wither because of the extra demands preaching made on him. 'It had exactly the opposite effect,' stressed Thomson, who felt what he labelled as 'spiritual liberation' was turning Liddell into 'a happier and a fitter man'.

That Liddell was reaching a new peak of performance became brilliantly clear in the unglamorous setting of Stoke, where the red-bricked bottle kilns of Wedgwood and Doulton squatted across the landscape like sumo wrestlers about to grapple one another. After the AAAs, sapping mentally as well as physically, no one expected another gala run from Liddell in a triangular international between England, Scotland and Ireland. The tournament was perceived as nothing more than a chance for the town's pottery and ceramic workers to glimpse the champion. Liddell adhered to that script. He won both the sprints, never shedding much sweat.

Less was expected of him in the 440 yards. He'd been entered only out of necessity. Scotland drafted Liddell into it to fill the lanes: the selectors weren't flush with athletes capable of competently covering that distance. He could have coasted through this obligation and claimed afterwards that he'd been too fatigued to make a fist of things. No one would have complained. What he did instead was produce the race of that summer – and most other summers beside. Those who saw him felt Liddell had summoned up something other-worldly. The *Scotsman* – and not out of bias or patriotism either – described it as 'bordering on the miraculous'. It quoted unidentified 'veterans, whose memories take them back thirty-five years and in some cases even longer' – the sentence suggests a row of men with white beards and seamed faces who witnessed it through rheumy eyes. According to the *Scotsman*, these old salts of the cinder acclaimed Liddell's run as 'the greatest track performance' any of them had 'ever seen'. In fairness, the nitty-gritty detail of what he did makes the feat seem extraordinary.

The race began on a bend. Liddell, given the inside lane, had travelled less than 10 feet when another competitor came to the kerb, clipped his foot and also pushed him over. Liddell tumbled on to the grassy verge, breaking his fall with outstretched hands. Assuming that leaving the track had disqualified him, Liddell watched the rest of the field carry on without him. In the grandstand, his voice indistinguishable amid the cheering, Tom McKerchar yelled at him to start running again. Liddell, still unaware that the rules permitted his return, continued to look and linger until a suited official chivvied him along. The front-markers were already almost 20 yards ahead – a gap that seemed insurmountable unless Liddell strapped a petrol engine to his back. Liddell tilted his head upwards and started a long, long chase. The crowd began to watch him rather than the leaders, never thinking a comeback was even a dim possibility. But Liddell, blazing like a magnesium flame, slashed the lead to 10 yards and then to 5. At the top of the home straight, he was only two strides off the front. At the line he was 6 yards ahead of everyone else. Even to see all this wasn't to believe it. The crowd looked at one another incredulously.

Having poured everything of himself on to that Stoke track, Liddell then collapsed unconscious into its dirt and was carried into the dressing rooms. Half an hour passed before he woke again. His head throbbed. He was offered a sip of brandy. Liddell turned it down. 'No thanks . . . just a drop of strong tea,' he replied. Afterwards, Liddell said he'd felt something go 'bust' in his head, which led to his black-out.

That run confirmed Stamford Bridge as no flashy fluke.

Eric Liddell's sprint double at the AAAs, as well as the mesmerizing run at Stoke, brought him more than national recognition. With it came new friendships too.

Harold Abrahams could never be a bosom buddy with someone capable of licking him in a race. Liddell was the enemy, after all. But, post Stamford Bridge, the other past and present members of Alec Nelson's Cambridge running clique – the triumvirate of Lowe, Stallard and Butler, plus Arthur Marshall, a quarter-miler, and the hurdler David Burghley – effectively made him an honorary member of the group.

The unofficial chairman was Philip Noel-Baker, who'd become the non-participating captain of Britain's Olympic team. As 'Mr Baker' – his wife's maiden name was added to his own after their marriage in 1915 – he'd been a 1,500 metres finalist at the Stockholm Games in 1912, aged twenty-two. At Antwerp eight years later, he'd carried the flag and won a silver medal at the same distance. He was a former president of the Cambridge Union, a former president of the Cambridge University Athletic Club and a fellow of King's College. Noel-Baker, though only a dozen years Liddell's senior, dispensed fatherly wisdom and also pastoral care, as if he was village clergyman and the athletes were his parishioners. He and Liddell enjoyed an immediate rapport. Noel-Baker's mother came from the Scottish borders. He'd been raised as a Quaker. As a conscientious objector during the Great War, Noel-Baker drove ambulances in France and Italy, winning the Mons Star and Silver Medal. Liddell regarded him as a high-class fellow of unimpeachable character, one of those men other men are proud to know. He listened attentively when Noel-Baker spoke and would quote back the things he had said to him. Like Tom McKerchar and D. P. Thomson, he won Liddell's unqualified trust.

These companionships – and Noel-Baker's influence in particular – were to become important in the coming months. Liddell fitted in and found the company in Cambridge naturally congenial. Lowe and Butler were quiet and unflappable, and neither of them smoked nor drank. Stallard, Marshall and Burghley, the future 6th Marquess of Exeter, were hail-fellows-well-met. Liddell liked each of them enormously.

There were formal sessions for British athletes at the White City and Crystal Palace. McKerchar's friendship with Nelson made him open to the idea of Liddell using the Cambridge circuit at Fenners as a convenient stop-over during trips between Edinburgh and London. Liddell learned in the hothouse atmosphere that Nelson had developed. 'The analogy is similar to that of a three-year-old being put through his paces by an older horse,' he explained. His Cambridge pals encouraged him to train on the beach at Hunstanton in Norfolk during days out that were meant to be pleasurably recreational as well as work. In return he invited them to run with him on the sands of North Berwick, close to the place where his parents had once rented a house.

Cambridge also charmed him for another reason.

*

Raised in that all-male environment of Eltham, Eric Liddell, the boy, had been so shy that he'd dropped out of the tennis team picked to challenge the nearby girls' school. Liddell the teenager, while running for Edinburgh University, hadn't joined in when his fellow athletes waved back at half a dozen women in flapper dresses at a train crossing. But Liddell the young man had begun to call on the artist Eileen Soper at the home she shared with her parents and sister in Harmer Green, Hertfordshire, only 35 miles from Cambridge. Liddell had known her since his schooldays.

Eileen was born in 1905, the second daughter of the acclaimed artist George Soper, who illustrated children's classics such as *Grimm's Fairy Tales* and Charles Kingsley's *The Water Babies* before becoming synonymous with paintings of horses and the farmers and land-labourers who ploughed until the turned fields resembled wide bolts of brown corduroy. An early conservationist and botanist, with a special interest in ferns, he built the house that Eileen eventually christened Wildings. Its grey stuccoed walls were planted in 4 acres. It became the family's sanctuary, a small world within the world. The garden was deliberately allowed to grow semi-wild. There was a meadow, a lawn, a feeding ground for birds, a deer shelter, an orchard and a spinney, a rose garden, a water garden and a summer house on the property's western boundary.

Eileen inherited her father's talent. He taught her to paint, etch and draw, nurturing her into a child prodigy. Aged fifteen, Eileen became the youngest artist ever to exhibit at the Royal Academy, making her famous on either side of the Atlantic. *Good Housekeeping* magazine called her 'A Schoolgirl Among the Masters'.

Her face was elfin. Her hair, dropping almost to her waist, was a vivid red-gold and centrally parted. She often heaped it into side bunches. Her cheekbones were sculptured. As well as her looks, she turned heads because of her intelligence and a love of motor cars and driving. But she was a bit of a prude, recoiling from ribaldry, however harmless. She condemned even Shakespeare for his 'coarse expressions'. Eileen didn't swear. She didn't drink either. This didn't deter suitors, towards whom she could be picky and prickly, offering cold rebuffs on first sight.

Liddell was the exception.

She was smitten with him. He was intelligent, decent-looking, respectable, mannered and kind. The two of them talked, drank tea and strolled

Eileen Soper, who became one of the most prominent wildlife painters of her generation.

COURTESY OF THE CHRIS BEETLES GALLERY, ST JAMES'S, LONDON ON BEHALF OF AGBI AND THE SOPER ESTATE

in the garden and the surrounding countryside. Even though Eileen knew of Liddell's Christian beliefs and his intention to go to China eventually, she began to think that a formal courtship, engagement and marriage might come from the relationship.

Life now seemed set fair for Liddell; for him there were blue skies everywhere. He had found his religious direction. He had a new set of friends – and a 'girlfriend' too. He was among the favourites for the Olympic 100 metres title.

What could possibly go awry?

CHAPTER THREE

Coming to the Crossroads

THE MAN WHO ENDED 1924 as an Olympic champion began it as an Olympic scapegoat, a victim of others' incompetence.

From January to late June, some considered him to be a traitor. By mid-July, he was a role model and a crowd darling. In between those wild poles of opinion neither he nor his principles ever changed. To dwell on those simple facts now is to admire more than ever what Eric Liddell overcame to win that gold medal in Paris – the abandonment of two years' work on a point of principle, the gamble of tackling another event as a novice, the thick-skinned will to resist criticism and coercion.

This amateur sport required a professional outlook. The British Olympic Association, however, were slack and inconsistent about providing it. Comfortably settled in the upholstered leather of London's gentlemen's clubs such as the Garrick and the Carlton, the higher echelons of the BOA were supposedly the great and the good of society, anointed so automatically at birth without the inconvenient need for achievement to precede such status. The president was George Sutherland-Leveson-Gower, the 5th Duke of Sutherland, then the government's Under-Secretary of State for Air who had, conversely, been a Royal Naval Commander. Its committee was an amalgam of the upper crust: peers, knights and Conservative members of Parliament with country houses and swathes of land. There was the Earl of Birkenhead, then the Lord Chancellor. There was the 5th Marquess of Cholmondeley, a direct descendant of Britain's first Prime Minister, the periwigged Sir Robert

Walpole. There was Cholmondeley's brother-in-law, Sir Philip Sassoon, a cousin of the war poet Siegfried. Sir Philip's mother was a Rothschild and he had been Sir Douglas Haig's private secretary during the war. There was the courtier Lord Tweedmouth – his mother was Winston Churchill's aunt – and also Viscount Curzon, brother-in-law to Churchill's father, Randolph. So it went on – a parade of the gentry, who regularly appeared in *Tatler* and *Country Life* and basked in the advantages of the old boys' network, the snaky tendrils of which spread throughout the British Establishment. As a group, the BOA was nevertheless pretty damn pathetic.

Lavish dinners were held at the Savoy, where peers invited other peers. The problem was this: most of the BOA's upper crust existed for show, seldom dirtying their white-gloved hands. Birkenhead, though initially the face and voice of the Appeals Committee, didn't do much heavy lifting. The grind of the work fell chiefly on the chairman – Gerald Oakley Cadogan, the 6th Earl of Cadogan – and the secretary, Reginald Kentish, a Brigadier General with a DSO. At least Kentish was an enthusiastic grafter. In the war he'd also been solicitous towards the plight of the ordinary Tommy in the trenches. In contrast, Cadogan was a Grosvenor Street toff from the tip of his long nose to the toes of his hand-made shoes. He was the sort of man for whom appearances mattered. He was fifty-five, but already looked well past sixty. When the royal photographers Bassano Limited snapped Cadogan in 1921, his hair was so sparse that his high forehead gleamed, beacon-like, in the overhead light.

Funding for the British Olympic team was generated through public subscription. In spats and a flat-topped silk hat, the cane-carrying Kentish toured towns and cities eliciting donations. In some of them the response was apathetic. 'No one seems to know or care about them,' he said, exasperatedly, of the Olympics. Despite the enormous personal wealth of the BOA's blue-bloods, and also its friends in high places, raising £30,000 for Paris proved arduous. The King, George V, tried to set an example. He gave £100. The Prince of Wales, the future Edward VIII, chipped in £50. The *Daily Mail* handed over 1,000 guineas and published numerous articles, each swaddled in the flag of patriotism, asking readers to contribute for the sake of Britain's competitive pride. But, less than seven weeks before the Games began, the BOA was still £2,000 adrift of its target – an amount most of its grander big-wigs would have spent without a quibble on the annual hunt ball.

From day one the preoccupation with money and the arrangement of peripheral matters in Paris, such as hotels for dignitaries and glad-handing on the cocktail circuit, consumed the BOA's thoughts. To judge from the minutes of Association meetings, as well as its public proclamations, the business of winning medals was almost secondary. There was a debate about who should travel first class – certainly not the athletes – and the choice of coloured ribbon to decorate the straw boater of the official uniform. The Association hired the London department store Gamages to make these uniforms. It was a penny-pinching option. Clothes didn't maketh the British men or women of these Olympics. The team went to the chicest city on the globe in outfits that looked to have been cut by a myopic tailor with a grievous grudge against both them and the Games. 'Ghastly,' is how Harold Abrahams described his blazer and white flannels. In one photograph Abrahams resembles the silent movie comedian Buster Keaton. Nothing fits him. His three-button jacket is too tight, even straining around the flatness of his belly. His trousers are too short. The turn-ups rise almost above the ankle, exposing his black socks. His boater is too big, casting such a wide shadow across his eyes that he seems to be wearing a mask that pre-dates the Lone Ranger's. It's as if Abrahams has borrowed each of these items from men of a different shape and size from him. The Association seemed chuffed with itself nonetheless. Cadogan called the uniform 'serviceable and neat' – presumably because he didn't have to wear it – and the Association boasted that 'no undue extravagance' had been permitted in purchasing it.

Hotel accommodation in Paris didn't compensate for the cheap tailoring. The Moderne on Place de la Republique was a budget affair into which competitors were corralled. According to Abrahams, it was a 'little miserable'. The bedrooms were functional. The walls were as thin as cigarette paper.

The selection of the uniform and the choice of the hotel seem harmless irritations. To complain about them could even be construed as being over-finicky. But both illustrate the BOA's tendency to regard the athletes the way a dog regards its fleas. Both also explain why, after failing to place the competitors first and foremost, the BOA either missed or ignored the crisis looming ahead of it.

Its arrogance, neglect and complacency were to blame for the predicament Liddell faced.

*

In *Chariots of Fire*, Eric Liddell is seen climbing the gangplank on the boat to Paris when an American journalist hollers at him, 'Mr Liddell, what about the qualifying heats on Sunday?' We then see Liddell on the quarter-turn. The expression on his face forms a question mark of concern, as though he's been asked something in a language he only half-comprehends. His mouth falls open. 'What did you say?' he asks, without waiting for the reply. On the boat he's told the programme of events for the Olympics has appeared in that morning's newspapers, and that to race in the 100 metres requires him to compete on a Sunday.

The film moves on to the gilt and chandelier finery of the British Embassy in Paris. Liddell has been summoned to a meeting, where the Prince of Wales, the Duke of Sutherland, the Earl of Birkenhead and Lord Cadogan attempt to force him to compete. Liddell is in white tie and tails. He looks like the head butler about to take a drinks order. The Prince goes into a small speech, designed to appeal to the heart: 'We share a common heritage, a common bond, a common loyalty. There are times when we are asked to make sacrifices in the name of that loyalty. Without them our allegiance is worthless. As I see it, for you, this is such a time.'

Liddell resists the argument. The Prince looks slightly askance. Cadogan glowers and becomes irascible, a cartoon version of a grumpy old man. You sense the room freezing over.

Then enter 'Lord Lindsay', whom *Chariots* has earlier depicted winning a bronze medal in the 100 metres hurdles. Lindsay apologizes for the intrusion, appreciates and respects Liddell's position and so proposes a kind of hey-presto escape for him. Lindsay has his medal. So, for Liddell's sake, he will give up his place in the 400 metres. The solution elicits handshakes and smiles.

Each scene is an invention. There was no revelation on the gangplank. No smoky conclave in the British Embassy. No 'Lord Lindsay', a fictional concoction based on Liddell's friend David Burghley. And Burghley could not have donated his 400 metres spot because he'd never been entered for the race.

The truth is much more prosaic, and the complications arising from it were avoidable – if Cadogan and Reginald Kentish had been administratively alert.

The draft timetable for the Games was shaped early in 1922. The

British Olympic Association paid only the scantiest attention to it. Liddell was then barely a contender and the English-dominated BOA didn't consider a Scot, still to race in front of them, as an important figure. That oversight was prejudiced but understandable. Future oversights, however, were inexcusably slovenly.

The BOA received the Games' revised timetable in the first weeks of spring 1923. No one matched the dates of the 100 metres to the days of the week. Only when Liddell received his copy – in late autumn that same year – did he and Tom McKerchar realize the calendar was against him. He alerted the BOA, which was still blithely unaware of the conflict of conscience confronting him. Not only did the schedule prevent Liddell from running in the 100 metres, he couldn't run in the 4×100 metres or 4×400 metres relays either because both involved Sunday competition. Only the 200 metres, in which he'd always planned to compete anyway, and the 400 metres events didn't encroach on that day.

The BOA didn't understand Olympic history. Paris was merely following the template laid down in 1920 in Antwerp, where the 100 metres heats and the relays had also swept through Sunday. The International Olympic Committee was generally unsympathetic towards Sunday non-combatants such as Liddell too. Disputes about it had scarred previous Games. In 1900, coincidentally in Paris, the American Sabbatarian John Cregan declined to run in the 1,500 metres. Another American, Robert Garrett, withdrew from the shot and the standing triple jump. A third American, long jumper Myer Prinstein, though Jewish, found himself barred from the final because his university, Syracuse, was against Sunday sport.

Much of the controversy was entirely of the IOC's making. The Sabbatarians in Paris were originally promised that field events beginning on Saturday could be completed on Monday. The IOC was guilty of committing two howlers. First, the policy was abruptly reversed. Second, either through cowardice or cock-up, news of that decision wasn't communicated properly; a few athletes even turned up on Monday unaware of the committee's U-turn. A well-run movement would have learned lessons and found a decent compromise thereafter. The IOC was intractable, even though the loss of athletes from Sunday events distorted the results. Even in London's 1908 Olympics, the American hurdler Forrest Smithson ran, and won, with a Bible in his left hand, carrying it in protest at being 'forced to compete' on the Sabbath, and to demonstrate his faith in God.

Liddell wouldn't run clutching the Bible; indeed, he wouldn't run at all on a Sunday. This was scarcely classified information. He'd already stated his opposition to Sunday competition 'in toto' and had quoted both the Fourth Commandment – about keeping the Sabbath holy – and the book of Revelation, which identifies it as the 'Lord's Day'. Anyone doubting Liddell's conviction was surely enlightened in July 1923 when he dropped out of an international against France in Paris's Stade Pershing because of its Sabbath staging. As Britain beat the French that day, Liddell was preaching at an open-air gathering in Greenock, where he had cantered through a 100 yards race the previous afternoon. In his sermon he said there 'could be no neutrality [where] Christianity was concerned'. His explanation was succinct. 'Each one comes to the cross-roads at some period of his life and must make his decision for or against his Master.'

Aware of this, the BOA ought from the outset to have been negotiating to make sure the 100 metres steered clear of Sunday. It ought to have said that Paris in 1924 shouldn't duplicate the errors of Paris of 1900. And it ought then to have added that Liddell's absence would detract significantly from the spectacle. The BOA did none of this – at least not until it was too late.

In November 1923, Liddell told them of his withdrawal from the 100 metres. Weeks later, so slow on the uptake that the attempt to tinker with the timetable seemed almost posthumous, the BOA finally wrote a begging letter to the IOC. It wasn't brave enough to specify the scheduling of the sprint as its motivation. Attempting to disguise its embarrassment, the BOA faked a wider altruism, as if it were a megaphone for other countries too timid to speak up. This made it look more imbecilic than ever. The BOA called for 'any athlete who objected to running or taking part in any game on a Sunday' to be allowed to rearrange his event. Predictably the IOC saw through the ruse and reacted contemptuously. Their reply was terse, the written equivalent of a slap across the jowls. The IOC said it couldn't ask Paris to 'make any such arrangement'.

Presuming Liddell was vulnerable to tender but firm persuasion, the BOA tried to apply it. There was no use appealing to his vanity. He was neither self-possessed nor interested in athletic posterity. There was no use playing the nationalism card either. He answered to a higher calling than country. Demonstrating a woeful ignorance of his background and his character, the BOA took a third tack, thinking his religion was malleable.

Liddell received a lecture about the loose strictures of the continental Sabbath. In France, he was told, the Sabbath ended officially at noon, which would enable him to pray in the morning and compete in the afternoon. Liddell deflected the insult of that suggestion with a put-down dressed decorously. 'My Sabbath lasts all day,' he said. The BOA then tried to find common ground through catechism. Since God had made him fast, wouldn't he be doing His will by competing? And wouldn't it be a slight against Him if he didn't? Such an approach seemed entirely appropriate to anyone non-devout – and entirely misguided to those who were. Liddell liked to recite what he called 'the three sevens'. This is the seventh verse in the seventh chapter of the seventh book of the New Testament: 'Every man hath his proper gift of God'. Liddell was adamant where his gift had come from, and equally adamant that the Bible forbade him to use it on a Sunday. The answer continued to dumbfound the secularists on the BOA, each incapable of seeing the world as Liddell saw it.

The BOA wasn't alone in its lack of understanding. Britain was hardly a puritan culture. As Peter Fryer points out in his book *Mrs Grundy*, a study of English prudery, the new century – and particularly the war – brought rebellion against the starchy gloom of the Sundays before. What Fryer described as emancipation from 'scriptural guidance' was gradually taking place. The Lord's Day Observance Society had been influential in Victorian Britain, attempting to crush underfoot anything that interfered with churchgoing. It protested against Sunday cinema, music hall and theatre, and even the running of Sunday trams. The Society's determination to tell everyone else how to behave shut pubs, art galleries, markets and fairs and also banned concerts and dances. The Society didn't like housewives hanging out washing on a Sunday, or their husbands reading a Sunday newspaper either. And it took the dimmest view possible of sport of any kind – even recreational cycling. The British Sunday under the old Queen was bleak and boring, the dread of most of the population. Attitudes changed incrementally following her death and gathered a ripping speed after 1918. Sunday strictures were shunted aside. The Society's members were seen as busybody 'Mrs Grundys', the censorious gasbag of a neighbour in Thomas Morton's eighteenth-century play *Speed the Plough*.

That modern mood worked against Liddell. Some of the public saw his attitude towards Sunday as anachronistic, dismissing him as holier-than-thou – a Mrs Grundy of the track – and a sap of a Society of which it erroneously assumed he was a card-carrying member. Some thought he was using religion as an excuse to duck a scrap with America's sprinters, who were odds on to beat him. Some believed he was sabotaging Britain's Olympic ambitions for a stance that seemed hollow and pointless to them. And some – expressing an opinion that chimed with the BOA's own – couldn't comprehend why Liddell wouldn't sacrifice one Sunday of kneeling prayer when a long lifetime of other Sundays stretched ahead of him.

The newspapers were initially slow off the mark, hardly recognizing Liddell's predicament as a headline story. The *Evening Standard*'s sports gossip columnist, signing himself 'Olympian', wrote at the end of December 1923, 'I learn from authoritative Scottish sources that Liddell will only compete in the Games . . . if the day of his heats is changed.' The *Sporting Life* ran an almost identical item in the same week.

Eventually the penny dropped, the full implication of Liddell's decision falling into focus. Reporters were dispatched to his rooms in George Square. One of his housemates saw a knot of them on the pavement. 'They hammered on the door demanding to see him,' he said. The housemate, sent down to clear them off, heard cries of 'he's a traitor to his country'. The atmosphere was 'quite menacing', he added. He also thought Liddell had become 'the most unpopular man in Britain'. The religious newspaper *Life of Faith* remarked on the 'icy criticism and cheap gibes' that it said were 'heard on every side' about him. The word 'heard' is significant. Liddell was slandered rather than libelled. The *Daily Mail*, for instance, level-headedly lamented only the 'severe loss' to Britain's Olympic prospects and refused to revile him. The *Edinburgh Evening News*, in favour of the local boy, announced that 'every Scotsman . . . respects the champion's view on this subject'.

The BOA continued under the misapprehension that Liddell could be turned. Alfred George was appointed manager of the Paris team. George was a fifty-six-year-old ex-runner who had won a dozen titles in England and North America during a career overshadowed by the Herculean feats of his older brother Walter, one of the first superstars of the sport. Walter was an AAA champion before turning professional, clocking a world record in the mile of 4 minutes 12 seconds in 1886. No one beat that mark for twenty-nine years. He drank beer excessively, smoked cigars and a pipe regularly and gambled away his prize money. But fame meant his face appeared on cigarette cards and he was hailed as 'The Champion of Champions' in a colourful caricature published in *Vanity Fair*. The artist Ape depicted him as giraffe-necked and knitting-needle thin. Alfred, always six steps behind him as an athlete, turned himself into a po-faced administrator and freelance writer, signing his articles 'A. B. George'.

He had a lofty view of his own contributions in the *All Sports Illustrated Weekly*, as though his pronouncements on the Olympics had been typed atop Mount Olympus. In one piece about Paris, George said the team 'feared we shall lack the services of E. H. Liddell', who 'hesitates to compete on the Sabbath'. Liddell had never hesitated. And George knew he'd scratched from the 100 metres already. The BOA wouldn't explicitly criticize Liddell in public. But nor – and this was glaringly apparent – did it offer support in public either. George's line, slipped in like a long blade, was mischief making.

Not everyone was anti-Liddell. A vicar in Aberdeen addressed his congregation on 'World Wide Christian Patriotism' and advocated that Liddell upheld 'the best traditions of the country' with his adherence to his faith. He was likened to 'Daniel', pushed into the lions' den because of his refusal to abandon prayer. The lyrics of the Salvation Army hymn were even quoted in his honour:

Dare to be a Daniel,
Dare to stand alone,
Dare to have a purpose firm,
Dare to make it known.

In a widely syndicated column called The Way the World Wags, a collection of gossipy titbits and wry asides, the unidentified writer waved another flag for him. He wrote:

The French artisans are content to work six days a week, and then to
hold their sports, their races, their football matches and all other forms
of sport on Sunday afternoon. Churchmen claim a free hand after
High Mass and non-churchgoers take no notice whatsoever of Sabbath
observance. We have travelled too far ourselves on that same road, and
it is refreshing to see a young man abandon his chance of success at

the greatest sports meeting in the world rather than compete on a
Sunday. He will be laughed at; but we are certain it takes more courage
to stand up for conscience sake than to win the Olympic sprint.

He ended the piece with the words 'Good Luck'.

Luck could take care of itself. What Liddell needed most of all was
sensible advice and good coaching. Without it Paris would be purgatory
for him.

CHAPTER FOUR

I Wonder If I'm Doing the Right Thing?

Paris expected nothing from Eric Liddell. He had chosen the 400 metres only because no other replacement distance was feasible for him.

The prospect of transforming a sprinter into a quarter-miler over only five months of competition – and shaping him into an Olympian – would have pushed most coaches into squawking panics and sleepless nights. Had the voluble Sam Mussabini been asked to do so, on Harold Abrahams' behalf, there'd have been a pyrotechnical display of agitation, a stomp and a strop and then several weeks of agonized planning.

Tom McKerchar was a phlegmatic as well as a practical man. The logistics of this late challenge didn't fluster him. He wasn't whiny or pessimistic about Liddell's chances either. And, aware of Liddell's devotion to the Church, he didn't attempt to change his mind about Sunday competition. This was not only important to their partnership, it also demonstrated his loyalty. McKerchar was a British Olympic Association coach. The BOA expected its interests to be promoted. In declining to act as an advocate for them on the issue of Liddell's withdrawal from the 100 metres, McKerchar risked its wrath and possible excommunication from the coterie of officials bound for Paris. To his fabulous credit, McKerchar accepted Liddell's situation, changing tactics on his behalf as easily as a commuter might change trains. He even thought that the 400 metres would be a better fit for him than the 200 metres, immediately making it their priority. As Liddell would later confess: 'What his knowledge meant to me . . . can hardly be set down in cold print.'

No one is immune from needling criticism. It always leaves a trace, even if the mark isn't visible to the naked eye. Liddell had been naive. He'd expected his decision to be seen as an honest matter of integrity. He consequently assumed it would pass without much adverse comment, which goes to show that those incapable of malice rarely suspect it in others. However much he pretended otherwise, the backlash wounded him. Only much later did Liddell admit this to a friend. He was 'hurt', the friend said.

He made an ally in the *News of the World*'s athletics correspondent, the bespectacled, trilby-wearing Joe Binks, a former world record holder in the mile who'd become an authoritative voice in the press box because of his knowledge rather than the gleam of his prose. Unlike most London-based writers, Binks had taken the train to Scotland to study Liddell long before the AAA's championship made him an Olympic candidate. The two of them exchanged letters, and Binks occasionally quoted these in his weekly column. He alluded to Liddell's puzzlement and his sensitivity towards the flak the papers and the public had fired at him. In a letter to Binks he had complained tartly about those purporting to know 'somewhat more about me than I do myself'.

The textbooks said that Liddell was physically unsuited for the 400 metres. According to the coaching experts, the stamina and speed needed for it could only be produced from a slim, spare build. The runner had to be at least 5 feet 10 inches to 6 feet tall and not too heavy around the shoulders. The body had to be well balanced and the body-angle for one lap was reckoned to be a slight, forward inclination of the trunk from the waist. The step had to be lithe and springy. Liddell ticked none of those boxes. Only McKerchar and Binks sensed that he possessed the staying power to equal his sprinter's thrust.

Liddell was a greenhorn beyond 220 yards. In 1921 he'd competed over 300 yards at Ibrox, finishing third. In 1922, at Craiglockhart, he'd won a 440-yard event during the Edinburgh University Athletic Club Annual Games in 52.6 seconds. In 1923, again at Craiglockhart, he'd taken first place in another 440-yard contest, though his time was 0.2 of a second slower than before. Only Liddell's sensational comeback at Stoke suggested he could conquer the distance. McKerchar was unperturbed. The sole target was peak performance in Paris; nothing else mattered. Every appearance for Liddell now, whether as a student or as an athlete of the AAA's, was geared towards that fortnight in July. Times were insignificant to McKerchar, who was canny enough to know that there was a psychological advantage to be gained from holding back the cards of a winning hand. If Liddell built up his strength, he'd be ready for Paris and be capable of winning there.

Through his Cambridge connection, Liddell was invited to guest for the Achilles Club in the University of Pennsylvania Relays at the end of April 1924. The trip cost him £28. The BOA looked unfavourably on it, believing a transatlantic passage at the start of the season would disturb his Olympic build-up. Liddell, disagreeing, explained to Binks: 'I have studied myself every way and I know how I can get fit to produce my best form.' Recognizing the brotherhood that had formed between Liddell and the Cambridge set, Binks made an equally valid point about his keenness to travel. 'He wishes to go with his Varsity chums,' he said. The Achilles team included Douglas Lowe, David Burghley and Arthur Marshall.

The bare details make the journey seem horrendous. It was as if, like the Ancient Mariner, Liddell had shot an albatross at sea and been cursed. He lost one suitcase going out and another coming back. The first crossing was rough, making him badly seasick. Still queasy when the competition began, Liddell was an inadequate fourth in the 100 yards and second in the 220 yards. The *Athletic News and Cyclists Journal* reported the Americans' dismal opinion of him. Its Olympic coaches saw nothing to fear – 'unless he promptly corrects his mechanical faults', said the newspaper. Among journalists, Binks was isolated in his opinion that Liddell would win the 400 metres. 'In my day the more I was told I didn't have a chance, the more I would go out of my way to do something extra,' he wrote. He was convinced Liddell possessed that 'something extra' too.

Those runs in Pennsylvania, so feeble on paper, were part of a broader strategy. Liddell had told Binks that 'if I should get beaten it will be an ordinary event'; and this is how he subsequently saw it. 'I merely regarded it as an incident in my preparation for Paris,' he said. Liddell thought he 'ran well enough' anyway, despite never finding his 'land legs' in America. He was obeying McKerchar's instructions. Before sailing, Liddell said his coach was 'careful to insist anyway that I should not overdo things in order that I should be perfectly fit three months later'.

There were social consolations too. On the ship home Liddell met two sisters called Freddie and Edith, colourfully different from the conservatively attired and conservatively spoken Eileen Soper. The 'girls', as Arthur Marshall called them, were travelling to 'do Europe'. In cloche hats and sleeveless dresses, long strings of pearls around their necks, Freddie and Edith were the epitome of Jazz Age fashion, flaunting underarm hair as a matter of rebellion. Their skin was pale, which accentuated the kohl-black eyeliner each wore and their equally black, fashionably bobbed hair. 'They said they were going to be in Paris for the Olympic Games,' remembered Marshall, 'and we said if we were there at the same time we hoped we could meet.'

Liddell came home motivated by a quotation he'd seen displayed at the University of Pennsylvania. On several occasions Philip Noel-Baker had recited it to him at Cambridge. 'In the dust of defeat as well as in the laurels of victory there is a glory to be found if one has done his best.' Previously he had referred to a more familiar saying as 'my motto'. It was embroidered on white cloth and modestly framed and hung in countless homes: 'If a thing is worth doing, it is worth doing well.' The University of Pennsylvania sentence had more poetic power. With the Olympics so near, the words resonated with Liddell. Even if defeat awaited him in Paris, he would accept it and recognize the 'glory' of losing honourably, he said. 'Those words expressed everything about the true spirit of competition. I thought about them often as the weeks went by.'

The British Olympic Association continued to act as though Eric Liddell was about to capitulate over Sunday competition. The minutes of its meeting dated 27 May – less than six weeks before the opening ceremony – included him in the team for the 100 metres rather than the 400 metres, ignoring his wishes. Before that month blew out, the BOA accepted it had all along indulged in wishful thinking.

On May's final weekend Liddell ran his first serious 440-yard race for a year – only the fourth of his career. The morning before McKerchar had asked to meet him at a deserted Craiglockhart, where the event was held. The two of them strolled around the full circuit of the track. As he walked the straights and bends McKerchar gave a commentary, passing on insights about how the race ought to be tackled. 'He plotted out the vital stages, telling me exactly how to run each part; and, doing so, I was able to win,' said Liddell. Without over-exerting himself, he registered a respectable 51.5 seconds.

Unlike Sam Mussabini, who could overcomplicate running, McKerchar didn't involve himself in fancy theories. His approach before Paris was plain and direct. 'Always, when running the quarter, I used the same method,' said Liddell, again crediting McKerchar for it. 'It was the same method every "sprint" quarter-miler usually runs: the first hundred yards almost, if not quite, "all out". The back stretch at well over three-quarter pace. The next bend, which one takes as the slowest part of the journey. The last hundred as a sprint.'

Liddell was taught something else by McKerchar, which he described like this: 'Slowness in becoming perfectly fit is always a help [and] a little each day is better than a lot in one day.' Liddell went to Powderhall twice a week and once to Craiglockhart. He did road-work on his own and occasionally sprinted on the lawns of the George Square gardens, which were surrounded by black rails and accessible through a gate almost directly opposite his front door. Liddell enticed his housemates to run against him, amid the flowers and trees, and gave them his old international rugby shirts to wear. He said he allowed them a 'good five paces handicap grace' to make it more competitive and then announced the start himself. About fifteen strides from the finish, he'd shoot past them.

Throughout late spring and early summer, Liddell said McKerchar was 'handling me beautifully', which made it sound as if his trainer was at the wheel of a Model T Ford. 'I was coming along steadily all the time,' he went on. His performances proved it. In the Scottish Championships in mid-June Liddell won the 100 yards in 10 seconds, the 220 yards in 23.2 seconds and the 440 yards in 51.2 seconds. 'My first ever clean sweep there,' he said. In the AAA Championships, staged at Stamford Bridge a week later, he won the 220 yards in 22 seconds and the 440 yards in 49.6 seconds, a personal best. Those championships were held in the shadow of Liddell's punishing final exams for his Bachelor of Science degree. In splitting track-time with intense book-work, Liddell admitted that he was not 'absolutely at my top' athletically.

There was a minor blip in the build-up to Paris. A few weeks before the Olympics, one of his housemates got into what he called a 'friendly tussle' with Liddell. He put a judo leg-hold on his right knee. In breaking free from it, Liddell strained his thigh. 'I learned what it is to be thoroughly unpopular,' said the housemate, who experienced 'immense relief' when Liddell recovered. Liddell was more concerned about whether academic stress had weakened him for the Olympics. Only in Paris did he realize that swotting up for his degree was 'not such a misfortune as I had first imagined'. Commitment to his studies meant he hadn't over-trained. His mind was relaxed for running because it had concentrated on essays and exam papers rather than races.

No British athlete, not even Harold Abrahams, was in better shape than Eric Liddell.

Either of two twenty-three-year-old Americans appeared a copper-bottom certainty to win the 400 metres nonetheless. The first was Coard Taylor, a Princeton student. The second was Horatio Fitch, a name so wonderful that Dickens could have invented it. His team mates simply called him 'Ray'. He'd studied at the University of Illinois and then become an engineer.

In the ivy-covered Harvard Stadium in Cambridge, Massachusetts, during the US Olympic trials, the lean, blond Taylor set a world record of 48.1 seconds. And Fitch, who ran in dark-framed glasses, was just 0.3 of a second behind him. These times were set in teeming rain too. Everyone expected Paris to turn into a private duel between Taylor and Fitch.

In America, Liddell's name had ceased to be taken seriously.

No Olympics had ever found itself at the epicentre of a carnival, which is what Paris had become. It had been the *fin de siècle* spot of the world – the capital of the free spirit and the sybarite. Consequently the marriage of event to place was treated like the rarest alignment of two planets. Paris sparkled, artistically and fashionably, and there was an obsessive compulsion to be part of it. Anybody who was already somebody – as well as those who aspired to make the acquisition of fame their life's work – made a beeline for it. Libertine attitudes made the place attractive. So did an exchange rate in which one dollar was worth more than 25 francs and one pound was worth up to three times more than that. The creative world packed its baggage and went to speak French. No one wanted to miss the party – especially Americans thirsty during prohibition. It was heady, gaudy and decadent, the craving for a good time never satisfied. Every joint jumped to the sweet thunder of big-band brass, the thump of trad jazz or the ragtime four-four of the Charleston. The pavement cafés were choked with impecunious writers, poets, painters and pretend philosophers. Even New York and London seemed drably provincial in comparison. It appalled the strictly puritanical, such as the Lord's Day

Observance Society, which saw nothing but louche living, debauchery and drunkenness.

We all know Ernest Hemingway's description of Paris as 'a moveable feast'. The writer Gertrude Stein – Hemingway's mentor and friend then – still put it best of all, saying: 'It was where the twentieth century was.'

This modern, popular city was determined to host a modern, popular Olympics.

No one was further removed from the bright young thing and the anything-goes bohemian than Eric Liddell. And an easy, but horribly flawed, assumption was made about him because of his character. His expression of religious faith was perceived as a sign of innate weakness. Because of his decision not to compete on a Sunday, Liddell was dismissed as a pacifist in top competition – a man with a soft centre. The notion was ludicrous. Once, when pointedly asked *how* he won races so often against the odds, Liddell answered, 'I don't like to be beaten.' On the track Liddell knew where to find the opposition's jugular – and he also knew how to rip it out.

Paris was a test of temperament for Liddell long before it became a test of speed, requiring qualities no one could coach: fortitude, integrity, forgiveness, stoicism, will. You either possessed these or you didn't.

Britain took seventy-three track and field athletes to Paris. In the pocket-sized handbook given to each of them, Lord Cadogan wrote what was supposed to be the standard rah-rah message on behalf of King, country and the red-blotched map of Empire. 'To play the game is the only thing that matters,' he said. Cadogan wasn't the sort of public speaker you would pay a nickel to hear; he tended to drone on a bit. But that single line stood out because the sentence came with a poisonous tip and the intended recipient was easy to trace. Cadogan's choice of phrase was a snide attack on Eric Liddell. His Lordship knew that in Britain the term 'playing the game' was bound up with Victorian and Edwardian honour and patriotism, sportsmanship and fairness. Conscientious objection to Sunday sport wasn't 'playing the game' as Cadogan saw it.

His loyal lieutenant, A. B. George, had already trashed Liddell's chances of winning so much as a tin button in Paris. George saw no conflict of interest in continuing to write his comment-based columns. In his preview of the Games, published a week before the opening ceremony, George patronized Liddell cruelly. 'Even late as it is, it may yet be possible for Eric Liddell to correct his fault at looking to the sky instead of to the track ten yards ahead,' he wrote. 'No wonder American critics found fault with his style. It is a pity he ignores the most ordinary rules of balance.' The subliminal message contained in that paragraph needed no elucidation. As George saw it, Liddell was a lost cause, not to be taken seriously. George was disingenuous too. He knew it was impossible for Liddell to overhaul his approach to running inside seven days. Given the context of the piece, his ostensible expression of 'pity' reads like condescension, so poorly concealed as to make certain its true motive and meaning are glimpsed. George's position as part motivator, part organizer and part general factotum of the British team ought to have been untenable after that. The BOA chose to ignore it.

A lot of men would have made Cadogan's teeth look like a heap of broken crockery. A lot of others would have confronted George. Liddell looked at both of them with a tranquil eye.

Philip Noel-Baker was particularly supportive. Clutching a cup of tea in each hand, he regularly sought out Liddell for 'a chinwag'. As a conduit between the top brass and the ranks, he was a mollifying presence. He didn't consider Liddell's stance to be detrimental to his character. Nor did he see it as a snub to Britain. His decision not to fight in the war meant Noel-Baker knew more than anyone else – even Liddell – about the courage necessary to go against the grain.

The rest of the Cambridge athletes wrapped themselves around him like a protective blanket too. He roomed with Douglas Lowe. He roamed the streets of Paris in the company of Arthur Marshall, who had travelled as a reserve. He trained with fellow 400 metres runner Guy Butler, who had most to lose from Liddell's entry into his territory. We tend to admire those who admire us. So Liddell made a new companion, the cross-country runner John Benham, a sprite of a figure who became a cheerleader for his talents. Liddell also had the unflappable Tom McKerchar, who told him to ignore the distractions and concentrate on winning, which would muzzle his critics. McKerchar had gone to Paris knowing he was about to become a father for the thirteenth time. That baby could wait; he had to nursemaid Liddell first.

Liddell still had to overcome stabs of self-doubt. He was heard muttering them to himself. 'I wonder if I'm doing the right thing?' There was the shortest of pauses before he assertively answered his own question: 'Yes, I'm sure.' The witness who overheard Liddell's dialogue with himself was Philip 'Christie' Christison, one of the team's 'assistant managers', all of whom were gophers for George and those above him. An army captain, Christison was in charge of the 2nd King's Own Cameron Highlanders, the musical accompaniment to Britain's Olympic march. Christison was a war hero, winner of the Military Cross at Loos in 1915. He was then awarded a bar in 1917 for conspicuous gallantry. Among his principal functions was arranging transport to the Colombes Stadium. This was a daily trial of wits because dollar-rich Americans commandeered an armada of black cabs, monopolizing the ranks with the guarantee of a double fare. Sometimes Christison had to frantically flag down open-topped trucks or private cars to ferry his stranded athletes. As a fellow Scot, he felt an association with Liddell and, after avidly following his career, wanted him to succeed. Christison tried to convey this. His good intentions led briefly to bad consequences only because he lacked two attributes: the finesse to compose his homage so it wouldn't be misconstrued, and the nous to appreciate that Liddell was supersensitive to even the subtlest effort to manipulate him. Christison blundered in, telling Liddell how 'sad it was' that the 100 metres would go ahead without him. Liddell misinterpreted the sentiment of regret. He saw it as a Trojan horse, containing an army ready to argue with him. So he got his retaliation in first. 'Don't pressure me,' he told Christison. 'I've made up my mind.'

Liddell knew what Christison didn't. He said he felt 'cherry ripe' for the 400 metres, calling it 'my pet event'. Even the circumstances that had forced him into it appeared pre-ordained now.

In retrospect, Paris was hailed as the first 'modern Olympics', a tag that seems half-preposterous to those of us who have grown up with the meretriciousness of the modern Games – a festival of advertising and commercial branding – and compare them to the black and white photographs and silent, scratchy film of 1924. The opening ceremony of today's Olympics is an amalgam of concert and cabaret, bedazzling Broadway and ballet. The opening ceremony in Paris looks like amateur dramatics in the church hall. There are no lights in primary colours, no barrage of flash fireworks, no great blasts of music – except from a brass band – and no grand choreographed dances. In fact, there's no hoopla at all. Everything in Paris is ordered and politely well mannered.

The flag bearers advance in a half-circle and gather in the grassy centre of the stadium. The Olympic oath is read. Trumpets are blown.

Flocks of pigeons, rising like specks of ash, are released from wicker baskets. A cannon goes off, the faint wisps of its smoke lost in the glare of the day. The embroidered flag is run up the pole. The dignitaries – among them the President of France, the Prince of Wales, the Shah of Persia – sit stiffly, like mannequins. The lack of corporate uniformity strikes the eye too. The track perimeter is devoid of adverts. The athletes are devoid of sponsors' logos. The Olympic rings, now everywhere at every Games, adorn only the flag.

There is a picture taken from an airship of Colombes Stadium which captures a near-pastoral scene around it. Trees in full foliage decorate the land. The wide Seine meanders westwards. The soft greenery of the countryside spreads towards the horizon, made fuzzy because of a heavy haze. Any artist would paint out what disfigures the serenity of the scene, which is a factory with four tall, spindly chimneys stuck on the river bank, each belching polluting fumes, and also the grim concrete oval of the stadium itself with its enormous square clock and 100-foot-long scoreboard.

During the parade of athletes Eric Liddell was jammed against the kerb of the track. A photographer caught him with his head turned towards the dignitaries, his straw boater laid formally across his chest.

The newspapers still concentrated on Lowe, Stallard, Butler and Abrahams – particularly Abrahams. At breakfast the athletes went briskly through the thin pagination of those papers and read stories aloud to one another. Correspondents christened Abrahams 'The Cambridge Cannonball', the alliteration rolling nicely off the page. Abrahams responded to it. He had only two narrow squeaks in the 100 metres. In his opening heat he clocked 11 seconds, describing his movements as resembling 'a dilapidated cab-horse'. In the second he sped up. It was as if he'd swallowed a whole jar of that Easton's Syrup: he ran 10.6 seconds to equal the Olympic record. In the semi-finals, however, he was left on the start line. A yard behind after 10 metres, Abrahams heard a 'small voice inside me'. It was crying, 'Don't panic,' he said. At the halfway mark he was a stride down. At the three-quarter mark he was nearly level. At the end, through an adherence to technique, he was in front. An exchange with Abrahams afterwards convinced Liddell no one would catch him in the final either.

LIDDELL: 'You were badly off.'

ABRAHAMS: 'Don't talk about it. I saw five in front of me. But I won't be left a second time.'

As Liddell put it: 'There spoke the match-winning temperament. It was not boastfulness at all. It was the conviction of a man who realised our hopes rested on him and who intended to live up to them.'

So it proved.

In the final, Abrahams was at the apex of his dip before the tape snapped against him, billowing across his upper torso. His head and chest were thrust forward and his arms were straight back, almost level with his shoulder. In this pose he could have been one of those very early aviators who believed that man-powered flight was possible with a pair of cane wings. Abrahams looked as though he were about to take off from the edge of a cliff face. The silver medallist, the slim-shouldered American Jackson Scholz, fell and flailed across the finish. There was something of the dying swan at the Bolshoi about him. The stopwatch timed Abrahams at 10.6 seconds.

Liddell was pleased for Abrahams and also relieved for himself. If Abrahams had lost, Liddell expected more criticism. Because he had won, no one much cared that Liddell hadn't. As far as the newspapers were concerned, he receded further into the middle distance. Abrahams was the show's star, a British soloist.

Aware of the form of Coard Taylor and Horatio Fitch, A. B. George had claimed 'Liddell's main hope would seem to be the 200m', reflecting his lack of confidence in a successful metamorphosis from sprinter to quarter-miler. George was essentially arguing that Liddell lacked the lung and leg power to stay with an international field over 200 metres, let alone 400 metres. Another reason was Liddell's sluggishness out of the holes. 'The papers now and then reminded me that my weak point was the slowness with which I started,' said Liddell, accepting it self-consciously. The consensus was that Liddell wouldn't beat Butler; and that Butler wouldn't beat Taylor or Fitch. The smart money was still on one of them to dominate the field straightforwardly. Apparently, the Americans thought so too.

Fitch kept an Olympic diary, which he called 'When You Get It Done'. Read between the lines of the early entries and you'll detect that either through complacency-cum-arrogance or, more probably, from poor tactics and poorer preparation, the coach responsible for the 400 metres, Amos Alonzo Stagg, blundered. Having reached Paris, after eight days at sea, Fitch wrote about meeting Hollywood's golden couple: Douglas Fairbanks, known for roles as a swordsman and swashbuckler in films such as *The Mark of Zorro*, *The Thief of Bagdad* and *The Three Musketeers*, and his wife Mary Pickford, regarded as 'America's Sweetheart', her movies regularly grossing a million dollars. And, rather than a programme of constant training, he recorded the daily 'pitching of horseshoes' for recreation, the bowls of strawberries Stagg's team ate 'morning, noon and night' and also a lot of sight-seeing, including a day at the Longchamp horse races. In the beginning the Americans hardly went near the track. Fitch had wanted to do some 'over-distance' work. He found the coach was 'against it'. Known as 'the Old Man', the sixty-two-year-old 'Lonnie' Stagg was a gridiron guru and the sportsman's sportsman: a football end at Yale and also an outstanding pitcher, who'd once turned down a contract with the New York Giants. Stagg had co-founded the American Football Coaches Association only two years before the Games. He saw no need to overtire his athletes, affectionately called 'The Gang'. But at the outset of the competition Fitch didn't consider himself 'in shape', blaming it on 'poor eating, charging around Paris too much and insufficient hard work in training'.

Britain didn't anticipate a medal because Butler, ranked above Liddell, was running with a handicap. He'd pulled a muscle in his thigh in mid-June and had walked on crutches until receiving ultra-intensive electrical treatment. He'd barely practised before the Olympics and used the heats 'as training spins'. To avoid aggravating his injury, Butler decided to start his races from a standing position instead of from the holes, which put him at a further disadvantage.

Newspapers said that Liddell would be fortunate to finish fourth. A typical forecast appeared in the *Sunday Chronicle*. Reflecting on his decision to swap the 100 metres for the 400 metres, its correspondent concluded: 'I am inclined to the view that the change will be detrimental to him – but that cannot be helped now.'

Such low expectations worked in Liddell's favour. He prepared himself without the pestering attentions of His Majesty's press. The 200 metres, expected to catapult Abrahams towards stellar fame, emphasized the value of that. Abrahams' entire reason for breathing had been to win the 100 metres gold and take the title of the world's fastest man. The physical and nervous effort required to achieve his goal siphoned off his strength. Euphoric afterwards, he'd headed to a café on the Boulevard des Italiens to unwind and overdid the beakers of beer and cigars of which he was so fond. He was a spent force, unfit mentally and physically. Abrahams finished sixth and last in this second event, shamelessly shovelling a proportion of the blame on Sam Mussabini. Abrahams had complained of feeling 'very tired' during the semi-finals; Mussabini attributed it to an overly fast start. Abrahams said that diagnosis persuaded him to take the final 'rather more slowly'. In this willing surrender, ground was given up that instantly became unrecoverable.

Next morning Liddell read reports about Abrahams' 'loss of nerve'. He condemned the writers as 'critics ignorant of the real facts'. He thought the bone-weary Abrahams was just 'quite run out'. Liddell had finished third in 21.9 seconds, behind Scholz, whose 21.6 was a new Olympic record, and Charley Paddock, a double gold medallist four years earlier. He admired both of them for racing 'like angels'. His bronze medal was obscured beneath the rock-fall of criticism that buried Abrahams. Stories were slanted towards his failure, which was treated as a calamity. The columns were all but trimmed in funeral black. Liddell hardly got a look-in. His success was a footnote. Even the *Scotsman* and the *Edinburgh Evening News* ran headlines that forgot where Liddell lived: 'Abrahams Fails' and 'Blank Day for Britain: Our Failure in the 200 Metres'. The *Glasgow Herald* at least exhibited basic news sense bespoke for a Scottish audience. But what it published – 'Liddell Home Third' – relayed the facts without putting out bunting and balloons.

Statistics from the 200 metres increased scepticism about Liddell's capabilities in the longer race. He'd run 22.2 seconds to win his first heat; 21.8 seconds to finish second in the quarter-finals; and 21.8 seconds again in the semis. None of these times suggested Liddell was about to be dealing in 400 metres gold.

Nor did the first two stages of that competition.

The seventeen preliminary heats were boringly routine. Coard Taylor, Horatio Fitch and Eric Liddell, drawn apart from one another, merely went through the motions to qualify. Taylor came home in a sedate 50.4 seconds. Fitch was able to set his own pace because only he and another runner competed, ensuring that both of them would go through anyway. 'I could not have gone any slower unless I stopped to pick violets on the way,' he said of his 52-second effort. Liddell clocked 50.2 seconds, inspiring no one to rapture.

The earthquake came in the quarter-finals. Every Olympics produces a surprise. Paris had Josef Imbach, an anonymous Swiss locksmith, who ran a world record of 48 seconds. Since no one had heard of Imbach, no one had considered him a threat. He startled Liddell – 'he ran so smoothly', he said – but petrified Fitch and Taylor because neither knew how much faster he could go. Again, the Americans completely ignored Liddell as a possible threat. He'd clocked a competent, though hardly conquering, 49.3 seconds to reach the semis, which made him almost invisible to them.

He became more irrelevant than ever after the semi-finals.

The 400 metres seemed crazy to those who observed it unwind in such unlikely turns and twists, fortune cloaking one runner and then another. Now the hot property was Fitch, who broke Imbach's world record barely before the Swiss could celebrate the holding of it. 'It surprised me as

The power and the glory: Eric Liddell commands
the 400 metres in the Olympic Games in Paris.

much as anyone, especially since I eased up in the last thirty yards to save myself,' said Fitch.

Things were suddenly different for him. With a time of 47.8 seconds, he was the undisputed number one over the distance; even more so because Taylor had faded badly, lucky to finish third in the other semi. And Imbach, though ahead of him, had come second. As for Liddell, the man who had beaten both of them, he'd registered only 48.2 seconds.

On the evidence of these times, Fitch was going to waltz it.

In the three and a half hours that separated the semis from the final, conversations in the American camp briefly focused on Imbach and excluded Liddell. Still a little wary of the relatively unknown Swiss runner, the Americans asked themselves whether Imbach had been saving fuel for the final, which would explain his loss. They finally decided otherwise, concluding he hadn't much energy left. Liddell, so familiar to them, wasn't labelled as a danger at all. Guy Butler, progressing stealthily, had been on Fitch's shoulder at the tape. He, rather than Liddell, was seen as the chief British contender.

Just one voice among the Americans thought differently.

With his rimless spectacles, double-breasted suit and well-combed whitish hair, Jack Moakley looked more like a bookish college academic than the sports godfather of Cornell University. Moakley, then sixty-one, had fifteen years' experience as head track and field coach there. More pertinently he'd also coached the United States at the Antwerp Olympics, where twenty-nine medals – including nine golds – had made them the most successful nation. Moakley advised his countrymen in Paris, often watching events from a seat near the press box, where he liked the company as well as the vista. He'd taken in the whole of the 400 metres competition. Every critic will spot something different. The best discern detail that others lack the insight to see. Dwelling on excellencies rather than imperfections, Moakley looked at Liddell and rated him far higher than a bit player.

'That lad Liddell's a hell of an awful runner,' he told the American team, having winced at his misshapen running style, before declaring, 'But he's got something. I think he's got what it takes.'

No one listened to him.

CHAPTER FIVE

Dancing the Tango Along the Champs-Elysées

T HE THRILL OF SPORT can lead us into a giddy loss of perspective. In attempting to describe the drama of it, there's always a risk of dissolving into romantic hype. Those who watch it and those who write regularly about it have been equally guilty on that charge because sport appeals to the heart. We want to become emotional about it. And, since the aesthetic and visceral experience is the point of being there, we surrender willingly to that emotion. Time doesn't darken sport's notable past deeds; nostalgia instead slings halos around them wider than Saturn's rings. That's why sometimes sports history prints the legend and perpetuates the myth, burnished even when the facts are disputable.

But the opposite is true of Eric Liddell in that hot summer of 1924. His win was worthy of every sensational phrase attached to it.

There were headline performances in Paris, particularly from the trio who became known as the Flying Finns: Paavo Nurmi, who claimed five gold medals after running seven races in six days; Ville Ritola, winner of the 3,000-metre steeplechase and the 10,000 metres; and the marathon man Albin Stenroos, who, wearing a white skullcap over his black curls, remained fresh in oppressive heat. There was also the Michigan long jumper William DeHart Hubbard who, at nineteen, became the first African-American champion; the decathlete and high jumper Harold Osborn of Illinois, a double Olympian despite being practically blind in his right eye; and the muscularly handsome Johnny Weissmuller, who won three golds in the pool and, much later, a seven-year Hollywood film contract with Metro-Goldwyn-Mayer that made him the loin-clothed Tarzan of the jungle.

Harold Abrahams' blue-ribboned run put him in the same category as the Finns and the Americans, but also highlighted what Liddell had voluntarily given away. Anyone who had picked up a newspaper or listened to a crystal set knew about the principled stand he had taken and also his unfamiliarity with the 400 metres. So no individual story was as poignant as Liddell's; and no win was as popularly celebrated.

For most of the Games, Paris broiled, as if trapped beneath a thermal blanket. The sprinters and middle-distance runners could just about tolerate the conditions. But to run further than a few laps was to risk heatstroke, dehydration, hallucination and physical incapacity. At the end of the marathon one athlete ran about as though demented and another hared into the stands for no reason. A third came into the stadium and turned the wrong way. An official pointed him in the right direction. The man was so disorientated that he began to run in small circles, like a human corkscrew, until he made himself dizzy and crumpled to the floor. Alongside the Seine there was no shade and the smoke from the factory choked the air and turned it black. On the exposed parts of the course, skin reddened quickly and then burned. To compete was almost suicidal. In temperatures of 113 degrees only fifteen of the thirty-two athletes who started the team 10,000-metre cross-country event reached the Colombes Stadium. John Benham was found dazed in a field by a small boy, who ran a couple of miles to the stadium and, grasping the first British figure he found, spluttered in panicky, broken English, 'Come quickly, your comrade is dying.' An injection of strychnine kept Benham alive. Liddell, sitting in the covered stand, said others' lives were saved by the 'narrowest margin' as doctors and Red Cross ambulances 'dashed into the arena'. He observed the shirt-sleeved crowd consuming 'all the available cool drinks and ice-cream blocks' and queried whether most of them realized 'what the athletes were going through in the fiery heat'.

Liddell was fortunate. The temperature in Paris on Friday, 11 July – a date he said was 'more vividly imprinted on my memory' than any other – was only 79 degrees. Shortly before 6.30 p.m., after the electric bell called the finalists from the dressing rooms, Liddell found the sting had been drawn from the day. He could breathe without feeling as though the air had been cooked. He'd learned a lesson from Abrahams, who said the three-hour wait he endured between the semi-final and final of the 100 metres made him feel 'like a condemned man just before going to the scaffold'. The changing room was cavernous, but almost pit-dark. Athletes leaving it adjusted to the harshness of the light outside by blinking furiously. Competitors and coaches constantly came and went again and the noise of applause and cheering from the crowds reverberated around the place. The highly strung, twitchy Abrahams escaped all this and also the pungent reek of others' liniment, sweat and massage oil by hiring a private hut nearby. Liddell still overheard him squabbling with Sam Mussabini. 'He had wanted to go around the outskirts of Colombes in a car – "just for a blow" as he put it. Mussabini knew his French taxi drivers and was not going to risk the fruits of a year of patient effort just to satisfy the passing whim of his charge. So he recalled the car just as it was about to start and made Abrahams sit down and sleep instead.' Liddell sat down and slept too, finding the quietest corner and passing the hours 'pleasantly enough', he said.

When he woke up Tom McKerchar slowly massaged his limbs, more out of routine than necessity. 'Heat makes the muscles loose, so there was no need for massage,' said Liddell. McKerchar worked in silence. 'We hardly spoke to one another. Our tactics were agreed.' Abrahams had been agitated and short-tempered, over-eager for his race to start and then be over. Liddell was serene and amiable, content to let the clock's hands carry him there. He did not wish Time away. 'Curiously enough I was quite cool,' he explained.

That morning he had been handed a folded square of paper, a gift from one of the team masseurs. Liddell was setting off from the Moderne and slipped the piece of paper into a pocket, promising to read it later. He found a benediction of good luck.

In the old book it says: 'He that honours me I will honour.'
Wishing you the best of success always.

He recognized the slight misquotation from the Bible – 1 Samuel, chapter 2, verse 30 – and this small, private expression of faith and hope moved him profoundly. Someone other than McKerchar believed in him and also in the stance he'd taken.

Horatio Fitch was still odds on to win; and he expected to do so in a no-nonsense way. The opposition didn't look formidable to him. Coard Taylor's confidence had leaked away. Guy Butler's sore thigh was strapped beneath his shorts. A Canadian, David Johnson, lacked the pedigree to upset him. Josef Imbach was like a once-invincible superhero who had been unmasked. And Liddell? Well, Fitch – forgetting Jack Moakley's endorsement – never imagined Liddell matching him. Amos Alonzo Stagg told Fitch there was 'no need to worry about Liddell' and dismissed him as 'a sprinter' who would 'pass out 50 yards from the finish'.

But being a sprinter actually gave Liddell two distinct advantages. The sun had baked the cinder hard, making it ideal for him. Also, the six-lane Colombes track was 500 metres long. The 400 metres race, beginning on the last straight, was run in a horseshoe shape. Liddell was best equipped to exploit the single bend. Everything had been thought through. Liddell hadn't wanted to be talked about as the favourite; and he hadn't intended to burn his energy low in the heats or the semis when qualification alone, not records or adulation, mattered. 'Despite the times the others had put up, I felt fairly confident. I had been running well within myself, and I felt absolutely keyed up to run the race of my life,' he said.

Already half-thinking of himself as an Olympic champion, Fitch realized none of this. The American newspapers didn't realize it either. Those with European editions published tables awarding the US team the 400 metres winner's points in advance, believing it to be a foregone conclusion.

Liddell was digging out his start holes when Joe Binks wandered down from the press box, wanting to pass on good wishes and a hunch about tactics. Binks always remembered what he said: 'I suggested an occasion on which he should "run mad", keep in front and make all the other five come after him to the tape.' He always remembered Liddell's reply too: 'I think that's a good idea.'

Pathé newsreel film of the 1924 Olympic 400 metres final lasts one minute and twelve seconds. The cameras used were static and positioned at ground level. There is no sound, but what the cinema audience saw, only a few days after the newspapers and the radio had told them of the outcome, conveyed the strength of Eric Liddell's running.

He's seen in close-up at first, the light falling flatly across his face. Hands on hips, his long fingers with their well-cut nails are stretched across them. His kit looks a little rumpled, as if he's slept in it – though his dark eyes and the baggy lines beneath them suggest he hasn't been sleeping nearly enough. His lips are pursed so tightly that the mouth almost disappears until his head swivels, ever so briefly, towards the camera. He licks his top lip to moisten it. Then his expression becomes a study in concentration again. He stares with a firm fixity down the outside lane, which is where the ballot has consigned him – the worst possible position because he won't know until the last straight whether he's in front or behind the others. The number 451 is stencilled on to a rectangle of cloth, which is pinned to his short-sleeved white running shirt. The imprint of the Union Jack, depicted rippling on a pole, is stitched above the number.

Behind him the crowd, predominantly male and predominantly middle-aged, are assembled in front of narrow benches beneath the upward slope of a roof. No one wants to sit down. The back of the stand is in shadow, the faces indistinct. Those at the front press against a high-pointed metal railing and are caught in a bloom of bright sun. The men wear three-piece suits; there's the odd glint of a watch-chain roped across a waistcoat. Most are in trilbies or newsboy caps as broad as dinner plates. Others, more conscious of elegance and the weather, wear straw boaters. One woman stands out. Amid the swell of dark suits she is resplendent in white – white calf-length dress, white hat, a pair of white elbow-length gloves. It's as though she's wandered in from a Manet painting. In the uncovered part of the stadium, where there is only shallow terracing, some spectators have put up umbrellas to shield themselves against the drop of the sun. There's a noticeable cross-wind, the flags of the nations at the southern end blown almost straight, like the one on Liddell's chest.

The camera doesn't capture what oral evidence preserves as fact: that, as ever, Liddell walked over to each of his rivals and shook hands with them before settling into the starting holes, which Joe Binks had seen him dig with a tiny silver trowel; that, as Liddell recalled, 'the vast crowd seethed with emotion', a hubbub so loud that the bowler-hatted starter had to ask the tannoy announcer to yell for silence because he feared the athletes wouldn't hear the call to their marks; that the silence he got after the appeal was like the hush of a church; that then the evening air was filled with the blast of the Cameron Highlanders marching band, who broke into eight bars of 'Scotland The Brave' – a cheeky indulgence breaching protocol; and that officious stewards attempted to stifle it, tearing towards Philip Christison, who on a whim had given the order to play the battle hymn to inspire his countryman.

Liddell is about to meet his moment. On the red scoria cinders of the Colombes Stadium, a nice guy is about to finish first. You know it as soon as the gun cracks.

He goes off as if he's been catapulted from the line. He makes everyone else look perambulatory. He burns up the track and burns off those chasing him, who see nothing but the arch of his back and the kick of his heels, which throw up puffs of cinder rising as high as his ankles. The toes of his black shoes leave a trail of scuffing as small as a child's footprints along a sandy beach. 'I got the perfect start,' he said.

The textbook approach was to begin the race with a sprint, constituting an all-out effort, before easing off slightly at 40 or 50 metres and settling into an even stride until the three-quarter mark when the muscles of the upper torso and the shoulders begin to power the final thrust of the body. He did what no one else had ever done. Because he was in the outside lane – and because he thought Horatio Fitch and Josef Imbach 'were the best placed' on the inside – Liddell said he gave himself this single instruction: 'Go all out – and don't be behind at the last straight.' Liddell and McKerchar decided on these tactics long before Binks came to the same conclusion. The shape and the hardness of that track was one reason. The stamina in Liddell's legs was another. The certainty that he would soon exhaust the field was a third.

Sluggish out of the blocks? Slow to get going? Not today.

Free tickets for the competitors offered only an angled view, which made it impossible to judge the state of the race. So Harold Abrahams has paid an exorbitant 10 shillings for a ticket opposite the finish line. Sitting beside Sam Mussabini, he is aghast at the risk Liddell is taking: 'He went off at such a terrific pace that it seemed as if he must crack before the end . . . it seemed impossible that he should last the distance.' Arthur Marshall can't believe what he's seeing either. 'He just pounded along,' he said, comparing Liddell to a super-fast train. And Guy Butler, already lagging 10 yards behind, is telling himself that no human can sustain 'an all out sprint' like this.

Even Liddell conceded he was thinking: 'Can I last home?'

His split time is a phenomenal 22.2 – just 0.6 of a second slower than Jackson Scholz in the 200 metres final.

Fitch has begun 'the way I always did – coasting a little'. Everyone still expects him to take gold; Fitch still expects it too because of his 'good kick'. He is waiting for Liddell to slow, absolutely sure his coach's prediction is about to come true. Liddell will buckle and pant along the home straight. He will rue the decision he's made. Countering the bias of the bend, distorting his advantage, is certain to tire him.

But Liddell does not tire. He accelerates, his head – as it always is – tilted heavenward as he runs, as though in prayer to the skies. In the 200 metres Liddell conceded that he couldn't increase his speed 'by a fraction of an inch'. Now it comes to him when he summons it. He gets a second wind and then a third. Fitch makes his own burst and closes in. He thinks he is going to draw level and overtake Liddell; that the prize belongs to him now. The thought comes and leaves him in a nanosecond. For what he sees next destroys it and in retrospect makes the idea delusional. Liddell first senses Fitch's approach and then sees him in his peripheral vision. He puffs out his cheeks, throws his head further back still and, from somewhere, finds an even fiercer fire within him. 'Not until I got to the top of the straight did it suddenly dawn on me that I was several yards in front of the field,' he said.

At 70 yards from the tape, still feeling that Fitch is nearest to him, Liddell pulls away again – pushing himself unstoppably on, as though sheer will is supplanting strength. The lead seized at the start is his at the finish. And in the closing strides what Liddell feels is liberation, justification, triumph. He knows he's uncatchable. He knows he's about to win. 'A comforting thought flashed into my mind. I could no longer see the second man behind me,' he said. He doesn't see the tape either. He simply feels it break against his body, his eyes still fixed on the sky.

Coard Taylor pulled a muscle and stumbled in his bid to throw himself after Liddell and a consolation medal. The front of his shirt was stained with cinder the colour of blood. Imbach had fallen after becoming ensnared in a line marker, those loops of white string attached to thin, 8-inch-high metal poles that divided the lanes and made them look like a market gardener's plot for sowing peas. Butler took advantage of both misfortunes to finish third. And Fitch, who had thought of himself as the predator, had become the prey, a silver medal hardly satisfying. The best in the world had beaten the rest of the world; Fitch had no option but to accept it. 'I had no idea he would win it. I couldn't believe a man could set such a pace and finish.' He likened Liddell to someone 'possessed'.

'I was amazed to find that I had won by six yards,' said Liddell. He

A second from glory. Eric Liddell about to burst the tape and win his Olympic gold. Closest to him is Horatio Fitch. The other American, Coard Taylor, struggles to his feet in one of the middle lanes.

confessed to being 'more amazed' at his time – 47.6 seconds, another world record. Inside twenty-six wild hours it had been broken, re-broken and broken again.

For this piece of live, unscripted theatre the applause – a landslide of noise – rolled down from the stands and on to the track. There were whoops and cheering. Flags were waved. Hats were thrown. Kisses were blown. Mussabini said the spectators went 'crazy mad' for Liddell, who acknowledged so modestly the acclaim Paris gave him. There was a smile, a wave, a raised arm, a nod of the head. Within a minute of taking the tape Liddell stopped breathing heavily, rose from a stooped position, hands on knees, and straightened himself up to look around, as if savouring a sight he never expected to see. He appeared fit and fresh, like a gentleman who had just come back from a bracing constitutional. The others were wrung dry and still semi-stooped. 'The strange thing was that, despite the race I had run, and the time I had run it in, I was quite cool and collected and not in the least distressed. I felt perfectly strong,' said Liddell.

The reporter from the *Glasgow Herald* was in shock. He consequently gave his readers the impression that Liddell belonged to a super-species, capable of achieving what the mere mortals among us would find physiologically impossible. He likened the Christian to 'some demon'. He confessed that watching Liddell tear away from everyone else early on

The victor and the vanquished. Eric Liddell
crosses the line well ahead of his nearest rival,
Horatio Fitch.

had alarmed him. As if expecting the heart to burst or the body to fracture under the strain, he explained, 'I feared that he would kill himself by the terrible speed he had set up.'

The most poetic and rhapsodic account of the race was penned by Grantland Rice in the *New York Herald Tribune*. He was then – and for a good while afterwards too – the most famous sports correspondent in America. When *Collier's* hired Rice as a columnist during that Olympic year, it said of him: 'His name spells colour, dash, action, drama – as well as honesty and soundness.' Rice was Wordsworthian in his prose. In celebrating Liddell he also celebrated everything that was tartan; or, at least, everything that was stereotypically Scottish. 'The Olympic atmosphere,' he wrote, 'was rife with the resonant melody of Scottish bagpipes, thistles, braes, bluebells and a new world record ... from Highland to Lowland it was Scotland for Ever ... the fluttering kilts took another twirl in honour of one of the greatest runners any nation ever sent to glory.' Rice saw Liddell as the 'Scotch meteor, flaming along' with 'whirring feet' and added: 'Fitch and the others may as well have been chasing an antelope startled into top speed, or some high powered motor driven by a Paris taxi-driver.' He thought 'some divine power' had dragged him along.

A few minutes after the Olympic final. Horatio
Fitch still looks as though he can't quite believe
Liddell's ferocious pace has beaten him.

Liddell and Fitch posed together, shaking hands for the photographers, who gathered in a semi-circle in front of them. Their long, pale shadows stretched across the field. Fitch wore an expression mid-way between a smile and a grimace. Strands of Liddell's hair had been blown awry. Otherwise, he was so composed he could have been asking Fitch whether the two of them might race again purely for the fun of it. Fitch found him somewhat formal. 'I'd guess you'd say stiff,' he said. 'You'd congratulate him and he'd just say "thank you".'

In the aftermath of the 400 metres final, Eric Liddell looks fit enough to run another race immediately.

The Olympics didn't indulge in ceremony in 1924. There was no medal presentation because there was no medal for him. There was no podium and no national anthem either. His gold would be engraved and posted on to Scotland later, wrapped in brown paper and string. So once the photographers had finished with him, and the crowd had begun to scatter homeward, Liddell slipped back into the dressing rooms with the minimum of fuss. The British team was waiting for him at the head of the tunnel leading to the changing room. John Benham was the first to extend his hand in congratulations. 'Before I knew where I was he grabbed me and got me upon his shoulders. I was carried by a big, excited crowd of my fellow country-men,' said Liddell. 'It was an experience I will always remember.'

Tom McKerchar made him lie down and rest and then began the post-race massage. 'He thought I needed a little quiet after the wild reception I got,' said Liddell. Knowing Liddell's habits so well, McKerchar expected him to go back to the hotel and stretch out on the bed. For once, Liddell surprised him. He dispatched a telegram to his parents in China, telling them of his win, and then announced he was 'going on the town' with Marshall. Freddie and Edith, the two sisters Liddell had met on the boat home from America in April, were on the Paris leg of their Grand Tour. The four of them headed for a Tango Tea Dance on the Champs-Elysées. The girls drank champagne. Wearing his Olympic blazer and flannels, Liddell sipped apple juice, the colour of hard liquor, and trod the floor with gusto. He was a nifty mover. Wanting to celebrate, Freddie and Edith suggested that Liddell ought to toast his entry into the Olympic pantheon with a tiny swallow of champagne. 'That would mean less for you,' he said, remaining abstemious and offering to dance as long as his legs would let him. The evening wore on and the adrenalin of his victory got Liddell through it. Near midnight, Marshall and the two women peeled off into a night club. Liddell made his excuses and said his goodbyes.

Everyone revels in a winner. The newspapers, so apathetic about Liddell beforehand, treated him exultantly the next morning. The *Scotsman* wrote of the Union Jack flying in 'proud majesty', the 'gasp of astonishment' Liddell's running inspired and the 'frenzy of enthusiasm' for his win. The *Edinburgh Evening News* announced that 'thrill followed thrill' for him. The French anointed him 'L'homme à vapeur' – the man of steam. To the Americans he was 'a thin legged Scotch divinity student', the 'spindly preacher' and, most colourfully, 'The Flying Parson' after being mistakenly identified as an apprentice Church of England minister. He didn't mind either the inaccuracy or that sobriquet, which conjured an image of someone running in a dog collar. 'If the papers want to call me the Flying Parson to lend another touch of picturesqueness to their copy, I certainly have no quarrel with them on that point,' said Liddell, describing it as a 'little additional touch' of licence that 'did no harm'.

The news agency Reuters captured the mood best of all. 'Liddell has made himself one of the most popular men in Paris,' it said. 'Certainly there has not been a more popular win.'

Asked about his triumph in its immediate aftermath, the popular man of Paris was shyly circumspect. Not wanting to boast or gloat, Liddell claimed, as if regarding himself as an accidental champion, that he'd been 'very fortunate' to have 'touched the top of my form at just the right moment'. However fortunate he felt, the Olympics were more fortunate still to have him on the roll of honour.

He was a poster boy, and how sorely the Games needed him.

Almost every Olympics closes with the encomium that it has been 'the Best Ever'. After all, it is always a guest's polite obligation to flatter the host. Paris was different.

These Olympics were the first in which the motto 'Faster, Higher, Stronger' slipped into common usage as a commitment to unimpeachable ideals. But, like so many that have followed them, the 1924 Games became enmeshed in ugly rows and recriminations through an amalgam of pig-headed pettiness, arrogance, pride, oneupmanship, score-settling, cheating and, above all, a warped sense of patriotism.

Paris got the Olympics to feed the vanity and self-interest of Baron Pierre de Coubertin, who got the idea to revive them in the 1880s. He wanted to mark the Games' 'proper' rebirth in his own birthplace. He wanted to atone for the pantomime shambles staged there in 1900. And he wanted to show off. The 1900 Games had been grandiose in ambition but farcical in execution. Had Coubertin been the head of a corporation, he'd have been sacked afterwards for gross negligence. The Games were supposed to complement the World's Fair. But there was no signage or logo to promote the term 'Olympic'. There was no new stadium, which Coubertin had promised. The Games embraced sports such as ballooning, cricket, croquet and Basque pelota and stretched from May until the last week of October in a marathon of public uninterestedness. The total number of spectators some of the sports attracted wouldn't have filled the Folies Bergère.

Now Coubertin was sixty-one years old. He looked seventy-five. His hair was milk-white. So was his moustache. About to retire as president of the International Olympic Committee, Coubertin had imagined a comfortably grand ride into retirement, a kingly parade of affection for services rendered. What he got were barbed questions about whether the Olympics were worth preserving.

Colombes was less than a hundred miles from the mud of the Great War. For the second successive Olympics, Germany's invitation was never posted. So the Americans initially took the brunt of French hostility and xenophobia. Their rugby team was refused entry at Boulogne and then also refused the use of the Olympic Stadium in which to train. The players were barracked and spat at along the shopping boulevards. Their money and jewellery were stolen during a training session. The rugby final, pitting them against the French, should have been held in a roped ring. It degenerated into brawls on and off the pitch. American fans were beaten. One was smashed in the mouth with a walking stick. After America won 17–3, there was mayhem. Bottles and lumps of rock as big as fists were thrown on to the field. A police escort was necessary to shepherd the gold medallists to safety.

This explicit anti-Americanism was not an isolated incident either. The *New York Times* reported that 'every losing stroke' by Helen Wills – then the US champion – 'was cheered' in the women's tennis final. 'Far from serving the cause of French popularity [the Games] have left in the mind of not a few of the competing teams and with the public a feeling of irritation and distaste,' it concluded. *The Times* was much blunter: 'In contrast with the persistent hostility to the Americans . . . our treatment . . . has seemed almost cordial.'

The crucial word in that line is 'almost'. Britain's middle-weight boxer, Harry Mallin, wiry and curly-haired – he looked like a floor-mop sent into battle – was bitten on the chest and ear in a bout against a local fighter. The partisan crowd, which saw slights everywhere, later pelted a referee with coins after a decision went against another Frenchman.

These were minor scuffles in comparison to the infamy of the fencing competition. Italy and Hungary became embroiled in a conflict so rancid that it sullied both of them. Four months later, in a sequel that belongs to the age of Dumas's Musketeers, two competitors slashed and badly wounded each other in a duel staged as a consequence of the bad feeling Paris had stirred.

The *Times'* Olympic correspondent was sixty-four-year-old Sir Harry Perry Robinson, who had won the Legion of Honour and contributed to the publicity machine behind William McKinley's successful presidential campaign in 1896. The Olympic shenanigans disgusted Robinson, who damned the 'uproars' and 'quarrels' he saw. 'Nothing has been generated except international ill will,' he wrote. 'The sum total is deplorable . . . The Games are a grievous failure.' His piece appeared below the headline 'The Olympic Games Doomed'. Robinson's muscular attack particularly impressed the *New York Times*, which quoted him before asking the question it insisted any 'thinking Frenchman' was asking himself: 'Were the Olympic Games worthwhile?'

Coubertin spluttered an unsatisfactory reply to that. He cited 'unprecedented successes' – without adequately cataloguing them – and then celebrated their competitors as 'gentlemen'. As an example of dreamy imagination, it was heartfelt. As a robust and coherent defence, it was nonsense on stilts.

Among all the grubbiness, Eric Liddell stood out more virtuously than ever: the personification of athletic prowess on the track, the embodiment of self-sacrifice and sportsmanship off it. He was a walking advertisement for Olympian ideals. Performances such as his own, especially seen against the back-story of his personal convictions, answered the *New York Times's* question better than Coubertin.

Liddell was the hero, feted for proving the Games weren't irrevocably rotten at the root.

CHAPTER SIX

Not for Sale at Any Price

Eric Liddell expected only a handful of well-wishers at Victoria station. What he saw instead, through the steam, smoke and smuts, was the crush of a crowd, heaving between the ribbed Ionic columns planted along the platform and also pushing against the door of his carriage. At the sight of him, there was cheering and a chorus of 'For He's A Jolly Good Fellow'. The song echoed beneath the soaring canopy of the partly glassed roof. It was so loud, according to the *London Evening News* reporter dispatched there, that 'every other noise in a noisy station seemed quite quiet'. He said he couldn't 'recall such a demonstration' for previous Olympians. 'Liddell was the biggest lion,' he added, making it clear who the fans favoured. Flags were waved – both the Scottish saltire and the Union Jack. Phosphorescent flash bulbs went off like summer lightning. Liddell was swept up and carried shoulder-high for some distance, somewhat unsteadily at first. At one point he glanced behind him, afraid his trunk and two cases would be lost or left behind in the confusion. A British Olympic official, brandishing a Union Jack, eventually pushed him into a taxi, which the man from the *London Evening News* saw become 'the centre of outstretched hands until the driver got going'.

Liddell was taken aback. He now knew what Jim Thorpe felt after returning from the 1912 Games in Stockholm as pentathlon and decathlon champion. New York threw him a ticker-tape parade. 'I heard people calling my name,' said Thorpe. 'I didn't realise how one fellow could have so many friends.'

Liddell was a celebrity, made so in part because of a new medium. The Paris Olympics were the first widely available on radio. The BBC, created less than two years earlier, incorporated reports from the Games into its evening news bulletins at seven and ten o'clock. Anyone with a crystal set no longer had to wait until the newspaper presses rolled overnight to find out the results from Paris. Memory is a fickle beast, always liable to play a trick or two. One of Liddell's housemates in George Square swore the 400 metres final was broadcast live and even offered a verbatim account of the commentary, insisting it contained tally-ho and golly-gosh exclamations such as 'Oh, what a race!' When Liddell ran, the BBC was broadcasting *Children's Corner* – specifically the second part of *Treasure Island*, a quite different pursuit of gold. But, though still in its screaming infancy, the novelty of radio impacted on the consciousness of those who heard it and so lifted Liddell's profile. The BBC's listeners bought the newspapers more eagerly than ever next morning and then wanted to see Liddell in the flesh, a scenario he had never envisaged.

What greeted him at Victoria was repeated at Waverley on his arrival in Edinburgh – another mass of people, another serenade of triumph, another thousand and one autograph books stuck in front of him.

Serendipity dictated that Liddell's graduation as a Bachelor of Science came only six days after winning in Paris. Demand for tickets was unprecedented. In the tiered, domed auditorium of McEwan Hall, the inside of which is cathedral-like, the university turned the ceremony into an ostentatious Olympic occasion.

Oleaster sprigs from the Royal Botanical Gardens were entwined into a chaplet to imitate the laurel crown of ancient Greece. Pindar, the cantata poet of Thebes, wrote fourteen Epinician odes to celebrate Olympians such as Diagoras of Rhodes and Xenophon of Corinth. He observed that no one ever looked 'askance' at the praise lavished on them afterwards. What was true in Pindar's classical Greece remained true for Liddell in the motorized age of George V, for the university penned a Pindaric pastiche on his behalf, which was put on a scroll and read aloud. The epigram spoke of Liddell's 'laurelled brow', the speed he'd displayed in Paris as being 'as none hath shown till now', and said of the chaplet: 'While you wear it, may Heaven never frown.' The Vice Chancellor strove to craft an apt sentence of his own, delivered the way a vaudeville comedian delivers a gag. 'Mr Liddell,' he said, 'you have shown that none can pass you but the examiner.' The *bon mot* was treated like a piece of razory wit from Oscar Wilde.

A recipient of an honorary degree that morning, the writer, socialist and social reformer Beatrice Webb complained sniffily in her diary about the 'lengthy process' and the 'endless procession' of speeches and presentations. She refused to attend the evening function because of it. Webb was alone in her dissent.

There is a photograph of Liddell being carried afterwards through the partly cobbled maze of Edinburgh's Old Town on a sedan chair, like a sultan of the East. It conspicuously demonstrates the affection towards him and also the pride others felt in his achievement. He stares barrel-straight into the camera lens. The face is noticeably tanned after the burning his skin took in Paris. Those around him appear as pale as parchment, as if the beauty of the summer has never crept that far north. Liddell's long dark gown hangs in creased bunches around his shoulders and upper arms like puffed sleeves. His right elbow rests on the wooden arm of the chair. His left hand grips the scrolls he's been given, the knuckles bony and prominent, and his wing-collared shirt and bow tie give him a stylish, if raffishly insouciant, air. What strikes you most about the picture is the joy in his smile. For once Liddell, basking in the light of his own glory, is absolutely at ease. The men in striped ties and three-buttoned wool suits, their hair shiny-slick with brilliantine, are privileged

Laurels for the scholar: fellow students chair the Olympic champion after his graduation ceremony at Edinburgh University.

to bear him aloft. You see it in their expressions, reflecting the distinction of this volunteered task, which is something to be boasted about in old age.

Liddell was pressed into giving a minute-long speech from the worn top step of St Giles Cathedral. Framed in the deep raked mouldings of its Gothic arch, he stood as still as the stone statues stacked in the niches above him. He then quoted the 'dust of defeat' motto at the University of Pennsylvania. It encapsulated what he knew to be fact: the gap between coming first and coming nowhere was infinitesimal. His own race was proof of it – the stagger of Josef Imbach, the collapse of Coard Taylor and Guy Butler's strapped leg. Each of them had lost when he had won; but Liddell appreciated how easily it could have been otherwise. And if the 100 metres heats had not been run on a Sunday, he'd still be a stranger to the distance that now belonged to him. History has a habit of either denigrating losers or ignoring them altogether, as if finishing second is a sackcloth-and-ashes disgrace. Liddell wanted to highlight the injustice of that. So he told his audience what the University of Pennsylvania motto meant to him in the hope that it would mean the same to them too. 'There are many men and women who have done their best, but who have not succeeded in gaining the laurels of victory,' he said solemnly. 'To them, as much honour is due as to those who have received those laurels.'

He was thinking of one athlete in particular.

Every day Paris had toasted exemplary track performances, chiefly from the Finns, who with modern training techniques, a dried-fish and black-bread diet and astute tactical thinking turned competition into a science. Their athletes ran like automatons. As Eric Liddell said of them, 'You could almost hear the purr of their engines.' He labelled Paavo Nurmi as 'a freak . . . a marvellous piece of intelligent mechanism'. But Nurmi, despite his remorseless accumulation of gold medals and records, wasn't the Olympics' stand-out man for Liddell. Neither was Harold Abrahams.

Liddell's role model was Henry Stallard, a true 'hero'.

Among myriad definitions of that word, *The Shorter Oxford English Dictionary* lists 'superhuman strength . . . distinguished by performance . . . an illustrious warrior'. In Paris the newspapers automatically slotted any gold medallist into those hoary categorizations. But, like beauty, heroism is in the eye of the beholder; and qualifying as a hero as far as Liddell was concerned had nothing to do with winning and everything to do with sportsmanship, which he quantified as 'playing for your side or country and not for yourself'. He wavered only once from that rule. When Philip Christison had gone to offer his congratulations in the dressing room at the Colombes Stadium, Liddell thanked him for that unexpected piped fragment of 'Scotland The Brave' before adding, 'I don't think it put an extra yard on me.' In cold type the quotation reads like a sharp put-down. In reality, it was a tutorial. 'Don't forget,' explained Liddell, 'I wasn't running for Scotland. The Olympics aren't like that. They are individual events to find out who is the best in his particular event. I ran for myself to prove that I was the best in my event.' Running 'for myself' sounds not only selfish but also like a fundamental contradiction of his core beliefs – until Liddell provides qualification for it. 'We've had enough struggles between nations,' he said to Christison. At Eltham College, Liddell had become all too familiar with morning assemblies that began with the reading of a name, the sombre marking of another casualty of a war that was supposed to end every other; a war, moreover, that burned its brand even on the lives of those who were only distant spectators. A total of thirty-four former Eltham pupils were killed in the fighting. The youngest was barely twenty years old. Liddell didn't want the Olympics to become a substitute for nationalist conflict minus the shooting. The war had taught him to handle the term 'hero' with extreme care.

Stallard won only a bronze in Paris. What mattered to Liddell was the way he won it. 'No one brought more lustre to our achievements,' he insisted.

Stallard was the overwhelming favourite for the 800 metres. 'Many of us were hoping that he would finish first,' explained Liddell, aware of his friend's declaration that Paris would be his farewell to the Olympics. What Stallard concealed, however, was the reoccurrence of two old injuries to the arch of his right foot and to a bone near his ankle. Leading the race on the final bend, he faltered. As Douglas Lowe zipped past him, Stallard yelled, 'Go on. Win it. You can do it.' Stallard trailed in fourth and afterwards needed morphine to numb the extreme pain. He hobbled back to the team hotel on a walking stick. 'No one for a moment dreamed that he would run again,' said Liddell, also convinced that Stallard, knowing he couldn't win himself, had engineered Lowe's success with a speedy first lap designed to tire the Americans.

Stallard had already reached the final of the 1,500 metres – another of Nurmi's events – and the prospect of scratching from it was inconceivable to him. Philip Noel-Baker attempted to persuade him not to compete. He pointed out, as if Stallard couldn't count, that it would be his fifth race in five days. Noel-Baker also stressed the long-term damage Stallard might do to his health. Stallard appreciated the risks. The physiology of the human body was his trade: he was a medical student at St Bartholomew's. Stallard saw it as his duty to take on Nurmi. Not to do so would be disappointing Britain, a mortifying prospect for him. Stallard received another dose of morphine and Liddell watched him bind up his foot and ankle with a roll of sticking plaster and crêpe bandages. 'Every time he put his foot down he was in agony,' he said.

Nurmi was unbeatable. His only opponent was the clock. With 120 metres to go, Stallard ruptured a tendon. He chased on regardless, taking himself beyond the edge of exhaustion. As he crossed the line, in third place, he staggered and collapsed head first on to the track. He was carried off on a canvas stretcher and remained unconscious for more than thirty minutes. Stallard awoke with no recollection of completing the home straight. No matter how hard he tried to dredge up a solid memory of those last ten seconds, nothing would come to him, either then or in the future. The picture in his mind was always blank. 'My brain suddenly went red hot,' he explained. 'The next thing I remember was someone rubbing my temples with ice.' When Stallard came round on the massage table, he found Noel-Baker standing over him with a furrowed brow and a hand on his shoulder. Noel-Baker was about to express his concern when Stallard spoke first. 'Sorry for the very bad show,' he said.

Thinking Stallard's bronze medal was equal in worth and weight to his own gold because of the circumstances in which his friend fought to win it, Liddell described the display as 'one of the most heroic things in the history of athletics'.

The music accompanying the modern gold medallist is the bell-ring of the cash till. Sponsors await him. Commercial brands are ready to bear his name, and there is an agent to barter on his behalf.

Eric Liddell had only D. P. Thomson.

What Thomson recognized was the chance to capitalize fully on his pupil's pulling power. Liddell would altruistically rake in people rather than money, though there would be pass-the-hat donations – mostly copper coins rather than silver – as a consequence of his speaking engagements. Early on Thomson, in charge of the events diary, contributed an article to the *Glasgow Herald* that was part personal profile and part advertisement. 'The name E. H. Liddell is fast becoming known as a speaker to young men,' said Thomson, as if appealing for bookings.

The Sunday after winning his gold medal Liddell spoke in the Scots Kirk on Rue Bayard. If an Olympic champion went into the pulpit today, less than forty-eight hours after his race, the regular congregation would find the pews filled with reporters, the aisles snaked with television cables and the glare and heat of arc lights upon them. Liddell's appearance was relatively unobtrusive. All that survives is a shadowed photograph – Liddell shakes hands with the elderly minister after the service – and the briefest of agency reports, thought so inconsequential that Britain's high-circulation newspapers spiked it. The Kirk was full: 'The Olympic record breaker . . . drew almost as many admirers . . . to hear him preach as went to Colombes to see him run,' said the correspondent who listened to him.

In *Chariots of Fire*, Liddell is shown reading the passage from Isaiah 'They shall run and not be weary, and they shall walk and not be faint'. The text he actually used was from Psalm 119.18: 'Open thou mine eyes, that I may behold wondrous things'. Those 'wondrous things' are the commandments, for the Psalm ends with the declaration: 'Thy testimonies also are my delight and my counsellors.' The Psalm was the springboard for Liddell to encourage worshippers to read and re-read the commandments because he also warned there 'were many ways in which men might blind themselves to the truth' of them. He then compared Christians – attempting to spread the Bible to the sceptical – to 'Columbus and other discoverers and pioneers' who had to 'toil before they succeeded in their task'.

That evening the British Olympic Association held a reception for any athlete of any nation who wanted to attend. Liddell went out of courtesy. So did a Scottish female admirer – women always seemed drawn to Liddell – who had heard him speak in the Kirk. During the war she had been a motorcycle dispatch rider 'all over England'. Now she wanted to dance 'all over' the ballroom floor with him. Her wish was unfulfilled; the man who wouldn't run on a Sunday wouldn't waltz on it either. The content of his sermon, as well as his refusal to dance, reaffirmed Liddell's priority, which was the divinity classes about to start at the Scottish Congregational College.

The same critics who thought it ludicrous for Liddell not to run on a Sunday now thought it equally ludicrous for him to go to China after his studies were over. Couldn't he tend to the poor and downtrodden of his own country instead? Weren't there moral lessons to be taught in Glasgow's Gorbals or London's East End? Why didn't he prolong his athletics career and exploit the publicity the Olympics guaranteed him to spread his message?

There was sense in these arguments. The end of the war had given the public a craving for the glamour and escapism of sport as never before. Wembley's first FA Cup final, between Bolton Wanderers and West Ham United, drew three hundred thousand to a stadium with a 125,000 capacity. The centre forward David Jack, who scored the opening goal, was later transferred for £10,000, a world record sum large enough to buy a property on London's Park Lane and employ a Downton Abbey-like staff to run it. In the era of the maximum wage for footballers, Jack was earning a basic £468 a year – plus several hundred more from undeclared bonuses. Britain's highest salaried sportsman was cricketer Jack Hobbs, the prolific run-maker. Queues around the Test match grounds confirmed the idolization bestowed on him. As well as owning a sports goods shop, Hobbs endorsed tailored suits and armchairs, fountain pens and breakfast cereal, cigarettes and energy tonics. He annually banked about £1,500, which was £500 more than a doctor or provincial solicitor and £1,000 more than a headteacher.

In America the big-gun sportsmen were better off still. Sport is almost always in the midst of a golden era of one sort or another. Only the sobriety of hindsight either judges it as authentic or condemns it as a dud. Most golden eras turn out to have been tin underneath. But this one was exceptional and glittery, made for writers such as Grantland Rice. There was Babe Ruth, whom Rice described as 'a bolt-heaving Jupiter' because he put pitches where he liked, which was usually at the back of a stand or out of the stadium altogether. There was Bill Tilden with that cannon-ball serve booming off sheep-gut strings from a racket head sized only 65 square inches. Rice thought Tilden 'the perfect tennis player' and 'one of the few invincible figures in sport'. There was the showman golfer Walter Hagen, who liked silk shirts, cashmere sweaters and fine wool plus-fours. And there was Jack Dempsey, whom Rice christened 'the greatest fighting tornado' and 'the most spectacular champion of them all'. His press box colleague Paul Gallico also saluted Dempsey, thinking no more popular prize-fighter had ever lived. Like someone over-fed on caviar, Gallico retreated from sport, becoming a successful novelist instead, after losing his taste for it. His valediction remembered a 'dizzy, spinning sports reel of athletes, events, records, personalities, drama and speed, a geared-up, whirling golden world'. That 'golden world' made those at the apex of it alchemists too. Tilden collected $25,000 per annum from writing syndicated columns alone. Hagen was paid $30,000 for an ambassadorial position at a golf and country club, which amounted to a heap of loose change compared with the monies Wilson Sports shovelled his way for designing equipment and then sliding it into his bag. Ruth never earned less than a basic $52,000 salary. Dempsey, who once adorned the cover of *Time*, became a million-dollar ex-champ and a folk hero after Gene Tunney pummelled him to pieces and he responded afterwards to his wife's worried question of 'What happened?' with that unforgettable, off-the-cuff reply 'Honey, I forgot to duck.'

Liddell was never interested in chasing money or acquiring possessions. Surviving on a peppercorn stipend was no hardship to him. He didn't mind the sort of impecuniousness that made the Morningside Church mice look like millionaires. Throughout his life he'd never earn more than £300 per year. The makers of Liddell's track-shoes rushed out a line advertisement in the *Athletic News and Cyclists Journal* to proclaim that a hand-made pair of spikes, similar to his own, started at 17 shillings and sixpence, which was almost half the average working man's weekly wage. Liddell made no financial gain from these shoes. As an amateur, he could not advertise a product even tangentially connected to his sport without infringing his status. The AAA would have banned him immediately. Only ex-athletes beat the drum for Phosferine and Wills Salts, supposedly remedies for everything from constipation to insomnia. Nor would Liddell – as others did – navigate around the regulations by accepting sly payments, which could be speciously dressed as travel and subsistence expenses.

He was even less interested in being a celebrity – at least for its own sake. He'd found himself one nonetheless. Letters and telegrams piled up. He couldn't walk through Edinburgh without being pointed at because his photograph was still appearing in the newspapers, and in the city's cinemas that strip of Pathé News film from Paris was shown, as if on an endless loop, half a dozen times every day for more than a fortnight. There have always been personalities who hide only where the press and the photographers are certain to find them and plunge into fame, letting its rip-tide carry them away. Liddell wasn't one of them. Fame was only worthwhile because it made him much more likely to be listened to. He wasn't one of those Bible-bashing preachers who, the good book in tow, had to wander peripatetically in search of audiences. The audiences came to him. The problem was finding meeting halls big enough to accommodate them.

Liddell could have gone anywhere, especially to the United States. The Americans were fascinated with the ostensibly quirky but morally unimpeachable Flying Parson, a tag that stuck to him even in small-town newspapers. 'Runs for Six Days a Week. Worships on the Seventh' proclaimed one headline, inferring he was 'God's Runner'. Another said he could 'preach' as well as he could 'run'. The *Literary Digest* reported what was being said about him elsewhere: that he was 'possibly the most prominent representative of the muscular school of Christianity in modern times' and that he constantly demonstrated that it was 'quite possible for one to be both muscularly and spiritually strong'.

America was bruised from the beating it had taken in the 100, 400 and 800 metres in Paris. It sought revenge and wanted Liddell, Douglas Lowe and Harold Abrahams to sail over, compete again in Pennsylvania and then undertake an East Coast tour, the highlight being a showdown in San Francisco. Liddell, it was proposed, could break away when he chose and give a sermon or lecture wherever he liked. He would get more invitations than could possibly be accepted, through the cachet of being an Olympic champion and also because he needed no introduction. After Paris, Johnny Weissmuller had toured Europe and swum against all-comers in stunts to foster good will. Why couldn't Liddell do likewise, using staged events to promote his beliefs? His character was also an advantage in attracting Mr and Mrs Middle America. He was wholesome, squeaky clean. Unlike Ruth and Hagen, he didn't have 'whisky fingers' and he wasn't as randy as a dog. Unlike Dempsey, he hadn't been accused of evading the war draft.

There was no shortage of offers to sift through. He could have written an instruction book about athletics with Tom McKerchar. He could have put his name to newspaper columns or opinion pieces on topics both sporting and spiritual. Edinburgh University was willing to accommodate him in a capacity of his choosing. There were businesses – banks and insurance companies – that wanted him as a figurehead. 'He declined several attractive and lucrative offers,' said a friend. Simply allowing organizations to add his name to their letterhead would have earned Liddell twice Hobbs's salary *at least*. With ads, written work and paid appearances, he could have quadrupled it. Hobbs was so shy he could barely look at himself in the mirror and declined parts in films because of it. The camera took to Liddell. Those close-up Pathé shots of him in Paris are evidence of his impact on screen.

His Cambridge chums, though recognizing the offer as futile, offered to pull strings for him, each of them golden. He could affiliate himself with the light blue of the university. There'd be additional perks. He could train with Alec Nelson, assisting him to school the next Olympic champions. On a Sunday he could preach in the yellow candlelight of King's College Chapel, amid what the future poet laureate John Betjeman described as the 'shadowy silence of canopied Renaissance stalls'. In return Liddell would be a glorified public relations executive, though the public the university wanted him to woo was pressed between the pages of *Who's Who* and *Debrett's*. He could butter up distinguished visitors at formal functions or casual soirées. The arrangement would be mutually beneficial. The university could bask in the kudos of an association with the country's favourite Olympian. The champion could relax because the bonds tying him were silk-made and slack. This was an Arcadia that most would have murdered for. If he preferred, Noel-Baker, now a professor at the University of London, could solicit openings elsewhere.

A lesser figure would not only have given in to temptation, but also convinced himself that it was the right thing to do. Excuses weren't in hard-to-reach places. Each would have been viewed as plausible too. Liddell could have said he wanted to absorb himself more fully in study before breaking into the wider world. He could have said there were urgent missionary tasks to be undertaken in his own backyard. And, most convincingly of all, he could have said that winning one gold medal had given him the ambition to try to win another. Liddell never contemplated it. He wasn't for sale at any price. Liddell told one congregation that 'the greatest danger was victory', which he further defined as 'bringing a man up to a level above the strength of his character'. He appealed to another to 'keep sport free from anything that tends to lower its purity and value' and to 'engage in it' for 'the sport's sake alone'. He revealed to a third that no cheering from athletics crowds had given as much pleasure as his religion. The kernel of each speech was the same. He wouldn't allow himself to become swollen-headed. He wouldn't use sport to make money or advance a career. Athletics was essentially over for him now.

His friends from the Olympics team settled into congenial lives. Douglas Lowe, with his natural legal bent, became a barrister. Arthur Marshall became an aviator, creating his own company, and earned a knighthood. Harold Abrahams became a journalist, an author, a BBC broadcaster and then a sports administrator. Guy Butler became a journalist and author too. Henry Stallard became what he'd always intended to be – an ophthalmic surgeon. And Philip Noel-Baker became everything – Labour MP, Cabinet minister, life peer, lecturer at Yale and winner of the Nobel Peace Prize. The rosy path wasn't to Liddell's liking. He had promises to keep. He'd sworn his allegiance to missionary work in China. His obligation was to join his family, who were everything to him. He'd initially wanted to do so without delay; only D. P. Thomson's intervention changed his mind. Thomson persuaded him to study theology and combine it with evangelistic appeals to the 'youth of the country', arguing that the opportunity 'might never come again'.

There were those who thought that he should postpone his journey for another reason: simply to live a little. Liddell was asked why he was so willing to give up everything the Olympics now offered him. 'Because I believe God made me for China,' he always replied.

Liddell had settled for a modest post. He'd agreed to teach science and take sports lessons at the Anglo-Chinese College in Tientsin, the city where his father had been reassigned after Siaochang. Most athletes quit after seeing the moment of their greatness flicker, afraid of a vertiginous decline. Liddell was about to retire at least four years before his prime for the sake of the country to which he'd become devoted.

This seemed perfectly logical to him and perfectly illogical to those who didn't understand his faith.

Part Two

Higher

CHAPTER SEVEN

Goodbye to All That

THE OLYMPIC FLAG HADN'T been lowered from the pole when speculation began about Amsterdam in 1928. The newspapers, which had
questioned whether Eric Liddell was a quarter-miler at all, now predicted
that no one in the foreseeable future would beat him over the distance.
Suddenly he was the Invincible Flying Parson.

While the Games were still hot in the memory, A. B. George began
touring the provinces like a repertory actor. He put together a lantern
show about Paris, the advertisements promising black and white slides
and 'expert' commentary and insight. The hypocritical George endorsed
Liddell as being 'capable of anything'. He made no mention of the pre-
Games ridicule of both his chances and his running style.

As well as Liddell's gold medal, George offered further evidence of his
infallibility over the 400 metres. He'd seen him run again, only eight days
later, at Stamford Bridge. The United States squad stopped over for an
exhibition against the British Empire. Without Liddell, Britain had lost
both relays to them in Paris. In the 4×100 metres, the quartet took silver
because the still-fatigued Harold Abrahams ran the first leg sluggishly
and the final baton change was botched. In the 4×400 metres the team
claimed bronze; though, in a peculiar move, Guy Butler, far faster than
his compatriots, ran the third leg rather than the anchor. 'With him,'
Butler said of Liddell, 'we'd most certainly [have got] gold.'

Liddell had proved one point in Paris. Now he proved another in the
4×400 metres in London. To counter him the Americans added his

adversary, Horatio Fitch, curiously excluded from the Olympic relay team too. Liddell considered this race to be 'at least as good' as the Olympic final. Others thought it was better. Charley Paddock had watched Liddell 'run the legs off' Fitch in Paris. 'No athlete ever came closer to being inspired by competition,' he said of him. 'He spread-eagled the field.' But what Paddock witnessed at Stamford Bridge he regarded as 'the most phenomenal quarter anyone ever saw'.

Olympic fever set the turnstiles clicking. More than forty thousand came, though twice as many would claim to have seen Liddell's stupendous run after the attention it attracted.

In another Stoke-like performance, Liddell estimated that Fitch was 'ten yards' in front of him at the change-over. 'It seemed an impossible start to give a man who only a week earlier had broken the world's record,' he said. Liddell began to chase Fitch down. In Paddock's telling, he caught up on the final curve before going 'gloriously mad', out-sprinting him to the tape in 47.7 seconds as his 'native bagpipes' played him home. The 10 yards lost to Fitch at the start were no handicap to Liddell, who was 10 yards in front of him at the end. All Fitch saw was Liddell's back. The first-hand accounts of the race – especially Paddock's – suggest that all Fitch felt was the whoosh of a side-draught as Liddell passed him in the next lane. 'Englishmen and Americans alike went crazy,' said Paddock. The *Daily Mail* announced it as a 'piece of running that electrified everybody'. Even Liddell admitted: 'For a long time I thought I could never close the gap. The effect of being behind gradually helped me get on terms and he cracked just before the finish.'

Liddell wrecked Fitch physically and psychologically. The *Athletic News and Cyclists Journal* published a front-page photograph taken at the tape. Liddell seems under no strain at all. Fitch, his legs about to buckle, looks breathless and haunted. Liddell didn't gloat or grandstand. Knowing how depressed Fitch must be, he sought instead to soften the defeat for him. 'Probably he was feeling the effects of Paris even more than I was,' he said. Liddell never mentioned the non-stop ceremonial hoopla of his own hectic week, which rendered him so exhausted that he'd travelled to London from Edinburgh less than twenty-four hours before the competition. Paddock could scarcely believe Liddell's stamina. 'He had enough wind left next morning to preach a long sermon in a London church,' he remembered. To those watching him, it seemed Liddell's jokey reply to questions about 'the secret' of his 400 metres success wasn't altogether tongue-in-cheek. 'I run the first 200 metres as hard as I can. Then, for the second 200 metres, with God's help, I run harder,' he'd said. He'd run so hard that, afterwards, the Americans contemplated the obvious. If Liddell was too quick for them after only a handful of 400-metre races, what else would he achieve with practice? Wyndham Halswelle's win in the London Olympics had come at twenty-six years old – the same age Liddell would be when the 1928 Games began. Liddell, fitter and speedier, could have strolled to Amsterdam, no one threatening him.

Liddell was constantly asked whether he'd offer himself for selection. While publicly never ruling himself out, he privately didn't regard it as a realistic possibility. Without Tom McKerchar, he couldn't train satisfactorily at the Anglo-Chinese College. Having signed a four-year tenure there, he couldn't travel back and forth to Europe and America for meetings either, denying him proper preparation. So Liddell simply said he couldn't tell, until reaching China, whether teaching and missionary responsibilities would be compatible with the Olympics. He imagined his spare time would largely be devoted to evangelistic work.

Liddell was counting the days until he left. None of these went unfilled for the workaholic. When he wasn't attending classes or writing theological essays, Liddell went on the road either alone or with D. P. Thomson. He was inexhaustible. His schedule was crammed with preaching – weekend after weekend and frequently on successive nights as well, observed Thomson. The requests mounted up. An eight-day week wouldn't have been enough to satisfy demand. Sometimes, risking laryngitis, Liddell spoke four to six times in twenty-four hours. 'No man found it harder to say no,' added Thomson. 'No place was too small. No meeting house too insignificant. No audience too unpromising.'

The Church sorely needed him. As the war had begun, service numbers swelled because people sought succour. After the war ended attendances eroded, slowly and then drastically. Some soldiers became agnostic, criticizing passive religious leaders for not doing enough to end the slaughter sooner. In the search for solace, spiritualism became an alternative to the Church. The bereaved relied on séances, Ouija boards and clairvoyance in attempts to communicate with the dead. As the 1920s rolled on, it was estimated that only fifteen out of every hundred went to a church service in Britain. A. J. P. Taylor summed up the general attitude in the *Oxford History of England*: 'The dogmas of revealed religion – the Incarnation and the Resurrection – were fully accepted by only a small minority. Our Lord Jesus Christ became, even for many avowed Christians, merely the supreme example of a good man. This was as great a happening as many in English history since the conversion of the Anglo-Saxons to Christianity.' The Moderator of the Assemblies of the Scottish Churches was more candid still. The Church, he said, 'stood at the crossways with the signposts somewhat obliterated'. One minister believed the 'dread of Hell' was dead, for Hell had been seen, garbed in scarlet and black and smelling of cordite and gas, at Bazentin Ridge and Arras and Ypres and Passchendaele and in innumerable shell-holes and rat-infested trenches that were now unmarked graves for unknown soldiers. Another claimed weekend motoring had slashed the size of congregations; his church planned to provide garaging and car wash facilities. A fact-finding report concluded that complacency was infesting the clergy, which it said was too tolerant of Sunday 'sport and games' and also lacked 'live wires' to speak on its behalf.

The live wire who wasn't tolerant of Sunday participation preached on. Wherever he went – theatres, music halls and public auditoriums as well as churches – anyone who couldn't find a seat gladly stood. There were 1,700 at one meeting in Kilmarnock. Another thousand came to a service in Paisley. As many as six hundred wedged themselves into Glasgow's Dundas Street Congregational, the small church where his father James had been ordained. To prove Liddell had a cachet beyond Scotland, a further thousand heard him at a YMCA gathering in London. One Sunday the prohibition-supporting Liddell was even given a hearing by lunchtime drinkers in a pub. Thomson's verdict was: 'We reached audiences not readily accessible to any other type of evangelist.'

Liddell sounded like John Wesley, the father of Methodism, in his pronouncements. His approach was also comparable. Adept, like Wesley, at open-air preaching, Liddell spoke wherever there was a need and irrespective of the surroundings. Like Wesley, he did so without flummery, and the plain props of his philosophy were compassion and rigour.

Wesley's instruction to his congregation had been the austerely altruistic 'Do all the good you can. By all the means you can. In all the ways you can. In all the places that you can. At all the times you can. To all the people you can. As long as you ever can.' This was Liddell's ambition too. At each event there was a loose script which, like a politician's stump speech, Liddell tweaked to suit audience and place. Thomson called it 'a straightforward and manly message'. Liddell introduced himself as being from the third or fourth generation of non-smoking teetotallers. 'Seldom does a proper athlete come from a drunken family,' he'd warn. Comparisons between sport and the demands of everyday life were then drawn. He talked about faith, prayer and the spirit of competitiveness and fairness on the field. 'The good team sportsman', he stressed, didn't backslide or bend the rules. Nor did he play purely 'for his own sake'. He had high ideals. He was concerned for others ahead of himself. He was forever striving to be 'the best' – even if his best didn't win him a medal. Whatever the outcome, the mind and the body were scrupulously maintained at 'the highest pitch of perfection', he added.

Always Liddell welded sport to sportsmanship, calling the first element of it 'courage'. This, he thought, reached 'its very highest form' in the trials of ordinary life. 'The man who had got the spirit of sportsmanship in his game would be able to carry that spirit into everyday activities.' The example he gave was going on 'day after day without work'. The crucial line was still looming. 'The good sportsman is in all of us,' said Liddell, urging those who heard him to become one.

Since the men who heard him say all this were generally the impoverished or the pitifully low-paid for whom a weekend luxury was a full pouch of tobacco, Liddell went on a tightrope walk whenever he gave that speech. He could have come across as pompous and condescending, another hectoring interferer from the island of the relatively well-off. But Liddell had a lambent quality and he qualified the sportsman analogy, tempering its ambition with an understanding of what it took to bind a family together in the mid-1920s. It seemed as if Britain had lost the Great War. Industry was ailing, blighted by strikes and walk-outs and shortages. More than 1.2 million of the male-dominated workforce were registered as unemployed. Row upon row of mid-Victorian houses were dank, insanitary, half-lit hovels. Ex-servicemen, still traumatized from shelling and the taste of death, suffered abominable neglect. He told them nonetheless: 'No man who really is a man ever cared for the easy task. There is no enjoyment in the game that is easily won. It is that in which you have to strain every muscle and sinew to achieve victory that provides real joy.'

Liddell was also concerned that 'to many people, Christianity [was] something that came out with the Sunday clothes and did not affect the rest of their daily life and work'. Unlike other preachers, he was convinced that 'no amount' of churchgoing could turn anyone into a true

Christian. 'Only intimate contact with God through Jesus,' he said, could achieve that. He described it as a 'free gift' from Him – 'the greatest of all sportsmen'.

Like every British medal won in Paris, Liddell's Olympic gold was delayed in the post because a dozy French official miscalculated the cost of the postage. The package got stuck in transit until someone in a sorting office realized what it must contain and organized delivery without excess charge. After receiving so many requests to look at the medal, Liddell occasionally took it with him when he travelled. The chance to see it was another incentive to go to hear him.

When asked about the Olympics, he referred to them in the past tense. He'd remember Paris sweetly as a 'crowded and glorious week' and 'the greatest experience of my life'. But he'd then add, as if no one knew of it, that irrevocable change was coming for him. 'I am needed in China,' he'd say. 'And I am going to run a different race there.'

There were goodbyes to say and debts to pay before Eric Liddell left.

His brother Rob had married shortly before the Olympics. In December he and his wife, Ria, sailed for Shanghai. In January 1925 Tom McKerchar's wife gave birth to a son. The boy was named Eric Liddell McKerchar; Liddell became the baby's godfather. He also secured an Olympic memento for his coach. Edinburgh's city grandees had presented Liddell with a second piece of gold to add to his medal, a half-hunter pocket watch with a barley-twist chain. He arranged for McKerchar to receive an identical timepiece. The inscription, which Liddell also chose, thanked him for 'faithful service' from 'Scottish Athletic Friends'.

Liddell then travelled to Wildings, having agreed to a last favour for Eileen Soper.

The length of her hair made Eileen the Rapunzel of the house; though, unlike Rapunzel, she didn't want to escape her confinement. Her reluctance to stray far from that sheltered home was a consequence of her father George's well-meaning mollycoddling and his exaggeration of some of the dangers lurking beyond its high hedges. George had a phobia of germs and disease. Eileen's nanny had been ordered never to allow *anyone* to lay a hand on his daughter during her infancy. Nor was she ever to take her into an unfamiliar house. Stricken with appendicitis as a girl, Eileen even underwent an operation in her father's studio because of his morbid fear of hospitals. The gardener scrubbed down a wooden table for the surgeon to work on. Those childhood experiences turned Eileen into something of a hypochondriac as an adult. So she worked relentlessly in self-imposed isolation, seldom leaving her studio except for a car ride into the countryside.

She'd become successful nonetheless, establishing herself as an artist without the patronage of her father's circle of influential friends. Only eight weeks before Liddell won in Paris, Eileen received a letter from the Royal Academy. Her dry-point painting called *Flying Swings*, depicting three young children in a playground, had been sold for £4.14s.6d. The buyer was Queen Mary.

Liddell would have made the ideal husband for her – if he'd been willing to forgo China.

The romance Eileen had envisaged for them was unrealistic. She did, however, prolong the relationship for a few extra weeks, persuading this least vain of men to sit for a portrait. Eileen asked Liddell to pose in his civvies rather than in his Olympic vest and shirt. She wanted to convey the studious thinker and scholar she knew rather than the brawn of the athlete. Eileen hadn't attempted a serious portrait before and usually preferred to work in watercolour rather than oil, the medium she chose for Liddell's painting. She laboured out of love; and the subject of that love was captive in her studio for a while, a patient sitter in front of an L-shaped window. At the end of each session the two of them walked and talked, which meant she had the memory of those last days together, as well as the portrait itself, to console her after he'd gone.

In Eileen's painting Liddell wears a three-piece grey suit, a tie of Scottish blue with thin red stripes, and a white shirt fastened with a slender gold pin across the collar. In his left hand he is holding a letter, which has been folded twice. The background is, oddly, almost the same shade of soft grey as his suit. Liddell looks much younger and fresher in art than he does in photographs. Eileen paints him as she saw him: handsome, wise and with a virtuous gleam. His hair is the colour of corn. His eyes are an iridescent cerulean. His flesh contains no crease, wrinkle or blemish apart from sharp scores beneath those eyes. Eileen purposefully allows strong light to bounce off Liddell's high forehead and along the lines of his cheekbones, which gives him a sort of celestial glow. The art critic Andrew Graham-Dixon regards the picture as 'no masterpiece' and adds that Eileen's inexperience and relative lack of aptitude for painting in oils is reflected in the portrait's 'uneven quality'. Only

Captured in oil. Eileen Soper's painterly homage to Eric.

COURTESY OF THE CHRIS BEETLES GALLERY, ST JAMES'S,
LONDON ON BEHALF OF AGBI AND THE SOPER ESTATE

one aspect redeems it in Graham-Dixon's opinion. 'It seems to catch Liddell better than any surviving photographs of him,' he says. That is arguable, but the gaze Liddell gives the viewer is undoubtedly pensive and intense. Graham-Dixon believes it makes him 'seem distant, as if entranced by some vision . . . perhaps it was that spark of divinely inspired purpose'.

Eileen adored the painting. She hadn't received a commission and there was no prospective purchaser for the 29-by-25-inch canvas. This was just as well: she had no intention of parting with it.

Eileen was an amateur poet too. She admired John Masefield and was drawn to the rural life and landscapes that Edward Thomas and John Clare depicted. Reading them persuaded her to write verse of her own.

She concentrated on what moved her, the fauna and flora, the birds and the animals she saw in and around Wildings. These were love poems to Mother Nature. Only one poem expressed love for a man. Entitled 'To E. L.', it begins 'We walked the fields of June'. She evokes a perfect day of 'lifting skies / Blue as the speedwell'. The clouds she sees are 'flying / Over the hill's rise'. What she hears is a 'peewit crying'. According to Eileen, she and Liddell climbed the hill, looked across the valley and then walked into a 'leaf-chaliced gloom', where the two of them found the white bell flowers of Solomon's Seal, its blossom drooping 'like tears upon the spray'. She regarded the walk as an advanced stage of courtship; and she is explicit in her opinion that Liddell did too. For the poem records that he took a silver key from his pocket and – 'though loath to mar / The beauty of the tree' – engraved their initials, lichen-deep, on the bark of a beech, where Eileen insists 'Many names were carved / For lovers' past delight'.

For someone so appalled by bawdiness, written or verbal, the prospect of physical intimacy can only have been contemplated with trepidation. So her use of the word 'lovers' is significant. Evidently Eileen thought that she and Liddell were about to become a loving item; that the carving was like an unspoken proposal; and also that she was willing to be a wife. So do another two lines:

> You wrote that Time might spell
> The letters E and L.

This suggests she'd more than contemplated becoming Eileen Liddell rather than staying as Eileen Soper.

The poem is undated, but was almost certainly composed after his departure from her life and almost certainly, too, discusses the summer of either 1923 or 1924. Its closing verse is wistful and melancholic:

> On fallen leaves
> The beech is lying.
> Nothing remains of that fair day
> Save a lonely peewit crying.

Preserving Liddell in poetry as well as in paint proved how much she cared for him. There is a yearning for the past about 'To E. L.', the sense of a time that cannot come again. With Liddell's departure, Eileen had lost something precious and unrecoverable. Only the sweet pain of remembrance remained.

Like a great racehorse handicapped by dropping slate weights into the saddle it carried, Eric Liddell could only be beaten on the track if he was disadvantaged first. So his last athletics season was a long lap of honour. Between mid-May and the end of June 1925 he ran in twenty-three races, winning nineteen of them. Of the four he lost, three were handicaps and the other was a relay. His final appearance came in the Scottish AAA Championships at Hampden Park. His 10 seconds for the 100 yards equalled a Scottish record set in 1884. He predictably won the 220 yards and 440 yards as well. At the end of the meeting barricades were erected to hold back the crowds wanting to mob him. The response was identical when he preached from the pulpit.

D. P. Thomson ambitiously booked Edinburgh's Usher Hall and saw no contradiction in taking the temperance advocate to a concert venue built from the profits of a whisky distiller. Classically designed, with a dome and circular walls, Usher Hall held between 2,500 and 3,000. No city auditorium was bigger. Thomson was warned that Liddell wouldn't fill it. 'You've made a big mistake,' a critic told him. To avoid the embarrassment of Liddell addressing empty seats, Thomson agreed to a solution. An evening service nearby would be shortened, its congregation briskly marched to Usher Hall to guarantee a decent turn-out. The reinforcements were never necessary. Liddell was due to speak at 8 p.m. At 5.50 the queue stretched for 50 yards. At 7.20 plans had to be made for an overflow meeting. Just over half an hour later, when the prearranged rent-a-crowd appeared, expecting to choose a seat almost anywhere, Thomson said Usher Hall was 'as tightly packed as we had dared'. Hundreds were being turned away from the overflow meeting too.

In Glasgow, another thousand came too late to see him and were stranded on the pavement, forced to wait for an overflow meeting later. This was a pity for them because Liddell's speech there was his most heartfelt. He wound back the clock. What Liddell gave wasn't so much a sermon as a chronological autobiography, as if wanting to explain both his life and his motivations. He had never spoken so expansively about himself before. He revisited Thomson's surprise arrival at George Square and the offer to go to Armadale. He revealed his own doubts about speaking in front of strangers. He disclosed the crucial details in that letter from his sister Jenny and recited the quotation it contained from Isaiah, which he'd seen as a light-beam illuminating his path. Liddell talked without drama or exclamations, never hammering out the message he wanted to convey. The facts did that for him, and each was laid next to the other like bricks.

The play St Joan had been premiered less than two years earlier. In it George Bernard Shaw imagines the scene between the doubting squire, Robert de Baudricourt, and Joan, who is questioned about the voices she claims to hear. 'They come from your imagination,' he tells her. She replies, 'That is how the messages of God come to us.' In speaking of how the message had come to him, as surely as if it had been an audible command, Liddell told the audience how it might come to them also. This had been an awfully big adventure for him. It had begun, as all big adventures do, with straightforward steps: that knock on the door; that letter next morning; that short ride to a nondescript spot – a spot, moreover, that was so like others his audience knew with a neighbourly familiarity; and then that first speech, which was no more than nervous throat-clearing before he found his voice. Now the adventure was taking him to China.

A week later, the news agency reporter sent to record his 'impressive send off' from Edinburgh highlighted 'the large following of women' trailing behind his black landau cab, which was decorated in streamers of red, white and blue. The specific mention of these female supporters, who would nowadays be categorized as groupies, illustrates Liddell's wide appeal. It was as if he were a movie idol heading to California to star beside Mary Pickford. Hundreds of fans followed him to Waverley station. Another thousand-plus were already waiting there, most of them flooding on to the platform. In the briefest of speeches, his voice 'rising shrilly above the noise of the station', Liddell said he was going to China as 'an ambassador'.

For the ordinary man and woman, who seldom went beyond their own communities, China was as distant as a planet; and the land and sea separating it from them seemed as vast and as unnavigable as the Milky Way. The Chinese alphabet, their clothes and their food were alien to Westerners too. There was bafflement over why Liddell should want to go there. He was like an explorer, heading off into the kind of uncharted territory on to which the earliest cartographers had scrawled the warning 'Here Be Dragons'.

In one of his best-known essays, entitled 'Boys' Weeklies', George Orwell pointed out that Britain had a tendency to slot citizens of non-English-speaking nations into categories. These were crude and offensively condescending. There was the 'Froggie' Frenchman, the 'Dago' Italian, the 'stupid' Scandinavian. The Chinese fared worst. The 'Chinaman', explained Orwell, was forever portrayed as being 'sinister' and 'treacherous' – a 'nineteenth-century pantomime Chinaman, with saucer-shaped hat, pigtail and pidgin-English'. Orwell omitted the other stereotypes: the drooping moustache thinner than a rat's tail, the long gowns with huge drop sleeves, the curly-toed slippers and the slits for eyes. Orwell also argued that few of Britain's population thought 'what happens in foreign countries is any of their business'. This was certainly true when he wrote it in 1940. It was truer still when Liddell went back to China.

There were reports of famine in the Kweichow Province, where it was claimed that 'people were eating the leaves off trees and selling their children for a handful of rice'. An earthquake in Talifu had made it uninhabitable, reducing homes there to cinder and splinters. But one headline starkly portrayed Western priorities about faraway tragedies: 'Earthquake Destroys Town in China: Foreigners Safe'.

Foreigners, however, weren't safe elsewhere. On the day Liddell left Edinburgh at the end of June, a single-column story on page fourteen of *The Times* put this into perspective. The disorder in China was described as 'very serious'. The writer said a 'campaign of barefaced misrepresentation' was being orchestrated by 'professional agitators' who specialized in the spread of a single and 'maliciously exaggerated' allegation. The Chinese believed treaties forced upon them in the past were cut from crooked timber. 'Foreigners' were being blamed for it, he said – 'particularly the British'.

China and the lineage of power there had grown thickly tangled in the eighteen years since Liddell's last sight of the place. The Xinhai Revolution had overthrown the Qing dynasty in 1911, breaking a hold first established in the mid-seventeenth century. In January 1912 China became a republic under Sun Yat-sen, its first provisional president. Sun was immediately forced to relinquish power to Yuan Shikai, an autocrat who failed to restore the monarchy and install himself as Hongxian Emperor. Sun went on to lead the Kuomintang, the Chinese Nationalist Party.

From 1916, a fragmented China drifted under the rule of warlord coalitions. After the war, the Treaty of Versailles awarded German rights to Shandong Province to Japan. China was apoplectic. It had entered the struggle in 1917 supporting the Allies on condition that Shandong and other German territories would be returned to it. Reneging on the agreement stoked terrible resentments, the Allies damned as duplicitous. From the backlash grew the student-led May Fourth Movement and also a feverish spread of nationalism. The anti-Christian movement was active again and fiercely intolerant. Under Russian influence, Communist propaganda was proliferating too. The newly formed Communist Party of China held its first session in 1921. Among the thirteen attendees was the twenty-seven-year-old Mao Tse-tung.

Missionaries had distributed more than eight million Bibles, established churches and hospitals and served impoverished communities. But now to be pro-Christian was to be anti-Chinese.

Liddell was willingly walking into all of this.

CHAPTER EIGHT

There Are No Foreign Lands

CORRESPONDENTS SENT BACK ALMOST daily dispatches that told of the instability in China and the hostility towards non-nationals, which convulsed the country.

The sense of betrayal over the post-war treaties grew worse; petty hierarchies, spites and rivalries existed even within the competing factions that sought to have them torn up or rewritten. There were strikes and riots, demonstrations and looting, military banditry and shootings. In late May 1925 nine students and workers were slain in Shanghai after colonial police fired indiscriminately into a crowd of several thousand, attempting to disperse a violently anti-foreign protest. Four more were shot dead the following morning. As the week progressed, foreigners were specifically targeted and 'badly mauled', reported *The Times*. Tram-cars were stoned too. Finally martial law was enforced. These incidents begat others elsewhere, temporarily closing schools, including the Anglo-Chinese College in Tientsin. The instability drew dire predictions of massacres to come. North China was on fire, and the sparks were flying everywhere when Eric Liddell got there.

His father, James, hadn't tried to pretend otherwise or coax him on false promises. At the end of every year the missionaries of the London Society were obliged to put together a state-of-the-nation review, including tentative forecasts about the next twelve months. Most of these, attempting to trap history as it flew, were staid documents. In the mid-1920s the worsening social and political climate made prediction a fool's task anyway. The uncertainty was reflected in the reports James Liddell sent from his own mission. These were uncommonly vivid compared with the efforts of his colleagues. In 1924 he referred to China's 'sad condition' and said: 'The feeling all round is one of suspense, not knowing what will happen next.' He discussed the 'perplexity, alarm, trouble and distress' of the upheavals around him and also the 'needless suffering, destruction and waste' as a consequence of them. One sentence implies his hopelessness. 'Oh, the horror of it all!' he added, the exclamation mark flung down to convey sights whose details he didn't want to share on the foolscap page. His 1925 report was darker still; so dark, in fact, that it made the previous one seem as cheery as a birthday card. 'The waters are boiling,' he wrote of the unrest. Liddell's father spoke of 'China's grievances' and 'the crushing load' under which its foundations were bowing. 'A nation is in travail,' he said.

None of this deterred his son. From infancy, Liddell's bond with the Chinese went far beyond the fact of his birth in the country and the hymns his father sang for it. The landscape and the life he had briefly led across it still gave him a sense of firm belonging, which he felt nowhere else at that stage. China was indisputably home to Liddell. Missionary work constituted the family business, and this was the only place he had ever envisaged continuing it, whatever the sacrifices. To believe – as Liddell did – that God had given him a task was also to accept that considerable hardships, sorrows and separations must be endured to complete it.

He could have sailed to China, a sedate journey lasting six weeks. In a decision that illustrated his keenness, Liddell instead took the boat train from London to Paris and then stopped off in Berlin on his way to Moscow, where he boarded the Trans-Siberian Express. The entire trip, from his old country to his new one, lasted a fortnight. The Trans-Siberian was not the Ritz on rails, however ornate the decorations of its gilt, peacock-blue rolling stock. The train was dirty, cramped and cold. There were usually three stops per day – at places such as Omsk, Irkutsk and Verkhneudinsk – and the countryside was mostly monotonous. The engine had a habit of breaking down, usually in remote spots, such as the Ural Mountains. Sleeping was difficult because the beds were as hard as red-brick. The traveller Peter Fleming, reflecting on his experience on that line less than a decade later, wrote of leaving 'the shoddy suburbs' and then seeing a vista 'clothed in birch and fir'. He reflected on the 'nondescript smell of the upholstery, the unrelenting rattle of our progress, the tall [glasses] of weak tea'. He liked the railway, admitting nonetheless 'You are a prisoner, narrowly confined.' Liddell called his voyage 'splendid' and told a friend, 'All along the way I was most fortunate to have as my companions Germans, Russians and Chinese who could all speak English.'

Afterwards he recuperated by stepping back into his childhood – those cosy days of beachside living beneath the sun. The Liddell family gathered together again for the first time in three years, in a bungalow with a shady veranda at Peitaiho, where there were long conversations and walks, reading and swimming, the leggings of Liddell's full-piece bathing suit longer than the shorts he wore in Paris. Seven of them were there: Liddell, plus his brothers Rob and Ernest, his sister Jenny, his parents and also Rob's wife, Ria. The Liddells weren't the only holiday-makers. Nor was Liddell the only freshly arrived Scottish missionary.

Annie Buchan was on the cusp of her thirtieth birthday. Born above the family bakery in Peterhead, Aberdeen, she had trained as a nurse and as a midwife in Dundee and Edinburgh before applying to the LMS. 'The work was hard, the training and discipline that of Miss Florence Nightingale,' she said. Her intention to go to China was the talk of her town. 'I might have been going to the moon,' she explained. Arriving four months before Liddell, Buchan had been based in Peking, where she was instructed in Mandarin Chinese. Peitaiho gave her the briefest of breaks before her studies resumed intensively. On the outside she was a comely, compassionate woman with a brisk, matronly manner. On the inside she had a flinty core and a capacious mind – prerequisites for dealing efficiently with ghastly medical emergencies. All this was contained within a bird-like frame, giving her a deceptively passive appearance. She was just 4 feet 11 inches tall. She had a thin face, hazel eyes and greyish brown hair parted wide on the right. She wore a pair of wire-framed glasses, the lenses as circular as the bottom of a milk bottle. To husbands who mistreated their wives in rural China, and also to wives who mistreated their children, she looked certain to be a push-over in a verbal fight, like a mousey librarian who daren't tell anyone to shush. That impression vanished as soon as she confronted them. Buchan's disapproving glare could have cracked ice.

She knew almost everything about Liddell and he knew almost nothing about her. Buchan's father had heard Liddell speak in Glasgow and asked one thing of him: would he deliver a letter to his daughter that told her how much he missed her? 'I was so thrilled, and not without emotion,' said a tearful Buchan after receiving it from Liddell's hand.

The LMS would soon be sending her to Siaochang. She'd already witnessed unsettling scenes in Peking, where student marches made the streets impassable. She'd watched the flourishing of banners and clenched fists punching the air in protest. She'd heard the chanting and the impromptu speeches – all anti-Western and especially anti-British. Buchan wasn't sure what awaited her in Siaochang. She was, however, steeled for it.

Liddell often quoted Robert Louis Stevenson's assertion 'There are no foreign lands. It is the traveller only that is foreign.' At that time – and in that place – Liddell was certainly a 'foreigner' because even the normally pacific and pro-British locals of Peitaiho were restless for change. Some were openly antagonistic. Liddell saw propaganda posters slapped everywhere. The messages were unsophisticated. The British government was accused of being arrogantly interfering and conspiratorial charges were levelled against it. Its politicians were nefarious. Its businessmen were exploitative. Its missionaries were there to lure the unwary into un-Chinese ways. Listening to Buchan talk about Peking, Liddell became aware of how softly he would have to tread. 'There is a prejudice against the British,' he said.

People drift in and out of everyone's life because friendships aren't always kept in constant repair. But Liddell and Buchan saw missionary work similarly, and each instinctively took to the other because dedication of service had brought them both to China. Their casual introduction on the sands of Peitaiho was the beginning of a good companionship. Over the next twenty years Liddell's life would intertwine with Buchan's in ways neither could have foreseen.

In a photograph snapped to celebrate the Liddells' reunion, the family poses half-formally at the bottom of the steps outside the front door of their two-storey brick home in Tientsin.

Eric Liddell, the right side of his face caught in the light of the sun, wears white flannels and matching shoes, socks and a button-down shirt. In a dark blazer, slightly loose at the shoulders, he resembles a day-tripper about to embark on a sea-front stroll. Sitting in front of him, James Liddell is like the archetypal Victorian, the sagacious patriarch who dispenses advice and signs the cheques. Beside him Mary, now a woman with a

Together again. The Liddell family in front of their Tientsin home in the French Concession after Eric's arrival in China. (Back row, from the left): Eric, Jenny, Rob's wife Ria, Rob; (front row): James, Ernest, and Mary.

fuller figure, seems much more energetic than her husband and looks a decade and a half younger than him. Her hair is as black as it ever was. Ernest sits cross-legged in front of his parents, like a team mascot. He has a schoolboy's parting, a lank of hair flopping across his forehead, and his ears stick out. Anyone coming to the photo without prior knowledge about anyone in it would assume Rob was the athlete. He is bolt-straight and as lithe as a hurdler.

Nothing in the picture suggests it has been taken in China. That is because the London Missionary Society and the Anglo-Chinese College, both as fixed as compass points in Tientsin, were settled in the city's French Concession, one of eight areas cordoned off for foreign residents. The other seven belonged to Austria-Hungary, Belgium, Britain, Germany, Italy, Japan and Russia. These territories were created as a consequence of China's military defeats – primarily against the British and the French – and existed outside local law, functioning largely as independent states in policing, taxation and government, like an early version of Hong Kong. The architecture within them was an indulgent, eclectic mix of styles, among them Greek, Tudor and Edwardian. Residents such as the Liddells were free to live or socialize anywhere in the Concessions, using the shops, banks and libraries created for them. There was even a racetrack, where Ascot-like ladies' days were arranged, and a country club that offered a genteel Home Counties atmosphere abroad. You could play tennis there. You could swim. You could dance in its ballroom to classical orchestras, big bands or jazz musicians. You could eat and drink and entertain clients and friends alike. The cooks and the waiters, responding to a finger-snap, were Chinese.

In this landscape, the Anglo-Chinese College looked like a Gothic fortress of learning. It had grey-stone towers with turrets and an 8-foot wall. The founder and principal was Dr Samuel Lavington-Hart. *The Times* called him 'a pioneer of western education in China'. The son of a Congregational minister, Lavington-Hart was a physicist as well as a missionary and he had originally gone to China in 1892 as a shooting-star prodigy. A graduate of both the Sorbonne and Cambridge University, Lavington-Hart was said to be capable of achieving anything after his graduation. As a student at Cambridge he'd made his own version of the penny-farthing bicycle, developing the curved front fork. He rode it between the colleges with his hands tucked into his pockets, speaking aloud his ideas for essays as he pedalled. Like Liddell, he had heard the missionary call early. To go to China wasn't career advancement for him, it was a compulsion. He refused academic chairs and research fellowships; he also refused to leave China despite the wrenching death of his brother – and his brother's wife – from dysentery within twenty-two months of their arrival there.

He began the college in 1902 with fifty pupils. His aim was to school and shape the boys of Chinese politicians, civil servants and businessmen, hopefully guiding the decision-makers of tomorrow towards a Christian baptism. It was said, ad nauseam, that the Battle of Waterloo was 'won on the playing fields of Eton', a twisting of something that the Duke of Wellington only half-said. An echo of this misquotation nonetheless existed in Lavington-Hart's approach to both scholastic excellence and biblical teaching. The playing fields of Tientsin were his Eton, and he intended to develop a Christian spirit on them.

The roll had since swelled ten-fold, and Lavington-Hart was almost sixty-seven. The tip of his white beard was short and wispy, like a goat's. He was an avuncular figure but protectively precious about the reputation of the college. He hired only on ability. The fact that he knew Liddell's father did not influence his decision to recruit Liddell. He did it because he believed Liddell, even without his status as an Olympic champion, was made of the right stuff. Another of his trusted masters had told him so. More than a decade after teaching him science, history, English and classics at Eltham College, A. P. Cullen was now Liddell's staffroom colleague.

Liddell easily swapped athletics for academia. He took the attic room of the house and filed his old life away like exhibits from the past. As an assiduous record-keeper, Liddell had always clipped out and saved newspaper cuttings and press photographs in a box. With a sense of finality, thinking nothing more would be written about him, he placed these inside two large scrapbook albums and became the curator of his own mini-museum. He hired a carpenter, who made a small cabinet with shallow drawers in which were placed almost two hundred medals, including his Olympic gold.

Liddell, given the twin responsibilities of teaching science and sport, learned how to control a classroom. He did so alongside another new recruit, Eric Scarlett, who moved into the laboratory with him. Scarlett was twenty-eight and also had missionary ambitions. After a disillusioning war, serving with the Royal Engineers, he'd sought some meaning from the whiz-bang of shells and the carnage of the Western Front. As well as taking science at Manchester University, he became travelling secretary of the Student Christian Movement. Liddell rubbed along with everyone because he searched for common points of interest. With Scarlett, it wasn't difficult. As another colleague said of him, Scarlett was 'a delightful person', a look-on-the-bright-side sort of chap who sought perfection for his blue-gowned pupils and wanted them to know why science was relevant even to non-scientists. In church his wife Dorothy played the piano. At home Scarlett liked to sing comic music hall songs to her accompaniment.

Lavington-Hart taught the theory of physics. He did so occasionally, as if giving a paper to the Royal Society. These classes were like obstacle courses for the mind. Liddell and Scarlett drafted more practical lessons to make science seem less daunting. Sometimes Liddell would reveal his mischievous side to lighten things. He'd brew up a chemistry solution and make a show of tasting it, telling his pupils 'it's wonderful'. He'd then invite one of them to dip his finger into the liquid too. The pupil found

Taking tea. Eric Liddell plays host to his Union Church congregation in Tientsin.

that Liddell's solution was actually so foul-tasting you had to spit it out. The class hadn't noticed the trick. With a deftness of hand that disguised it, Liddell had placed his forefinger into the glass but licked his middle finger afterwards.

Twice a week Liddell and Scarlett had a tutor of their own. Conscious of the need to speak Chinese well, Liddell had begun to re-learn the language and sought out a teacher, whom Scarlett shared. Liddell even studied the Bible and the mission hymn book in Chinese to familiarize himself with its characters.

He soon fell into a timetabled routine. He taught his classes. He took his turn on the rota for Morning Service. He went to the weekly evening prayer meetings. He read lessons as Sunday school superintendent. He took Bible classes. Occasionally he preached at the Union Church, which served the British and the American communities. As if the Amsterdam Olympics of 1928 remained a possibility, he continued to train too. The six-lane cinder track at Tientsin was planted into a piece of prime fenced-off parkland fringed by low trees overlooking the high windows of the college buildings. When Liddell raced against his pupils, he did so under a severe handicap, generously surrendering a huge yardage to them. He was glad to lose, for the credit awarded to whoever beat the Olympic champion improved morale. He'd often be seen playing tennis against

*What the smartly dressed science teacher should
wear. Eric Liddell in Tientsin in the early 1930s.*

himself too. He'd lob the ball from the baseline and chase it around the
net. He'd then lob it back again before the shot bounced twice.

Colonial life was well ordered for Liddell. His teaching duties were a
pleasure. His preaching duties weren't over-strenuous. Every August there
was the bonus of another holiday in Peitaiho and days of sea-bathing,
shell-hunting and beach picnics. But even in his cosy existence, Liddell
was conscious of Tientsin's 'other face', which some of those around him
tried to pretend did not exist.

Commercialism had made Tientsin wealthily and vibrantly cosmopolitan. Electric trams rattled along broad arterial roads and merchant
ships and steamers crawled into the congested docks, backing up bow to
stern. But the finery their trade brought only accentuated the rank poverty existing alongside it. Illiteracy and a lack of basic hygiene were
commonplace in the populated suburbs to the west and to the north

where rickshaws and wooden handcarts, their wheels 3 feet wide, crawled along the streets beside donkeys, bullocks, packhorses and camels. The houses were shacks. Those who lived in them scrabbled for a living as coolies, carpet-weavers or manual labourers on the roads, at the docks or in the agricultural fields, the crops in them fertilized by human excrement toted in metal buckets. In the outlying villages – both there and elsewhere – the conditions were far worse. Confirmation of that for Liddell came not only from his father but also from his new friend.

A train and then a springless mule cart carried Annie Buchan to Siaochang, where she shook the sand off her clothes. Dust storms, sweeping in from the Gobi Desert to the north of the Great Plain, covered the soft, brown, powdery earth. The eye saw only flat land. That flatness turned the sky into a vast canopy that was icy blue in summer and metallic grey in winter. 'No fleecy clouds like back home,' said Buchan. Hundreds of mud-brick villages were spread towards the flat edge of the Great Plain, which she said 'had a glory of its own'. The furthest of them shimmered like a mirage. Each village had a dotted copse of weeping willows and, in rare shady patches, peaches, hard pears and apricot trees bore fruit precious to the half-starved.

Buchan called Siaochang 'not a very important place, just one of many small communities linked by dirt roads'. She saw 'one or two market towns'; though the term 'market', suggesting a hectic to-and-fro trade, didn't chime with the sight of a few shops that were 'dark and dingy inside' and displayed meagre and mediocre goods on the open street. The rhythm of the villages was cyclical, tied to the seasons. In the short spring Buchan followed the progress of the farmers, who on plots between 1 and 5 acres grew *kao liang*, a dark wheat that sprouted between 14 and 16 feet high, and also millet, cotton, sweetcorn, watermelons and peanuts. She sweltered in early summer, the temperatures reaching 110 to 116 degrees and causing a lassitude noticeable in everything and everyone. Buchan said that even the birds were 'in distress . . . their beaks open and feathers drooping'. In mid-July came the annual miracle of meteorology in those parts. 'A cloud the size of a man's hand would appear on the far horizon and literally, while one watched, the cloud would grow bigger and more clouds gathered and came thick and fast.' The wind accompanying these clouds could be hurricane force, and Buchan would always hear a 'loud bang' – the opening note of a thunderstorm. The rain came in a

Annie Buchan, who became one of Eric Liddell's most avid supporters and closest friends in China.

dam-burst and would last 'for weeks', she said. 'To our amazement with one night of rain frogs would be deafening us with their croaking.'

The farmers feared the uninvited guest. Buchan watched locusts arrive in their thousands, spreading over the fields in a black mass and stripping the crop to bare stalks in less than an hour. The farmers and their families ran pointlessly into the fields, shouting and banging together tools and sticks in an attempt to save a scattering of grain for the harvest. The locusts feasted and flew on.

And then the winter came. Snow and frost lingered because it was so dry. The thermometer dipped below zero. Buchan wore padded clothes stuffed like a mattress. The farmers swathed themselves in goat-, sheep- and cat-skin coats. The fur was worn on the inside, leaving exposed the pink-brown skin of the animal from which the pelt had come. The farmers didn't care how this looked; nor did they care if their coats smelled of rotten hacked-away flesh.

While working as a nurse, Buchan ran into other customs she found impossible to reconcile. In the factual accounts she kept, both contemporaneously and decades afterwards, Buchan looked at Siaochang the way Pepys had looked at London. Her typewritten records, though never sensationalist, are unflinching, which is why readers come across passages that make them stop suddenly, appalled and incredulous. 'The people were primitive in their mode of living. They had not moved on with the passing years,' she said, attempting to provide perspective as well as mitigation.

There were horror stories. A father hacked off one of his son's arms for disobedience. 'The father would not be in trouble legally for that,' Buchan commented. Daughters had it even tougher. Those who got pregnant before marriage could be buried alive. 'No one questions it because there is no law against it,' said Buchan. She remembered one case in which a woman was rescued from that fate after being kidnapped and gang-raped. 'Rogues and bandits did terrible things,' added Buchan, alluding to frequent instances that went uninvestigated. The woman hid in the hospital and gave birth there. The baby was adopted so she could return home without the fear of being murdered by her father. Some cases were tragically hopeless. A baby's fingers were bitten to the knuckle by a hungry rat. A man who lost a fight was 'so cross', said Buchan, 'that he cut off his own right hand so as to put the blame on his opponent'.

Health education was rare. There was also a reluctance among the Chinese to be treated in a Western hospital. Villagers tried to heal themselves with concoctions of leaf and stem, the recipes inherited from previous generations. Cataracts would be ignored until the eyelid turned inward, threatening blindness. Arthritis or osteoporosis had already bent a spine or withered a hand before a doctor was sought. Opium addicts raged and sweated and wiped their black-rimmed, yellow eyes. Women – even among some of the poor – were disfigured for life after foot-binding, the hideous custom of soaking cotton bandages in animal blood and herb water before repeated, vice-like swathing of the feet broke and re-broke the toes and disabled the arch. Even acute pain and swellings were tolerated, which meant cancerous tumours and growths were at a late stage before an operation attempted to cut them out. One man, complaining of indigestion, was found to have peritonitis. Buchan also recalled a seventy-year-old widow who admitted her daughter to the clinic. The daughter was pregnant and suffering from an advanced abdominal tumour. The baby died. The widow became 'almost demented', said Buchan. 'Her grief was terrible to witness. She screamed and screamed.

She thumped her head with her fist. She tried to drag and shake [the baby] back to life. She then lashed out and kicked. She cursed us all.'

Buchan knew that the baby's death, though no fault of the doctors, would deter prospective patients from attending the hospital. Word of mouth would take the news around the villages, each re-telling gingering up the details so that in the end the story bore little relation to the truth. Buchan was used to such setbacks. She had learned that being a missionary meant overcoming the mistrust of those you were trying to help. She had learned something else too: there were some things she could never change and others that could not be eradicated in one decade or two.

It wasn't uncommon, for instance, for baby girls to be abandoned shortly after birth. The male was the more highly prized in a family. But Buchan once found a baby boy, wrapped in a dirty rag, who had been placed on a roadside dump. His mother already had four children. She couldn't feed any of them, let alone herself. The baby, ailing from malnourishment and exposure, died two days later.

Domestic violence was common too. The men claimed 'devil spirits' were responsible for their veniality. Buchan said that 'culture, pride and history' made the truth ungraspable for them. She slogged intrepidly on. In Siaochang, there was no other way.

In Tientsin, where she sometimes travelled to collect supplies and meet Eric Liddell, the expatriate community was sheltered behind its iron-studded gates and crenellated walls. Afternoon tea was always served. Everyone dressed for dinner. The elegant urbanites saw themselves as a civilizing presence. The only crisis for them was a shortage of tonic for their gin. The rest of China was viewed with detachment, as if through glass. Liddell once caused a social kerfuffle after appearing in the Union Church pulpit wearing a pair of shorts. He'd thought it too hot for trousers. This was considered to be a shocking breach of protocol – proof that priorities were sometimes warped within Tientsin's smug bubble.

But the rudest of awakenings there wasn't far away.

CHAPTER NINE

Will Ye No Come Back Again?

T HE PHOTOGRAPHER FROM THE *Tientsin Times* wanted an action image of Eric Liddell at full speed.

He set up his heavy camera on the track, its wooden tripod like a spider's legs, and then began focusing the lens. There was a minor, but critical, flaw in this plan. He had no conception of how fast an Olympic champion was capable of running. The clueless photographer was still trying to frame the shot when he discovered the gold medallist bearing down on him. Like someone attempting to sidestep an avalanche, the photographer tried to remove his camera – and himself – from Liddell's path. Liddell tried to swerve out of the way too. Neither man was successful. Liddell crashed into the photographer, flattening him and tipping over the camera. The smack of heads knocked both of them unconscious. Annie Buchan, sitting in the stand, saw Liddell slump 'flat on his face'. He was carried into a tent, where he awoke and woozily announced that he was 'just winded'. That incident, which reads like something from a slapstick film, proves that what one newspaper said of Liddell in the late 1920s was not flannel meant to flatter. He hadn't lost 'any of his wonderful speed' in China.

Another eyewitness confirmed it shortly afterwards. He saw Liddell in a relay race, competing in the Min Yuan stadium. Min Yuan, opened in 1926, was partly Liddell's design; he'd modelled it on Stamford Bridge.

'He stood, hands on hips and thin hair blowing above his high forehead,' said his admirer. 'He received the baton last, but then flew around the track, overtaking all opposition.'

What he'd given up for China was apparent during the preparation for the 1928 Amsterdam Olympics, and then the Games themselves.

There'd been regular updates in Britain about his fitness. One telegraphed dispatch, from the Anglo-Chinese Mission Sports, said he'd won the 100 metres and 400 metres – no one referred to track yards any more – and had also 'wiped out' an enormous deficit to take his team home at 'a canter' in the last leg of an 800 metres relay. The writer didn't spoil a decent yarn by pointing out the catch in his story. The Mission Sports provided shabby opposition for Liddell. It was like running a pedigree greyhound against a cocker spaniel. During the 400 metres he could have stopped for a cup of Earl Grey and still taken the race in a dip finish.

Liddell avoided reporters as much as possible. Once, seeing a group of them waiting for him on a dockside, he borrowed a huge conical cork hat and wore it to cover his face, sneaking past his would-be interrogators. But now, almost a year before Amsterdam, he couldn't dodge the newspapers and so had to give a pessimistic answer to a straightforward question. Asked about his Olympic prospects, Liddell listed the difficulties of reclaiming his peak without the presence in China of anyone to push him. He explained that the Chinese wouldn't agree to stage handicap events, believing them to be uncompetitive. That meant he couldn't make competition deliberately tougher for himself. As a consequence, Liddell implied, he was considerably short of top form. The British Olympic Association appeared casually indifferent about the matter. No one bothered to contact Liddell, either directly or indirectly, about his physical condition. To the BOA, out of sight really did mean out of mind, his gold medal in Paris like a memory lost to them.

Britain's Amateur Athletic Association paid attention to Liddell only to mildly rebuke him after the publication, mid-way through 1926, of a series of ghosted articles in *All Sports Illustrated Weekly*. In one of them he implied that Alec Nelson and Sam Mussabini would have been useful in the Colombes Stadium dressing rooms. Immediately the AAA replied in a huff. As Nelson and Mussabini were professionals, the two of them 'would possibly have aroused discontent amongst the officially appointed trainers', it said high-handedly. Liddell outlined the importance of Philip Noel-Baker as well. In its letter to the newspaper the AAA were dismissive of him too. 'I fear your correspondent is rather at fault,' wrote the Honorary Secretary, who added condescendingly that Noel-Baker 'no doubt' had done 'good work' before proceeding to denigrate it. Nothing Liddell said could be construed as rabble-rousing. The message from the AAA was unmistakably clear, however. Even a gold medallist didn't have the right to express an opinion.

Along with a dozen other sportsmen – including Harold Abrahams, Douglas Lowe and Guy Butler – Liddell was signatory to a letter published in the *Daily Mail* five and a half months before Amsterdam. The letter called for voluntary donations to ensure that British competitors were 'afforded every chance to give of their best' there. The BOA, who couldn't have missed it, still didn't float an invitation to the Games in front of him. This was despite the fact that most of its home-based 400 metres runners could barely break 50 seconds. Since it wasn't in his character to force himself on anyone, Liddell didn't approach the BOA either. Doing so would have been a meretricious shout of 'Look at me!' which Liddell would never have justified to himself.

In April 1928 the *Daily Mail* reported that the BOA 'thought he wouldn't get leave' for Amsterdam and so consequently continued to do what it did best, which was nothing.

May was the pivotal month. In its first week Lowe, who received letters from Liddell, let slip that his friend wouldn't be in Amsterdam. His 'absence', said the *New York Times*, 'removes from the forthcoming competition . . . one of the most colourful figures'. On the 12th, the time Liddell had recorded in Paris was finally beaten by the twenty-two-year-old American Emerson 'Bud' Spencer, who ran in a pair of dark spectacles after a car crash robbed him of his sight in one eye and damaged the other. Spencer clocked 47 seconds flat at Stanford University, a performance as unexpected as it was accomplished. Less than a week afterwards Liddell confirmed Lowe's original statement. It was impossible for him to participate, said a report, because he couldn't take a furlough from China. This went unchallenged, though top-notch investigative journalism wasn't needed to enquire why, if the Anglo-Chinese College wouldn't release him, he hadn't come clean about it well beforehand to end all the speculation. In fact, Liddell could have gone to Amsterdam; but, rather than the BOA's apathy towards him, his decision to forsake the Olympics turned on personal factors.

The first was the deteriorating situation in China. Disorder and lawlessness continued to blight the country; and two of the people Liddell most cared about found themselves ensnared in the worst of it.

In the previous twelve months Annie Buchan had not only been shot at – she was caught in bandit crossfire, the bullet passing through the raised peak of her cap – but also forced out of Siaochang with the other missionaries. When rival warlord armies began lashing out indiscriminately, causing more deaths there, the London Missionary Society staff loaded mule carts and escaped. Buchan, fearful for the locals left behind, admitted, 'We felt ashamed to go free.' In the villages she saw the soldiers kick down doors or thrust swords through the gaps in the brittle wood and heard 'the cries of the terrified' inside. A platoon of these soldiers soon caught up with the missionary carts, commandeering them and forcing Buchan and her colleagues to walk. When the mission reopened in Siaochang in September 1927, Rob Liddell moved from Shanghai to continue the rebuilding of the hospital, which a flash flood had previously swept into a jagged ruin. That reconstruction, as well as tending to traumatized peasants, made the effort of acquiring another gold medal seem a puny waste of energy to his brother. 'He didn't think it was fair to leave for such a long time in those circumstances,' said a friend.

Liddell had come to the conclusion that he was too ring-rusty for the Olympics anyway. No one had coached him since Tom McKerchar. No one had stretched him on the track since the Scottish AAA Championships in 1925. No one – not even Liddell – knew what another week and a half on the Trans-Siberian railway might take out of him on the way to Amsterdam. As unselfish as ever, Liddell also didn't want to take a place someone else might use more profitably; an athlete, moreover, who had been through the selection races and wouldn't be chosen purely because of his status as the defending champion.

It was a miscalculation. Another American, Ray Barbuti, beat Spencer in the Olympic trials and then went on to win the gold medal in 47.8 seconds, slower than Liddell's performance in Paris. In agency reports, filed from Amsterdam, Liddell's absence was viewed as a 'great misfortune'.

Exactly how much of a misfortune became apparent that October when Liddell ran a race in the port city of Dairen on the southern tip of the Fengtien peninsula. He sailed there across the Bohai Sea. The South Manchurian Railway Celebrations, staged to commemorate the Emperor of Japan's coronation, were planned as a contest between Japanese and

French Olympians. Liddell, a guest runner, outshone them. Reports of what he did – both before and afterwards – differ because of the fractured nature of news distribution in the 1920s. According to one dispatch he took the 400 metres in 47.8 seconds. If that is true, he equalled Barbuti's Olympic time in Amsterdam without training for it. More plausible is an alternative account. In a wind so strong that it almost blasted the athletes backwards off the last bend, Liddell won in a 'fraction' over 51 seconds. The captain of the French team was an Olympic bronze medallist from 1924. He'd seen Liddell's race in Paris. Watching him again, he calculated Liddell would have crossed the line in 48 seconds – if that gale hadn't hampered him.

There was a bizarre coda. The race was run at 2.45 p.m. Liddell's boat was casting off half an hour later. The docks were a twenty-minute taxi ride away. Still wearing his kit and his spikes, Liddell grabbed his coat and bag and was attempting to leave when the band struck up the British national anthem. 'I had to stand as still as a post,' he said. As the last note sounded, Liddell was ready to 'leg it' again. This time the band played the Marseillaise to honour the second-placed Frenchman. The taxi reached the wharf as Liddell's steamer was pulling out. The wind that had slowed him on the track tossed his boat towards the dock again on what he described as 'a bit of a tidal wave'. Liddell hurled his bag on to the wooden deck before a hop and a step launched him into an enormous leap. He cleared at least 15 feet of water. 'I tried to remember in the very act how a gazelle jumps . . . and I made it.' Like the standard fisherman's tale, the distance Liddell covered grew appreciably as the years passed. Before long he'd straddled half the China Sea without getting a toe wet.

Everyone who saw him that afternoon thought Liddell should have run in the Olympics. There was also consensus about what would have happened: he'd have taken a second gold medal. Because his legs, his shoulders and his upper body were stronger and had developed with age, he possessed more stamina than before. It is easy to extrapolate extravagantly when contradiction is impossible. The claims made on his behalf were, however, given more credence in autumn 1929.

Dr Otto Peltzer, born in 1900, was a Teutonic track hero in the 1920s – skinny and tall and as blond as white sand, his hair parted high on the left. He was a world record holder in three middle-distance events and had set German bests in eight different disciplines. He'd captained the team in Amsterdam and had been the favourite for the 800 metres until,

Showdown in Tientsin. Eric Liddell lines up beside Dr Otto Peltzer for their exhibition race.

during a game of handball, someone stepped on his foot accidentally, fracturing a bone. He was labelled 'Otto the Strange' because of his training methods. Like a disciple of Max Sick, Peltzer insisted the elasticity of the muscles was vital. He took hot baths and found a coach in the McKerchar mould to massage him before and after races. Peltzer liked to sunbathe nude. He was able to sleep for a few moments at a time, dropping off even minutes before a race began. He also developed jumping exercises to strengthen his legs. From a standing start, Peltzer could leap from the bottom to the middle step of a flight of stairs. He even went to Finland to glean insights from Paavo Nurmi. In 1926 he beat him in Berlin over 1,500 metres and also snatched the world record.

When it came to sport, Peltzer shared Liddell's outlook. After triumphing over Nurmi, he turned down $250,000 from two entrepreneurs who asked him to re-stage the race across America. The notion of it went against his principles. 'A sportsman does not need financial compensation since the act carries its own reward,' he said. 'You can't turn it into a job without taking away its ideal root, and the inner joy in doing it.' You can almost hear Liddell yelling 'hear, hear' in reply.

Peltzer was promoting German athletics around the globe, which pulled him into Liddell's path in Tientsin. The contest between them was a double-header over 400 metres and then 800 metres.

The wind got up, making both races tests of endurance. Liddell still comfortably bested Peltzer in the 400 metres. He then pushed him to a near photo finish in the 800 metres, finishing only 0.1 of a second behind. Afterwards the conversation between them turned towards the next Olympics, the Los Angeles Games of 1932. Almost every athlete will dig out an excuse for failure. Liddell found reasons – always charitable ones – to explain his opponents' defeats. Peltzer wasn't at his slickest, he said, because the German had been 'travelling a good deal'. Peltzer knew differently.

To beat him over any distance was remarkable. To beat him as Liddell had done – in this outpost where competition of calibre was virtually non-existent – astounded Peltzer. He'd expected the two races to be an exhibition rather than a showdown. He judged Liddell against the Olympians of Amsterdam, finding them inferior. Considering him to be his prime rival in Los Angeles, Peltzer asked Liddell to confirm he'd compete there. No, said Liddell, claiming he was already 'too old' to do that. Peltzer was taken aback. He'd be thirty-two by the next Games, which made him two years Liddell's senior. Why, for pity's sake, wouldn't he run? In slightly imprecise English Peltzer advised him, 'You train for the 800 metres and you are the greatest man in the world at that distance.' Liddell's attitude was inconceivable to a fanatic such as Peltzer, for whom the track meant everything.

But Liddell was withholding one significant fact. It was like hiding the last pieces of a jigsaw underneath the box. Without them, Peltzer couldn't see the picture properly.

Eric Liddell admired no man more than his father, whom he regarded as the model missionary. Work, rather than words, defined James Liddell, and he went about it dedicatedly, the betterment of his congregation always put before the betterment of the self. Even his hobby of photography was used for the sake of the Chinese peasants. His pictures, exposing the level of poverty in the countryside, swayed hearts and minds among the administrative members of the London Missionary Society who were ignorant of it.

Early in Liddell's life, his father shared the biblical passage that most influenced him, which was the Sermon on the Mount. With poetic flair, the Sermon distils the main tenets of Jesus's sayings and teaching – including the Beatitudes and the Lord's Prayer – into chapters five to seven of the Gospel of St Matthew. Even non-churchgoers find the Sermon familiar, though sometimes without knowing it, because quotations from it have passed into common usage: blessed are the poor; the meek shall inherit the earth; turn the other cheek; give to him that asks for it; love your enemies; judge not that you be not judged; seek and you shall find. Through his father, Liddell adopted the Sermon as his manifesto. One passage summed up in only three words what he attempted to achieve daily: 'Be ye perfect' – the same thing he'd preached ever since that Friday night in Armadale beside D. P. Thomson.

Liddell knew perfection was unobtainable; but he also thought that shouldn't dissuade him from striving for it. If he fell short, he would strive again tomorrow. His father set the example for him. He'd loved his enemies. He'd turned the other cheek. He'd blessed everyone, however antagonistic. He had striven to be perfect.

His moustache had long since gone white. His hair was thinning badly. Gastric trouble had forced him to cancel trips – his first debilitating sickness since arriving as a probationary missionary more than thirty years earlier. Most children still tend to believe their parents are indestructible; Liddell supposed so too. The Boxer Rebellion hadn't forced his father from China. Nor had flood and famine. Nor had the initial scepticism and indifference of the locals he'd been sent to convert. He'd survived the dust storms, the diet and the daily slog of riding on mules and carts to remote places, which awaited cartographers to properly recognize them.

But, at the beginning of 1929, James Liddell had gone to Tsangchow to participate in one of the LMS's district meetings. There he'd suffered a stroke, which briefly affected his speech and the movement of one arm. He was fifty-eight. James wanted to recuperate in Tientsin. His next furlough was due in June. The doctor, despite the patient's delicate state, told him to convalesce in Scotland immediately.

James, regarding the LMS as brethren, had no intention of retiring, which would have put them to the inconvenience of replacing him prematurely. He was certain his recuperation wouldn't last long. He'd see China again within eighteen months. His son, though convinced of that too, felt his absence keenly. What separation nonetheless brought was a sharper sense still of what must come next for him. For Liddell, the coming decade was mapped out as surely as if the route existed in an atlas. He planned to become a member of the London Missionary Society. At the end of the following summer, he'd return to the Congregational College in Scotland and be ordained in Edinburgh after another period of theological study. He'd then come back to China, where he and his fit-again father would complement each other. That was why, unlike Peltzer, he'd be content to read about the 1932 Olympics from afar.

Liddell had a capacious memory. It closed around information as tightly as the leaves of a fly-trap plant and devoured it, allowing him to memorize long stretches of his sermons. As well as the Bible, he could also remember, often verbatim, sections of novels, verses of poetry and sequences of numbers and chemical formulas. During what were called 'the entertainments' – party pieces for house guests – he'd give recitals of Dickens or Robert Burns.

Burns' most quoted line is a warning about the unreliability of planning for the future:

The best-laid schemes o' mice an' men
Gang aft agley,
An' lea'e us nought but grief an' pain . . .

So it proved for Liddell.

Missionaries moved through China with increasing trepidation, always walking in the shadow of terror or death. These instances harked back, like a banshee echo, to the Boxer Rebellion. In April 1929 pirates killed three American bishops in Chenki in West Hunan. Less than two months later brigands held hostage five British members of China's Inland Mission, plus a baby, in Shekichen in Honan. Whole streets were burned. Inhabitants were 'beaten, tortured and shot'. Widespread looting took place. The hostages were finally released.

Innocents elsewhere were not so fortunate. A missionary was stabbed in the back while riding in a rickshaw in Chang-tu-fu. Another was stabbed in the stomach for failing to hand over money from a safe. In Lungyan, in south-west Fukien, bandits took 'a fiendish pleasure in torturing those they were about to slay', said *The Times*. 'Some were disembowelled. Some hanged. Some drowned. Some brained.' Some were also beheaded, dismembered or buried alive. 'Women were killed with tortures that cannot be written down,' added the newspaper. So it went on. Early in 1930 two Italian bishops and three nuns were murdered in Hong Kong. The headlines read like the covers of those popular but sensationalist Victorian penny-dreadfuls. Some told of 'Lootings Along the Yangtze' and 'China on the Rampage'. Two in particular – 'The Outrages of Murder' and 'Foreigners in Peril Again' – cropped up monthly. In Yunnan Province, for example, those who either couldn't or simply refused to pay bandit bounty were soaked in paraffin. 'They burned like torches,' said one account.

The missionaries of the London Society in and around Tientsin still thought of themselves as relatively safe. The city was fearsomely fortified. There were 8,500 foreign troops stationed there. The Americans, responsible for almost half of that number, could call on an assortment of aircraft, five tanks and five field guns. Only the certifiably insane would have taken them on.

An atrocity spilled into the colonial enclave nonetheless in April 1930. It changed everything, especially for Eric Liddell. A. P. Cullen and Eric Scarlett were travelling to Peitaiho. Their brief was a pleasurable one: the LMS wanted them to check whether the beach-front bungalows needed repairing. The journey from the railway station to the coast was barely 5 miles. Cullen and Scarlett each rode there on a donkey. Halfway along the route a gang of three men, their faces covered in scarves, brandished short pistols at them in a surprise attack from the high thickets running on either side of the rough pathway. Cullen and Scarlett listened to the demand for valuables and money. Cullen, a couple of yards in front of Scarlett, began to unthread the gold watch and chain that hung from his waistcoat pockets. He tried to reason with one of the robbers, who he supposed was as 'inexperienced' as the other two. The men seemed to him to be 'considerably flustered', as though this – a stand-and-deliver highwayman's hold-up – was their baptism in serious crime. The stress of the moment made one of the men pull his trigger without provocation. The shot Cullen heard instinctively sent him swivelling in his saddle. He saw Scarlett drop to the ground. The bullet had hit him a couple of inches above the heart. The sight of Scarlett bleeding affected the gang as much as it did Cullen. The men began an agitated scramble to take what each of them could hold or stuff into a canvas bag. Cullen was yanked off his donkey. The watch chain, still looped through a button hole, was torn from his waistcoat and a robber made a successful grab for his wallet, which contained only a few notes. The suitcases and a briefcase, which the donkeys had been carrying as a tied pack, were ransacked. Clothes and papers were scattered across the path. Another shot was fired – more as a warning to Cullen than an attempt to murder him too – before the gang vanished, leaving nothing but footprints behind. Five minutes later Scarlett died as Cullen cradled his head.

In the first nine months of that year a total of ninety-seven missionaries were reported kidnapped; thirty-three of them were murdered. Seen as just another statistic of the unrest, Eric Scarlett was soon forgotten except by those who knew him in Tientsin. His murderers were never caught. Liddell was a coffin-bearer at the funeral. When reflecting on Scarlett's killing, he referred to the 'darkness of the days we have passed through'. Those days had direct consequences for Liddell.

When his train had left Waverley station in 1925, his friends had sung an old Scottish ballad to him from the platform: 'Will Ye No Come Back Again?' His answer, shouted from the carriage window, was that he'd be back 'soon enough'. As Liddell began teaching some of Scarlett's classes, he realized his planned return would have to be delayed because of the murder. There'd be no possibility of seeing Scotland or his father again for at least another twelve months. To stick to his original schedule would have put the college and the LMS 'in a very difficult place', he said.

In deciding to postpone his homecoming, he acted exactly as his father would have done.

In his diary for 4 September 1931, D. P. Thomson wrote of seeing Eric Liddell again for the first time in half a dozen years. Thomson noted that he looked 'a little yellower and balder' than before.

The newspapers were more interested in his athletics than in his missionary ambitions. As Thomson stressed, 'For tens of thousands he was still a national hero.' Would Liddell train throughout the winter? Would he, approaching thirty, enter the Scottish AAA Championships the following summer? Liddell explained that he hadn't competed seriously for nearly a year – he'd won the sprints and the quarter mile in the North China Championships – and had no intention of reviving his career because an impossibly crowded twelve months of learning and preaching were his priorities instead. The clamour to see and hear him was so 'very great', added Thomson, that 'almost every pulpit in the country would have welcomed him'. Invitations for Liddell to speak piled up months before the date of his arrival became known. A committee was formed to arrange a workable timetable for him; otherwise Liddell would have been exhausted within weeks. On top of his regular Sunday sermons there were public 'welcome home' gatherings, temperance and Sabbath obser-vance rallies, sportsmen's services, London Missionary Society and Women's Institute meetings. As ever, overflow areas had to be created for him as he criss-crossed the country.

Thomson, ordained only three years earlier, had become closer than ever to Frank Buchman and the Oxford Group. Liddell now became a convert too. Buchman, born in Pennsylvania in 1878, had gone to China during the First World War. Some loved him, hailing a far-seeing Christian statesman. Others loathed him, reaching for words such as 'autocrat' and 'fraud' and hurling them like rotten tomatoes. South African newspapers had given Buchman's apostles the Oxford tag in 1928 because so many of them were current or former students of the university. 'Those who disliked the movement and valued the good name of Oxford accused Buchman of accepting the sobriquet to give [it] a cachet,' wrote *The Times*.

The group had 'four absolutes' – honesty, purity, unselfishness, love – which it said 'Jesus Christ kept to . . . in their fullness'. Buchman, who compared mass evangelism to 'hunting rabbits with a brass band', instead held house parties, intimate gatherings where the public confession of sins was encouraged.

Liddell's programme of engagements soon became a slog for him. As a respite, he went to his parents' home to listen to an Oxford Group member and found himself refreshed. He said the 'four absolutes' clarified the teachings of the Sermon on the Mount and that the movement itself gave him a 'greater willingness to share the deepest things in my own life' and also 'a greater power' as a speaker.

He needed that power to convince his audiences of China's relevance to them. Stories that appeared during his first months back reinforced the British public's derogatory impression of it. Everything there seemed anarchic and anachronistic.

A woman was condemned to die after being found guilty of mistreating her mother-in-law, who had committed suicide with an opium overdose. The punishment was *ling chih* – death by a thousand cuts. Yet another group of missionaries was abducted to elicit a blood ransom. Almost simultaneously, a nineteen-year-old from Britain was abducted by police, bleeding from the chest and the face. Within forty-eight hours of his capture the teenager was shot by an interrogator who lost his temper during questioning. These events hardened prejudices about China.

Liddell acted as an educator. He conceded that one crisis was perpetually overtaking another and even that the Chinese 'did not want foreigners'. He explained, however, that the extremes of climate created a level of poverty unimaginable even when compared with the foulest slums in Britain. These contributed to the political instability. He also made it clear that China was convinced 'other nations', especially Britain, had 'taken from her what should be hers'. Liddell said he still believed in the fundamental decency of the Chinese. Despite all the trouble he'd seen and all the trouble reported to him, the British and Foreign Bible Society were handing out nearly five million shilling texts per year in China now. Too many families, trying to survive off the parched or flooded soil, were illiterate because wielding a hoe was still considered among farmers to be more important than reading a book; but a Bible in the home was an incentive to learn written language at last. Liddell compared handing them out to sowing seed. Something would grow from it, even if it took another generation. However unpromising that task seemed to outsiders, his mission was to fulfil it. That is why he'd be returning to China as an ordained minister.

For Liddell, studying was relaxation from talking. His knowledge of theology was already encyclopaedic, so to read formally what he always read informally anyway never seemed like a chore to him.

The other pleasure was seeing his father again. The LMS had compulsorily retired James Liddell because of further bouts of ill health, which were slowly worsening. The old Reverend Liddell was resigned to never seeing China again. All he had left of that country were his photographs and his memories and also the satisfaction of knowing that a new Reverend Liddell was about to replace him.

Liddell's furlough seemed so short. He'd originally asked for a twenty-four-month-long leave. The LMS, ignoring his family circumstances and his father's generous service, allowed him only half that. James Liddell was given some consolations. He sat proudly in the front pew when his son preached in Drymen, the church of his childhood. He was also present at his ordination and then stood on the platform at Waverley station to see him off, promising to be there again when the train brought him back from China at the end of the decade.

No matter how many miles separated them, Liddell always felt extremely close to his father. The feeling was particularly powerful over Remembrance weekend in 1933. His father was in Drymen, he was in Tientsin's Union Church. Later he'd reveal how his father had seemed so 'very near to me' as he preached that day. The overwhelming sense of his presence was inexplicable to Liddell then. Next morning he received a telegram from Scotland. His father had died twenty-four hours earlier.

The circumstances of his death came only afterwards. He'd settled into a comfortable chair, intending to take an afternoon nap. He'd never woken up. He died as good men ought to die – peacefully. Another stroke had claimed him.

In the awful silence that enveloped him after slitting open the telegram and reading the brief factual message it contained, Liddell said he thought of 'all the love, sacrifice and service' his father had given during his 'devotion to missionary toil'. Short obituaries appeared. James Liddell was mentioned in the newspapers because his son was famous. There was a terrible misprint in one of them, which called him 'Mr Riddell'. Fifteen days after learning of his death, Liddell received his father's last letter. In it he reassured his son that he was 'full of energy'.

Liddell had comforted and counselled hundreds of men and women through grief. Only now had death's hand touched him directly. In response Liddell did what he knew his father would have demanded of him: he hurled himself into his classes and his congregation, grateful for long hours immersed in other people's concerns. Writing to his mother, he confessed it was a coping mechanism. 'I have just kept straight on with my work here,' he said. 'It has been the best thing possible for me.'

He had used his father's life as the template for his own. He'd been his friend as much as his mentor. Without him, the world could have fallen in on Liddell.

What saved him was something that has saved many men both before and since.

A woman.

CHAPTER TEN

There's Something I Want to Talk to You About

IT IS NOT ONLY a single man in possession of a good fortune who is in want of a wife. The missionary, with meagre funds and scant worldly goods, eventually is in need of one too. In that regard, Eric Liddell's celebrity preceded him. He received invitations to cocktail parties and coffee mornings, dinners and smart suppers, church fairs and poetry recitals.

What we are travels with us always. Never able to say no in Edinburgh, Liddell was unable to say no in Tientsin either. He was on every guest list. The morning post brought formal invitations to speak or appear at an event so his name would add lustre to it. The informal invitations were delivered during a stroll through the compound. There were requests to attend a dinner or a tea or simply an offer to 'drop by' whenever he liked. Tientsin's Union Church Literary and Social Guild, the community's upper crust, even pressurized him into telling his Olympic story to them.

On every occasion Liddell found himself steered towards an eligible woman in the hope he would find her irresistible. But he was choosy and patient. Eileen Soper, still painting in the seclusion of Wildings, was aware of that fact more than anyone.

From observing his parents' own marriage, Liddell understood what it took to be a missionary couple in China and also how tightly bound husband and wife needed to be. Everything his father and mother had experienced – danger, disruption and absences – Liddell expected to experience as well. His parents had come through all of China's turmoils. That's because the marriage was a true partnership, said Liddell. Each was the other's spiritual soul-mate, best friend, confidant and unconditional supporter. He knew his father could never have devoted himself so comprehensively to the mission without his mother. Never drawing attention to herself, she shaped the conditions that made it possible for him to focus on his field-work. In the wider world her unglamorous endeavours on his behalf – the practical structures she built around him – went unnoticed. Her sympathetic counselling of some of the local women, who approached her rather than him, also went unacknowledged. It was as though her responsibilities were taken for granted except by those, like her son, who saw that labour close up. Inspired by his mother's example, Liddell searched for identical attributes in his bride.

To find a wife wasn't difficult in Tientsin. There was no shortage of attractive women who would have volunteered to become Mrs Eric Liddell. But to pick, as his father had done, that 'true partner' required discernment. Liddell searched for beauty beneath the skin as well as beauty itself.

He chose Florence Jean MacKenzie. Usually called Flo, she was 5 feet 7 inches tall, auburn-haired, hazel-eyed, athletically energetic and vivacious. Liddell said he came to appreciate how much 'fire' was in her too. She was the eldest of seven children. Her father Hugh MacKenzie and his wife Agnes were both missionaries from Canada. He was the reliable Man Friday and chief mechanic of the creaky London Society machine. Around him almost everything turned, especially financial bookkeeping and travel arrangements, which could be labyrinthine. Agnes had originally come to China as an evangelist and now ran the MacKenzies' eight-bedroom house in Tientsin and also a staff of servants. Missionaries with bulging cases came and went there like commuters crossing the concourse of Grand Central Station.

Liddell and Florence first met during the autumn of 1926 in the Union Church. His courtship of her didn't begin, however, until three years later. The delay seems inexplicable without another piece of information: Florence was only fourteen years old when she arrived in Tientsin. She shared a classroom with Liddell's brother, Ernest. Liddell taught her in Sunday school. When he fell in love with her, Florence was approaching her seventeenth birthday. She was established as a church organist and a pianist and had also begun leading some Sunday school lessons, shepherding infant classes through Bible stories. Occasionally Liddell invented an excuse – the need to borrow a book; the need to rifle through the store cupboard; the need to pick up something that had been 'forgetfully' left behind – to go into the room where she taught. Apart from catching a glimpse of her, he also wanted to eavesdrop. What impressed him was Florence's empathy with her attentive but always difficult-to-please young audience, which got bored easily and would have squirmed on the polished wooden floor if Miss MacKenzie hadn't held their imagination. The more he saw of Florence, the more he liked her. He liked her sense of independence. He liked her feisty, get-up-and-go approach to the challenge of each fresh day. He liked the way she spoke, perceptively and without pretension, about what she saw around her, which emphasized a mature outlook.

His courting of her was nonetheless painstakingly circumspect. D. P. Thomson described Liddell as 'one of Nature's gentlemen', which isn't surprising because the same was said of his father. He was strictly proper in his pursuit of Florence. He was a timid suitor more akin to the late

Portrait of Florence taken in the mid-1930s.

eighteenth century than the early twentieth. Indeed, you could hardly call it courting at all. The two of them drank tea and exchanged friendly conversation in a crowd of other people at the MacKenzies' or spoke to each other in church. When his sister Jenny gave Florence advanced piano lessons, Liddell cleared his diary and came home early to make sure he never missed them. So much for passionate wooing. Liddell's crush on Florence walked softly on tip-toe so as not to reveal itself conspicuously and scandalize one or both of them. Behind the clean lace curtains of middle-class respectability, Tientsin society could be sternly censorious, always watchful for those who used the wrong fork. Even when Florence broke into her late teens, he was nervous about the age gap – almost ten years – between them. Liddell didn't want to be perceived as plucking her from the reeds of the Moses basket. It would have been less troublesome to date and marry anyone else. But, sensing the woman Florence would become, Liddell refused to compromise.

In the summer of 1929 the two of them went on a holiday-cum-expedition into the mountains near Peitaiho. Lasting four days, it involved walks along steep paths and the dry beds of streams strewn with boulders. Florence wasn't so much chaperoned as guarded. Among the party of ten was one of her sisters and one of her brothers. But, back at the beach, Liddell finally summoned the courage to meander to the front door of the MacKenzies' bungalow and invite her to accompany him along the shoreline alone. The couple had still to hold hands, and what Liddell felt for her went unspoken until circumstance forced him to express it at the end of that same year.

Florence had turned eighteen only a few weeks before. Like Liddell's mother, she wanted to become a nurse. She planned to train for three years in Toronto. He had been coaching her in mathematics, which she needed to pass to attend college. The question of what – if anything – would happen after she achieved her nursing diploma now needed to be asked and answered. Liddell had no idea whether or not Florence was considering returning to China once she had earned her qualification. He wasn't entirely convinced she'd want to wed him, or that she had even considered the prospect of doing so. One evening, when she was unable to concentrate on her mathematics, which exasperated her, Liddell suggested a breath of fresh air, concealing his real motive for it. For him, it was now or never.

There was a butterfly-delicacy about the way he floated the matter of marriage, as if afraid of being rebuffed. From him there were prevarications and hesitations, qualifications and reaffirmations. From her there was a request for him to repeat what he'd said and then to confirm it again to avoid the possibility that she'd either misheard or misconstrued him. Florence, though confessing that she was 'terribly in love' with Liddell, had never expected him to discuss marriage. She'd supposed there were more obvious candidates; and that each of them was far ahead of her in the queue for a ring. Years later she recalled what Liddell had said so awkwardly to her:

'There's something I want to talk to you about. Now I've been thinking about this for a long time . . . I have thought I would like you to be my wife. I know you're very young.'

She asked him two things: 'Are you sure? Do you really mean it?'

If Liddell was sure, the second question was superfluous. 'Yes, indeed,' he replied.

The couple then kissed for the first time.

His fiancée announced herself as 'stunned' by the proposal. 'I was naive,' she said. 'I knew I was special to him because he was spending so much time with me. I didn't ever imagine he'd propose. There were a lot of women who were his own age. I thought they'd kill me after finding out he'd popped the question.' Her family was equally taken aback. 'We thought: "Why is he marrying Flo? She's so plain",' said one of her brothers, proving that familiarity means siblings don't always appreciate one another's merits.

Liddell bought Florence an engagement ring almost identical to his mother's, a band containing five diamonds.

That she instantly said yes to Liddell showed the age-gap didn't bother her. What counted were his character and his demeanour and the commonality between them. The date of his birth and hers was immaterial. Anyone who arched their eyebrows in shock didn't know Liddell and didn't appreciate the sensitive way he'd conducted himself. She loved him all the more for it. Mind you, it was easy to love Liddell. In the same sentence Florence once described him as 'a very good man' and as 'a naturally good man', which had the benefit not only of establishing that fact – as if it were in doubt – but also of explaining it. She was sure Liddell had been born good, which was an intrinsic part of his appeal to her.

Before friendship turned into a marriage commitment, Florence had observed him as intently as he had observed her. A lot of people pretend to be what they are not. They superficially put on an act designed to impress or flatter. They behave in a way that their social antenna tells them will suit either the company or the circumstances of the moment. Florence saw that Liddell wasn't like this. He was just himself and nothing more. He didn't change his accent or his manner, and he didn't compromise his beliefs, so that a dinner-table audience or a roomful of strangers gained a false impression of him. The boldest lines of the sketch Florence always drew of him conveyed his gentleness and tolerance.

She called the quiet, private hour he spent every early morning in Bible study 'the mainspring of his life'. The implacability of his faith still didn't make him solemn or preachy whenever he spoke about the practice of it, she said. He didn't bore or brow-beat anyone who failed to share his religious certainties either. One of Florence's friends, recovering after an attempt to commit suicide, was fearful of meeting Liddell again in case he cold-shouldered her. Florence provided reassurance. He would understand and be sympathetic; he judged 'no one', she said.

Liddell was also 'strict on himself', Florence explained. He was restless after leaving tasks unfinished. He chastised himself for squandering so much as an hour, which made him more determined to 'do better' next time. He seldom rested because he was 'always doing something for somebody'. He was also 'a peacemaker', she added. 'I watched him settle disputes and misunderstandings between friends and colleagues, and even strangers.' Afterwards, a few of them milked his generosity appallingly and others, knowing Liddell wasn't confrontational, were arrogantly obstreperous towards him. 'It used to stagger me the way people would disagree violently with him and say the bitterest things. He would smile and pass it off. He was incredibly forgiving and thought nothing was accomplished by losing one's temper.' Florence felt that what truly set him apart was the one quality so few possess. 'He was so understanding of other people. He always seemed to be able to put himself in the shoes of somebody else.'

Small acts illustrated this. D. P. Thomson heard about two instances.

Flies were a menace in China because of the illnesses these insects were capable of spreading. Liddell had been invited to the home of some friends for coffee and biscuits. When a fly settled on the topmost biscuit, Liddell was told not to touch it. He ignored the advice. 'His action was not intended as a rebuke – that would never occur to him,' Thomson was told. Liddell was instead making certain 'that no one else should suffer discomfort' as a consequence of eating the one biscuit the fly had 'defiled'.

The second example of Liddell's concern for others was even more touching. In the visitors' book of a church where he'd been preaching, Liddell wrote in Chinese: 'Keep Smiling'. After the local minister read it, he approached Liddell about a member of his congregation who had been injured in an industrial accident. Her scalp and one eye had been torn out. The primitive grafts to restore the skin had taken two years of surgery. She was deaf and suffered intense headaches. The eyelashes on her remaining eye had to be pulled every month to stop them from growing on to the eyeball. She nonetheless scribbled 'Keep Smiling' on the bottom of every letter she wrote. She would feel, the minister said, that Liddell's own message had been 'left especially for her'. Liddell offered to meet the woman. 'Busy though he was,' explained the minister, Liddell spent 'an hour with her in her little room'. Afterwards she wrote a long letter of thanks to him.

The sequel to that vignette seemed to everyone who heard it – and to Liddell himself – to be providential rather than coincidental. Her letter arrived shortly before Liddell set off to catch a train. In an otherwise empty carriage he sat facing a much younger man who looked lonely and troubled. Gradually, a distressing account of adversity, failure and personal defeat bled out of him. The man explained he'd 'lost all belief and hope'. He was 'seriously contemplating suicide'. Liddell admitted that for a minute or two he 'did not know what to say or do'. So he produced the letter from the woman from his pocket and said, 'Read that.' Liddell then spoke movingly of the woman's 'grinding hardship, her accident and her faith'. As the minister put it: 'Before that journey ended, a new journey had begun for that young man.'

Two strangers on a train had been connected through a letter from a third stranger.

This was the Liddell that Florence loved.

One of the most curious and ridiculously anachronistic of the London Missionary Society's strictures was the clause in its contract relating to matrimony. Managing to sound manipulating and morally superior, the LMS declared that its directors must approve of a couple's choice of each other before 'completing any engagement with the view to marriage'. It implied the LMS would veto those it regarded as unsuitable. These self-appointed judges and juries of the heart didn't bother Eric Liddell. The

*Cream is the colour for both Eric Liddell and
Florence during his furlough in Toronto.*

only thing concerning him was the reaction of his own parents – his
father was still alive then – and Florence's. Hugh MacKenzie, describing
his future son-in-law as 'very unassuming and so gentle', placed only one
barrier between Liddell and his daughter. Florence had to finish her training before the banns could be read.

The flame of most other relationships would have flickered out, all
passion long spent, in the three years and four months separating Liddell's
proposal and the recital of the wedding vows. From mid-June in 1930
until early 1934, Liddell and Florence saw each other only twice for a
total of eight weeks. He bookended his furlough to Scotland with sea
voyages to Canada. Otherwise ink took the place of speech and sight.
Liddell wrote to her about the Bible classes he organized and the 'memory
cards' he had designed, each containing a daily scripture reading that
could be slipped into a pocket and be absorbed wherever the recipient
wanted to read it 'for meditation'. She wrote to him about making

hospital corners with the bedsheets, emptying chamber pots and her aching feet after ward-patrol in several departments as diverse as children's care and psychiatry. When Florence finally arrived back in China, Liddell was waiting for her on the dockside at Taku. Watching him, pacing with his hands behind his back and staring out to sea for the first sight of her ship, one of Florence's brothers realized how dearly her fiancé loved her. 'I'd never seen Eric so animated. He couldn't wait to see her. He was bouncing around like a rubber ball. When the ship finally appeared, he was beside himself. If he could have swum out to meet her, he would have done.'

Eric Liddell and Florence MacKenzie were married on 27 March 1934 in Tientsin's Union Church, where the two of them had originally met eight years earlier.

In the official, typically stuffy wedding album shots, snapped outside the church, Mr Liddell is impeccably smart in the sort of matrimonial uniform his ancestors would have worn: top hat with a silk sheen, starched wing collar and frock coat. A pink carnation blooms in his left button hole. The new Mrs Liddell carries a cascade of pink carnations and a heap of greenery so enormous that the florist's shop in Tientsin must surely have seemed very bare after the bouquet was collected for her. The comet trail of that bouquet looks as long as the train of her lace and satin dress.

The two best photographs of man and wife were taken informally. There are couples who even on their wedding day seem still to be getting used to the idea of being together. The Liddells were different. These pictures tell you everything you need to know about the marriage. It is frequently said that a man can win over a woman simply by making her laugh. This was true of Liddell. Florence said her husband was an 'incurable romantic' with a 'fantastic and very unconventional' sense of humour. The evidence is in these pictures. Preserved in them is much more than his character and spirit and also the joie de vivre of a morning about to break into a long celebratory afternoon. What the photographs transmit is the ease between the Liddells and the absolute contentment each feels in the other's company. In the first, Liddell is wearing his wife's wide hat, made from light, wispy material, which she wore for a friend's wedding. The pleasure on his face is like the pleasure on a child's; a child, moreover, who has suddenly been given what it most wanted. Florence's smile at her husband's larking about is instinctive, unforced. The second

Here comes the couple. Eric and Florence leave the Union Church in Tientsin after attending the wedding of a friend (above) before their own wedding day there (below) in March 1934.

picture is even better. What it captures is unscripted – the very second when Liddell tries to tickle his wife and she pretends to resist being tickled. Her semi-turn, in a mock escape, obscures her expression; but his is exultant.

The Liddells spent a ten-day honeymoon at an LMS cottage in the Western Hills, close to Peking, before returning to Tientsin. Their newly decorated three-room flat was filled with furniture bought for a pittance from departing missionaries. Like all newly-weds the Liddells were wrapped up in themselves and thankful at last to have an address that belonged to them alone. Nothing mattered more than being together. But around the bliss of it all hung the black menace of everyday life in China.

Sometimes the landmarks of history, disputed or otherwise, are less telling in retrospect than its footnotes or the newspaper reports at the bottom of a column. The perfect example is three short paragraphs from *The Times* in mid-June 1934. The piece appeared beneath such a familiar

Eric Liddell reveals the carefree element of his nature by pulling on Florence's hat, which she wore at a friend's wedding.

A sign of love: Eric playfully attempts to tickle Florence . . . and she pretends to try to run away from him.

headline – 'Missionary Killed in China' – that it looked like recycled news. The sub-heading – 'Struggle with Bandits' – reinforced that idea. The slain missionary was seventy-five years old. A veteran of the Boxer siege in Peking, he had spent almost half a century in China tending to its huddled poor. He'd pioneered work in medicine and surgery for native doctors, writing textbooks for them in Chinese. He'd been called one of the country's 'best foreign friends'. He'd also put together manuals for non-Chinese speakers who wished to learn the language. His robbers neither knew this nor would have cared. He was shot twice in the head at midnight. He'd been attempting to protect his wife and two grand-children. The salient – and most sobering – detail of the dispatch was the location of the shooting: the missionary was staying in the holiday cottages in the Western Hills, where the Liddells honeymooned only ten weeks earlier. Here was another sign that the size of the country offered no protection to anyone.

China hardly seemed to be a place to build a home and start a family. A home was built nonetheless; and a family was soon begun too. Liddell was in his early thirties. His friends had been fathers long before him, and so had his brother, Rob, whose son was born in 1930.

Barely sixteen months after the wedding, Florence gave birth to a girl, christened Patricia. A second daughter was born in the first week of January 1937. The Liddells couldn't agree on a name. The baby was originally due in late December, and Florence wanted to call her Carol to chime with the season. Liddell preferred Heather, reminding him of Scotland. Eventually, a compromise was agreed. A draw would be made to resolve the impasse, and Liddell volunteered to organize it. He placed two folded squares of paper inside one of Florence's cloche hats and invited her to pick out one of them. She did so, reading aloud her blind choice to him: Heather. She accepted defeat until Liddell, unable to tell even the whitest of lies, made a confession. The contest had been a fix. He'd written Heather on both pieces of paper. 'I picked up a cushion and threw it at him,' said Florence. 'Then I reckoned that if he'd wanted the name Heather that much, I wasn't going to stand in his way.'

With two children, one just two years old and the other in the cradle, most parents would have settled into the quietest of family routines. But another path beckoned Liddell like a hooked finger; and where it led promised nothing quiet or cosy.

*

A bicycle made for a family. Eric, dapper in his straw hat,
prepares to pedal through Tientsin. Florence, Patricia (left)
and Heather see him off.

Eric Liddell planned to be a country missionary like his father; only the timing of the move remained in doubt. The London Missionary Society nagged him into it much sooner than he had expected.

As early as 1935, less than fourteen months after his marriage to Florence, the LMS became concerned about what it called 'the smallness' of its ranks in North China and the 'consequent inadequacy to meet the needs of the country fields'. The solution was to transfer evangelists such as Liddell to fill up the numbers. The LMS wanted him to go to Siaochang, his boyhood home and his father's former district. His brother Rob was still doctoring there. His friend Annie Buchan was still the hospital's matron. The LMS turned the screw on Liddell in an un-Christian manner. Its executive committee traded on both his conscience and his obligations to God. It asked him to 'consider' whether the 'serious emergency' over staffing did not 'constitute a Call to him to give temporary help'. The enquiry, though polite, was as loaded as a gambler's dice. The capitalization of the word 'Call' – and what it implied – piled on the pressure. He initially resisted it, thinking the LMS's timing wrong for him and Florence. The Anglo-Chinese College needed his teaching, he said, and to go to Siaochang would be a 'big waste' of his educational work at that stage. His Chinese wasn't fluent enough to cope in the remotest of the rural areas either. Noticeably he didn't summon the excuse about bringing up a young family and not wanting to leave them; after all, missionaries complaining about the agony of separation sounded like sea captains complaining about the sea. Above all, Liddell stressed that he then didn't 'feel a definite enough call' to abandon the college just yet.

The LMS was peeved. The executive committee did what autocratic organizations always tend to do when someone or something doesn't bend to their will. It first moved the goalposts and then gerrymandered the outcome it wanted. In a pincer movement, it decided to review 'the whole policy and work' of the college and pledged to reduce staffing there as soon as 'circumstances' allowed. The meaning of these announcements didn't require translation. Liddell would be steered towards Siaochang eventually. Within another twelve months the LMS made its second attempt to engineer the move, proposing that Liddell go there 'on loan' either in the autumn of 1937 or the spring of 1938. The earlier date was preferable to the impatient LMS.

Liddell continued to waver, mulling over the move at enormous length. The future prosperity of the college, which he had served for more than a decade, bothered him. Liddell also thought he was still 'more equipped for educational work, both by training and temperament' – at least for another year or two. With the LMS adamant, however, Liddell went into a period that Florence described as 'much prayerful consideration' because 'all his decisions were made in light of what he felt was God's will for him'. After those prayers, Liddell's opinion changed. 'It took him a long time to be sure he was doing the right thing,' said Florence. 'But eventually he felt God was calling him to the country.'

That call could not have come at a more dangerous time.

Long before he began chronicling the making of American presidencies, and winning the Pulitzer Prize for it, Theodore H. White reported on China for *Time*. Casting his eye across the churned battlefields of its history, White reflected that successive dynasties were 'born of upheaval and fermented in the brew of revolution'. Those, such as Liddell, who were there during the 1920s and 1930s lived through one of them, each a witness to civil war during a decade of mass death and madness. Liddell saw the Nationalists and the Communists fight over ideology and he picked his way gingerly through the wreckage both of them scattered.

The Nationalists, under Sun Yat-sen, and the Communists, under the intellectual Li Dazhao and his party co-founder Chen Duxiu, had become allies in 1922, a coming-together of convenience designed to rid China of its warlords, who ruled and duelled as arbitrarily as those maverick king-commanders in George R. R. Martin's *Game of Thrones*. When Sun died of liver cancer in 1925, Chiang Kai-shek, then thirty-eight, eventually replaced him, turning himself into the organizing brain of the Kuomintang. Within eighteen months Chiang had shrewdly married the Christian Soong Mei-ling. Her sister was Sun's widow. Chiang read Mei-ling's Bible daily, and prayed with her after becoming a practising Methodist. Of him, White said: 'He cloaked himself in the sanctity of a deacon . . . his utterances rang with the sincerity of a Puritan . . . [he] frowned on sin with the intensity of one who has sampled it and found it less rewarding than piety.' White then smashed apart the picture of Chiang as the saintly Christian soldier with the mallet-swing of this line: 'His ferocity was that of an Old Testament Joshua . . . as a politician Chiang dealt in force rather than ideas . . . any concept that differed from his own was treated with as much hostility as an enemy division.'

The warlords were said to have a total of 1.5 million followers when Chiang's 'Northern Expedition' began against them in 1926, an action dismissed as 'hopeless folly' by the correspondent of the *New York Times*. As Jonathan Fenby points out in *The Penguin History of Modern China*, Chiang was more wily than his critics at home and abroad ever believed. 'He grasped the importance of finance and resources, of political control and coalitions which, however temporary, isolated opponents.' With the support of the Communists, he substantially weakened some warlords and toppled others, reunifying the bulk of China under the National Government, based in Nanking.

But even victors are by victories undone; and so it proved now. Political and military fault-lines as big as chasms remained, and China was an ungovernable Gordian knot of intrigue and corruption, pride and ego, feuds and resentments in which the self-serving and the power-crazed were unimaginably entangled. Things fell apart. Without a common enemy to unite them, the 'understanding' that had existed between the Nationalists and the Communists rapidly disintegrated. In April 1927, what became known as Chiang's 'White Terror' began. Communists and dissidents alike were purged; five thousand were slaughtered in Shanghai alone as Chiang – aided and abetted there by the criminal organization the Green Gang – strove to establish an unbendable capitalist state beneath the tent of his dictatorship. As White observed, there were 'riots, bloodshed and butchery'. Chiang even placed a bounty on the heads of Communist leaders: $50,000 alive and $20,000 dead. Li Dazhao was hanged after being captured in Peking. Dazhao's political partner, Chen Duxiu, lost his influence and was subsequently expelled from the party.

That summer, out of the chaos, the Communists created the Red Army and made Mao Tse-tung its commander-in-chief. In one photograph he is thin and distinctly oval-faced, his thick black hair centrally parted and cut almost flush against the tops of his ears. Mao looks as if he is wearing a clown's skullcap and wig.

Just as the Boxer Rebellion had done, the civil war became convenient cover for hate-crimes against foreigners. Missionaries were wedged between rival armies and rival warlords and also the bedraggled but belligerent assortment of bandits who took advantage of the anarchy.

Every fresh year brought another boiling point. Between the end of 1930 and September 1931, Chiang orchestrated three 'Encirclement Campaigns' designed to isolate Communist troops and gain supremacy. He intended to starve them of food and deprive them of military hardware. The Red Army repelled each assault. But what neither it nor the Nationalists could prevent was Japanese expansionism.

Japan's Kwantung Army waded into and then conquered Manchuria in September 1931 to take advantage of the instability elsewhere. This was done on the false pretext that China had blown up part of a railway line that Japan commercially owned. The Kwantung had actually set the explosives itself. Manchuria became Manchukuo, the invaders installing a puppet leader with long strings, who was controlled from Tokyo. Western governments and the League of Nations were impotent against the land-grab. So was Chiang, unable to strike on a new front and retain those he held already.

China's fury was articulated in the lyrics of a song called 'Kill the Enemy', which appeared in the *China Times*, reflecting the mood for revenge. The Japanese scoffed at it. Less than four months later came the abomination of the Shanghai Incident. Outrage was piled on outrage. The Japanese smashed and gutted swathes of the city through relentless bombing, first from naval destroyers and then from low-level air raids, the circumference of which was gradually widened. In the inferno, roads became wide pits. Homes and shops and factories became charred shells. White-eyed corpses of men, women and children were laid out and photographed among the rubble. Some civilians were hauled to a race-track where the army bayoneted them to death.

By 1933 China, still in conflict with itself, was pressed into defending the Great Wall against the Japanese, who provoked another dispute. The Boxer Treaty had given them control of a garrison. The Japanese fabricated the discovery of two bombs inside it. In the aggression that followed, the town of Jehol was shelled, clearing a path to the wall for them. To avoid an attack on Peking, the Chinese agreed to the removal of troop battalions from almost 120,000 square miles.

China was a tinder box, always ablaze somewhere owing to either the Japanese or the civil war. A further two Encirclement Campaigns took place in March and October 1933 as part of Chiang's attempt to crush Communist resistance. Even as the Liddells settled into their marriage during the autumn of 1934, the Communist retreat that became the Long March – lauded as an 'epic poem' to its cause – began unwinding in a monumental exercise of endurance on a route from southern to northwest and northern China. The 368-day trek passed through twelve provinces, crossed twenty-four rivers, went over eighteen mountain ranges and occupied sixty-two cities. Depending on whose calculations you prefer to believe, it covered between 4,000 and 6,000 miles. Afterwards myths and fictions were entwined into accounts of it, which Mao propagated. Mao didn't march much of the way – porters carried his privileged backside on a litter like a Roman emperor – but he spun stories to glorify his Red Army, anointing his retreating soldiers as 'heroes'. He invented battles and exaggerated derring-do skirmishes for the purpose of politics, grandeur and posterity, chiefly his own. It is said that eighty to a hundred thousand took part in the Long March. Less than one in ten is thought to have survived. The civilian casualties – murdered, starved, beaten or abused – went uncounted.

The civil war caused Liddell inconveniences and irritations at the Anglo-Chinese College. These became more pronounced in the months following his wedding. The Nationalist government made attendance at a two-week soldier camp mandatory for those aged fourteen. Afterwards, a twice-weekly drill became compulsory too. Also, the college had to hoist and lower the national flag daily and gather the entire roll call in front of the pole to witness it, as if the ceremony of rope and silk were symbolically sacrosanct. Government interference continued incrementally. To refuse a decree would have shut the college and seen it reopen under entirely new and more malleable management. New orders steadily encroached across the educational timetable. At the beginning of 1935 it obliterated three months of blackboard work for one class, which was marched off for 'national service'. The government's next move was more sinister: the college was instructed to provide Scout uniforms for pupils belonging to its junior middle. This was not an altruistic, Baden-Powell-like attempt to encourage self-sufficiency and spark the outdoor spirit. No one wearing the uniform was collecting campfire badges. The Scouts was a preparatory class for the infantrymen of tomorrow.

Every omen was dark. The differences between the Nationalists and Communists were irreconcilable. Japan continued to devour territory, further infiltrating North China, where it ignored Boxer protocols, strengthened its fortress forces and assumed control.

The outcome was predictable.

The first Sino-Japanese War had started in late summer 1894, and lasted only nine months. The second, beginning in July 1937, was far bloodier. In his *Penguin History* Jonathan Fenby writes two sentences that require reading at least twice because the figures contained within them are so horrifying. You re-check them to make sure your eyes really have sent the information correctly to your brain. Writing about the second Sino-Japanese War, he says, 'The death toll of soldiers and civilians . . . will never be known. Estimates range from ten million to twice as many, with most in the fifteen to twenty million range.' He adds that the official history of the Nationalists, which omits Communist–Japanese encounters, calculated 1,117 'major' battles and 38,931 'lesser engagements'.

Like so many wars, the beginning of it turned on a minor disturbance. The scene was the stone Marco Polo Bridge, which spanned the Yungting River. A unit of Japanese soldiers was involved in a field exercise on a night when the moon over Peking could barely be seen between galleon-sized clouds. A shot was fired and returned. A Japanese messenger went missing temporarily. In the game of claim and counter-claim that followed, the Japanese blamed the Chinese for aggression. More gunfire came with the dawn. A ceasefire, token and shaky, was cobbled together. Nineteen tense days passed. Japan gave China an ultimatum: remove two divisions within twenty-four hours or face the consequences. It didn't bother to wait for a reply. Attacking the Summer Palace, its ground and air forces mowed down and bombed hundreds of Chinese troops.

A day later Liddell, already planning for Siaochang, was walking casually through Tientsin. In the distance he heard what sounded to him like the pop and crack of fireworks, the sort that might greet a New Year. An explosion, loud and hard enough to shake buildings, blew away any thought of celebration. The Japanese had dynamited the university. Next came the drone of twenty-eight planes. For four hours Tientsin came under siege from the sky and also from the deadly arc of artillery shells. More than seven hundred died. More than a thousand homes and public buildings were destroyed. More than two thousand displaced Chinese attempted to move into the Concessions, which weren't shelled to avoid foreign wrath.

Afterwards, an agency report said that there was an 'unearthly quiet' in the city, which was 'broken only by the crackling of the blazing buildings'. On a hot, windless afternoon black-grey smoke rose in straight funnels all around Tientsin. Liddell watched the carnage from a rooftop, knowing a new reality had come to China.

A new reality loomed for him too.

CHAPTER ELEVEN

Everywhere the Crows
Are Black

Eric Liddell was precise and clear-eyed about the sort of missionary he intended to become. He didn't want to be seen only as a do-gooder, who dispensed the scriptures competently enough but remained dispassionately aloof from the world in which his words were heard. As Liddell saw it, religious zeal alone didn't qualify you to be a missionary anyway. You had to ally it with a solid purpose; and you had to know how that purpose would be achieved. He believed missionaries ought to ask themselves one thing before venturing overseas. The question was particularly relevant in China.

'What exactly had one got to give?'

'Anyone going to China had to think that over a long time,' explained Liddell. 'For in China one was dealing with a people who had produced great philosophers, who had given to them a way of living which had enabled them to continue down through the centuries.'

From his father, Liddell appreciated that change in China would never be wrought suddenly. Even the distant past, belonging to Lazoi, Confucius and Sun Tzu, influenced the present integrally there. This wasn't a straightforward case of honouring the country's heritage or adhering to old customs. It was bone and blood and breath to the Chinese. But everything will retrograde if it does not progress, and Liddell was conscious, well before returning to his homeland, how much China required 'a push' to place it on a different course – and also how gently persuasive that push needed to be. Otherwise he'd alienate the locals.

Liddell publicly announced that he'd always 'felt destined' for China, which allowed him to develop a plan for it and also list those things he sought to achieve.

His primary task was to pass on 'The Great Message', he said. Liddell went so far as calling that message 'so great that it was worthwhile trying to add to what those great philosophers had already given to China'. He summarized it in a sentence: 'What we [have] to give the Chinese [is] the love of God in their hearts.'

The first step was education. Illiteracy was the enemy. 'Until they were taught to read, the Bible was a closed book to them,' he said of the converts his father had made. The second step was education too. He wanted equality, respect and better treatment for the less fortunate. Knowing that the well-off disparaged the poor – sometimes appallingly – Liddell was determined to show China 'the value of life and an idea of service' which would correct 'the absence of help for those unable to help themselves'. The disabled, who were denigrated in China as being near worthless, were a priority to him. China must 'look with sympathy on those who were infirm', he said.

Liddell was convinced any programme should start with the young, which is why he taught at Dr Lavington-Hart's Anglo-Chinese College for so long. Now the first part of his missionary life was over. He could barely wait for the second part to begin.

His original reservations about being posted to Siaochang vanished as soon as the decision to resign from the college was made. Afterwards China seemed to open up afresh for him. Nothing could change Liddell's mind about going into the country at last – not even the awful escalation of the Sino-Japanese War.

In August 1937 Chiang Kai-shek proclaimed that China's 'limits' of 'endurance' had been reached with the Japanese. There was no option but to fight them 'to the bitter end'. Without pause or mercy, the next six months brought weekly accounts of Japanese progress and Chinese collapse, particularly in the north. Peking was captured and the fight for Shanghai began along a front stretching for 40 miles. In a forty-eight-hour spell, 2,526 bombs fell on that city. The coast was bombarded too and then attacked through amphibious landings. After thirty thousand men piled into Hangzhou Bay, the Japanese began a rear assault as well.

'Towns on the route were devastated – dogs grew fat on the corpses,' wrote Jonathan Fenby. The Rape of Nanking was not far away, and as a prelude to it the farmland between that city and Shanghai was turned into a graveyard containing almost 'a million' corpses.

Obscenities followed the taking of Nanking, a savage and deliberate slaughter of soldiers and innocents alike. It is said, but still disputed, that three hundred thousand Chinese died in the massacre. Other figures, taken from contemporary records, estimate that a hundred thousand or fewer perished. Inarguable is the fact that entire families were wiped out. Some people were buried alive. Often a head was left poking from the soil to allow hungry dogs to tear at the face. The Japanese also tied victims to posts or nailed them to boards before bayoneting them. Nanking was a torture chamber. 'Martial arts swordplay was practised on defenceless civilians,' wrote Fenby, who listed other methods of murder there: 'run over by vehicles, mutilated and disembowelled, sprayed with acid or hung up by their tongues'. In the first month of occupation approximately twenty thousand women and girls were raped and then put to death to cover the original crime. 'Some died with sticks rammed into their vaginas. Foetuses were ripped from the bodies of expectant mothers,' said Fenby. 'The killers felt no shame at their savagery. Some photographed the killings, and sent the negatives to Shanghai to be developed.'

The Anglo-Chinese College opened at the start of the academic year, as though impervious to the ramifications of the new war. Nearly six hundred pupils enrolled, and Liddell continued to teach them. There was another consolation for him, which cultivated a sense of normality, however false: Liddell had the company of his brother. Well before the Sino-Japanese conflict began, blocking roads and railways, Rob Liddell had brought his sick son to Tientsin from Siaochang for an X-ray. This revealed tuberculosis of the spine. No Chinese hospital had the facilities to treat him. The boy was placed in a body-cast and sent back to Britain with his mother. Rob planned to return to Siaochang alongside Eric and Florence, who had been safely in Peitaiho with the children when Tientsin fell to the Japanese. As unafraid as her husband about the prospect of Siaochang, she'd resolved to go there with him. 'I'd been brought up in China,' she said. 'I knew what to expect from a place like Siaochang.'

Full of brio, Florence began packing as Liddell made transport arrangements for three adults and two children. She gathered up the family belongings and cleaned her home. She said goodbye to friends. In a disgraceful act at the eleventh hour, the London Missionary Society, as if possessing the moral right to assert control over Florence, forbade her to travel. The LMS decided it was 'too dangerous'. That arrogance failed to take into account two points: the risk was hers rather than the LMS's, and she deserved to decide for herself whether or not to take it. Florence was livid. Not wanting to create a scene, she instead went into the bedroom where the luggage was already roped together. She took her fury out on the cases. 'I kicked them all around the room,' she said.

The best photograph ever taken of Eric Liddell captures him in his absolute prime. He's wearing creased civilian clothes rather than his athletic kit, and he's gazing directly into the lens. The picture was taken with a standard box camera, and Liddell didn't pose for it. It's as if the photographer – his brother Rob – has surreptitiously loaded a roll of film and then slyly framed the shot before shouting at Liddell to turn towards him. It's almost noon on a particularly bright day. Liddell's lampblack shadow doesn't fall far. He's sitting on a mound of scruffy earth in a dark polo-neck sweater and an equally dark calf-length overcoat, its wide lapels slightly upturned against the cold. He also wears a pair of thick grey flannel trousers, badly in need of pressing, and woollen, fingerless gloves. On his head is a straggly-looking fur hat, which lies slightly below the tips of his ears. He resembles an explorer, who could be walking across the Russian countryside rather than China's. The landscape immediately behind him is bare and stony. Only in the middle distance is there any sign of vegetation: the scrub of short hedges, winter trees without a leaf, uneven fringes of grass and tufts of old crops. The sky appears milky white, making the distant scene indistinct. Nothing more than the shape of buildings and a grain store is visible.

The compelling aspect of the photograph is the look on Liddell's face. The eyes are squinting against the glare of the sun, which is reflected off the baked soil. He's unshaven, the dimple in his chin accentuated by fine stubble. The firm set of the mouth gives him a rugged appeal too. What strikes you most about Liddell nonetheless is something very traceably poignant in his expression. In this square, amateur snap you see the determination within him. It's as though he's been interrupted momentarily from some deep, hard thinking; and, during the half-second that lapses before he can return to it, the thoughts in his mind can be read on

Portrait of a missionary: Eric Liddell, resolute but slightly dishevelled and unshaven, on his way to Siaochang in late autumn 1937.

the face he presents to the camera. Liddell is in the midst of one struggle and there are others, much more arduous, ahead of him. To appreciate that properly requires an understanding of the story behind the photograph.

He has left behind Florence, Patricia and the baby Heather.

He is on his way to Siaochang at last.

As the conflict between the Chinese and the Japanese grew ever more violent, it was originally impossible for Eric Liddell to break out of Tientsin and fill the post the London Missionary Society had given him.

That autumn he and Rob had made two early attempts to reach Siaochang, much of which had been devastated by flooding. In the chaos so many bridges were either badly damaged after bombing or partially dismantled – the Chinese attempting to check the march of the Japanese – that dead-ends were frustratingly common for the traveller. The

Siaochang compound scarcely functioned. Only one staff missionary remained to oversee it. Overworked and anxious, he wrote to the Liddells pleading for reinforcements. His appeal never reached them, the letter lost in the confusion that had enveloped everything. Aware of his difficulties nonetheless, the Liddells piled a few essential belongings into black canvas bags and set off. The railway timetable was erratic because sections of track had been ripped out – again to hamper the Japanese – or destroyed during fighting. Knowing that the fickleness of the service could maroon them anywhere along the route, the Liddells still took a chance that a train might get them close enough to Siaochang to make the latter stages of the journey walkable. The route was not direct. The first train carried them only as far as Tsangchow, a distance of 600 miles. A week later the Liddells got as far as Tehchow – 100 miles further – before the Japanese blocked them again, refunding the brothers' fare and actually apologizing for the inconvenience.

Since neither road nor rail could get them to Siaochang, the Liddells decided to think laterally. The two of them would sail there instead. The option was risky. Parts of the river were still swollen after the floods and stretches of embankment had also crumbled away. The unrepaired bridges made the waters harder to navigate because strewn debris turned them into an obstacle course. There was also the question of the river pirates, who patrolled the unpopulated banks the way Blackbeard had once patrolled the Caribbean seas. These armed men weren't inclined to take no for an answer and then wish you a breezy so-long. Nothing deterred the Liddells, however. The result was a daring escapade not unlike the sort John Buchan could have put into one of his adventure-cum-spy novels.

In ten days, starting in late November 1937, the Liddells were twice robbed at gunpoint, the awful evidence of the war always around them. A five-and-a-half-page account of the journey was neatly typed and sent to the LMS afterwards. Although authorship was shared – and Liddell's name came before his brother's at the head of the document – the writerly credit belongs to Rob. He described the drama in a casually deadpan manner, as if near misses with death were no more traumatizing than a paper cut. 'We thoroughly enjoyed the whole affair,' he concluded, also remarking that the 'fresh air, the long sleeps and a healthy amount of exercise' amply made up for the bothersome interruptions of bandits brandishing weapons at them. To read the narrative is to appreciate the closeness of the brothers, who were so supportive and caring of each other and relished being together, even in a situation as treacherous as this one. The Liddells simply muddled through.

To reach Siaochang required two boats. The captain of the first was a local character called the Chief of the West River. He was proud of that grand epithet, and wore it like a campaign medal. It was bestowed on him because the boat's 55-foot mast ranked as the tallest in the region. The mast was the boat's only virtue. The unprepossessing 110-foot-long wooden vessel resembled a pair of ramshackle boats welded together. Its sail, said the Liddells, was 'quite a complicated affair' and looked as though it had 'weathered many a storm'. The Chief gave the brothers his cabin, tucked away at the stern. Like the sail, the cabin had been patched up to make it presentable. This was not luxury cruising. The ceiling and the walls were so cracked that the Chief had plastered them with paper, a botched piece of DIY that constantly needed repairing. His attempt at a homely touch was a bolt of cloth that decorated the lower part of one of the walls. The trailing end of the cloth was draped across a section of boarded floor like ill-fitting carpet. The rest of the floor was covered in straw matting. There was no heat, obliging the Liddells to sleep in most of their winter clothes. The boat lacked speed too, the Chief piloting it along the Hutuo River as ponderously as a Sunday motorist driving a brand-new car. To stretch their legs the Liddells merely had to jump off and walk briskly beside it. At various stages the brothers – and their travelling companions – helped to pull the boat ropes from the towpath because 'it was going too slowly for our liking'. At other times the Chief and his crew used long poles, as though punting, to navigate those areas where the floods had smashed or blistered the mud banks, clogging the black water.

The detritus of war littered the countryside. Its effect on the Chinese, predominantly the farmers, was ruinous. The Liddells had a better view of this than the newspaper correspondents, who were trying to make sense of Japanese dominance and Chinese defeats and give both an accurate shape on maps of the fighting. The intelligence was frequently unreliable and often contradictory, which meant their grasp of the war was incomplete. The truth leaked out only in fragments. The Liddells saw for themselves the dark trail the Japanese had cut through the agricultural lands. Silhouetted against the sky were wrecked or abandoned cars, trucks and buses – the discarded junk of battle. Although there was 'little' evidence of 'actual fighting', said the Liddells – resistance trenches had been dug but seldom used – what the brothers found instead troubled them because the short- and long-term ramifications were dreadful to contemplate.

The floods had protected some villages and a few of the small towns from invasion. Others were so primitive that, apart from the odd ancient rifle or small firearm, the population had been defenceless and hadn't attempted to put up much resistance in case the consequence was unnecessary shooting and a lot of casualties. Their huts and shacks, and also a few concrete buildings, stood intact and mostly unmarked because no cannon or bullet had been fired to claim them. The mere presence of the Japanese had been enough to guarantee surrender. The men had stayed behind, forming a human barrier initially to protect the women and children and then to allow them to escape. What horrified the Liddells was the fact that these communities were then systematically 'stripped of everything' valuable or useful. Homes were empty shells. Food was picked clean from the shelves and larders. Furniture was confiscated and chopped for firewood. Doors and windows were torn off and taken for kindling too. Utensils and farming equipment were commandeered. And any livestock – hens and chickens in particular – were immediately whisked away as bounty, destined for a Japanese cooking pot. Those who remained because there was nowhere else for them to go collected the splinters and scraps of what was left, setting it alight for flickering warmth. There was almost no food; and there was no prospect either of getting fresh supplies because these victims of Japanese looting now had nothing to trade or barter in return for them. 'Poverty will walk through the countryside this winter until it is possible for those who have been able to plant wheat to reap it in the spring,' was the dire forecast of the Liddells' report to the LMS. 'There was not a hen to be seen, an egg to be purchased.'

The brothers had taken ten brown loaves of bread and ate two meagre meals per day. At certain points vendors appeared from the hedgerows and trees and the boat pulled close to the bank, allowing them to leap on to the deck and sell food such as the grain *kuo tzu* from baskets and trays. One of the vendors fell into the water after the boat lurched, and he narrowly avoided being crushed under the hull in his attempt to claw back supplies that were floating away from him on the river tide. That he was willing to risk his life for his livelihood demonstrated the scarcity of basic food. The Liddells watched him retrieve a package and knew he'd be able to sell it, however water-soaked the goods were inside.

The iron rations, the snail-like progress of the transport and the uncomfortable chill of the conditions on and off board were still minor inconveniences compared with the menace of the bandits, who lurked near bridges and hid on bends.

War is a perpetual excuse for a multitude of misdeeds, an open invitation to slide off the moral scale. The bandits sometimes cloaked themselves as Robin Hoods, claiming theft as philanthropy on behalf of the underprivileged. It was a lie, but propagating it satisfied their own idea of fairness and justice. These thugs were the worst kind of opportunists – vicious and exploitative even towards their fellow countrymen and women. The Liddells had prepared themselves for the possibility of such an encounter and were coldly composed when it arose. A doctor and a missionary were seen as small-fry and safe prey for bandits because neither concealed a gun and wouldn't be inclined to fight back.

On the morning of the brothers' first brush with banditry, the Liddells wrote of being 'very rudely awakened'. The Chief's boat was approaching a bridge when a roughly dressed group claiming to be self-appointed 'peacekeepers' blocked the way. No one could protest. The bandits were clutching rifles, evidently knew how to fire them, and stood 20 yards apart to ensure the boat couldn't manoeuvre beyond them. 'We could do nothing but draw to the edge of the river,' said the brothers. One of the bandits had covered his nose and mouth with a muffler. The small firearm he waved about was hidden behind a handkerchief. He was the ringmaster of a motley crew. To prove it, and liking the sound of his own voice, he dashed along the bank shouting orders at the other bandits and also at the Liddells' boat. His main accomplice came on deck, a riding whip in his hand. The Chief attempted to sweet-talk him. 'Don't take the luggage,' he asked, which only made it sound as if the cases contained something highly prized. Realizing his mistake, the Chief tried bribery instead. He was immediately beaten for it. The bandits snatched $700 worth of cigarettes and stole $70 from the passengers.

The Liddells, who had emerged from their cabin as soon as the commotion began, were told to return to it. After what the brothers called a 'bit of a pow-wow together', the two of them decided to try to negotiate with the man disguised beneath the muffler. The bandit refused to remove it and 'gesticulated' at the brothers with his revolver whenever he spoke. 'He met us with sarcasm and courtesy, which do not mix well,' said the Liddells. He stole a further $20 from them and then irrationally returned $1.60 without explaining why. Equally irrationally he also gave them a box of cakes and a carton of cigarettes. They got off lightly. 'Another boat, much smaller than ours, was in their hands at the same time,' said the brothers. One of its Chinese deck-hands was shot before the bandits even boarded it.

The Liddells and the Chief had to transfer the bandits' gains from both plundered boats on to a third and watched the masked leader sail clear of them without a backward glance. 'We parted silently from our friends with no great demonstration of affection, not even the kindly words *tsai chien* – see you again,' said the Liddells, insouciantly summoning humour to play down the severity of a scrape in which only diplomacy and acquiescence had saved them from harm.

Another wasn't far ahead. Having left the Chief, who was heading in a different direction and gallantly refused the offer of payment from them, the Liddells found another captain to take them to Siaochang. During the brief stop between boats, Rob took that pensive photograph of Eric. On what the brothers called a 'never to be forgotten day' more bandits targeted them. Again the Liddells were confronted with a row of rifle barrels. The men claimed to have the right to 'borrow from all people and boats passing that way'. The Liddells explained 'who we were [and] what we were doing'. That explanation wasn't entirely successful. The bandits snatched at the brothers' identity cards and marched them to a checkpoint. The Liddells called it a 'veritable stronghold' because everyone there seemed to be armed. Those who didn't have a rifle carried a revolver. One of the bandits gleefully toted a machine gun. Far from keeping the peace, the men were in the business of disturbing it for anyone who had the temerity to stray into their territory. The Liddells were held until the boat was ransacked. 'We found that nearly everyone had lost something – a little money, some clothing or goods.'

Less than 10 miles further on there was a third armed gang awaiting them. Wary and weary and also convinced that the tense cycle of these ordeals would never end – the bandits parroted identical threats and commands at them – the passengers disembarked, wanting the thing to be over as quickly as possible for the sake of their nerves. When one of them gave what the Liddells regarded as an unintelligent answer to a question, a shot was discharged into the far distance. The bang and ringing echo of it was enough to bring the quarrelsome traveller to heel. Hearing about the earlier checkpoints, this gang eventually parted, like an open gate, and let the boat through, believing there was nothing else worth taking from it.

The closer the brothers got to Siaochang, the more peaceful their passage became because flooding had made much of the land impassable.

Reporting on the final third of their passage, the Liddells slipped a colourful local into their writing. Her name was Ta Chiao, an inn-owner, and she appears in print the way a good soldier might make it into dispatches from the front. The translation of Ta Chiao is Big Feet, which is scarcely complimentary: in China small feet were still considered to be an important sign of feminine beauty. The Liddells described Ta Chiao as being of 'large dimensions'. She was 'capable of holding her own at any time and fearless in what she said', and they compared her to 'a hurricane'. Ta Chiao spoke without pause or punctuation at incredible speed and blew the listener backwards with the force of her words. Those who heard her, the Liddells added, felt like 'the rustics' who appear in Oliver Goldsmith's seventeenth-century poem *The Deserted Village*, which is written in heroic couplets. To sum up the extraordinary sight of Ta Chiao, as well as her garrulousness, the Liddells quoted a line from it: 'And still they gazed and still the wonder grew'. However formidable, she impressed the brothers, who thought of her as 'businesslike'. Inherent in the paragraphs about her is relief. The worst of the Liddells' trials were over now. Ta Chiao's inn was a safe haven.

The brothers, bedraggled and dirty, walked the final 10 miles to Siaochang. At journey's end neither their clothes nor their skin had seen soap and water for almost a fortnight. The dust of the fields clung to their big boots. Their beards were unkempt and straggly. The lone missionary who greeted them initially thought he was hallucinating. He'd supposed no one could possibly reach him until well into the New Year. The two men standing in front of him looked like tramps in search of a soup kitchen; both of them certainly smelled like tramps in need of a bar of carbolic. He hugged them nonetheless. So did Annie Buchan, perplexed to see Liddell in particular because, she said, 'everyone was surprised' that he had decided to become a missionary.

She was not surprised for long.

Since Eric Liddell did his talking from the pulpit, and spoke mildly there, others failed to appreciate the resilience behind his gentleness. Stuck in a district that Annie Buchan described as being 'infested with bandits

On the road. The brothers, rugged-looking,
have still to wash the dust off themselves after
reaching Siaochang.

and soldiers', he now showed he could be as hard as hand-made nails because the conditions forced him to reveal it.

On his arrival, he'd said undramatically, 'So this is Siaochang.'

It was only half-familiar to him, most of the images of his infancy now cloudy. Behind its high wall, the mission compound contained a stone church, a boarding school for primary pupils, four detached dwellings, normally used as houses, and a hall capable of hosting an audience of five hundred. The roofs were made from corrugated iron. The men's and women's eighty-bed hospitals, as well as a dormitory, lay beyond the main buildings. There were no tennis courts here. No tinkling piano to signal the start of the cocktail hour. No excuse-me dances to the accompaniment of a twelve-piece orchestra. In fact there were scarcely any activities that allowed the compound residents to fritter hours away festively. Nearby, however, was a Japanese fort.

The geography of the Great Plain was still as Buchan had discovered it more than a decade earlier: the mud-brick villages and the scattering of towns around which the agricultural year of reaping and sowing progressed slowly, and only when nature gave its permission. War had considerably worsened conditions during the months immediately before Liddell's arrival. That deterioration continued apace now, the Japanese always in the ascendancy.

Buchan gave Liddell a graphic account of what she'd seen and heard. The sword-carrying Japanese kicking open doors and terrifying those behind them. Villages cleared before being torched. In one of these only a barking dog remained alive, yelping for its owner. In another she calculated that a hundred were killed and 'a big number' wounded. She'd watched groups of bound prisoners being paraded through the streets towards an executioner whose 'long carved knife' was already 'dripping with blood' from earlier beheadings. 'Every so often the column [of them] stopped,' she said, 'and he lopped off a few more heads, tossing them into a basket.'

Frequently the Japanese stomped into the Siaochang compound unannounced. Men either awaiting an operation or convalescing from one were seized from their beds. The soldiers claimed to be arresting known Communists or guerrillas. Doctors were interrupted during surgery, the Japanese demanding to take the patient even before his incision had been stitched. On one occasion Buchan searched in vain for a surgeon, who was needed to examine a desperately sick man. As a last resort she went into the operating theatre where she found a Japanese soldier beating the surgeon over the head with a baton. Buchan instinctively swatted the baton out of his hand and calmly said that she required the surgeon urgently. The soldier, rather than attacking her, stepped back, agog that she wasn't afraid of him. Another soldier, bored and badly drunk, once staggered into Buchan's quarters and pushed her aside on his way upstairs. With Buchan screaming at him to leave, he stood in front of her full-length mirror and saluted his reflection before turning around and departing wordlessly. She also told Liddell something else: he was more likely to see dead bodies than flowers along the roadside.

Liddell's mission in Siaochang was no more than a needle point in this ghoulish tapestry. There was heavy fighting to the south and skirmishes to the east and west. The outskirts of Siaochang had what Liddell said was a 'small taste' of what was happening there. The population was still cowed and afraid. Seldom did a day pass without the unmistakable, if distant, noise of guns, which sounded like cackling. The infestation

Buchan had talked about meant missionaries such as Liddell were trapped in the middle of the competing sides, comprising Japanese and Nationalist soldiers, the troops belonging to the Communist Eighth Army, and the bandits and chameleon mercenaries, who changed their battle colours when it suited them.

There were two main rail tracks, which ran parallel to each other. The first connected Tientsin to Shanghai, 40 miles to the east of Siaochang. The other ran from Peking to Hankow, a similar distance to the west. The Japanese had claimed both of these lines. The Chinese had taken most of the land in between them. The complications for those, like Liddell, caught within it increased after each country banned the other's currency in the territory it controlled.

Leaving the relative civility of Tientsin, even under the Japanese flag, for the volatility and desolate austerity of Siaochang was traumatic. The place had become a pit, and problem upon problem was being piled into it.

A sign hung over the gate, having been placed there after the Boxer Rebellion. It read 'Chung, Wai I Chai' – Chinese and Foreigners All One Home. As Liddell discovered, the sentiment was no longer true because of the deprivations war had inflicted. 'The floods are only a small part of the sorrows of the people,' he said. The bigger sorrow, he added, were those 'bands of irregular soldiers' who were 'all over the countryside', squatting in a village and then 'living off it' through 'repeated demands' for grain and money. He went on: 'Fear reigns everywhere and the bitterest thing of all is to think that this trouble comes to them from their own in the midst of a great national tragedy. Every day brings its stories of distress, suffering . . .'

Liddell said that the people in Siaochang were 'burdened by the struggle to live'. Crops had failed. Cholera was rampant. An eighty-year-old carpenter, who Liddell thought possessed 'the fine courtesy of old China', found himself constantly cutting wood for paupers' coffins, supply always behind demand. The peasants' homes were mostly identical: three curtained-off and sometimes whitewashed rooms, measuring 8 feet square, and a kitchen half that size. One brick-based bed was set aside for the mother, grandmother and children. The houses were slightly raised off the ground as rudimentary protection against flooding, and each family owned at least one rowing boat. The only furniture was a table, a couple of chairs and occasionally a chest. The second room was more private, containing the family shrine. Most of the cooking was done on an outside stove and the aromatic scent of woodsmoke hung overpoweringly in the air. Inside, thread and cotton and cloth were perpetually spun. The windows were box-shaped and covered in rice paper, meaning the light was 'so poor', said Liddell, 'that its rays only lit up nearby things and the further parts were just dim objects'. In the three-quarter darkness he heard the 'click, click, click' of the spinning wheel, which was as necessary for survival as water and bread because the women made clothes to trade.

The pressure was relentless. Shells frequently flew over the compound rooftops during Japanese attacks on the bandits. Mortars exploded close to the walls. Wherever Liddell went – either to conduct services or administer pastoral care – he risked being accosted, harangued or needlessly searched and questioned by whichever army stopped him on a whim or pounced in an ambush. There was always the chance that a bullet, either a stray shot or one fired deliberately at him, would wound or kill. Villagers were afraid to give Liddell basic directions in case of reprisals from the Japanese on the grounds of collaboration. That anxiety was evident everywhere he went. The apprehension that some new cataclysm was waiting for them permeated daily life. Some villages were scared enough to station a guard at their entrance. The guard would hold up a slate on which two or three characters were chalked. Like the pronunciation of the word 'shibboleth', the characters had to be correctly spoken before the traveller was allowed inside.

There was no hiding place from the war. On the Sunday before Christmas, Liddell was performing a baptismal service in an outpost town. The 'distant rumble of guns', he said, had been heard twenty-four hours earlier. On the morning of the service, a Japanese scout plane began circling the sky. With rumours spreading about an imminent attack, the numbers who came to the church were 'considerably less' than Liddell had anticipated. He was in the middle of his address when the barrage began. Shells went off with a 'terrific' racket, he said. One shell fell 'just around the corner' from him. 'There was silence for a moment and then we continued,' he explained, which meant he continued and everyone else listened and pretended to ignore the shelling. When the service came to a close, none of the forty-strong congregation wanted to leave the church. Liddell organized hymn singing until thirty-one truckloads of soldiers arrived. Notices were put up in the main street telling the villagers not to be afraid. The Japanese were seeking Chinese bandits rather than hounding them – a spurious statement to say the least. Liddell noted there was comparatively 'little' looting during the full-scale, three-hour search that took place, which should not be read as a tacit thank you for small mercies. The soldiers were still stealing from people who couldn't afford to lose anything in the first place. One member of the church returned home to find a huge shell-hole in the front wall of his house. His belongings were gone.

The graver the situation in Siaochang, the more determined Liddell became to head into the countryside every day, which he did unflinchingly. His fellow missionaries said he possessed 'an utter fearlessness'. There was nothing swashbuckling about him. He worked in a patient, placid way, tending to small lives in that big war so that each good deed was a counterstroke to the bad ones he saw around him. In winter he wore an old sheepskin coat or a plaid quilted jacket. In summer he'd be seen in a short-sleeved shirt, shorts and a pair of calf-length socks. The soldiers had guns and trucks. He criss-crossed the treacherous, potholed paths of Siaochang on a bicycle and wore a Red Cross armband to signify his neutrality. When another missionary wanted to arm himself, stuffing a hand-gun in his pocket, Liddell persuaded him against it. 'Put it down. Don't even handle it. You will be shot long before you get to your pistol.'

In his rucksack Liddell carried only what he considered to be essential – a Bible, a prayer book, a compass. In his head he carried something else: the Chinese proverb that said 'Everywhere the crows are black', which he interpreted as 'Everywhere human nature is the same'. Wherever he went, whatever he saw and whoever he met, Liddell remembered that saying, believing wholeheartedly in the truth of it to comfort him.

But war warps whatever it touches, and one of the first things to bend is human nature. A specific case highlighted that fact more than any other he would ever face.

CHAPTER TWELVE

The Sharpest Edge
of the Sword

COUNTRY EVANGELISM WAS ERIC Liddell's forte. He had been born for it. Within six months, after his Chinese began to improve markedly, he was certain that leaving Tientsin for Siaochang had been a 'destiny-fulfilling' decision for him after all. Once asked outright by the inquisitive Annie Buchan whether he ever regretted his move, Liddell replied 'Never' and then explained why: 'I have more joy and freedom in the work than I have ever experienced before.' Liddell said it was 'wonderful to feel one with the people'. Florence Liddell saw the change in her husband. 'It was quite obvious he did the right thing,' she said. 'He loved the work . . . and I think he blossomed out in a new way.'

Liddell considered the Chinese to be 'calm, patient, willing to suffer a great deal with very little complaining and content with very little'. He could have been describing himself as well. Predictably he became confidant, comforter, grief-counsellor, social worker, diplomat and problem-solver in Siaochang – inside as well as outside its walls. If there was a quarrel, he was 'used as a buffer', recalled Buchan, whose initial scepticism about whether Liddell could transform himself from classroom teacher to missionary quickly passed. To the Chinese, who looked on him so fondly, he became Li Mu Shi: Pastor Liddell. When any decision had to be reached – and especially if it was likely to stir controversy or required mediation – Buchan would hear someone say, 'Ask Li Mu Shi

The formidable Annie Buchan marches through the Concessions in Tientsin.

what he thinks about it.' The preachers, the nurses, the students and the Chinese 'hung on his words', she added.

His surname gave him an advantage among the locals that was denied to other missionaries. He wasn't a stranger to them. As Buchan pointed out, Liddell's father James was 'still revered and loved' in Siaochang. The children James Liddell had known now had children and grandchildren of their own and remembered his kindnesses and also his fierce commitment to China. Liddell never spoke to them about being an Olympic champion. There was no point. No one in the outback of Siaochang had any concept of the Games and its ribboned gold medals. His prestige came from his lineage. To talk about his father was like presenting an impeccable character reference. There was an instant connection, which brought an instant trust, because stories could be swapped about a shared past.

Buchan also said Liddell possessed his father's 'winning personality' and was always thorough and organizationally innovative in his work. He drew maps of the area because none except the most rudimentary had previously existed. These highlighted safe short-cuts that ducked away from known Japanese patrols. According to Buchan, he compiled charts and schedules too, which enabled him to 'systematically' visit churches and regularly hold meetings there. No one in his parish felt neglected. Space was created in his diary for ordinary house calls, dropping in on parishioners to whom, Buchan insisted, 'he never expounded elaborate theories but suggested the possibility of a way of life that was Bible-based and God-governed'. Buchan, a loud bell-ringer for Liddell, thought he 'had the sympathy and patience needed' to convert 'a slow-moving people' and also the 'seething masses who tax one's strength from dawn to midnight'. What Florence identified as her husband's blossoming was actually renewed confidence in himself, which stemmed from the sense of purpose Siaochang provided.

It was as if everything that had gone before was preparation for this.

Liddell liked to teach the Chinese hymns. He'd cycle the back roads singing them to himself. He was keen on both 'God Who Touches Earth With His Beauty' and 'There's A Wideness In God's Mercy'. His particular favourite, which he sang repeatedly in both English and Chinese, was 'Be Still, My Soul'. Written in 1752 by the German Katharina von Schlegel, an expressive Lutheran, 'Be Still' wasn't translated into English until a century later, which made the Church rather slow on the uptake. Liddell's infatuation with it began in 1927 when von Schlegel's lyrical four verses were attached to Jean Sibelius's symphonic poem Finlandia. Liddell said it was 'a calm, restful, beautiful tune' and he never tired of hearing it. 'Be Still' also contains a line that embodies the message Liddell was always attempting to press on his congregation: 'Through thorny ways lead to a joyful end'.

Thorny ways were a part of life in Siaochang. The letters Liddell sent to friends and the annual reports he filed to the London Missionary Society continued to illustrate the awfulness of the situation and also the resourcefulness, mental strength and raw courage required to cope. 'The scenes have changed so quickly and the problems have been so varied that I almost wonder if I have been looking through a kaleidoscope,' he said of Siaochang. If so, the image within that kaleidoscope was a vile one. For Liddell there were intensely sad cases to handle and intensely tragic scenes to witness. He came across men shot dead and thrown into ditches and dykes or left hanging from clumps of hedgerow. He found women, their starving bellies bloated, begging for food. He discovered babies and children naked and abandoned. That sight distressed him most because he thought of his own daughters. Three instances were so especially harrowing to him that he recorded them briefly, as though needing to bear witness. A small girl, unwanted by her parents, suffered frostbite so extreme that her feet had to be amputated. A carpenter made her replacement feet out of blocks of wood. Another young girl was sold as a slave and 'ill-treated so badly that she became very ill', said Liddell. After her rescue, she was taken to the hospital, her body 'marked and dreadfully bruised', to be nursed back to health. When a house was torched after guerrilla attacks, he was told of two malnourished families huddled in the blackened shell that remained. Liddell walked into what he said was 'one of those pathetic' scenes of war – a wooden house set alight and gutted except for two rooms. The blaze left only 'great long pieces of burnt timber' among which two widowed mothers and two children lived. The Japanese had taken one of the husbands and demanded a ransom for his return. When the wife could not pay it, the Japanese had executed him. 'At no other place did the horror of war strike me so much as there,' said Liddell.

Commercially and culturally, Japanese influence was becoming unbreakable. Goods from Japan dominated the Chinese market and their non-competitive pricing excluded other importers. A Japanese bank was established, which issued its own banknotes and raked in Chinese currency in exchange. In many schools pupils were pressed into marking Japanese military victories with parades. The children were given either Japanese flags or the old five-barred flag of China to wave. 'The invaders were trying to convince the people that they had not come as conquerors, but merely to establish a new China,' explained Liddell.

Communication was haphazard. Rarely did English-language newspapers reach Siaochang. The Chinese editions were either closed down or censored and the rabid propaganda of the Japanese-controlled press dominated the market. The Chinese were forced to take these newspapers, which were thrown into their homes. Payment for them had to be given, like a tax on information, at the end of the month. Radio signals also drifted weakly across the Great Plain, and no newsreel could ever be seen there. Accounts of the fighting on the home front came spasmodically, delivered whenever a new face arrived at the mission or a familiar one returned. Accounts from Europe were patchier still, a piecemeal passing along of information down a human chain, which meant words and whispers could be lost, misunderstood or mistranslated. The Anschluss in Austria, the claim on the Sudetenland, the Munich Agreement, Neville Chamberlain's waved sheet of worthless paper promises, the smashed windows and the scrawled graffiti of Kristallnacht: Siaochang heard about these belatedly and incompletely. Still, no one doubted the implications of them. Hitler told you what was on the way. But what was looming elsewhere was then less important to Liddell than the aggression and oppression on his own doorstep.

Nothing betrays the character of a man like his manners – a phrase slightly misquoted from the poet Edmund Spenser that Eric Liddell never forgot. He even extended his courtesies to the occupying force in Siaochang – and not only because it pays to be polite when someone is pointing a gun at your head. Liddell followed two self-made rules in his dealings with Japanese soldiers. The first, he said, was 'Take it all with a smile', referring to crudely deliberate attempts to rile and intimidate. The second was 'However troublesome, don't get annoyed'.

The Japanese wanted rid of the missionaries without upsetting Western governments. The first commander in Siaochang had been raised in California and spoke impeccable English. Out of earshot of his own troops, he'd refer to the doctors and the missionaries as 'buddy'. The commander's mother was also a practising Christian, which meant he gave the mission a lot of leeway, often turning a blind eye to comings and goings there. His replacement was different. His tactic was hardly a bright one, but nonetheless proved effective because it rubbed on the nerves. He implemented a policy of daily disruptions. He organized an anti-British demonstration outside the gates of the compound. He even built a stage so the sound of propaganda speeches could be heard over the wall; a strong wind fortunately blew the stage down before a word was spoken.

He was more successful in turning travel into a trial for the missionaries. Patrols were increased and a policy of stop-and-search to niggle them began. This was carried out in a passive-aggressive way. The Japanese commander mistakenly believed that Liddell and his ilk would close down the mission out of sheer exasperation; alternatively the missionaries would be worn out by these petty inconveniences and minor persecutions. The plan was to goad them and spark a gung-ho incident somewhere – disobedience, the discovery of contraband or a loss of control – that could be used as a legitimate excuse to remove them permanently.

The soldiers were told to demand identification papers 'on sight'. These would be checked and re-checked laboriously, as though each was a possible forgery. What ought to have been a five-minute process was often stretched to half or three quarters of an hour. The papers were held up to the light. The missionary was frisked. His bag was opened, the contents tipped unceremoniously on to the ground, like hurling down a sack of rubbish. Each thing in it was examined with an aching slowness. Even the saddle of a bicycle was searched. Liddell moved so extensively around Siaochang that the soldiers always recognized him. The same procedures were followed with him nonetheless. There'd be tiresomely predictable questions too. Where was he heading? Who did he plan to see? Had he spoken to anyone else? When would he be back? Interrogations occurred at least twice per day. The most awkward soldiers would claim there was something amiss either in the papers presented to them or in the answers given. The missionary would be instructed to go to district headquarters, an errand designed to humiliate. The Japanese were playing a game.

Fortunately Liddell knew how to play back, and he also had the verbal flails to bamboozle them. He met malevolence with compassion, which threw the soldiers off stride. The angrier someone became, the more measured his response. Liddell behaved towards them in war exactly as he would have done in peace because he knew no other way to act. Tact, cheerfulness and the warmth of his personality defused confrontations. He made open-palm gestures. His smiles were undoubtedly sincere, signalling forbearance. As protocol demanded, he bowed to the Japanese – though from the neck rather than the waist. He was canny too. Slid into his wallet were two square photographs of his daughters that he'd show to the family-oriented Japanese, who automatically became friendlier towards him. Some took out pictures of their own families in a like-for-like trade of love and longing for home.

He even refused to condemn or criticize the soldiers who attempted to bully him. One of his colleagues put it perfectly. For Liddell, the Japanese were 'not to be feared or hated, but sought as sheep far from the fold', he said. He forgave them their trespasses. The Japanese came to accept him because he was efficient and ever present. He tramped and cycled the Siaochang roads endlessly, never missing a church service.

Staffing shortages eventually meant Liddell was appointed acting superintendent of the hospital. 'Don't laugh,' he wrote, adding that his new title was 'rather a joke' because the use of 'iodine and magnesium sulphate' represented the range of his medical knowledge.

The post enabled him to make short visits to Tientsin to collect medical supplies or Chinese currency, which meant he could spend the odd day with Florence and the children. On the way there and back again, he confessed, 'I think that I have had nearly every type of experience.'

The Japanese searched his shoes to check whether he was carrying secret letters in them. One soldier tried to filch his compass. Liddell phlegmatically told him the instrument was of 'more value' to him and so the request was dropped. On another occasion a soldier came across his copy of the Chinese New Testament, a book Liddell said he 'constantly carried about with me'. Speaking to him in slow and broken English, the soldier managed an ungrammatical three-word question: 'Bible. You. Christian?' Given his Red Cross armband, his nationality and also the physical evidence of the Bible, the soldier already knew the reply Liddell would give him. After hearing it, he shook Liddell's hand and turned away to allow him through.

The scarcity of coal made it as precious as diamonds in Siaochang. Every lump of it the Japanese unearthed in village raids was appropriated for their own soldiers. Liddell volunteered to head to Tientsin and haul back 60 tons on a chugging black barge. No one else wanted to go because the prospect of being successful was dismissed as negligible and the chance of being clubbed or shot for the cargo was considered highly probable. 'People said it couldn't be done, which is always a good starting point,' he remembered. Navigation of the rivers had become even more difficult since his trip with the Chief. Dodging the bandits was necessary on every turn of those hazardous waters. And Liddell seemed to attract them the way a magnet attracts metal filings. The journeys there and back again proved tortuous. The Japanese held Liddell for thirty-six hours. The Chinese detained him too. On four occasions he was stopped and robbed, which whittled his finances to nothing but a few coins. On the return leg to Siaochang Liddell had to hastily organize a U-turn and sail back to Tientsin for more money. Until the Japanese became interested in his footwear, he had hidden cash in his shoe. But, as Edgar Allan Poe proved in his short story 'The Purloined Letter', the best hiding place is always in plain sight. Eventually Florence had one of those eureka moments that solved everything. She suggested that Liddell hollow out a baguette-shaped loaf of bread and wedge rolled-up notes inside it. She told him to make sure the bread protruded from his rucksack. She argued two things: no one would ever split open a loaf of bread to check it had been baked through; and something so obviously in front of the Japanese soldiers' eyes would never arouse suspicion. She was right. 'He didn't have a problem after that,' said Florence.

That war is a pollutant on character was reaffirmed for Eric Liddell when he went to tend to one of the casualties of it. What he saw always stayed with him. What he did in response to it required cold courage. No medal – though he unquestionably deserved that recognition – was awarded to him afterwards. Liddell played things down, believing he'd done nothing more than react compassionately to a chance situation. If the London Missionary Society hadn't been so fastidious about record-keeping, no one would have even heard about it. But, like everything significant that happened to him in Siaochang, Liddell was obliged to inform the LMS about it. His account was handwritten in blue-black ink, rather than typed, as though he'd hastily composed and posted it to London on the move. The story Liddell told is essentially broken into two parts and demonstrates how perilous the countryside had become; how ferociously malign the Japanese soldiers were; how imperturbable Liddell was under fire; and, finally, how lucky he needed to be to avoid detection and punishment.

At the beginning of 1939, Liddell was travelling back from Tientsin to Siaochang. On the way he heard of a man, shot and wounded, who had lain for five days on a thin mattress in a derelict temple 20 miles from the mission compound. Liddell said it was 'a filthy place open to the wind and dust' which 'no one ever cleaned'. There was no heating, and the nightly temperatures there fell to freezing point. None of the locals who owned big-wheeled wooden mule carts had dared ferry the man to a hospital because he belonged to the military. The prospect of meeting a Japanese soldier scared them too much. Such an encounter would have meant death for the man, and torture before death for them. Liddell finally managed to persuade one carter to break ranks. The carter attached a proviso to the agreement. He wouldn't go alone: Liddell would have to accompany him. Typically Liddell said it was 'quite dangerous' for the carter rather than for himself, which was patent nonsense. If either had been caught, the Japanese wouldn't have discriminated between them.

Their small train set off. The carter led the way and Liddell cycled after him. After a few miles Liddell overtook the cart and went on ahead to the village where the temple was located specifically to 'see the Headman . . . and make arrangements' to transport his patient. Liddell discovered that the nervous villagers wanted the wounded man gone as soon as possible. No one would take him in, though one friend went daily to feed him. As Liddell explained: 'If the Japanese descended on them and found that a home had anything to do with the military, it would be destroyed at once and the lives of those in it would be in danger.' He was told that the nearest Japanese troops – plus a tank and ten motor lorries – were stationed less than a mile from them.

Liddell went into the temple, marvelling that the man had survived the bitter nights. He told him to hang on; the cart would be there at dawn. Wrapped in his sheepskin coat, Liddell settled down to sleep, his mind turning over the practicalities to come. He remembered asking himself: 'Suppose I met the Japanese? What would I say?' Liddell reached for his Bible, which he said 'fell open at Luke 16'. He read verse ten – 'he that is faithful in that which is least is faithful also in much; and he that is unjust in the least is unjust also in much'. Those lines, he said, 'seemed to me to bring me my answer'. From them Liddell drew this meaning: 'Be honest and straight'.

The Japanese were closing in. Next morning he and the cart went through one village as soldiers in vehicles simultaneously went around it. 'We fortunately missed each other,' said Liddell. The roads were difficult because deep tracks and pot-holes had been worn into them. Some of these were 'like enlarged trenches' according to Liddell. At one point a wheel slipped into a trench and the cart swayed and creaked before over-turning. Liddell and the carter righted it again and then made a rest-stop at another temple.

Their cart and its passenger rolled in as the old Chinese year was rolling out, the new one about to be born. During the celebrations for it Liddell learned of another victim of the war – a second 'wounded man whom we could pick up by going out of our way a short distance', he said.

Behind that bland sentence was a tragedy far more grotesque than the first.

The Japanese had rounded up a gang of six men who were supposedly members of the underground resistance. There was no evidence against them, and no trial for them. An officer yelled charges; he was judge, prosecutor and jury, and his verdict was execution. The Japanese soldiers ordered the men to kneel in front of them. Five did so, and were swiftly beheaded with a sword. The sixth refused to kneel and remained standing. Instead of forcing him to the ground, he and the officer stood eye to eye. The officer then drew back his blade, still bloody from the previous murders, and slashed at him twice. The man dropped into the dust. Assuming he was dead, the Japanese marched away, leaving the villagers to bury his corpse and the others' too. But the swing of the sword had delivered neither a clean nor a fatal blow to him. The blade left instead an angled and horribly deep gash stretching from the left to the right ear. After regaining consciousness, the man began to moan and whimper. The villagers, still convinced he would die through loss of blood, hid him behind an idol in the temple before carrying him to a bed in a dark shack. Dirty rags, wrapped around his neck and face, were used as makeshift bandages.

When Liddell and the cart arrived, the man had already been there for several days. Liddell promised to take him to the hospital at Siaochang. 'I could not guarantee his safety,' he said. 'If we met the Japanese, he would have to take his chance.' Liddell also explained that the cart 'was only a small one', constructed for one person. So the man agreed to be placed in its shafts. The cart trundled on for another 18 miles, the weight of the two passengers slowing its progress through the narrow, jarring pathways, which Liddell chose to avoid the regular routes. At the outset Liddell stared skyward and saw a Japanese aeroplane, which he said was 'circling round slightly south of us'. He was all too aware of what its presence meant: 'Japanese troops were moving almost parallel to us a mile or two away.' The odds of avoiding them, as well as the other patrols, were unfavourably long. Liddell, constantly expecting to be apprehended, could only have pleaded for mercy, which the Japanese were unlikely to grant him. He'd be considered as the enemy's friend. The Siaochang hospital was strictly humanitarian. War didn't taint the Hippocratic oath, and the doctors there didn't take sides on the operating table. Chinese and Japanese combatants, as well as rebels and guerrilla fighters, were treated alike. Impartiality and medical ethics was only one of two hopeful cards Liddell could have played in his defence. Another was to claim that he'd found both men on the roadside and considered them to be innocents caught in the fighting.

Miraculously, Liddell didn't have to reach for any excuse or explanation. The carter and his cart, Liddell and his bicycle and the victims of the war arrived safely, without encountering a solitary soldier on the way. That outcome seemed both outrageously freakish and fantastically mysterious to those who heard about it afterwards and knew, first-hand, the difficulty of travelling half a country mile in Siaochang without stumbling into the Japanese.

The first man died two days later. The second lived, his face for ever scarred. He was a stout character and what saved him was his unusually thick, muscled neck. Not only the compassion Liddell had shown him, but also the fact that he'd agreed unhesitatingly to go across terrain as perilous as a minefield on his behalf, turned the survivor into a Christian. Pretending he'd only been a distant observer, rather than the protagonist, Liddell used the man's conversion as an inspiration during subsequent sermons he gave for the LMS.

If only the Society had done as much for him as he consistently did for it.

Apart from a few days eked out in Tientsin, plus a holiday in Peitaiho, Eric Liddell had barely seen Florence, Patricia or Heather for more than eighteen months because his obsessive sense of duty made him an absent husband and father. 'It was hard for him,' said Annie Buchan, who saw the agony Liddell went through because of that separation. Once he'd settled into Siaochang, Liddell had again pressed the LMS to allow Florence and the children to move to Siaochang. The Society, initially more sympathetic towards his situation, first said yes and then said no for the second time. The organization's general secretary was travelling on a train with Liddell when a segment of blown-up track forced the carriages to an abrupt halt. It unnerved him. Afterwards he decided unilaterally that the rural areas still weren't 'safe' for Florence. There was no opportunity to make a third application.

Bad timing dogged the family now. With Europe sliding into war, Liddell was due his second furlough, the outline sketch of which he'd already drawn. The family intended to sail to Canada, spending a month in Toronto. The next stop was Scotland. D. P. Thomson had arranged numerous personal appearances and speaking engagements for him.

Liddell's mother was waiting to see the grandchildren, who to date had been no more than framed photographs on the mantelpiece to her. Rob Liddell, who had come home eight months earlier, was waiting there too. With his son still requiring specialist treatment for his spinal condition, he was forever turning over a question in his mind: should he go back to China at all?

Hitler rearranged Liddell's itinerary. The sequence towards the Second World War – the occupation of Czechoslovakia, Germany's Pact of Steel with Italy, the invasion of Poland – is so well known as to require no elaboration. But, as Liddell weighed up which move to make, he saw each flashpoint in isolation. What is historical record to us was daily experience to him. There was no chance to appraise it objectively because no one could foresee the next event or know exactly how it would precipitate another. Like everyone else fed on this daily diet of bad news, Liddell hoped beyond hope that what he feared would be avoided through rational negotiation.

When Neville Chamberlain arrived back from Munich, he'd looked like an Edwardian butler smugly announcing that his employer had guaranteed him an improvement in below-stairs conditions. When he gathered the country in front of the wireless to hear him declare war on Germany, he sounded like an undertaker explaining the procedure for a state funeral. By then the Liddells were in Toronto.

Liddell sent an air-mail letter to the London Missionary Society. His suggestion was sensible and logical: he should take his furlough in Canada because German U-boats had turned the Atlantic into a shooting gallery for ships. Only eleven hours after Chamberlain's broadcast, the 14,000-ton liner SS *Athenia* was torpedoed and sunk 250 miles off the north-west coast of Ireland, killing 117 passengers and crew. It was carrying no bullion, no guns, no munitions of war. Winston Churchill, then First Lord of the Admiralty, ordered armed convoys to operate along the route. Liddell still thought it 'most unwise' to travel. The reply was glib and insensitive. Always impecunious, the LMS rattled on about 'maintaining the Society's income', which was a sideways nod to Liddell's abilities as a fund-raiser. The man Liddell had saved in the cart was an artist. Liddell had procured paints and paper for him during his convalescence and got in return a watercolour of a peony rose. Hundreds of lithographs were made of the picture and Liddell planned to sell them in Scotland at a shilling each for the LMS. But why couldn't he sell them in Canada instead?

The answer the LMS gave is essentially summed up in the thirty-eight words that concluded its letter: 'We shall have to leave the final decision with you, but we are anxious on the one hand to have you in England and, on the other, to avoid unnecessary risk of travel to your wife and family.'

The sentiment the LMS expresses in the second half of the sentence contradicts that expressed in the first. If genuinely wanting to 'avoid unnecessary risk' – and, pointedly, Liddell himself isn't mentioned in relation to it – the LMS ought to have unequivocally told him to stay in Canada. Or at least the organization could have made it clear that remaining there was perfectly understandable in the circumstances and didn't reflect poorly on him. But concern for themselves overrode concern for their loyal missionary. The opening, 'we shall have to leave the final decision with you', reads like the weary gasp of a parent towards a child who is being a bit awkward. The next part, 'but we are anxious . . . to have you in England', is a blatant appeal to his conscience and his weighty sense of obligation. This was a craven and manipulative response from the LMS, which was too afraid to say outright what it really wanted – presumably on the basis that it could rinse its hands of responsibility if things went wrong. Instead it gently implied, as if to cultivate some guilt within Liddell, that he would be letting the team down. It was shameful anyway that the LMS didn't contact Liddell before he contacted them. As it turned out, the letter took so long to reach Canada that he was forced to make his decision before receiving it. Liddell felt there was no option but to go alone to Scotland, breaking up the family again, because he couldn't endanger Florence and the children.

Liddell reached Edinburgh in November 1939. Thomson found him 'different in many ways from the man we had farewelled some seven years before'. Once, while swimming in Peitaiho, another missionary had slapped him across the top of his balding head: Liddell was breaking the waves and his colleague mistook his glistening pate for the domed body of a stinging jellyfish. He looked noticeably older to Thomson because of that baldness. Liddell was also 'more serious' in his approach, added Thomson, who wasn't privy yet to the scale of the traumas he'd either witnessed or endured in Siaochang.

For the next nine and a half months Liddell did what he could in a country clothed in khaki, amid black-outs, gas masks, the fear of bombings, the introduction of rationing and other hardships. The posters implored the population to Make Do and Mend and Dig for Victory. Liddell's youngest brother Ernest had gone into banking. The prospect of becoming a missionary had never interested him. Now twenty-seven, he volunteered for the army. Liddell himself tried to enlist in the Royal Air Force – despite never having flown in a plane – as a member of the flight crew. At thirty-seven he was deemed to be too old for service. The RAF, thinking of Liddell as a motivational figure, offered him a uniform and a desk instead, which he declined. He could inspire as easily from a pulpit in his suit and tie.

'Deputation work in war-time was a very different thing from what it had been,' said Thomson. The swarming rallies could not be replicated. The men attracted to them had signed up as soldiers. The women had gone into the factories to replace them. The black-outs had curtailed night-time assemblies in the winter. A further three Olympics had also come and gone since Liddell's gold in Paris. Thomson nonetheless saw no slackening off in the interest surrounding him. 'Everyone still wanted to shake his hand,' he said. Liddell lectured on China, principally because the war in Europe had made the conflict there seem more irrelevant than ever to his audience and he wanted to remind them of it. He was convinced the missionaries were within sight of a 'breakthrough' in Siaochang. 'At no time have we had such a great opportunity as we have now. Every home is open to us. The people feel as though we are working with them and they will listen to our message everywhere,' he said in a speech.

In the spring of 1940, Liddell gave in to an appeal from Florence. The Atlantic had become a little less volatile. The armed convoys had shielded passenger ships. The Royal Navy and the German U-boats had been shadow-boxing each other. So the family sailed from Canada at last. Florence and her daughters were among only 147 passengers on a White Star liner capable of carrying more than two thousand. The serene furlough the Liddells had originally imagined in Scotland began belatedly and would be fleeting – a mere 140 days.

The zenith of it was almost a month at Carcant, a spread of 600 acres 20 miles south of Edinburgh on the Scottish borders. It belonged to Liddell's brother-in-law; Jenny had become Mrs Charles Somerville eight years earlier.

One translation of the name Carcant is 'a collar of jewels', which is how it appeared to the Liddells that summer when the Meteorological

Office reported 'abundant sunshine'. Scotland got sunburned, tanning itself in its hottest June for over eighty years. The highest recorded temperature was 89 degrees. Carcant was a countryside version of Peitaiho, an idyll concealed within the wider world. Instead of sand there was grass and parched heath and drystone walls. Instead of the sea there was the shallow lochan, the shape of it not unlike a shakily drawn map of Wales. Instead of the flatlands beyond there were the Moorfoot Hills, which changed colour as the seasons changed – from purple-blue to livid bronze and then lush, variegated greens. Apart from the sheep and rabbits and cattle, plus a scattering of small farms with corkscrew rises of smoke, the Liddells had Carcant almost to themselves. It was one of those places where the sky seemed bigger and all-enveloping. Their low bungalow was built from dark wood slats and had white-framed windows, which were shrouded in net curtains. There was a stone chimney, a coal fire, a big green copper bath. Rhododendrons dressed the veranda. There was an unbroken, shut-in hush about Carcant that made it difficult to believe that the curvature of the Earth was hiding two wars, which all too soon would melt into one. You could collect milk in metal pitchers, fresh from the dairy farmers. You could bathe in the lochan. You could drink cold spring water. If you were a child, you could behave like Enid Blyton's Famous Five, everything an adventure.

It seemed then as if summer would never come to a full stop.

Rob Liddell decided not to go back to China; his family needed him too much. His brother, however, was already committed to returning. At the end of one sermon he'd promised an Edinburgh congregation, 'We're going back and we'll stay as long as we are able.'

In early August 1940 the Liddells sailed from Liverpool, their ship one in a convoy of fifty-five split into five lines. It included other passenger boats, Royal Navy warships, merchant vessels and minesweepers. From the deck, Liddell called it a 'delightful sight'.

The convoy was barely clear of the Irish coast when, at 8.30 p.m., he heard the thud of something against the hull and then felt the ship shake. The family's leather trunk shot across the floor as the cabin listed and vibrated. A torpedo had hit them without detonating, the ship and its three hundred passengers unscathed. Liddell had three theories: 'Whether it was a dud, and only the cap exploded, or whether it had expended its energy, having been fired from too great a distance, or had exploded right below us, we are not sure.' Liddell, Florence and the children grabbed huge ring lifebelts and headed for the deck. The ship immediately began a defensive zigzag. 'We were running for our lives,' said Florence.

For the next two days, rolling on choppy seas, the convoy found itself under attack again. One of the ships at the rear was sunk and a small boat a quarter of a mile from the Liddells' own vanished from sight within two minutes of being blown up. Hearing the mighty boom of the explosion, Liddell was certain the 'engine boiler' had taken a direct hit. The passengers on Liddell's ship came on deck, half expecting to see the next torpedo cutting through the waters towards them. When nothing happened, the all-clear was sounded around noon and everyone was told to file in for lunch. Mid-way through the first course the alarm clanged again. A third ship had been hit. In the early evening a fourth and then a fifth were torpedoed too. By 9 p.m. the Royal Navy was locked in a fight with a German submarine that had risen to the surface. 'All night people slept in their clothes with lifebelts ready,' said Liddell, who added that ignorance of what was happening meant his daughters 'weren't scared at all' – a contrast to the adults around them.

Running at full speed – 'far above its average', said Liddell – the ship pulled itself out of range of the ordinary subs. 'Only an ocean-going one could come so far, and there were few of those,' Liddell explained. That Sunday he was asked to perform a service of thanksgiving in the first-class lounge. 'I only had my sports coat and flannels,' he said, as if sartorial elegance had suddenly become de rigueur in the middle of an ocean-going wartime convoy.

One theatre of war disappeared behind him. The one in front of him, however, had worsened considerably during his furlough. Approximately a million Japanese soldiers were now occupying China – fanned along the coast, the railway lines, and holding strategic positions in the centre of the country. While outnumbered man to man, the Japanese had superior communications, which was proving crucial. The Chinese were also pinned down because of unsuitable roads, insufficient troop transport and a lack of both general and military supplies. A mass of soldiers had to dig in around each vulnerable area to counter the swifter-moving Japanese divisions. The Japanese were muscling aside the opposition. Between May and September 1940 the Japanese dropped almost thirty thousand bombs on Nationalist-held cities. And, just as Liddell embarked for China, the Communist Eighth Army launched the Hundred Regiments

Tom McKerchar, a father of thirteen, with his family in Edinburgh. The boy in his lap is named Eric, after the Olympic champion.

Offensive, losing twenty-two thousand men in the fighting to Japan's three thousand.

Liddell was also coping with a piece of sad personal news, which awaited him in Toronto, the mid-point of his travels. His coach, Tom McKerchar, had died of a stroke, aged sixty-three. He'd been admitted to Edinburgh's Royal Infirmary on the very day the Liddells left the dockside at Liverpool. His death came less than twenty-four hours later. The paid advertisement announcing it in the *Edinburgh Evening News* made no mention of Liddell and the Olympics or even of McKerchar's career as a coach. When Liddell heard of his passing, McKerchar's cremation was over. The mourners present had been asked not to bring flowers.

It was late autumn when Eric Liddell saw the Siaochang mission and the hospital again. He described it as a 'garrisoned village'. The Japanese had poured across the area and were now more conspicuous than ever. Liddell was thankful that Florence and the children were in Tientsin, where he could see them during forays for supplies. He tried to continue as before and put the bravest of faces on his circumstances. He pedalled into the countryside, took services and tried to re-engage with communities, which had become fractured and tense. 'When I am out it is giving, giving all the time,' he wrote. He said this was his attempt to 'leave a message of encouragement and peace in a time when there is no external peace at all'.

Liddell felt powerless. Land was being 'ruthlessly' requisitioned without compensation by the Japanese, he said. Ancient burial mounds and graves were wantonly desecrated; soldiers drove or marched across them. The persecution Liddell had previously witnessed had escalated. The Japanese no longer made attempts to conceal it or to blame someone else for such aggression. The locals were simply ordered to hand over their possessions, their food and their livestock; those who refused were shot or beaten or, like the artist Liddell had rescued, given the sharp edge of an officer's sword. Men were commandeered for manual labour: digging trenches, making roads, building walls, and fetching and lifting for the Japanese. 'Watching them work makes you think of the old Roman press gangs,' said Liddell, his gloom and dismay detectable. He said the soldiers were stirring an 'increasing hatred and rebellious spirit'. The locals were defenceless against each humiliation.

There was a solitary spot of colour for Liddell. He presided at a wedding on a chilly, windy day. The bride was carried into the church on a sedan chair. She and it were traditionally dressed in red. The bridegroom wore a trace of red too, a sash looped around his waist and shoulder. 'Everyone loves a wedding,' said Liddell, so pleased to be there. The occasion, however, didn't stop a prolonged exchange of fire afterwards between the Japanese and the Communists. That evening, during the bridal feast, heavy gunfire was also heard only a mile away. The following day the Japanese shot twice at Liddell, who presumed the soldiers had mistaken him for a member of the Eighth Army on a bicycle.

The unequal struggle between the missionaries and the troops lasted so long only because the Japanese allowed it. But no one believed – least of all Liddell – that the Siaochang compound would remain intact indefinitely. Something was always going to give, particularly when another war was tearing up Europe and North Africa. Winston Churchill once dismissed China as a country of 'four hundred million pigtails'. So what happened in an obscure missionary station planted in an equally obscure region of it was unlikely to divert his attention; certainly not when London was under a nightly blitz from German bombs. The Japanese could commit any crime, knowing its disclosure would be low on the British government's agenda.

The missionaries were working under the eye of the clock, and time ran out for them early in 1941. Already there'd been rumours that deportation or internment was imminent. The Japanese then posted an unsubtle warning. Soldiers arrested the Chinese headmaster of the mission school and a handful of his staff. The allegation against them was anti-Japanese teaching. Even Liddell realized the position in Siaochang was untenable now. If the missionaries didn't go of their own accord, the Japanese would turn on them next. The sequence of events wasn't difficult to predict: false charges, questioning, harassment and imprisonment.

The compound closed on a cold morning in mid-February 1941, and the missionaries headed for Tientsin. The Japanese made an inventory of each piece of furniture and equipment, which was claimed as reparations for the inconvenience the missionaries had caused them. Annie Buchan said the soldiers 'didn't allow' her or anyone else to take 'anything' with them. She spoke of the 'awful feeling of emptiness, frustration' after being 'stripped of everything, most of all the work which was so dear to us'. Much later the mission was 'completely destroyed', said Buchan, 'with every brick and every piece of wood or iron scattered'. After the missionaries left, the headmaster and his teachers were released.

One forced retreat was always going to lead to another, and then another, until there was no ground left on which the missionaries could safely operate. The Japanese had made that much obvious. The London Missionary Society's decision-makers, still wearing blinkers, bafflingly announced that the situation didn't warrant 'any general withdrawal'. In Tientsin, however, Buchan saw another example of vindictiveness. Five months earlier the Japanese had signed the Tripartite Pact, which allied them formally with Germany and Italy. Pockets of anti-Semitism, though not common, emerged simply to satisfy the Germans, who encouraged them. Buchan witnessed the rounding up of several hundred Jews. Their passports were 'thrown into the waste baskets', she said. 'The Jews knew what that meant. They belonged to nowhere. Some turned away with wild weeping and wailing. Others stood with grey, ashen faces glued to the spot with a dumb fear gripping their heart.'

The LMS gave new assignments to the missionaries. Liddell was put back into the field, where he understood what his employers did not.

Soon Tientsin, a bomb waiting to go off, would be no safer than Siaochang. The missionaries would eventually be pushed out of there too – deported at best, imprisoned at worst.

And then Florence let slip her secret to him. She was pregnant again. Their baby was due in September.

Part Three

Stronger

CHAPTER THIRTEEN

The Man Who Isn't There

Eric Liddell had become a specialist in saying goodbye at the boat dock or the railway station, which can be such maudlin places for the leaving and left-behind alike. These farewells had been the theme of his life, beginning in boyhood. So had the routine and the rituals attached to them: the embrace, the kiss, the forced smile, the stock phrases of solace.

Nothing, though, had prepared him for this. For a fraught month Liddell and Florence debated whether or not she should take the children back to Canada. From the start, the parameters of the question were so narrow as to make the answer straightforward. Only that thing called love complicated it.

China was too volatile for Florence to give birth there. Liddell's contract with the London Missionary Society nonetheless bound him implacably to it. His conscience wouldn't allow him to sever that tie. However much heartache it brought to those he most cherished, Liddell had to remain in Tientsin. Always referring to the Chinese as 'my people', he declared he'd neither desert them nor renege on his obligation to his demanding employers. Liddell didn't need to make this clear to Florence. She knew duty came first for him; that, after all, was the sort of man she'd chosen to marry.

Whenever you don't want to face the obvious, you tend to put off seeing it. Whenever the head is in conflict with the heart, you pretend the head will eventually surrender to the heart's will. And whenever you're reluctant to make a decision, you cling to the fanciful hope that something – *anything*, in fact – will resolve your problem before you cave in to the inevitable. So it proved for the Liddells.

During the first months of 1941, the fighting in Europe was spreading apace into North Africa. The Luftwaffe was still bombing London. The German infantry tore into Greece and Yugoslavia. The war's rate of expansion made it unlikely that Asia could escape the conflict. 'It was like sitting on the edge of a volcano,' said Florence. Already the Japanese had secretly dispatched a spy to take notes about that spot on the map called Pearl Harbor. As well as the Allies' pursuit of Hitler, the draught of which would soon blow his way, Liddell became more preoccupied than ever with the conflict swirling around him, including the role of the mercenary bandits who were everywhere, like scavenging dogs. He grew increasingly afraid that he or his family, especially now with a baby on the way, would be kidnapped as other Westerners had been, forcing him into an untenable position.

The most rational and practical of men still equivocated about sending Florence home to Toronto; and Florence, also aware of what needed to be done, equivocated too. The thought of being separated from him again was agony for her. The couple had been apart from each other for more than half of their marriage, which was now in its eighth year. Those absences had been filled with letter-writing, a correspondence amounting to gallons of ink and forests of stacked paper. But the Liddells wanted more than love slipped into an envelope.

The LMS was maddeningly inept, insisting that neither the war nor the prospect of the Japanese entering it warranted a retreat from China. The aim, it said, was to work on until 'conditions render this impossible'. The LMS's lack of worldly awareness, plus its inability to understand China, suggested an organization possessing only the vaguest acquaintance with reality. Given the hazards, the LMS should have released Liddell and the other missionaries, allowing them to kick their heels clean of the country before escape became impossible. There was no gain in occupying areas where Japanese interference effectively made it an act of tokenism to stay.

The Liddells sorted through each option, which was a prolonged misery because the process was circuitous, always dragging them back to the depressing point where the discussion had begun. Protecting Patricia, Heather and the unborn child was paramount. Finally the Liddells accepted that splitting up the family was the sole way of guaranteeing its safety. 'I wouldn't have gone if it wasn't for the children,' Florence stated.

Liddell tried reassuring her that one of two outcomes was likely. Soon stability would return to China, allowing them to be reunited. Or, if the situation deteriorated irrevocably, the LMS would arrange his evacuation. Liddell told her about another of his ambitions. In the future he was sure awaited them together, he was planning to work with the tribes of native North Americans and Canada's First Nations people. Even seen at its brightest – Liddell attempting to make the best of his own and also Florence's sadness – his sunny optimism is the classic example of whistling through a thunderstorm. There was no possibility of peace between the Chinese and the Japanese. The hatred between them was entrenched. The top brass of the LMS had a wonky antenna for danger and were incompetent about responding to it even when the signal reaching them was strong and unambiguous.

Liddell's first decision was strategically shrewd. He booked a cabin for the family on the 17,163-ton *Nitta Maru*, a 560-foot-long fledgling ocean liner with a single black funnel and an impressive sweep of glass, which allowed light to pour into its upper decks. The ship had made its maiden voyage only two months before. The key piece of equipment on the *Nitta Maru* was the Japanese flag, guaranteeing its neutrality in the Atlantic. No submarine was going to take a pot shot at it. 'Some of our friends still thought we were asking for trouble,' remembered Florence.

Whatever the Liddells said, each striving to convince the other that a reunion wouldn't be far off, the couple packed as though the opposite were true. The show-cabinet, where Liddell had displayed his athletics prizes, was more than half-emptied. Florence re-boxed his Olympic gold and bronze medals and put them in a trunk – a move that didn't suggest confidence in Tientsin's long-term security.

The *Nitta Maru* was docked in Kobe and the family sailed to Japan across the Yellow Sea to meet it. The girls, Patricia and Heather, retain small fragments of memory of those clear May days: Liddell dressed in a uniform of white – short-sleeved shirt, long shorts and high socks, which were folded evenly below the knee; the grey bulk of the harboured *Nitta Maru*; their father boarding it to settle them and then embarking on an exploratory tour of the decks; their labelled luggage stacked in the cabin.

Words in such circumstances offer nothing more than palliative care. Nothing Liddell said to Florence could make either of them feel less wretched. Every reassurance sounded like a platitude, useless and uttered to fill a silence. Instead Liddell lifted Patricia on to his lap, gazed at her with berry-bright eyes and said, 'I want you to be a good girl. I want you to look after your mother. I want you to look after this new baby. I want you to promise you'll do that.' Nearly six months pregnant, Florence bowed her head, unable to choke back tears that were unstoppable now. She sobbed as quietly as she could. Liddell had staunched his emotions, telling his daughters that he'd see them again before either had missed him. But, when the moment came to part, he did something that betrayed his distraught state. He kissed his children and his wife and then left without lingering. He walked briskly down the gangway of the *Nitta Maru*, never giving it a backward glance; or at least none that his children could recall. He did not wave from the quayside. It was as though he couldn't bear to see the ship break away from him. 'We can't imagine the turmoil he must have been in,' said Patricia. 'At least my mother had us. He went back to Tientsin alone.'

On board, watching the dock recede from her, Florence was resolute for the sake of her daughters. 'I had to snap out of it,' she said of her sadness. 'I couldn't sit and only think about myself.' Before long the white-capped tip of Mount Fuji was glimpsed through a porthole. The angle of the setting sun through the glass splashed the snow in a rainbow of reds and greens as bright as the colours from a paint-box.

Florence never saw these shores again.

The telegram arrived in mid-September. Eric Liddell learned he had a third daughter, the baby christened Maureen. He cabled back immediately with two words and an exclamation mark: 'Wonderful news!'

He was living in a flat with A. P. Cullen, his friend and former tutor. Cullen's presence compensated for the loss of another sympathetic voice in Liddell's life. The Japanese had given Annie Buchan special dispensation to move to Peking, where she began caring for a sick friend.

Faraway incarceration precipitates a pining for home. Cullen liked to listen to the BBC from Shanghai because it played a patriotically rousing recording of Vera Lynn singing 'There'll Always Be An England'. He pictured country lanes and cricket matches, church spires and thatched cottages. The war blazed on through the broadcasts, the BBC reporting what government censors regarded as permissible. The accounts Liddell heard didn't suggest that either a swift end or a negotiated peace was possible. Winston Churchill had already warned of the impasse, using the emphatic rhetoric of the warrior-politician who understood that attempting to find compromises with a dictator was to scatter bad seed in lunatic handfuls. In mid-June Germany invaded the Soviet Union. As summer faded into autumn, the Siege of Leningrad began. In Germany the Jews were ordered to wear the Star of David. In America Franklin D. Roosevelt, responding after a U-boat fired on a US warship, instructed the navy to blast back if another ship was similarly threatened. But the isolationists and the interventionists remained as implacably opposed as ever there.

And in China, as Liddell learned of the arrival of his baby, 120,000 Japanese troops strode towards Changsha, also taking the heavy support of a hundred planes, twenty ships and two hundred motorboats in another attempt to wrest decisive control. Unable to match that firepower, the Chinese managed to beat them off with artful strategy. The Japanese undermined the missionaries, making the task of calling on the villages that ringed Tientsin as haphazard and onerous as it had been in Siaochang. There was no structure or timetable to Liddell's work because his travel plans could be disrupted on the say of a sentry who had woken up feeling cantankerous that morning. Only occasionally, after much bowing and the laborious presentation of his documents, did the soldiers allow Liddell to cycle to the distant farms. The lack of contribution he and other missionaries were able to make illustrated again how misguided the London Missionary Society had been in tethering them to Tientsin. Liddell would have been far more use to the LMS in Toronto or even in bombed-out London.

Then dawn rose on Sunday, 7 December, the date that changed the shape of everything.

The Associated Press announced the raid on Pearl Harbor at 2.22 p.m. Eastern Standard Time. Within minutes of ripping the bulletin off the wire national and local radio stations were cutting into live drama serials and documentaries, sports programmes and talk shows for one of those sombre, urgent announcements which back then were made only when a tragedy of genuine magnitude had occurred. This tragedy was still occurring, which is why nothing could be confirmed apart from the plain fact of the attack. The port was alight and the oil-black smoke from partly gutted or sinking ships obscured the detail of the losses and the number of dead. Early on neither could even be guessed at. Hearing breaking news can be a numbing and a chaotic experience, the repercussions initially hard to take in. But, as the reports were absorbed and the scale of the assault on the US Pacific Fleet became known, no one doubted what it meant for America; or how it would wash tidally into the war. Pearl Harbor would have been a day of infamy even if Roosevelt had not described it as such. Almost two hundred American planes were destroyed and eighteen vessels, including eight warships, were blown apart or damaged. The death toll, including the Japanese, was more than 2,500; a further 1,178 were wounded. The Pennsylvania-class *Arizona* was struck four times, killing 1,177 of the 1,400 officers and crew on board. *Time* regarded the raid as 'premeditated murder with a toothy smile' and the announcement of America's eventual entrance into the conflict – Germany declared war on the US after Roosevelt declared war on Japan – as 'a great relief'. The magazine likened the repercussions to 'a reverse earthquake', maintaining that 'One terrible jerk shook everything disjointed, distorted, askew back into place . . . Japanese bombs had finally brought national unity to the U.S.'

Roosevelt was lunching at the White House when reports of the carnage first reached him. Winston Churchill was at Chequers, dining with the American ambassador. During a telephone call, Roosevelt told his ally, 'We are all in the same boat now,' which was an insensitive metaphor to use in the circumstances. However maladroit the phrase, someone else was thinking of it too. After hearing of Pearl Harbor, Chiang Kai-shek put a gramophone record on the turntable. The record was 'Ave Maria'. He played it as a celebration, relieved that his enemy now had other enemies who would become his friends.

It was as though a shutter had slammed in Tientsin. Japanese reinforcements were wheeled into the city and uncoiled barbed wire to close off the foreign Concessions. A. P. Cullen saw Liddell's distress. Knowing now that there was no possibility of reaching Florence and his children, he 'just wandered the streets', said Cullen. Like everyone else, Liddell found himself under house arrest. Also like everyone else, he had to report for questioning. The Japanese wanted lists of valuables and hammered on doors to obtain them, taking whatever was deemed inappropriate for enemy aliens to possess. Cullen had to surrender his radio. There'd still always be an England for him, but from then on he could only sing along with Vera Lynn in his head. Had Florence not taken the Olympic gold medal the Japanese would have seized that too and melted it down.

Liddell was given a scarlet armband to denote his British nationality. He and Cullen were split up. Liddell was billeted with a family belonging to the Methodist Mission. Other restrictions were so prohibitively harsh that he found himself among the unemployed. He couldn't teach. He couldn't preach. Unless he was buying something in a shop or talking to a servant, he was forbidden to fraternize with the Chinese at all.

Pearl Harbor also denied Liddell the chance to see the face of his new daughter. It was the shallowest ripple from the aftermath of that attack, inconsequential to anyone but him and Florence.

In November she had arranged for a colour studio portrait to be taken of her and the girls. Patricia and Heather were scrubbed and put into their Sunday best, matching rose pink frocks with white Pilgrim collars. Florence, wearing an unfussy green dress with puff sleeves, sat between them. In her arms she held Maureen, wrapped in a christening shawl. The photograph is the sort every family had framed for the mantelpiece

The family without its father. A sombre Florence gathers together her children – (from left) Heather, Maureen and Patricia – for a picture she planned to send to Eric in 1941.

or to hang on the wall, a memento to mark a glad event. This one evokes absence rather than togetherness. To see it is like looking at a table with one place setting left unfilled. The group is sorrowfully incomplete. Florence doesn't even smile at the camera. It's as though she was caught thinking of her husband in the second the photographer's flash went off.

The plan to get the photograph to Liddell seemed infallible. Hugh MacKenzie, who had earlier returned to Canada, would courier it in his luggage. He'd decided to go back to Tientsin, ignoring the restrictions in the region, and had booked his passage on a ship leaving from San Francisco. A conjunction of two events meant he would never see China again. These were so implausible that a novelist would have thought twice about including them in a plot to avoid the charge of relying over-much on coincidence. Strolling along a foggy dock, MacKenzie was hit by a car. A few hours later, waking from unconsciousness, he was told his ship would not be sailing. MacKenzie had suffered his accident on the very day the Japanese bombed Pearl Harbor. He was one of the last people in America to learn of the atrocity.

To be shut in Tientsin was like being shipwrecked on a desert island. You could only hopefully await rescue and busy yourself in the meantime as a way of avoiding the effects of the isolation. The postal system in China was erratic. Like the castaway, you had almost more chance of getting a message in a bottle than a letter. And if a letter did arrive, the news it contained could be up to half a year old. Eric Liddell once got two in the same post from Florence. She received a bundle of five in one delivery from him.

Liddell managed to contact her through convoluted channels. He'd write to a friend in a part of China that wasn't under the heel of the Japanese. He'd ask for the letter to be forwarded to Canada. Clandestinely, through other contacts, he also ingeniously sent a few lines of correspondence through a radio relay. This began with the Chinese International Broadcasting Station. The next stop was a listening post in Los Angeles. The listening post then sent it on to Toronto's United Church Office. Florence, opening the message like a surprise package, got some reassurance. 'No need to worry,' wrote Liddell on behalf of himself and his colleagues. 'We are all in good spirits . . . You are constantly in my thoughts.'

A. P. Cullen became more supportive than ever of Liddell. Cullen said that 'almost every day' the two of them went on long walks. This closeness allowed him an exceptional insight into Liddell's thinking, much of which he spoke about freely to his friend. Cullen was subsequently able to talk about Liddell's religious beliefs more perceptively than anyone else.

The missionaries, though given licence to roam the Concessions, were forbidden to hold assemblies of more than ten people either indoors or out. Fortunately these orders, plus those given about preaching and teaching, couldn't always be enforced because the Japanese were under-manned. The missionaries continued to stage services and hold classes privately. There were also social gatherings in family homes, which became platforms for serious debates and lectures as well as a general trade of whatever scraps of news, reliable or otherwise, had filtered through the lines. On Sundays, when the soldiers were more vigilant about checking on the missionaries, the wives hosted afternoon tea-parties during which a sermon was read. Often Liddell wrote these, running sheets of paper through a mimeograph copier beforehand so each of the congregation could take one away.

Sermon writing was only a sliver of the self-improvement programme he devised. Liddell could have relaxed, backsliding into indolence, because the workload was whatever he chose to make it. There was no pressure to do more than the absolute minimum. He confessed as much to Florence in a letter: 'It would be easy to let this time go by with nothing done; nothing really constructive, and so have the days frittered away.' Liddell decided to treat his confinement as an opportunity to put himself through a second university education. He'd be his own tutor, reading and taking notes extensively. 'Persistent study' is how Cullen described the next fourteen months for Liddell. Cullen said that 'conscientious thoroughness' was 'manifested in all his work, his undertakings and his manifold interests and pursuits'.

Liddell was always scribbling on pads and loose paper on which he put down thoughts and ideas or short quotations that inspired him. His advice to everyone was 'Take a pen and pencil and write down what comes to you.' Liddell was widening his knowledge of theology and com-mitting to memory those few books of the Bible he couldn't already quote whole. He did so slowly. 'Don't read hurriedly,' he said. 'Every word is pre-cious. Pause, assimilate.' Liddell compiled an anthology of prayers, which was bound in smart navy boards. The prayers he chose and painstakingly typed out with two fingers, the borrowed machine perched on a tiny table, were printed on pitifully thin paper. The fledgling author produced another compendium called *Discipleship*, a collection of various readings arranged monthly over the calendar year. Later the title became *The Disciplines of the Christian Life*. 'If it never comes to anything it will have been useful for my own thinking,' he said.

Liddell considered *Discipleship* to be a 'companion booklet' to his daily prayers and took no credit for the contents, claiming he'd merely plucked out quotations for it from some of his favourite devotional books. Cullen disagreed, saying 'much of it is actually his own', and thought Liddell's 'personality and character breathe from every page'. The sight of these books confirmed something for Cullen. He believed Liddell's progress since arriving in China could be legitimately compared to the races he ran to become Olympic champion. As a runner Liddell was 'always a bit slow in getting off the mark', he explained, perfectly serious in the analogy he was about to make. In the same way, he continued, Liddell had been slow to make an impression as a prospective missionary. Indeed Cullen thought there was 'nothing remarkable' about his initial strides to become one. He was adamant that Liddell had established himself only as his 'momentum . . . steadily increased'. The assessment was accurate. Liddell admitted as much in *Discipleship*, writing that 'careful attention and repetition' should be 'the method' used in both learning 'any new subject' and also becoming 'proficient in any game'. Just as he'd trained himself to become a runner, gradually in the beginning and then with a ferocious intensity of purpose, so he'd trained himself to become a missionary too. 'The Christian life should be a life of growth. I believe the secret of growth is to develop the devotional life,' he said.

Cullen observed close up that such a devotional life meant Liddell was 'completely dedicated to the service of God and man'. He put it as plainly as possible. It was 'absolute surrender to the will of God'. Cullen had heard Liddell say 'absolute surrender' so frequently that he claimed categorically: 'The conception was always in his mind . . . God should have absolute control over every part of his life.' Liddell was emphatic about it: 'Every Christian should live a God-guided life. If you are not guided by God, you will be guided by something else.' He even outlined how he made this happen. 'If, in the quiet of your heart, you feel something should be done, stop and consider whether it is in line with the character and teaching of Jesus. If so, obey that impulse to do it, and in doing so you will find it was God guiding you.' For him, 'obedience' was always 'the secret' of that guidance.

Liddell took inspiration from diverse sources, such as Aristotle, who he said had kept 'the passion of resentment under control', and also the African-American educator Booker T. Washington, who eschewed confrontation even when he was vilely heckled for being black. Liddell cited one instance of it in *Discipleship*. An incredulous companion, who saw Washington treat his racial abusers with politeness, asked, 'Why raise your hat when they slight you?' Washington replied, 'Why should I stoop to be less than a gentleman because others do?' Liddell treated the Japanese in the same way.

The Sermon on the Mount remained the keystone of his faith. Liddell argued that each passage of it required reading 'over and over again'. He confessed how intimidating the Sermon had originally appeared. The strictures it laid down had seemed unachievable to him. 'The first time you read it you feel that it is impossible,' he said. Clarity came to Liddell only after he returned to the text, looking at it anew. 'The second time you feel that nothing else is possible,' he added. The Sermon became Liddell's manifesto, and he became the exemplar of it to a literal degree. He believed it constituted 'the technique of being a Christian' and also counted as a 'working philosophy of life'.

Liddell owned a postcard-sized picture of the Danish artist Carl Bloch's painting of the Sermon, one of twenty-three scenes commissioned at the end of the nineteenth century for the chapel at Frederiksberg Palace in Copenhagen. He used it as a bookmark. Bloch depicts Jesus in ankle-length red robes and a grey shawl half a dozen shades darker than the rock on which he sits. His right hand is raised. The multitudes are listening to him speak. Liddell's card was frayed and slightly bent over at the corners, demonstrating the number of miles it had travelled inside his Bible.

Liddell felt 'at least one good book' about Jesus 'should be read by everyone – Christian and non-Christian alike'. The book he recommended, cherishing it in an ever-expanding personal library housed in a blackwood bookcase, was *The Christ of the Mount*, published in 1931. Like the Bloch card, the pages became rather tatty and dog-eared after Liddell repeatedly referred to them and readily lent out the book. Written by the American theologian and missionary E. Stanley Jones, a confidant of both Gandhi and Franklin D. Roosevelt, *The Christ of the Mount* added enormously to Liddell's comprehension of the Sermon. Jones said that the Sermon, which he considered a 'portrait of Jesus', was as grand as an

'Everest peak'. His work was the catalyst for Liddell's decision to put together an earlier book, his own twenty-four-page analysis of the Sermon modestly subtitled 'Notes for Sunday School Teachers'. As the war widened, becoming all-engulfing, his opinions chimed with Jones's. 'The Sermon challenges the whole conception of force which militarism holds,' said Jones, arguing that 'blows could only beget blows and hate will beget hate, and you will find yourself in a vicious circle'.

Discipleship, finally completed in Tientsin, still stands as the most significant thing Liddell wrote because the Sermon permeates every thought presented in it. It is also the closest we get to hearing Liddell speak from the heart.

'Jesus' life is the most beautiful life there has ever been,' he said, explaining why his own became an attempt to mirror it in both 'character' and 'outlook'. For Liddell, this meant never 'willingly' being rude or 'irritated'. This meant disdaining pride, which he saw as 'the great enemy of humility'. This meant being 'ready to go out of [your] way to help' and to 'reduce people's burdens'. And this – once more – meant striving to 'be ye perfect'. Such high moral standards seemed unreachable – absurdly so – to some of those who heard Liddell espouse them; surely no one could be *that* godly.

But, within only a few months, he'd show under adversity that whatever he preached was always practised, irrespective of personal cost.

Late in the summer of 1942 the prospect of repatriation was dangled in front of the missionaries. Civilian Japanese held in American Relocation Centres would be swapped for Allied non-combatants in China.

By now the Japanese had bombed and forced the surrender of Singapore, cut the Burma Road, soon taking over the country, occupied the Dutch East Indies and were battling to either retain or assume control of South Pacific targets such as the Solomon Islands and Papua New Guinea. Air attacks had been launched on Australian towns, among them Darwin in the Northern Territory, where almost two hundred were killed in the first raid on the harbour and two airfields, and Broome in Western Australia, which was an aircraft refuelling stage and also a stopping-off point for refugees. Between seventy and a hundred people died there in a surprise assault lasting barely twenty minutes.

Against this backdrop the missionaries in Tientsin seemed inconsequential, so the plan to be rid of them made sense.

Eric Liddell had never relaxed. He'd delivered the mail, which was now a dribble, throughout the Concession. He'd participated with infinite patience in games that occupied the children of the missionary family with whom he lodged. The temperature rose oppressively high; sometimes it was 100 degrees in the shade. He played cricket with the boys and tennis with the girls nonetheless. He spent spare hours affixing Chinese stamps into albums for them too. If other missionaries needed someone to complete a four at bridge, Liddell never refused appeals to make up the numbers. He did chores to ensure the house was well run. He went to the bakery at 5 a.m. to buy bread. After a terrible dust storm – sand and grit sneaking through closed doors and windows to cover the floors and furnishings – Liddell got up before 4.30 a.m. to clear it with a pan, broom and duster, doing so as quietly as possible to wake up no one else.

Now, expecting to be given a departure date, Liddell wrote to Florence to say he'd volunteer for fresh tasks in Canada. The London Missionary Society, regarding his return as a foregone conclusion, also wrote to her. The LMS enquired whether Liddell had plans post-China, ending with the wildly presumptuous 'Best wishes to yourself and Eric if he has by any chance turned up yet'. Hope can bruise the spirit. Florence had tried to suppress her optimism; but the LMS was telling her that Liddell would be with her any day, and certainly before the Christmas tree needing trimming. She waited for the telegram telling her of a firm date.

The repatriations turned out to be a sham except for those who had money to bribe officials. Only the rich were guaranteed release, able to buy berths on the ships sailing away from China. The first batch of missionaries got only as far as Shanghai, where the position became depressingly apparent to them. The second batch, including Liddell, who lacked the funds to compete with wealthy businessmen, never left Tientsin. The Japanese decided to sweep up the stragglers. Instead of being given safe passage, the missionaries were going to be corralled in a camp where it would take fewer soldiers to monitor them.

Liddell once said that 'half the things we worry about never happen'. This was not one of them. In mid-March 1943, Liddell learned he'd have a little over two weeks to sort his personal affairs, his papers and his possessions. He was being sent to a Civilian Assembly Centre in Shandong Province.

This new home was called Weihsien.

CHAPTER FOURTEEN

No More Happy Birthdays

THE MOST TERRIBLE NIGHTMARES are those in which the dreamer believes himself to be awake. To be captive in Weihsien, especially during the early days there, was akin to that feeling. That proclamation over the main gate – Courtyard of the Happy Way – was a grotesque distortion of what awaited those who went inside.

No one old enough to remember the camp clearly ever forgot the first sight of it. Plaster had been hammered off walls. Water pipes and radiators had been torn out. Holes had been hacked in brickwork. Windows had been broken. Desks and chairs, once used in classrooms, had been smashed or split and then left to rot or rust uselessly in the open air. So had bed frames and wardrobes, tables and chests of drawers. The wells had been deliberately dirtied – used either as trash bins or toilets. What Weihsien had once been, an immaculately spick-and-span American Presbyterian mission, was now a wreck, every pathway cluttered with debris and heaped with garbage. It was as if something meteorologically freakish had swept across the place.

The truth was more prosaic. First Chinese bandits and then Japanese soldiers had ripped through Weihsien long before its designation as a Civilian Assembly Centre. Hooliganism had destroyed the fabric of the buildings. Looting had picked the camp almost clean of valuables from the hospital, the school, the kitchen, the church and the barrack-like accommodations. Even the latrines had been vandalized. None of them flushed, so the bowls overflowed. The stench of shit and piss was choking.

There was no running water. There was no heating either. Electric light offered measly illumination – no more than a mid-Victorian gas lamp.

There was a grey, 8-foot-high wall surrounding Weihsien, and later on electrified bands of barbed wire. In conical corner towers, from which searchlights could burn through the darkness of the night, guards stood with machine guns poking through slots. On the ground there were another thirty or so guards with rifles and bayonets, still wearing winter black uniforms and calf-length boots. Some of them held a German Shepherd dog on a chain lead and also had a sword in a sheath tied to their belts.

Eric Liddell hadn't known what to expect from the camp. Nor had he known who else would be there. The Japanese had given the new internees from Tientsin instructions rather than information. Liddell was told he could send a bed and a mattress to Weihsien in advance of his arrival. He could dispatch three other big pieces of luggage that way too. Everything else had to be carried either on his back or in his hands.

No one thought about seeing Tientsin again. If the war went well, the internees expected to be liberated overseas. If it went badly, who knew what tortures the Japanese would put them through? Whatever was left behind would soon be lost to them for ever. So those going to Weihsien wrapped sentimental keepsakes and small heirlooms as well as practical essentials. Liddell packed his clothes, his Bible, his prayer books and a selection of other titles, including E. Stanley Jones's *The Christ of the Mount* and a red, leather-bound edition of John Bunyan's *The Pilgrim's Progress*. As a precaution – the Japanese hadn't mentioned cooking utensils – he took cups and plates and a knife and fork. Soldiers checked the sharpness of each in case Liddell planned to turn them into weapons. He pushed sets of cushions and curtains into his leather cases. He reckoned the curtains could be used for extra bedsheets. He took photographs of his family. He gathered up what remained of his athletics medals and also two watches: the gold half-hunter that Edinburgh's city fathers had given him for winning the Olympic title and a stopwatch, which he had also brought to China almost twenty years earlier. Into one suitcase he slipped his university blazer and the pair of spiked running shoes – dark grey canvas uppers and long grey laces – that he'd worn in the late 1920s and early 1930s.

Liddell was lucky. He got to the camp with his possessions intact. Elsewhere internees found the Japanese brazenly stealing from them. The soldiers' excuse was always that something – especially gold or silver – counted as unsuitable cargo and could therefore be taken with impunity. It was pointless to argue. The internees had to placidly surrender whatever the occupying army fancied taking from them.

Liddell didn't escape the minor humiliations inflicted on everyone sent to Weihsien. The Japanese made sure photographers recorded the departing internees, glum-faced with apprehension and stooped under the weight of their suitcases. They trekked in a crocodile line like a regimented bunch of hobos. The Chinese, many of whom had worked as household servants, tearfully saw them off. This was done mostly in silence. The penalty for attempting to speak to a prisoner could be a rear or a frontal blow from a swagger stick or a rod of bamboo.

It was 300 miles from Tientsin to Weihsien. Liddell walked to the railway station wearing his fur hat and an overcoat. He climbed into a third-class carriage. After ten hours he changed trains. After a further five, the city of Weihsien loomed ahead of him at last. The final leg of his journey was a 3-mile, forty-minute truck ride. He and the other internees rattled and shook over cobbles and along rutted tracks. He arrived to find Weihsien already crowded with people exactly like him – pasty-pale, their complexion the colour of wet clay. The dishevelled groups were hollow-eyed, sorely in need of sleep. Some were distractedly sorting through the rubble. Some were peeling freshly dug vegetables, which were still half-covered in soil. These had been heaped in front of them the way a farmer dumps fodder for his livestock. Some were disoriented, still clutching baggage like travellers stranded at the wrong stop. Some, despairing and inconsolable, wandered without apparent purpose, the scenes of human frailty and lowliness too much to bear for them. On that same day, speaking in the chandeliered splendour of London's Waldorf Hotel, Winston Churchill declared that a 'bitter and inexorable war' was being fought to 'ensure that the spirit of liberty and human dignity shall triumph over the satanic forces that have set at nought all the laws of God . . .' Neither liberty nor human dignity was triumphing in Weihsien. The laws of God seemed to lie far outside its walls because within them there was only the chaos of almost 1,800 internees crammed in a space barely 150 yards long and 200 yards wide.

No one put the sight of it better than Langdon Gilkey, a Harvard-educated teacher who in the mid-1960s wrote *Shantung Compound*, an account of his imprisonment.

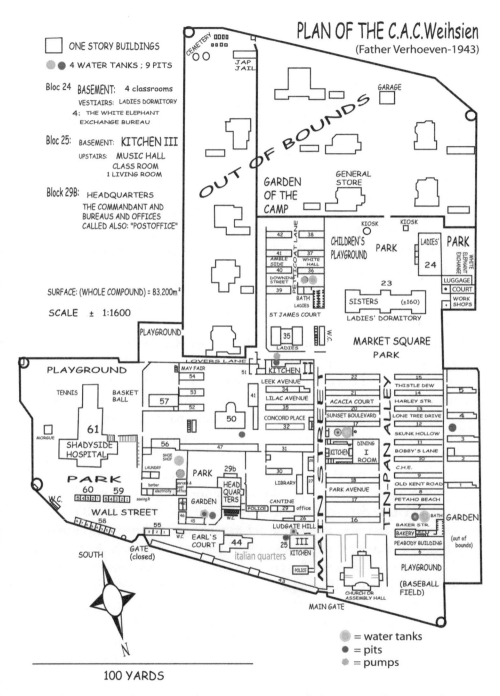

PLAN OF THE C.A.C.Weihsien
(Father Verhoeven-1943)

☐ ONE STORY BUILDINGS

◐ ● 4 WATER TANKS ; 9 PITS

Bloc 24 BASEMENT: 4 classrooms
VESTIAIRS: LADIES DORMITORY
4: THE WHITE ELEPHANT
EXCHANGE BUREAU

Bloc 25: BASEMENT: KITCHEN III
UPSTAIRS: MUSIC HALL
CLASS ROOM
1 LIVING ROOM

Block 29B: HEADQUARTERS
THE COMMANDANT AND
BUREAUS AND OFFICES
CALLED ALSO: "POSTOFFICE"

SURFACE: (WHOLE COMPOUND) = 83,200m²

SCALE ± 1:1600

CEMETERY

JAP JAIL

GARAGE

OUT OF BOUNDS

GARDEN OF THE CAMP

GENERAL STORE

KIOSK   KIOSK

CHILDREN'S PLAYGROUND   PARK   LADIES' PARK

42 38
41 37   24
AMBLE WHITE
SIDE   HALL
40 36   LUGGAGE
DOWNING   COURT
STREET   WORK
39   BATH   SHOPS
LADIES
ST JAMES COURT   SISTERS   (±160)
23
LADIES' DORMITORY

PLAYGROUND   35
LADIES

W.C.   MARKET SQUARE
PARK

LOVERS LANE

PLAYGROUND   MAY FAIR

TENNIS   BASKET BALL   54   51   KITCHEN II
57   53   LEEK AVENUE
52   34
41   LILAC AVENUE
35
50   CONCORD PLACE
32

56   47   31

SHADYSIDE HOSPITAL   SHOE SHOP   30
LAUNDRY   LIBRARY

PARK   PARK   29b
61
MORGUE   HEAD
QUAR
barber electricity TERS

60   59   parcels & post office   GARDEN   CANTINE
58   sewing R   45   POLICE   29
W.C.   46   W.C.   LUDGATE HILL
WALL STREET
55   W.C.
EARL'S
COURT   44   25   III
SOUTH   GATE (closed)   italian quarters   KITCHEN
POLICE
43

22   15   THISTLE DEW
21   14   HARLEY STR.   5
ACACIA COURT   20   LONE TREE DRIVE
SUNSET BOULEVARD   17   SKUNK HOLLOW   4
KITCHEN   DINING   11   3
I   BOBBY'S LANE
ROOM   10   2
18   C.H.E.
PARK AVENUE   9
17   OLD KENT ROAD   1
8
16   PETAHO BEACH
7
BAKER STR.   BATH   GARDEN
BAKERY   (out of
PEABODY BUILDING   bounds)
6

MAIN STREET   TIN-PAN ALLEY

PLAYGROUND
(BASEBALL FIELD)

CHURCH OR
ASSEMBLY HALL

MAIN GATE

◐ = water tanks
● = pits
◐ = pumps

N

100 YARDS

Weihsien, 1943. The map was drawn by a Roman Catholic priest, Father Leonard Verhoeven.

Facing him was a 'great crowd of dirty, unkempt, refugee-like people . . . coldly staring at us with resentful curiosity'. Gilkey noticed that their clothes looked 'damp and rumpled' and were 'covered with grime and dust – much as men look who have just come off a shift on a road gang'. He asked himself the question everyone there before him had already thought about: 'How can anyone *live* enclosed in this tiny area for any length of time?'

Ever the bright optimist, Eric Liddell focused on the positive; and never more so than in his letters from Weihsien. Acutely conscious of how his correspondence would be received back home, Liddell suppressed the truth about the camp because he believed telling it would serve no constructive purpose and that sorrow would be rust to the soul for his wife. The London Missionary Society informed Florence about her husband's captivity. He guessed she would fear the worst, so his priority was pretence, created to shield her from the awfulness of his surroundings.

Every month the internees were allowed one Red Cross message comprising twenty-five words. It was like the 1940s equivalent of a modern-day tweet. These had to be written in capitals on a white form, measuring 6 inches by 10, which was headed 'To The Comité International De La Croix-Rouge'. The sender had to include name, nationality and matriculation number – Liddell's was 3/88 – and the content was supposed to be 'family news of [a] strictly personal character'. That instruction, like every other, was set in blood red type. In both outgoing and incoming mail the Japanese learned how to spot double meanings, such as 'Can't wait to speak to Uncle Sam again' or 'John Bull might be seeing you soon'. The guards were less adept at picking out metaphor. One writer was eventually able to alert an internee about the bombing of Germany by writing about 'pigeons' that were 'flying into a troublesome neighbour's garden'. When the Japanese deemed a piece of information inappropriate, the sentences were redacted with a thick black pen. The letters and forms then became largely incomprehensible, the families struggling to make sense of them. Even holding the flimsy paper up to the light made no difference. Words the Japanese didn't want read were completely obliterated. Sometimes the guards found the work too time-consuming and tiring and simply destroyed the Red Cross messages or stacked them in a shed, never to be posted on.

Four of those Liddell wrote are typical of his chin-up-and-make-the-best-of-it attitude. The first, sent a fortnight after his arrival, began: 'SIMPLE HARDY LIFE UNDER PRIMITIVE CONDITIONS'. The second, dispatched shortly afterwards, repeated the phrase 'simple and hardy' and stressed the 'community life' he was experiencing in the 'open air'. The third, written to mark his tenth wedding anniversary, promised: 'I [AM] FIT, BUSY AND NO COMPLAINTS'. The fourth, composed five months later, said: 'HEALTHY, ENJOYING SOME READING . . . CONSTANTLY REMEMBER AND PICTURE YOU ALL . . . EVERYTHING SUFFICIENT'. If you didn't know Liddell was a prisoner of war, you might think he'd sent a seaside postcard. Apart from the word 'primitive' there's no suggestion that anything much is wrong. This wasn't entirely through self-censorship or the restriction on the number of sentences he could string together before running out of space. It's because Liddell's character and his beliefs never allowed him to be depressed or negative, irrespective of the hardships.

A fellow internee, remembering the 694 days Liddell spent in Weihsien, said he was an 'unruffled spirit' with a 'serene temper' and a 'constantly smiling face'. Another recalled him as 'always cheerful', as though to be otherwise set a bad example and counted as a dereliction of duty. 'He never let anyone see him downcast,' said a third. 'Every day to him was still precious. He threw himself into it to make others feel better about the situation all of us were in.' Langdon Gilkey remarked that Liddell 'didn't look like a famous athlete – or rather he didn't look as if he thought of himself as one'. Gilkey regarded him as 'surely the most modest man who ever breathed' and soon realized that this was 'one of the secrets of his amazing life'.

Weihsien was under the control of the Japanese Consular Service rather than the country's army or military police, and the guards themselves came from varying backgrounds and were either older or younger than those automatically sent to the front line. The atrocities and brutalities perpetrated elsewhere under the flag of the Emperor, such as forced marches, human experimentation, tortures and beheadings, and also the starvation of men to skeletal waste, were not repeated here. The conditions were nonetheless horrendous.

The Japanese hadn't thought through how Weihsien would work practically. What had appeared to them as the straightforward solution to one difficulty – coping with a civilian, non-combatant population – merely created others as a consequence of rushed and lackadaisical thinking. Internees were drawn into the camp from numerous points in China, including Peking and Tsingtao as well as Tientsin. But there had been no comprehensive pre-planning about what would happen once the Courtyard of the Happy Way had swallowed them up. From the outset Weihsien became a logistical conundrum, which the Japanese lacked the wherewithal, the will and the resources to solve. It was deficient in basic facilities. It lacked regular supplies. And, above all, it was impossibly claustrophobic.

Every stratum of society was locked into it. There were the seriously wealthy, who'd led almost an aristocratic existence. Their lives had revolved around chauffeurs, waiters and cooks. Amahs had cared for their children. Even the opening swish of the bedroom curtains each morning had been done for them. One was said to own at least two Rolls-Royces and several mansion-like homes. Others, regarding themselves as superior and upper middle class, came from well-to-do commercial businesses. There were bank managers and clerks, stockbrokers and company directors, chartered accountants and architects, government employees and merchants and mining engineers. Also caught in the Japanese net – beneficially so for the camp – were doctors and surgeons, nurses, dentists, lab pathologists, teachers and lecturers, tailors, cooks and those recorded as 'artisans', such as carpenters, masons and general handymen. Four black American jazz musicians had been brought to Weihsien from the stage of a nightclub. One woman listed her occupation merely as 'sewing teacher'. One man described himself as a 'lighthouse keeper'. The religious community was diverse. There were Roman Catholic and Protestant priests, Trappist monks and nuns, members of the Salvation Army and also lay teachers. Liddell was one of almost two hundred missionaries.

The nationality of the camp was predominantly American and British. The cosmopolitan mix – another twenty-seven different countries were represented there – nonetheless included Iranians, Panamanians, Palestinians and White Russians, the latter financially bereft and displaced after the Communists turned the country red in 1917 and left them stateless. Some internees were half-Chinese or even half-Japanese. Like every community Weihsien wasn't free of problem citizens either – the alcoholics, the prostitutes, the drug and opium addicts and also the downright lazy and the sort of devilishly rakish-cum-nasty personalities that ordinarily you'd cross the street to avoid. But, of course, it was impossible to avoid them in Weihsien. The consequences of overcrowding were entirely predictable. There were acute shortages, especially of food and fuel and clothes and soap. There were also interminable queues to receive them.

According to one internee, who remembered 'queuing for everything', the food line provided an almost daily example of 'the worst in people', a place where 'griping and surliness were a way of life'. Those serving the meals were frequently harangued about the portions. Accusations of favouritism could rapidly turn into shrieking rows too. Hair could be pulled. Balled fists could be brandished. Clothes could be torn.

There was no privacy, which led to disputes about personal space. If a husband and wife had two or more children, the family would be given a pair of 9-by-12-foot rooms. Each had a square window at the front and a clerestory window at the back. Often a loop of rope ran from one wall to another so a sheet could be draped across it, like a modesty screen, to divide living and sleeping areas. In winter, plaster peeled from the walls and the window frames splintered. The internees would cover gaps and cracks with papier-mâché; sheets of newspaper were pasted together with an unstable glue made from flour. Those alone in the camp – Liddell among them – were called 'the unattached' and grouped together in similarly minuscule rooms or the barn-like dormitories. Suitcases and bags were stored beneath the beds – some of which were propped unsteadily on bricks – or used as seats and tables. The dorms became so congested that the foot of one bed often touched the head of another. Territorial quarrels arose because beds were supposed to be 18 inches apart. Chalk marks were laid on the floor to demarcate occupancy after some internees began incrementally shifting their beds into a neighbouring space. A few went as far as rubbing out the chalk and redrawing the marks, expecting the fraud to go unnoticed and unchallenged. There were also internees without bed frames who slept on mattresses lifted on to trunks or cardboard boxes.

The sanitation, which essentially amounted to holes in the ground, worsened after diarrhoea, sickness and even worms spread throughout the camp. As one captive said of these crude latrines, 'It took a strong stomach to use them at all.'

The Weihsien commandant had only recently been a vice consul in

Honolulu. He had almost no English, and a memo sent from the American consul in Japan to the American State Department condemned him as 'a man of very ordinary intelligence' who was 'extremely incapable in practical matters' and 'not inclined to be helpful'. His language was so limited that a colleague who'd once lived in London had to speak to the internees on his behalf. Since the English had always treated him well, he promised reciprocal benevolence. There was a proviso. 'Remember,' he said, pausing for effect, 'you must co-operate. Provocation and disrespect will be treated harshly.' The internees were given a square of cloth on to which their camp number was stencilled. Everyone wore it – and woe betide those who didn't – because rebuilding was more important than rebelling.

The Japanese told the internees to manage their own affairs. Committees were promptly set up to administer day-to-day organization. These fell under nine categories. Seven of them were discipline, education, engineering, employment, health, quarters and supplies. The other two were finance and general affairs. Both of these attracted those men in the camp who had previously sat around boardroom tables and considered themselves to be 'big wheels'. The terms 'finance' and 'general affairs' each had a whiff of lordly power about them and, unlike some of the others, didn't seem to imply either getting your hands filthy or bending your back. The situation changed when the Japanese became aware that 'general affairs' was being seen as a soft number. The commandant decreed that latrine cleaning and maintenance would be part of it. Those who had previously taken two sharp steps forward to volunteer now went into a fast-pedalling retreat.

The rich businessmen, aghast at the prospect of unblocking toilets, were embarrassed by the nuns and missionaries, who did it with ungloved hands. The sisters turned up the long hems and the sleeves of their blue or black habits and pulled on boots to prove that cleanliness is next to godliness. Their starched white coifs were pushed further back with every exertion, revealing stray coils of hair. Among those known as 'the sanitary police' was Mary Scott, a self-confessed 'tomboy'. Scott was thirty-four years old and 5 feet 2 inches tall. She was both stoutly round-shouldered and round-faced. Her voice was calming. Her walk was a firm bustle. Her black wavy hair was brushed well back from her forehead. Just two and a half years earlier she had abandoned a comfortable teaching position in America to become a missionary for the Church of the Nazarene. Scott admitted that the odour from the toilets was 'so pungent' that her nose 'burned'. Some of the nuns held a scented handkerchief to their face to prevent them from vomiting. There were twice as many men's latrines as women's because the Japanese – in another sign of the army's defective planning – had miscalculated the number of females for internment. Once these became usable again each stall was hand-flushed with old washing-up water, which was stored in bulbous earthenware kangs.

The 10 p.m. curfew for internees necessitated the use of chamber pots. These pots were emptied next morning into unfenced cesspools about 12 feet in diameter. A priest, who had a deformity of the spine, slipped into one of them and had to be rescued. Another internee, who also fell in, suffered a severe panic attack before being heaved out with a rope. A river ran beside the compound. The Japanese told the internees to dig a trench that would allow the effluent to be swept straight into it.

The camp, however, did begin to take some sort of rough shape. The internees sorted through the destruction, rescuing what could be fixed and disposing of the rest. The pathways were slowly cleared of rubbish. The rooms and dormitories were spruced up a little. Some were even given cosmetic flicks of paint from half-full pots. The wells were dredged. The internees were inventive too. Stoves were built from discarded bricks. The fuel used in them came from scraps of firewood – snapped twigs and branches of trees and broken furniture. Scavenged coal dust and odd, precious fragments of coke were mixed with clay and water to create rectangular briquettes or round lumps the size of a pool ball after drying. The flues, which carried the smoke away, were crafted from tin cans. Crude candles were made by pouring peanut oil into shoe polish bottles and cutting a length of Chinese thread as a wick.

Everyone fit enough to work was assigned a specific task. The specialist skills of the qualified tradesmen were a boon. Those who lacked them were mostly given manual labour to do. Three kitchens, each capable of serving more than five hundred, were soon operational. These required cooks and support staff to either prepare or serve the food. Enormous brick bread ovens were constructed, producing around four hundred loaves per day. Strong-armed stokers fired up furnaces in both the kitchen and the bakery and then slaved to keep them alight. A rota was agreed on for pumping water from 6 a.m. to 9 p.m. The six well pumps resembled the metal handles on railway handcarts – and required the same amount of sweaty effort to operate. The water, held in 44-gallon storage towers, always had to be boiled before drinking – though the content of one well was so contaminated that even half an hour of boiling couldn't make it fit for consumption.

Elsewhere, the hospital hired orderlies to assist the doctors and nurses and each internee was asked to surrender medicines and bandages to create a central pharmacy. The hospital was made operational in less than three weeks, which counted as the most remarkable transformation of all. A laundry was set up in the basement, where women with boards, tin tubs and scrubbing brushes – the bristles of which soon wore away – eked out small bars of soap in marathon sessions of washing.

Liddell was officially the maths and science teacher. He was unofficially everything else.

His original role had supposedly confined his 'other duties' to arranging church worship and services, taking Bible classes and scripture readings and organizing sports on a bare patch of land in the camp's south-west corner. He scrupulously did all these things and became a ubiquitous presence. He was like the shepherd in 'Ninety And Nine', the hymn he continued to teach at Sunday school. Liddell was always looking for Weihsien's lost sheep.

His background in Siaochang meant he was used to roughing it. Liddell had often slept in the same clothes for days on end and washed in basins of cold or lukewarm water without soap. He'd camped in peasant homes on slate-hard beds. He'd eaten and drunk whatever his hosts had served, which in the poverty-blighted countryside wasn't much. Liddell saw Weihsien as an extension of his original mission. So he took extra turns at pumping water. He cleaned the latrines. He chopped wood and rolled coal balls before taking that fuel to the elderly. He swept floors. He took away garbage. He carted sacks and food supplies and helped out in the kitchen. He played chess to stoke the competitive spirit of those who seemed resigned to giving up as prisoners. He did numerous odd-jobs – shifting furniture, hanging washing lines, completing fiddly repairs. He put up a row of shelves for one of the prostitutes. She said afterwards that Liddell was the only man there to have come into her room without 'demanding favours'.

When Liddell wasn't engaged in fetching or carrying, he gave emotional support to the internees. He was the consoling Samaritan of the camp, the epitome of a good neighbour. Into his ears problems were poured, and Liddell listened to friends and strangers alike. 'He was the man we turned to when personal relationships got just too impossible,' said an internee. 'He had a gentle, humorous way of . . . bringing to one's mind some bygone happiness or the prospect of some future interest just round the corner.' The only way to feel half-alone in Weihsien – and ensure you weren't being overheard – was to ramble around the inside perimeter of the wall. Liddell was always being asked whether he'd be free to go for 'a stroll'. On these walks he dealt with homesickness and loneliness, depressions and resentments and fears the internees had both for themselves and for far-off loved ones. Liddell never spoke with those he cared for pastorally about his own apprehensions or the awful hurt he felt because of his family's absence. Hearing him pine or complain would only make them gloomier still, he thought. Nor did he criticize others or make disparaging remarks about them.

Recognized as an impartial and unimpeachably honest broker, he was called in to settle spats too – some of which threatened to become explosive. In one Red Cross message, Liddell had told Florence that 'everyone [was] a worker', as if the load in Weihsien was being shared equally. That wasn't entirely the case. Mary Scott said that 'men and women alike were soon known not by their outside occupations, but by the quality of their work, their spirit of willingness and their measure of enthusiasm'. She added that the camp 'judged people not by what they had, but for what they *were*'. Liddell had to mediate when squabbles began over whether or not someone was shirking his – or occasionally her – duties. Sometimes he'd mediate again in claims of petty pilfering. Food or fuel regularly went missing. So did possessions. When guilt could be proved without reasonable doubt, the thieves were named on notice boards. What was meant to disgrace and deter the light-fingered also increased tensions. Suspicions both real and imagined were stirred. Some were shunned after indiscretions committed only to stave off hunger or cold rather than to satisfy greed. This was, after all, the 1940s, a period when self-respect and particularly self-restraint were expected. Not to show them was considered to be bad form even as a prisoner of war. Cliques became tighter than ever. Those who considered themselves well-to-do avoided those regarded as the camp's underbelly. The strictly neutral Liddell was accepted on both sides of the social divide, which he shuttled between.

He never flagged. Liddell rose before it got light, well in advance of his companions, to pray silently. He sat at a table with the curtains tightly shut so the Japanese wouldn't see the low glow of his peanut oil lamp and think someone was planning to escape.

Liddell's advice was always 'First of all, have a prayer hour. Secondly, keep it.' He was rigid on the point because he believed that 'Anyone who, neglecting that fixed hour of prayer, [will] say he can pray at all times will probably end in praying at no time.' Liddell explained that the opening few minutes of his prayers were 'a sincere moral search' in which he waited for the mind to stop 'at anything' he had done wrong. His first prayers were then for Florence, Patricia, Heather and the baby Maureen. In his *Prayers for Daily Use*, Liddell carefully wrote each of their names in the margin beside the section titled 'Absent Loved Ones'.

Liddell compared his quiet period of contemplation and study to washing 'the dust' from his eyes. Once that was done, he faced the day to come.

Those who saw what Liddell did believed he came close to bucking the theory that no one is indispensable. 'I once saw him unloading supplies from the back of a cart,' said one internee, who was then an enquiring child. 'I said to myself: Why is he doing it? That's someone else's responsibility. Later I realized he did *everything*. It's said he was worth ten men. I can believe it.'

Another observer put it even better. 'I was amazed that anyone could carry such a timetable,' she said.

The internees tried to make Weihsien more like home. The pathways in the camp were playfully renamed. The central track was Main Street. The parallel thoroughfare became Tin Pan Alley or The Rocky Road, the name dependent on preference. Among the others were Wall Street, Downing Street, Sunset Boulevard, Old Kent Road and Peitaiho Beach. There was even a Lovers' Lane. That painter of weirdly fantastical images Hieronymus Bosch would have been the ideal artist to put on canvas the chaotically surreal scenes witnessed on them.

The Japanese never issued new clothes to the internees. What anyone wore soon became dirty, particularly when the torrential rains came and turned the main roads into mud-heaps, or were damaged through daily wear and tear. These tattered and patched clothes were repaired time and again until further repairs became futile. Replacements had to be cut and stitched from any available fabric – curtains, sheets, blankets, pillow-cases and, most commonly, the threadbare remnants of other garments. Nothing was ever wasted. A flower-patterned tablecloth became two pairs of underpants. A sweater, with gaping holes where the elbows ought to be, was gradually unravelled, the wool re-used to knit a new one. A pair of dining-room curtains was turned into a shirt. Shoes, the soles dropping off, were bound with long string or twine. Once that became impractical, strips of cloth were nailed on to wooden soles instead. In summer some of the men went around bare-chested and walked in bare feet too. In winter there were Chinese clogs to wear. No one cared about appearance; the aim was to make clothes last as long as possible and to dress functionally.

Either out of panic, or because no one had known precisely what to take, the internees had brought an eclectic collection of outfits from their wardrobes, which led to some curious and carnivalesque sartorial sights during the two and a half years of the camp's existence. The place could have been mistaken for a lunatic asylum in which everyone had free access to a child's dressing-up box. One woman wore a fur coat and pearls. Another put on a ball-gown, the wide ruff of the hem filthy and frayed before it was cut off and made into something else. A man dressed in his dinner jacket and evening shirt to wash dishes. His friend never seemed to be without his pink Leander boating scarf. Someone else usually wore his Ascot tie.

None of the clothes could be properly ironed. The internees laid them between the bedsprings and the mattress. 'When we took the clothes out, they were well creased but flattened at least,' said Mary Scott. Otherwise, she added, clothes were washed and simply hung out to dry 'hoping the wind would take out some of the wrinkles'.

Eric Liddell had arrived in Weihsien in a white shirt, long white socks and a pair of khaki shorts beneath his overcoat. The curtains he'd brought with him – one pair orange, another flame-red – were eventually cut up to replace the white shirt. He resembled the glowing tip of a match. He wasn't alone. Another prisoner wore shorts that had once been patterned curtains too. The outlines of the sun and the moon were apparent on each buttock. Liddell discarded his socks and wore whatever footwear would fit, including his old running shoes. He merely yanked out the spikes. Clothes were still the least of the camp's inconveniences for him and everyone else.

The internees were able to shower only once a week in austere communal blocks offering scant privacy for their nakedness other than sheets, which were no substitute for proper curtains. The exceptions were the stokers, covered in dust and grime, and the bakers, sweaty in the heat:

the camp allowed them to shower every day. Weihsien was also home sweet home to insects and vermin, which were ever-present and everywhere. No amount of fumigation could ever satisfactorily shift them. As well as the flies in the kitchen, and the rats scurrying around the garbage, there were fat maggots and mosquitoes, scorpions and several varieties of troublesome red-brown bugs, which regarded skin as a gourmet feast and left spots of blood behind on the sheets. The internees were meticulous in attempting to get rid of them, taking out and cleaning bed frames, mattresses and blankets as well as trunks and clothes. Walls and floors were washed. Water was boiled and poured over the bed frames. The bugs were squashed beneath fingernails. None of it worked. The bug population trooped back before the sun rose again, forever interrupting sleep as the internees strove to bat, slap or flick them away. There was no Pied Piper to combat the rats in Weihsien either. Elaborate traps were laid and hundreds perished, snapped to death or drowned; but, like the bugs and the flies, there were always more – scores upon scores, in fact – to replace them.

The climate worked against the internees too. The winters were so cold that those peeling vegetables in the kitchen sometimes couldn't feel a cut caused by a slipped knife; their fingers were just too numb. The summers were so hot that the perspiration fell off the workers, sapping them of energy. Whatever the season, Weihsien life was predominantly about the drudgery of a rigid routine. This was both wearing and also strangely necessary. The camp's strict structure forced the internees to engage with every day through the obvious need to survive. The tasks were grindingly dull, but at least none was ever senseless, each of them serving a bigger purpose – except the forced tedium of roll call, which was called *tenko*.

Liddell was a roll call warden. Every morning the bell called the internees to it at 7.30 a.m. It could be a laborious process. 'Often we had to stand in lines for hours,' said an internee. 'The guards had difficulty counting us. They would count the several long lines, compare notes, then count again.' It soon became obvious that simple mathematics was not the guards' only deficiency. They didn't possess cut-glass minds.

When several internees were discovered to be missing, another internee was told to locate them. The roll call then became such a protracted affair that some of the elderly fainted during it. Eventually the guards calculated that only one person was now absent. A further recount, dragging on painstakingly, took place before the truth finally became apparent. The 'missing' internee was the man who'd originally been sent to hunt down the others. He was still searching for them. Internees subsequently brought fold-up canvas stools or rickety deck-chairs to avoid standing. Others carried books to pass the time or small musical instruments, such as accordions or harmonicas, for a sing-along. Young boys dug shallow holes for games of marbles. Middle-aged women took their knitting. The fussiness of the roll call caused antagonism between the internees and the guards, each party blaming the other for the length of time it took to complete.

In the beginning the Japanese were an intimidating presence. 'A loud grunt and a pointed bayonet struck fear into the hearts of even the most recalcitrant,' was the verdict of a camp newcomer. The guards, few of whom spoke English, threw their arms around and barked orders incomprehensibly in what sounded like a choleric rant of confused abuse. The decibel level was the only guide to its urgency.

As the months went on, however, the internees grew less daunted, the guards becoming comic buffoons to them. Some of the 6 feet-plus-tall Americans and Europeans towered over these gaolers, making them look like small boys in costume. Sometimes the guards betrayed over-sensitivity, thinking general banter between internees – joshing one another and laughing at puerile jokes – was actually insolence towards them. The guards would then complain about lack of respect. To pacify them, internees were told to 'give way' on the streets, which meant altering 'course to port or starboard to avoid a head-on collision', said one.

This still wasn't enough. One of the guards was known as Gold Tooth because of the dentistry work on his left incisor and one other front tooth. He carried a swagger stick and his moods were described as 'obnoxious at best to downright sadistic'. His ego was said to have 'exploded beyond the bounds of reality'. Some went further, thinking he was 'mentally deficient'. He held sway over the stores and blamed any failure to understand what was required from them on the internees rather than his own poor grasp of their language. Gold Tooth would go into a dancing rage, padlock the stores and disappear out of pique. He hated internees who sang to get through a day's work, his swagger stick wielded against them.

Another guard became known as King Kong because – short and squat and square – he was the complete opposite of Merian C. Cooper's colossal screen invention. Like Gold Tooth, he also had an aversion to musical accompaniment. In his case a specific song grated on him. The internees, gathering in the canteens for meals, would sing 'Happy Birthday' to whoever was celebrating one. With so many people in the camp, it was always someone's birthday; and sometimes there could be half a dozen choruses sung on the same morning. The guards, who weren't familiar with either the tune or the lyrics, began to think it was a protest song or another way of criticizing them. King Kong put a blanket ban on 'Happy Birthday'.

The most unflattering label was pinned on a sergeant. He became Bo-shing-de, generally translated as either 'it's forbidden' or 'not do'. The sobriquet stuck because 'Bo-shing-de' was his answer to everything. The phrase was uttered aggressively too, as though some personal affront had been committed against him. The camp regarded him as a blustering bully. The children still mocked the sergeant incessantly, fearlessly trailing after him and shouting 'Bo-shing-de' before running off. When a pup somehow crept into the camp, it was christened Bo-shing-de, which gave them another chance to shout the name. The sergeant eventually captured the pup and threw it back over the wall. He grew indignant over his ribbing, insisting this notice was pinned around Weihsien on his behalf: 'By Special Order of His Imperial Majesty, the Emperor of Japan, "Sergeant Bo-shing-de" is NOT to be known as Sergeant Bo-shing-de . . .' The word 'not' was even underlined, as though Hirohito had left the Imperial Palace and dictated the sentence himself after considering the matter gravely important. He became more of a laughing stock than before.

The guards didn't endear themselves to the internees over the worst of the privations in the camp either. There was never enough to eat; hunger almost always sat in the belly of everyone. You either talked about food, dreaming aloud about the delicacy you'd most like to eat, or you said nothing because the thought of a favourite meal made the mouth salivate unbearably. Someone wanted fried oysters. Someone craved Dover sole. Someone else wanted a breast of chicken. A lot of internees spoke of sirloin steak and pork chops. Rations were appallingly inadequate; indeed to call them food was stretching the point to ridiculousness. Those who cooked the meals pinned up joke menus, which promised 'Medallions of Beef', 'Whitebait', 'Chicken in a Cordon Bleu Creamy Sauce' or 'Boeuf Mironton'. What appeared on the plate was slop and mush; though some didn't even own plates, eating instead out of tin cans, enamel mugs, saucepans and pots or frying pans and soap dishes.

The repetitiveness of the diet was crushing. Breakfast was the wheat grain *kao liang*, which grew abundantly and became a dietary staple. No more needs to be said than the fact that local farmers used it to feed pigs rather than themselves. There was also a bean, *lu dou*. Lunch was a greasy, tough stew. The internees called it SOS – Same Old Stew. The smelly grey meat and slabs of liver to make it arrived in a semi-rotted state from slaughtered horses and donkeys. In the summer flies came in dark swarms, like a sweep of heavy rain, and fed off the meat or laid eggs on it. The meat could stink so much that, as one internee remembered, 'it was noticeable some distance away even if a lot of pepper had been added'. Supper was usually soup made from watered-down leftovers, potatoes and stringy vegetables such as cabbages, cucumbers, carrots, white radishes and aubergine. There were also thin porridges, the basis of which was often sour-tasting bread containing weevils that could not be sieved from the flour. At each meal weak black tea was served out of pails.

There was plenty of bread in the camp because the Japanese had a decent supply of flour and yeast. But margarine and butter were scarce and the skimpy amounts available were frequently mouldy or littered with straw. The internees slightly amended the opening line of the Lord's Prayer, which was recited as 'Give us this day our daily bread – and some jam to spread on it'. Just occasionally that plea was answered. Early on, some of the missionaries were fortunate enough to get food parcels. A woman found Golden Syrup in her package. Sadly the joy of it didn't last long. Rats had infested her building. One of them fell into the tin, which she threw away, unable to contemplate either fishing out the rodent or eating the contaminated contents. After she told another internee about what had happened, and offered him the syrup instead, the tin was taken out of the rubbish. The sticky rat was removed from the syrup, which was then boiled for 'several hours' before being eaten.

No one really wanted to know where the food had come from; and no one really wanted to know either what condition it had been in before reaching them. The internees ate things we would spit out in horror. In error, one of the cooks, a Belgian priest, admitted he 'put a great lump of salt' in the soup and thought no one would eat it. 'Everyone did,' he said, 'because we had nothing else' and also because 'we had to chew on our mistakes or go hungry'. One family was fortunate. A pigeon flew through the front window. It was instantly plucked and cooked and then dropped into a pan of soup.

The Japanese were sometimes cruel. Once a horse died near the officers' quarters. The animal was putrefying before the guards allowed the internees to skin it and hack away the decay. A heap of potatoes was treated the same way. The Japanese put them off limits until the point at which rot took hold.

There were occasional treats. Roughly one tablespoon of sugar was the weekly allowance of each internee. That entire entitlement was collectively donated to the cooks, who, on high days and holidays, made something with a loose acquaintance to gingerbread, shortbread and cake. While not exactly mother's home recipe, these things nevertheless came hot out of the oven and were preferable to another ladle of over-boiled vegetables or a grisly forkful of donkey meat. When a few dozen oranges arrived, straws were drawn to determine who received them. Internees previously in Peking had fixed it for Chinese friends to dispatch parcels for them. These rarely arrived without having been partly picked apart, the choicest goods stolen in advance or even the entire contents of the box removed. The Japanese blamed the Chinese and vice versa.

However hard the kitchens tried, it was impossible to provide the internees with enough food. Some shed as much as 7 to 10 stones. Adolescent girls didn't menstruate. Children's teeth began to grow without enamel. Such a beggarly diet even took 'the spring' out of Liddell, said one internee, who noticed he began to lose weight at the same rate as everyone else. Liddell avoided telling Florence about it.

The Japanese allowed the establishment of a White Elephant Shop, which originally let the internees swap goods between themselves and then later sold dried fruit, toothpaste, toilet paper, cigarettes, peanuts and soap. Occasionally shoe polish was for sale, which seemed bizarrely superfluous because so few had footwear requiring it. To buy these 'luxuries' the internees used an allowance known as Comfort Money, worth only one or two Chinese dollars per week. The Red Cross provided it and the cash was supposed to be repaid at the end of the war; recipients even had to sign a promissory note.

The shop's limited range of goods was never sufficient to nourish the internees, who began to look elsewhere. The Japanese treated the Chinese who lived outside the camp as pariahs. Peasants with homes and farms nearby were considered untouchables, lower than the bugs and the flies. The only locals ever allowed inside the camp were coolies who carried 'honey buckets' to remove excrement from the latrines. The internees saw them differently. Those beyond the walls were capable of aiding those inside them – providing there was a decent incentive.

The Weihsien black market was about to open for business; and Eric Liddell willingly played his part in it.

CHAPTER FIFTEEN

You Can Run . . . But You Won't Catch Us Old Man

WHEN HE FIRST ARRIVED in Weihsien, Eric Liddell was asked by a fellow internee, 'Do you do any running still?'

It was a well-intentioned attempt to open a conversation. The tone of the question was badly off, however, making it sound like sarcasm. Those who heard it anticipated an acid response from Liddell, still a stranger to most of them then.

Nearly two decades had slipped by since his Olympic win in Paris. He was forty-one years old and bald. He hadn't run competitively since 1937. Anyone sensitively thin-skinned over glories long gone would have given back a burst of invective capable of turning the air Prussian blue. To ask such a thing anyway, given the state of the camp, appeared idiotic. But Liddell neither wanted to embarrass the man nor cause offence. He looked solicitously at him and said, without rancour, 'No. At my age I am a little past it.'

Being a 'little past it' meant something different to Liddell than it did to others in Weihsien. Of course, he couldn't run the 400 metres in under fifty seconds any more. As a former Olympic champion, he could nevertheless out-dash men in their early twenties. As late as 1939, during his furlough in Scotland, Liddell had demonstrated how much of his sprinter's speed still remained. There were no crowds cheering from the stands. In fact, there were only two spectators – his daughters Patricia and

Heather – and Liddell chased a rabbit across a field rather than an athlete around a track. He'd taken them for a walk at Carcant. The rabbit ran in front of them and Liddell went off in pursuit of it, thinking of dinner. You have to be particularly fleet of foot to catch a rabbit, which is capable of clocking between 25 and 45 miles per hour to avoid capture. In this contest, however, there was only ever going to be one winner. Liddell grasped the rabbit by the hind legs, and it went into a pie.

Soon enough Weihsien witnessed how quickly Liddell was capable of running too.

In those early months the camp was more preoccupied with sorting propaganda from truth – both of which 'passed through it like wildfire' according to an Australian Cistercian monk called Father Patrick Scanlan. In his mid-forties, Scanlan had previously been in a Trappist monastery north of Peking and had once taken a vow of silence lasting almost ten years. He was a bulky man with thinning red hair and a deliberately ponderous manner of speech, which didn't betray to the guards that his alert mind whirled as colourfully as a fairground carousel. Scanlan remembered that there were 'many ways of hearing or half-hearing' misinformation. The Japanese guards would talk among themselves and be overheard. The Chinese shouted news at the internees from over the wall. An English language newspaper, the *Peking Chronicle*, specializing in the spread of false gossip, came into the camp either whole or in bits, a few pages wrapped around supplies. That items the *Chronicle* contained shouldn't be taken at face value was evidenced from its description of Weihsien. The paper claimed the place was 'equipped with all facilities to make [living there] as comfortable as possible'. The writer then added: 'Inmates are allowed to lead lives as if they were in their own homelands.'

Misinformation about the war was non-stop, most of it preposterous.

The camp heard that the Japanese were advancing through Australia. London had been bombed so ruinously that nothing recognizable of it remained; all was rubble there and Winston Churchill was dead. The German invasion was only a week away. In Washington, Franklin D. Roosevelt was pleading for peace and reconciliation. On the West Coast, the Emperor's imperial navy was sailing into San Francisco harbour and his troops were preparing to march along the Golden Gate Bridge. There'd been a second revolution in Russia, far worse than 1917's. The

Allies planned to drop soldiers over the Himalayas and fight in the south of China. And Chinese irregular soldiers were poised to smash open the Weihsien gates in a daring rescue mission, forcing the Japanese to close the camp and dispatch everyone in it to Tokyo.

There were three stories even more bizarre than those. In the first, the Hollywood beauty and soprano Deanna Durbin – her film career began alongside Judy Garland – had died in childbirth. In the second, the dancer Carmen Miranda, famed for her exotic clothes and her tutti-frutti hat, had been involved in a car crash, resulting in the amputation of both her legs. In the third, Churchill and Roosevelt had set off to rescue the internees on camels before becoming marooned near the Yellow River. No matter how implausible that last tale sounded, the internees were still 'eager to hear the next one', said Scanlan, because the most far-fetched speculation was somehow invigorating, a way of emerging from the limbo state of Weihsien. Scanlan explained that the camp was 'always anxious to hear something that might show us that the end was coming, that our internment would be soon over' and so 'anything that aroused our hopes we grasped and welcomed – though we knew in our hearts that it was an idle grasping at a shadow'.

One maliciously mischief-making internee made it his business to disseminate a different rumour every day, which he passed on during his morning walk inside the wall. He'd then eavesdrop conversations over breakfast and lunch to discover not only how far his piece of nonsense had travelled, but also the amendments and elaborations attached to it during constant re-telling. One of Scanlan's colleagues, a Belgian named Raymond de Jaegher, retaliated, starting what he called equally 'wild rumours' that were 'mixed [with] items of real news'. These were aimed against the Japanese. He claimed the Emperor had been assassinated and that 'two hundred thousand of his soldiers' had been killed 'in one battle alone'.

De Jaegher managed to get letters out of Weihsien after procuring Chinese-style envelopes and addressing them to what he called 'loyal Chinese friends of certain prisoners in camp'. The envelopes were then tied to a brick and thrown over the wall. The replies de Jaegher received enabled him to plot troop movements. So did a scheme he created, equally cleverly, with the cesspool coolies. He rolled up letters and placed them in a sealed tin box. The box was dropped in the coolies' pails of human excrement, which the Japanese only later began searching by poking through it with a long stick. Coolies also brought in information on small pieces of silk paper. These were either deposited in their mouths and spat out or forced into their noses and blown out. De Jaegher collected them from the spittle and the snot on the floor.

For all its distortions – 'we presumed even its sports results weren't true', said a prisoner – the *Peking Chronicle* was useful, providing you were intelligent enough to read between the lines and dismiss the lies. According to the *Chronicle*, the Japanese and the Germans were forever trouncing the Allies. In saying so, the paper dropped place-names. 'The mention over a period of months in this newspaper of the Gilbert and Marshall Islands, Manila, Iwo Jima and Okinawa was an unintended admission that the Americans had the Japanese on the run,' observed an internee, who reached this conclusion: 'To be fighting there the Americans must have advanced there.'

The Japanese guards were inadvertently suppliers of snatches of information from the distant war too. Remarkably slow-witted, the guards discovered that a Russian internee was a wizard when it came to mending radios. He was even allowed to fix them unsupervised, which allowed him to listen to broadcasts. He'd either delay the return of the radio, claiming the job was a tricky one, or he'd complete a token repair on the set, knowing the guard would have to bring it back to him in a month or so. In this way the internees learned of the Allies' invasion of Sicily in July and August 1943. As a way of communicating it to the camp, some of them sang countless renditions of 'Santa Lucia', which was then changed to 'Goodbye Sicilia'. The guards never spotted the unsubtle code.

None of the broadcasts suggested the war would be over soon. So the acceptance that freedom – if it came at all – was years rather than months away took an awful hold. The prospect was frightening for some, disturbing to all others. 'Our forced inactivity and complete ignorance of what the future held in store weighed heavily on all,' said Scanlan.

Towards the end of that first, hot summer the internees were at a low ebb, morosely disheartened by the squalor, the lack of food and the monotony of the diet and also pessimistic about how long Weihsien would be their gaol.

So the camp decided to stage late-afternoon athletics races to raise morale. Often these were held on red letter dates, such as American Independence Day, Labour Day or British Empire Day. For a few hours

Weihsien's 'Sports Day' was a way of forgetting the world both inside and outside its wall. The internees who weren't working tumbled out of their rooms and their dormitories to see it. The question of whether Liddell still ran wasn't so empty-headed after all now. And the running shoes he'd brought – even minus their spikes – proved useful.

There was no space to create a track in the cramped camp. A convoluted route was agreed upon instead. The start line was close to the Church Assembly Hall. The so-called 'front straight' was the turn along Main Street. The competitors then went into Market Square and returned down Tin Pan Alley, which was the 'back straight'. The finish line was a corner of a recreational field, already used for baseball and softball, which was treeless. One circuit totalled approximately 220 yards. Liddell's race, which was the main event, comprised four of these.

He had once given Patricia a pep talk about competition. The two of them had run together in a father and daughter's race in Tientsin. Patricia was supposed to pass on a white handkerchief, a substitute for a baton. She completed the course, but continued to hold on to the handkerchief.

Weihsien camp's makeshift baseball and softball field, which also marked the finish line of racing during frequent 'Sports Days'.

Liddell couldn't begin running until he had ever so tenderly coaxed it away from her. Those seconds, lost in persuasion, made it impossible for him to come first. Afterwards he told Patricia that winning never mattered. The important thing, he stressed, was always to 'do your best'. Liddell, though absolutely sincere in what he'd said to her, seldom acknowledged his toughly competitive instincts, which were inborn. He didn't like to lose.

An Olympic champion doesn't only possess more talent than anyone else. He also has something extra in regard to desire and motivation, which pushes him past the rest. Liddell demonstrated it even in Weihsien. He was spindly. His facial flesh had sunk around his cheekbones. His shoulders had dropped slightly because of the physical loads his frame carried from dawn to darkness. He didn't resemble a runner any more, let alone one whose name and photograph had appeared on the pages of five thousand newspapers – from New York to Nairobi, from Montevideo to Moscow – as a world and Olympic record holder. Those photographs had shown him in his Great Britain vest. Now Liddell wore his loose short-sleeved shirt and his khaki shorts, shabby because of wear and grime.

Aubrey Grandon, nicknamed 'Muscles' because of his physique and his love of exercising.

Some of his rivals either hadn't been born or were toddlers in 1924. Chief among them was twenty-four-year-old Aubrey Grandon, powerfully built enough to be nicknamed 'Muscles'. 'He was always showing them off to us girls,' said one internee. 'You'd see him doing his exercises and playing sport whenever he could. That was his way of coping in the camp.' He was a stoker, which accentuated his impressive physique – wide shoulders, strong arms and well-defined abs and pecs.

Half-Chinese, Grandon became a bit of a heart-throb, the sort of handsome gent who would stop a lady in mid-conversation when he entered a room. He had considerable charm, winning over even the elderly ladies with a rendition of the Irish ballad 'Molly Malone'. He had a prominent jaw and his nose, equally prominent, looked sharp enough to guillotine cheese. An accountant, Grandon grew up in a family wealthy enough to have servants. 'You didn't pour your own coffee – even if the pot was in the same room,' he said. After Weihsien, his father's fortune long gone, Grandon let his hair grow into a dark mane. This was so unfashionable and socially frowned upon that his friends refused to sit beside him on the London tube. The British sculptor Jacob Epstein noticed Grandon nevertheless and subsequently used him as the model for his work *Manhood*, which was exhibited at the Festival of Britain in 1951. Epstein's contemporary, Henry Moore, also chose him to be Adam in his study *Adam and Eve*.

Sportingly, Liddell gave his opponents a slight head start, agreeing not to begin until those quickest off the line began to swing into Main Street. He had a dozen paces to make up on them after the starter climbed on to an upturned wooden crate and held a white handkerchief aloft, letting his arm fall after shouting 'Ready, set, go!'

Liddell's reputation preceded him. Everyone in Weihsien, aware of his background, expected him to win without much of a sweat. Only those with knowledge of athletics understood the challenge of pitting his middle-aged body against someone as fit and as fast as Grandon. The trauma of the previous six months, plus the lack of nutrition, had weakened Liddell. He knew nonetheless what his audience had come to see. He also knew his failure to deliver it would disappoint them acutely. Liddell went into competition mode, dragging a performance out of himself.

The narrowness of the pathways made overtaking difficult for him until the wider part of the course was reached. Main Street was

Tin Pan Alley in the Weihsien camp. The photograph was taken in the early 1900s.

particularly tricky because tall acacia trees grew on either side of it. Their branches, full of foliage, interlocked like fingers and draped a canopy over the ground. The dust and dirt whipped up from the dry surface also meant that blown-back grit clouded the eyes.

Liddell lacked the whip speed of his younger self. What he didn't lack was technique and timing. There were runners who could undoubtedly have bettered him in a short sprint. This, however, was more a trial of endurance. He knew when to lengthen his stride and make the decisive move.

Grandon went off like a firecracker. Liddell gradually made his way through the pack, taking the outside route whenever possible. The crowd urged him on with shouts and yelps. The guards in the watchtowers overlooking the field began to applaud, as though the result meant something to them. On the final lap Liddell went ahead in the gaping open space after the bell tower. He didn't need to glance over his shoulder again. The matter was settled. No one could catch him now; not even Grandon. The winner threw his head back as though it were 1924 again.

In that hot gale of speed Liddell took the race comfortably, endorsing the opinion Otto Peltzer expressed about him at the end of the 1920s. He could have stepped up from the 400 metres to the 800 metres and competed in the 1932 Los Angeles Olympics. Liddell also won in a way that didn't suggest he was a slick, cocky professional who had grandiosely conquered a bunch of game amateurs. He shook each man's hand afterwards, offering congratulations before receiving them. It seemed as though everyone in the camp wanted to slap him on the back.

The effect of the performance was calculable in the mood. In those few minutes of action Liddell had shown himself to be a battler,

The height of the wall around the Weihsien camp and the bank beneath it were a deterrent to would-be escapees.

unnaturally strong in heart as well as muscle. The internees became even prouder than before about having him among them.

The brief drama of that race would nonetheless be forgotten in the aftermath of another, which proved monumental.

Not every missionary and Churchman won the wholehearted approval of Weihsien. Some, unlike Eric Liddell, lacked the instinct to appreciate the anguish of others and consequently failed to make proper allowances for it. The standards of the High Church could never be imposed on the secular – especially in such a harsh environment. That still didn't deter the most overzealous missionaries and priests from trying to introduce them. The same missionaries and priests could be sternly unforgiving afterwards when these attempts predictably hit stony ground. A few of them, strictly anti-smoking, anti-alcohol and anti-gambling, thought all cigarettes should be burned, the camp ought to become teetotal and the card games within it prohibited.

Internees with vices did go to extreme lengths to satisfy their addictions. The compulsive smokers would puff away at roll-ups of dry tea when tobacco was unavailable. The compulsive gamblers would head for twenty-four-hour poker marathons as soon as their Comfort Money arrived. The compulsive drinkers were the worst, pressing sweet potatoes to make a pungent wine whenever the bottles of the Chinese brew *pai ka'erh* or *by-gar*, a whisky, couldn't be obtained through subterfuge. The drunks, dependent well before Weihsien, went after the hospital's quota of medicinal alcohol, distilled drink from wood shavings and cleared the shelves of 'hay rum' hair tonic in the White Elephant Shop. One man was desperate enough to swallow his wife's perfume; no one minded the missionaries and priests condemning him.

The mistake of the fundamentalists was to scorn the moderate tippler, the five-a-day smoker and the occasional bet too. There could be a hard stare of disapproval even when an internee was overheard swearing. Langdon Gilkey remembered that a missionary in his dormitory believed 'any deviation from his own doctrinal beliefs, or any hint of personal vice, spelled for him certain damnation . . . He would cheerfully assure us that anyone who smoked, cussed or told off-colour jokes was certain to go to Hell,' he said.

The internees, thinking the odd loose curse to be a triviality in comparison with the camp's other failings, would dismiss it as a pointless complaint from a pernickety and interfering busybody. Respect on both sides was eroded on such irrelevances and others, including another preacher Gilkey recalled insisting on extra space 'in which I can have quiet to think out sermons'. The internees considered those like him to be over-righteous and unctuously moralistic. Early on Gilkey was called to calm a dormitory of twenty-one single women. There had been a fight between an American missionary and a British secretary. The other secretaries complained about the missionaries 'praying aloud at night' and singing hymns at 6 a.m. The missionaries complained about the secretaries 'chattering endlessly' about 'all the lurid escapades in their pasts'.

The most divisive differences were nonetheless attitudes towards the black market. The Japanese had forced the internees to agree to one condition: not to make contact with the Chinese. There were missionaries and priests who thought opening up a channel to them was like breaking a solemn promise, which counted as a disreputable act. The fact that the Japanese weren't feeding them well enough was not an acceptable excuse. The further fact that the black market's ring leader was the ingenious and resourceful Father Patrick Scanlan made no difference to them either.

Aware of how the internees 'were in circumstances in which it [was] easy to lose courage', Scanlan decided to fortify them. Already men and women alike, but particularly the elderly, were losing weight at an alarming rate. Among them was eighty-two-year-old Herbert Hudson Taylor, the only surviving son of J. Hudson Taylor, co-creator of the China Inland Mission in the 1880s. H. H. Taylor had a beard like Tolstoy's and would eventually weigh less than 80lb. He was said to have 'one foot on earth and the other in heaven'. His granddaughter, Mary, remembered others asking him 'let us take in your clothes'. He'd simply reply, 'God is going to bring me out of Weihsien and I'm going to fit into these clothes again.' Scanlan was compelled to act on behalf of people such as him. 'We were not badly treated,' he said. 'The rules of the camp were reasonable enough and, if we kept to these, we were given no trouble.' The problem of food was nonetheless insurmountable for Scanlan unless he broke those rules. 'Had the meals been better, or even if we had been allowed to buy from the Chinese, there would have been no friction, or at least very little, between us and the Japanese,' he explained.

The priest had geography on his side. He roomed on the south-east side of the wall. Just beyond was a scattering of peasant homes. 'There was no place in the camp better suited for buying,' he said. The Japanese, paranoid about the internees signalling to the Chinese, banned the hanging of laundry that could be seen from beyond the wall in case the order or the colour of the clothes constituted a coded message. Scanlan was still secretly able to make initial contact and persuade the Chinese to trade. He was also fortunate that an iron-barred drain was located near his building. The drain became an exchange point. Usually after lights out, Scanlan would lift it open and crawl inside. The Chinese placed food, especially eggs, between the bars at the other end. A few bricks were also chipped out near the base of the wall to create a 'serving hatch' for him. At midnight, as soon as the goods had been checked and counted, he'd return with payment. There was a silent system to alert Scanlan of danger when exchanges were made over the wall and also under it. Under the pretext of facing the wall to pray, priests took up vantage points within sight of one another and then passed signals in a relay, using either a handkerchief or a prearranged gesture, such as bending over. Next morning Scanlan and the other monks would carry contraband in the large pockets of their black scapulars, delivering it to those who had placed advance orders. 'At first I made it a rule to buy for sick people and children,' said Scanlan, expanding those parameters only when 'people really in need begged me to get things'. He called the struggle to obtain them and the Japanese efforts to stop him a 'contest between us and them'.

Liddell fully supported Scanlan. He thought the ruses to obtain food were not only legitimate, but also without moral dilemma. The Japanese expected the internees to work. That work couldn't be done without strength and muscle, which was wearing away without sustenance. Relying only on the Japanese to provide it was neither sensible nor sustainable. Liddell willingly distributed what Scanlan brought – and took orders for more – for the camp's benefit.

Eggs were particularly important because the shells were ground to powder with the back of a spoon to provide pure, dry and much-needed calcium, which was sickening to swallow. 'It tasted like crunchy chalk dust,' said an internee. Tomatoes, apples, corncobs, jam and watermelons were among other foods regularly smuggled in. So were chickens and geese – both alive and dead. One live goose was hurled over the wall and went squawking down the streets in fright after landing. The recipient had to chase after it, finally covering the bird with a pair of pyjamas before smartly wringing its neck with a twist of his hands. In comparison with the sickly scrapings of normal Weihsien dining, Scanlan introduced gold-leaf living.

At first the guards neither noticed the food nor smelled the aroma of it cooking. But some of the Chinese grew irresponsibly bold, scaling the wall to barter inside the camp rather than outside it, and the Japanese soon identified Scanlan as the mastermind behind these negotiations. He was closely observed. On one occasion Scanlan, hiding five dozen eggs, was about to be apprehended by a sentry who had noticed the bulge in his clothes. Scanlan thought quickly. He began to squat on the floor and made anguished noises, telling the guard he had diarrhoea. The guard believed him and walked away.

He was a scrupulous black marketeer. Accounts were kept in a black notebook, which he called The Book of Life. Every purchase, no matter how small, was logged and dated. This was almost his undoing. He was once apprehended with both his list and a packet containing five hundred Chinese dollars. He was led away by the wrists to be searched and interrogated. Again he feigned sickness, falling to the ground with a low groan. As the guard reached down to drag him upright, Scanlan displayed the dexterity of a magician to remove the money and throw it behind him.

Eventually Scanlan was forced to shut down the operation temporarily to avoid further suspicion. When it resumed, however, the Japanese caught him on a moonless evening near the wall, where he'd been whispering to a dealer. Scanlan had taken his breviary with him as a prop. He now pretended to read it, turning the pages as a torch beam illuminated his face. Scanlan told the guards he was 'reading my prayers', which was hardly plausible in such enveloping darkness. The guards ordered him to read aloud to them, a test of whether he could see the words. 'The light was fading fast, and I really could not read the small print,' he admitted. Scanlan nonetheless knew the psalms by heart and merely recited them from memory, convincing them he was eccentric but also innocent.

Then his luck ran out. He was caught with a 10lb package of sugar in one hand and a bag containing fourteen tins of jam in the other. The Japanese hauled him off to the stone guardroom, sentencing him to solitary confinement. Knowing nothing of Scanlan's Trappist religion, the commandant thought solitary confinement was a punishment for him. Supposed to serve fourteen days, Scanlan was released after ten because he annoyed the Japanese so much. He sang hymns and chanted loudly in Latin throughout the early hours, interrupting the guards' sleep. Scanlan was so well liked that internees used to give him what he called 'a pleased and knowing smile' whenever he passed them in the mornings and 'saw and heard the eggs I had bought sizzling in peanut oil'. So his freedom was celebrated in an Independence Day-like parade. The guards looked on askance when the short route back to his room was lined with an enthusiastically cheering crowd, as though he'd beaten Liddell in one of the athletics races.

The risk of conducting business became more dangerous. And the ramifications grew worse. The Japanese panicked, becoming worried that the internees would start to purchase guns instead of food. The guards badly beat up two Chinese dealers. A third was hoisted by his arms and legs and an internee witnessed his body being 'swung like a battering ram against a brick wall until his skull was a bloody pulp'. A fourth was shot at, the bullets just clearing his head. A fifth was electrocuted on the barbed wire fence. The Japanese left the blackened corpse to hang there for almost a week to deter the Chinese and the internees alike. A sixth and a seventh were marched off to face a firing squad in front of other villagers. The rapid crack of rifle fire, killing both of them, could be heard inside the camp. There were numerous instances of water torture. One local, found packing eggs in his padded trousers, was subjected to it ruthlessly. 'When his belly was swollen like a barrel,' said Scanlan, 'the soldiers often kicked it, stepped on it and jumped on it.' Rice was sometimes tipped into a victim's mouth, which 'made the ordeal worse', added Scanlan, because 'the water caused [it] to swell in the poor fellow's stomach'. Scanlan and his team worked on, placing commitment towards the community ahead of personal safety. Scanlan also told one internee: 'If we are caught and executed for this, there will be one less priest. If one of the fathers of a family is caught, there is the added suffering of his wife and children.'

The ancient economic law of supply and demand was always stacked in favour of the Chinese, who openly exploited it. As Scanlan confessed, the dealers 'asked much more for their goods than the actual price'. A watermelon could cost $50. Fewer than half a dozen apples might be twice as much and were considered a delicacy. Once, after a supply was delivered, Liddell said cheerfully, 'Well, even if we don't have the money to buy them we can at least enjoy the smell.' Even a carton of eggs, abundant on the farms, fluctuated between $20 and $50 depending on the mood and the whim of the seller. Scanlan estimated that each night 'many thousands of dollars' were passed either over the wall or through the drainage system.

It meant the oldest economic principle – and also the most basic – became a factor. When outgoings exceed income, bankruptcy can follow. The Comfort Money, which was paid only spasmodically anyway, was never sufficient to consistently cover the sums the Chinese demanded. The internees began to swap jewellery and trinkets for food instead. Some went to extreme lengths, telling the camp dentist to pull out gold fillings. Others dealt with a hideously vulgar character named Jacob Goyas, a short, rotund Uruguayan with globed eyes, thick lips and a leathery tan. In his early forties, he called himself a 'merchant', which was the polite alternative to his real title – criminal conman and war profiteer. It was believed Goyas owned multiple passports and had been embroiled in murky and mostly illegal currency trading in North China, which made him fairly wealthy. He loaned money to internees, ideally preferring gold in return, and could often be seen counting a wad of IOUs.

Liddell stuck with Scanlan, as if declaring a solid oath of solidarity with him. He began willingly to donate the only valuables he'd brought into Weihsien – those medals and trophies from his athletics career that Florence hadn't taken to Toronto. Most of them had been won at relatively minor events, such as inter-varsity competitions, and small Saturday 'games' held around Scotland. The food Liddell got from exchanging his personal history was shared, the bigger portion always going to those he thought needed it. Much later he also had his gold watch and chain valued, intending to sell it to purchase new sports equipment to replace what had been lost or broken. A colleague called it 'a sacrifice willingly thought out and prepared for' simply so Liddell could 'give pleasure to scores of people'. He kept the timepiece only when a package containing long-awaited Comfort Money, delayed because of Japanese bureaucracy, arrived at last.

Scanlan didn't spend long in Weihsien. In the late summer and early autumn of 1943, the camp went through an upheaval. More than three quarters of the priests and nuns were released and taken to Peking after Pope Pius XII's officials declared each was a citizen of the neutral Vatican State and the Japanese accepted the argument rather than squabble with the pontiff. While Scanlan and most of his colleagues marched two abreast out of the camp – 'on many sides I saw tears', he said – a group of them stayed behind to minister to the needs of the imprisoned Catholics. Within a fortnight there were new arrivals to replace them. From the China Inland Mission School at Chefoo came teachers and more than three hundred students, aged between six and sixteen.

Liddell became 'Uncle Eric' to dozens upon dozens of them. 'If he'd told us the moon was square, we'd have believed him,' said one, remembering his impact on their young lives.

Trying to drag back childhood or early adolescent recollections can be maddeningly difficult. What returns often does so in flashes, appearing and disappearing again in the speed of a subliminal image. The pictures that settle in the mind are seldom completely whole either. That's why there are always irregularities in early recollections – discrepancies between what you are sure happened, what you think happened and what actually did happen. The past is like looking at a half-finished painting in which a corner is missing, a face is blurred, a distant scene is indistinct.

But the children and the teenagers of Weihsien who spoke or wrote about the camp afterwards had shared points of reference about the place. Each of them remembered the small, tight rooms and the barbed wire along the walls. Each of them remembered the food – the grain and the beans and the tough meat. Each of them remembered the flies and the bed bugs and rat-catching competitions, the first prize a tin of sardines. Each of them remembered the perpetual search for coal and coal dust and the endless pumping of water and the daily roll calls, which seemed endless too. And each of them remembered Eric Liddell, the memory of him as sharp as sunlight. Aside from their own family, Liddell was the one adult in Weihsien whose presence made an enduring impression on everyone who came into contact with him.

Separated from his own children, and so considering himself to be orphaned, Liddell adopted whoever needed him. Recalling his own unhappiness without his mother and father at Eltham College, he was especially solicitous towards the parentless in the camp. That title of unofficial 'uncle' was bestowed on him because of it. In his so-called free time, which meant whatever hours were left after his designated chores were over, Liddell gave himself willingly to the camp's children and teenagers. Worried about the psychological as well as the physical damage Weihsien would inflict on them, Liddell tried to make each day interesting to alleviate stretches of boredom and also educational to nourish the mind. Joyce Stranks, almost sixteen, became particularly devoted to Liddell, who she said was 'concerned about our concerns', never trivializing them or patronizing whoever raised them. 'He was so kind and so patient and always so gentle with everyone,' she said. 'All of us knew we could talk to him about anything, especially our difficulties, and he'd take what we said seriously and offer advice. Sometimes we could speak to him more easily than our own families.' A contemporary of Stranks's added that Liddell's one-to-one conversations made you feel 'as if you were the only person who mattered to him'. Stranks said simply: 'We youngsters went to see him whenever we could.' One of Liddell's friends in the dormitory, constantly pestered with the question 'Is Uncle Eric here?', carved a wooden sign which he nailed to the front of the door. It was an arrangement of two sliding panels. One panel told the caller that Liddell was IN. The other informed the caller Liddell was OUT.

In the chemistry classroom, where textbooks were scarce and the apparatus for practical experiments was virtually non-existent, Liddell found a solution. He hand-wrote an instructional book in blue and black ink on lined paper, which was then stitched together. The book, a hundred pages long, also exhibited his artistic talents. He drew sketches of instruments and also diagrams that explained an assortment of tests to be carried out using them. At the front of the book he wrote a dedication to whoever read it: 'The bones of inorganic chemistry. Can these dry bones live?'

Outside the classroom Liddell trained anyone who wanted to run, teaching them about stride-pattern and stamina and then timing them with his stopwatch. Shortly after arriving in camp, a group from Chefoo decided to stage a race. Liddell, overhearing them, said he would compete too. The teenagers saw a bald man rather than a former Olympic gold medallist. None of them imagined this 'old chap', which is how he looked to them, could possibly stay the course. In agreeing to let him jog along one voice rose above the others and said, 'You won't catch us.' The sight of Liddell coasting along beside them, never needing to accelerate, came as a revelation to them. Among those runners was Steve Metcalf, then fifteen. He'd been born in China, the son of a Protestant missionary who had translated the New Testament into Eastern Lisu. 'He won easily,'

Metcalf said of Liddell that day. 'He wasn't breathing hard at the end. We didn't find out until afterwards that he'd already beaten the adults in a proper race before we got into the camp. We didn't know his full history and I suppose weren't fully aware of what being an Olympic champion really meant. We thought we'd win simply because we were younger.'

Metcalf was dark, short – around 5 feet 4 inches – and slim too. The camp was initially overwhelming for him. 'It seemed so chaotic. The adults who were already there didn't know what to make of us at first. Some of the men were relieved to discover our lads were strong enough to pump water. We still represented mouths to feed and couldn't be as effective as the Catholic priests had been.' Liddell became Metcalf's mentor. 'He was my role model too,' said Metcalf. 'He was also everyone's hero.'

Metcalf admired Liddell's hatred of cheating. After catching one of his other athletes attempting to elbow a rival in the chest, he spoke to him about a hurdles relay race he'd witnessed at that Stamford Bridge meeting against America in 1924. This was the first time – but not the last – that Metcalf and his friends heard it. The first leg was run in two lanes. The remaining legs were run on the inside only, making the hurdle in the

Steve Metcalf, who received Eric's grey running shoes and considered the Olympic champion to be his mentor.

second lane redundant. Watching from the grandstand, Liddell saw the splendidly initialled Major E. G. W. W. Harrison open a 10-yard lead on the American Dan Kinsey, another gold medallist in Paris. Harrison's foot then flicked the top of an inside-lane hurdle, tipping it over. Kinsey had a choice to make. 'The fallen hurdle left a gap,' said Liddell, knowing Kinsey could run through it and gain easy distance on the shaken Harrison. 'In the fraction of a second at his disposal, a decision was made. He swerved to the side, jumped the hurdle next to the fallen one and then moved back in to the edge of the track again.' He remembered the thrill that 'went through me', and 'the cheer' rising from the crowd, which recognized the gesture. 'That was the finest thing done that day,' said Liddell, who believed Kinsey had been inspired 'by the spirit of sportsmanship' which was 'ingrained in him'.

Metcalf knew the purpose of the story: 'Those were his values and he wanted us to be like that in life as well as in sport.'

Liddell played hockey, football, basketball, baseball and softball too. He also made sure the equipment was well maintained and asked Metcalf to become his assistant in the repair shop, which was a white-walled space no bigger than a broom cupboard. Broken bats and hockey sticks were bound with either torn bedsheets or twine and glued to the wood. The glue stank like fish that had been left to rot for a fortnight. 'The smell was terrible,' said Metcalf. 'It made you feel sick until you got used to it.' Shut off from the camp, the door closed to contain the stench of the glue, the teacher and his pupil talked away, attempting to ignore it.

When Liddell occasionally spoke of his family, he did so with a quiet, touching pride. 'He missed them without ever admitting how much,' said Metcalf. When he spoke of the Olympics – only whenever Metcalf mentioned it – he usually changed the topic after a few sentences. 'He was concerned with the present rather than the past,' added his friend. Metcalf once asked Liddell about his refusal to compete on Sunday in Paris. 'He replied that it was just the natural thing to have done. He'd been following his beliefs and had never regretted it.' Ready to frame a follow-up question about the repercussions of that decision – Metcalf wasn't fully aware of the British Olympic Association's reaction to it – he heard Liddell turn the conversation in another direction. 'I took it as a sign that he didn't want to say anything else that afternoon. It was done very politely and graciously, of course.' Eventually Liddell did let slip that 'pressure' was applied on him to change his mind even after reaching Paris. In what can only be a reference to Lord Cadogan's 'playing the game' message in the official brochure to athletes, Liddell also added that the higher-ups in the BOA thought sporting 'principles' should come before personal convictions.

Things were different in camp. Weihsien pushed Liddell into making a concession over Sunday sport that no amount of brow-beating from the BOA had ever accomplished.

Liddell always locked away the sports equipment in a hut on Saturday night and then unlocked it again on Monday morning. The camp's elders accepted his stance, never disputing it, until one summer Sunday morning when Liddell discovered the door had been split, the lock hanging off. A handful of older boys, weary of the humdrum rhythm of that listless day, had broken in, taken the hockey sticks and begun a game to occupy themselves. Without a referee, the contest had disintegrated into quarrelling, rancour and brawling. The precious sticks were used as weapons. Fisticuffs and the odd bruise and black-eye were hardly the harbinger of feral anarchy to come. Weihsien's disciplinary committee was nonetheless spooked enough to ask Liddell to reconsider his position on strict Sunday observance. He didn't want to appear dogmatic, certainly not when conditions were so trying in camp. After forty-eight hours, during which time he contemplated the dilemma, Liddell adopted the middle-way. He agreed to arrange Sabbath sport, but only after the midday meal. And so it was that the continental Sabbath, which Liddell had refused to acknowledge during the Paris Olympics, came to Shandong Province. He even refereed the next hockey match, which passed with barely a cross word between teams amazed to see him there. No one had thought Liddell would contribute to the game, believing instead he'd only open up the equipment store and then either return to the church or conduct Sunday school. 'Everything he did was for the greater good, including that,' explained Metcalf.

If there was a problem anywhere, 'Uncle Eric' would be there to sort it out.

In the web of forced associations that Weihsien became, the usual rules about the birds and the bees and what happened as a result of them could never be suspended. The heart wants what it wants whatever the surroundings and the circumstances. Even the celibate priests and monks formed strong emotional attachments with women, who waved them a lachrymose goodbye after the Vatican secured those release papers for them. Sex in Weihsien was difficult because of the lack of privacy and also the lack of contraception. It was nevertheless not impossible after the lights dimmed. The statistical proof is irrefutable. There were thirty-three children born in Weihsien. There were also half a dozen weddings, the bride usually wearing a veil made from a mosquito net and a dress cut from a silk nightgown. Among the weddings was an interracial marriage between the jazz band leader and his attractive half-English, half-Chinese bride, who gave birth to a daughter ten months later. With the exception of a few loudmouth bigots, the internees were generally more enlightened and tolerant about racial integration than others in the 1940s. The camp was less forgiving about under-age sex.

With puberty came rites of passage – not only mild sexual experimentation but also intercourse between some of the more mature-minded teenagers. Langdon Gilkey claimed that a group of them gathered at night in an unused basement for 'what we could only term sexual orgies', which sounds very Sodom and Gomorrah. Gilkey added that 'horrified and furious' parents, who beforehand had 'taken no interest' in what their offspring were doing 'so long as they were out of the room', neither offered a constructive solution nor volunteered to find one. 'To no one's surprise,' he concluded, 'the crisis was finally dealt with by the missionary teachers.' Evening classes and dances were held and a makeshift games room appeared. Gilkey said he regularly saw Liddell bent over a 'chessboard or a model boat, or directing some sort of square dance'. He also witnessed the constant demands placed on Liddell and the way in which he responded to them – 'absorbed, warm and interested, pouring all of himself into this effort to capture the imagination of those penned-up youths'.

There was another notable example of it. Liddell encouraged a sixteen-year-old Greek called Alex Marinellis to pursue running. Marinellis, heavy-set, told a friend that his new tutor was 'coaching me almost daily' and thought 'I've got what it takes to be a great runner if I really work at it'. More accurately, Liddell believed athletics might reform Marinellis, who had been caught stealing coal and who spent too long as a minor henchman to Jacob Goyas during black market negotiations among the internees.

Liddell thought no one was beyond redemption.

*

In her memoir *God Remained Outside*, the French Resistance fighter Geneviève de Gaulle-Anthonioz tells of her imprisonment in the women's concentration camp at Ravensbruck, where around fifty thousand died. She prayed there, throwing herself 'on the mercy of the Father'. She remembers being 'answered not even by silence – but by the wretched sound of my own distress'. Certain she is about to be killed, de Gaulle-Anthonioz then asks: 'My God . . . Why hast Thou forsaken me?' – the question Jesus asks in the Bible.

Eric Liddell never felt forsaken even when Weihsien was at its worst.

His close friend in camp was another missionary, Joe Cotterill. In the first six months he and Liddell were next-door neighbours. After the camp's accommodation list was redrawn – following the departure of the priests and nuns and also the repatriation of over three hundred Americans and Canadians in exchange for Japanese prisoners – the two of them roomed together on the third floor of the hospital building. Cotterill, a stoker in one of the kitchens, awoke at the same hour as Liddell. 'We began to share our Bible readings and prayed together,' he said. Cotterill called them 'very special times'.

The twenty-six-year-old Cotterill was married in Weihsien – partly because of Liddell's influence. His fiancée, whom he met there, belonged to a different mission. 'We couldn't contact our respective mission bodies to ask advice about whether we ought to get married. And there were many people who didn't think the camp was the right place anyway to make a decision that would be binding for life. We decided to think seriously about that. We even stopped seeing one another, except casually, to give us more time to consider what to do.' Cotterill was unaware that his wife-to-be was seeking advice from Liddell, whose own courtship with Florence had hardly been orthodox. When Cotterill underwent an appendix operation, Liddell was the messenger who made sure his future bride was fully informed about it. She, rather than Cotterill, promptly announced their engagement at the beginning of his convalescence. 'I don't know what Eric did or said, but I am fairly sure he knew what was going to happen before I did,' said Cotterill, who found Liddell had a 'calming and very stable influence' in the camp. 'He was always so positive – even when there wasn't much to be positive about, and he carried the weight of others' worries and burdens without hesitation.'

As Weihsien deteriorated in every way, and the war ground on seemingly without end, internees who had led blameless lives began openly to question both their religious faith and the overall purpose of the Church. Some asked Liddell directly, 'What is the point of continuing to pray – for food, for comfort, for rescue – when those prayers aren't being answered?' Where was God? Why wasn't He listening? Also, why had He 'allowed' Weihsien to happen in the first place? Hearing him recite his daily devotions, Cotterill knew not only that Liddell's own belief never wavered, but also that he reassured those who had doubts. 'His faith grew stronger than ever in such troubled times,' he said. 'He didn't blame God for the situation we were all in. He believed God was in that situation with us. That was his message and he never stopped preaching it. He'd say to us all "Have faith".'

Liddell regularly read aloud from *Discipleship* and the Sermon on the Mount and dwelt on one passage: 'Love your enemies. Bless them that curse you. Do good to them that hate you. Pray for them which despitefully use you and persecute you.' Early in 1944 he began urging the internees to pray specifically for the men in uniform – the camp guards. Liddell told his congregation and also his Sunday school classes: 'I've begun to pray for the guards and it's changed my whole attitude towards them. When we hate them we are self-centred.' This was an extension of a sermon he'd originally given a dozen years earlier in Hawick on the Scottish borders. There he had told the story of the disciples who asked Jesus how many times someone ought to be forgiven. 'They had missed the whole point of His teaching,' explained Liddell. 'They could not forgive a person once. They must have the whole spirit of forgiveness.'

He resolved to give the guards his 'whole spirit' too. Some of them had tried to forge relationships with the internees. One pruned a tomato plant for a family, bringing it back to health. Others taught judo or played chess with the children. A handful performed small kindnesses, such as donating milk for a baby, giving a bottle of sake to the head of a household or presenting a watermelon to a seamstress in return for mending a pair of trousers. But, as Langdon Gilkey stressed, there were guards who took sadistic delight in being vile. 'They would rant and bark, slap and kick, as if the person in front of them were a hideous spider that had sent them into a panic and must be crushed,' he said. 'Anyone under their authority apparently inspired in them a streak of meanness, the desire to prevent another from doing what appeared fun, and on the contrary, to make him do what was unpleasant.' A sixty-two-year-old internee was slapped for merely 'bumping into a guard'. A thirty-eight-year-old woman was struck for no apparent reason. A sixteen-year-old was hit after being caught trying to buy honey from the Chinese.

Some thought prayer was wasted on such an enemy. Others considered Liddell's approach as either a step too far or sheer bloody lunacy.

If taken in isolation, there are aspects of Weihsien that make it seem less like a prison camp and more like a summer camp.

There were enough books to build a small lending library. You could find multiple copies of Shakespeare's *Collected Works*, the novels of Charles Dickens or the plays of George Bernard Shaw. You could wallow in a limited amount of romantic fiction or high-brow biography, such as Boswell's account of trailing behind Dr Johnson across the isles of Scotland. And you could read Jules Verne's *Around the World in Eighty Days* and H. G. Wells's *The Time Machine*. Someone put a copy of John Gunther's 1939 socio-political work *Inside Asia* on the shelves too. The cover was wrapped in brown paper in case the Japanese came across it and became hostile towards the content, thinking it subversive.

As well as the professional jazz combo, which played at dances, there were enough musical instruments – and a sufficient number of musicians – to form a Salvation Army band, a symphony orchestra, and a choral society. Joyce Stranks's father had packed an assortment of brass instruments – including a trumpet, a trombone and a euphonium – between bed mattresses in Tientsin. His eldest daughter had walked into Weihsien with a viola strapped to her back. Internees also brought cellos, clarinets, flutes and violins. Recorders were cut from sticks of bamboo. With a piano already in camp – dusty and in need of repair and tuning – the only instruments missing were a bassoon, an oboe and a double bass, which was too bulky to transport. Recitals included Mozart concertos, Handel's *Messiah*, Verdi's *Aida*, Tchaikovsky's *Swan Lake*, Mendelssohn's *Elijah* and Chopin's *Polonaise*. A Trappist monk beautifully sang 'If I Had The Wings Of An Angel'. A Welsh missionary belted out a marvellous rendition of 'I Know That My Redeemer Liveth'. The camp's commandant once arrived at a performance of Stainer's *Crucifixion* at the very moment the choir had reached the part that begins 'Fling wide the gates'. The commandant was oblivious to the irony.

The internees' choice of music wasn't always welcomed. The Japanese protested when the Salvation Army band played the Star Spangled Banner to celebrate American Independence Day in 1944. The guards were at least mollified when the jazzmen dedicated a concert song to Gold Tooth, who rose from his seat and made several low bows to the audience after the announcement. What the combo played was 'I'll Be Glad When You're Dead You Rascal You', which Louis Armstrong had popularized in the early 1930s. Gold Tooth, liking the foot-stomping tune but not understanding the lyrics, assumed he was being paid a compliment. 'He yelled and clapped and danced a small jig,' reported an internee.

There were enough would-be thespians to put on shows and dramas. Among them was Noël Coward's *Hay Fever*. The appeal for props highlighted the odd collection of impractical novelties and knick-knacks some of the internees had brought into camp, such as a cuckoo clock, a set of andirons and a Constable print in a gilt frame. Costumes were cobbled together. For a production of Shaw's *Androcles and the Lion*, the Roman guards' uniforms were made from tin cans.

Aside from culture, the other regular recreation was baseball or softball. The teams were given names such as the Peking Panthers, the Tientsin Tigers and the Priests' Padres. Before leaving the camp Father Patrick Scanlan had even created a side called the Black Marias to honour the black marketeers. Mary Scott got involved enthusiastically. 'No one thought it was strange or undignified for a woman in her thirties to be playing ball,' she said. Aubrey Grandon, a natural athlete, regularly thumped home runs over the wall, forcing either the Chinese to throw the ball back or the guards to go and retrieve it. The softball games, like the athletics races, were landmarks – benignly rowdy and boisterous affairs. The Chefoo pupils, said one internee, were told there was no such thing as a set of manners for the outside world and another set for the concentration camp. 'You were supposed to be as refined as the two princesses in Buckingham Palace all the time,' she said. That refinement was forgotten on the softball field. 'We whooped, we hollered, we flipped hand springs and slapped each other on the back. Our teachers shuddered.'

Those who weren't sporty, couldn't play an instrument, and couldn't sing or dance or act gave talks and lectures instead. The artists in Weihsien – one of them had work hung in London's Royal Academy – produced colourful posters to promote topics as widely different as atheism and agnosticism, the practicalities of woodwork and the works of the Greek philosophers. In the search for entertaining speakers Eric

Liddell was prodded into giving a lecture about his athletics career. He did so reluctantly, of course. As ever, Liddell made it sound as though becoming champion in 1924 had been a fluke, a combination of wild chance on his part and bad luck on the part of those who ran against him. The talk was based around others' achievements. Liddell said his success in Paris wouldn't have been possible without the influence of Tom McKerchar and the encouragement of his friends from Cambridge. He skimmed over his own race, as if it weren't worth dwelling on, and spoke instead about watching Harold Abrahams and Paavo Nurmi. His audience – about sixty-strong – learned of his admiration for Henry Stallard's courageously inspiring effort. Speaking about his head-back running style, Liddell wove in the story about his collision with the Tientsin photographer, who had knocked him unconscious. He told it against himself, as though he ought to have seen the camera on the track and avoided it. That part of the lecture, which seemed hilarious at the time, would return darkly to the minds of the internees soon enough.

Other ostensible signs of normality were dotted through the camp.

At Christmas Liddell organized the distribution of cards and goodwill messages, which were made from any scrap of loose paper the internees could find. Several months after Mussolini was deposed, a hundred Italians were arrested in Shanghai and brought into Weihsien. Liddell made sure the spirit of the season was extended to them too. He put the cards and messages in a vegetable sack and went on a delivery round like a festive postman.

One man planted gladioli bulbs and saw them flourish. One boy raised four peregrine falcon chicks. One woman painted watercolours of the camp's buildings and its flora and fauna; another kept a snowy-coloured kitten until a guard dog mauled it to death. Students sat Oxford Matriculation Exams, which were among papers carried into Weihsien. The university ratified the passes after the war. Girl Guides and Brownies, Boy Scout and Cub Scout troops were formed. Those in them earned badges for a selection of disciplines – tying knots and folk singing, sewing and fire-building, and reading and the study of nature.

Don't be fooled. This was still no playground of carefree freedom. The rigours of the place were always severe. The entertainments, arranged to bring a creative structure and a spirit to the camp, went on against a gruesome backdrop: the various sicknesses – malaria, dysentery, dehydration, scarlet fever, exhaustion, low blood pressure, long clinical depressions and short mental crack-ups; the lack of medicines with which to cope with them; the bickering that became bitterly intense between internees growing ever more irritable and desperate under the cumulative stresses of being locked up; the scurrilous behaviour, such as stealing, that those stresses initiated even among those who had previously shown impeccably solid morals; the shortages of food, the servings so meagre that eventually the enfeebled prisoners concluded that starvation would come before liberation.

How long can anyone live on crumbs? The average man will burn 400 to 500-plus calories per hour while doing heavy manual labour. Weihsien's calorie count fell to barely 1,200 per day. There were internees who foraged for weeds, boiling pigweed and dock after green vegetables ran out. One of the Japanese owned a nanny goat, which once strayed from the officers' and guards' compound. The animal was immediately milked before the guards realized it was missing.

Everywhere the camp was under pressure. In the kitchens the cooks couldn't cope with the lack of supplies. The stokers, constantly aching and dirty, wanted a break from firing up the ovens. Some of those who pumped water began complaining of pulled back muscles, arm strains and hernias, and also blistered hands. A few of them collapsed through fatigue. A few more claimed to be too sick to leave their beds. Gastric and bowel illnesses were common. So was gingivitis and other gum diseases. The internees sang a song called 'Weihsien Blues'. It ended with the lines:

Since we've come to Weihsien . . . they've worked us till we're dead,
Though now we're called the labour corps, we'll be a corpse instead.

Some were desperate enough to attempt suicide. Over two and a half years a clutch of attempts were made through slitting a wrist, drinking stolen morphine or swallowing painkillers from the hospital, ingesting match-heads and hanging. None succeeded.

Without the likes of Eric Liddell, the camp would have come apart. He was a singularity in it – a one-man task-force. Every morning he wound himself up for another great burst of work, often overheard singing one of three hymns during it: 'There's A Wideness In God's Mercy', 'Gracious Spirit, Dwell In Me' and 'God Who Touches Earth With Beauty'. 'The more he was needed, the more he did. I don't remember hearing him ever saying no to anyone,' said Joe Cotterill. 'You only had to wait your turn in the queue for his time.'

Weihsien thought Liddell was indestructible. After all, he was an Olympic gold medallist. He could come through anything, as though that medal were the equivalent of Achilles' shield. The grateful internees were too familiar with the sight of him – and also the diminishing sight of themselves in the mirror – to notice much difference either in his appearance or in his bearing. But throughout the spring and summer of 1944 he became progressively thinner. He became tired more quickly than before too. He found tasks, completed routinely in the past, were harder now. He discovered that easy sleep eluded him. He blamed the diet and assumed his condition was no different from anyone else's. It took an unweary pair of eyes to enter the camp, see Liddell afresh and register the changes in him.

Those eyes were Annie Buchan's.

CHAPTER SIXTEEN

Call to Me All My
Sad Captains

Eric Liddell was frequently seen staring at photographs of Florence and the children, as if contemplating the life he might have lived well away from war and Weihsien.

The letters he received from her came only fitfully, the mail travelling slowly across sea and land and then seldom reaching him anyway because the 6,000-mile chain bringing the post contained too many vulnerable links ever to guarantee reliability. A ship could be sunk or forced to change course. A truck might be blown up or ambushed. A lazy or indifferent hand might casually throw away or burn her words before the Red Cross received them. Florence wrote on regardless, hoping the next letter – or the letter after that – would get through.

The letter telling Liddell of her father's death in November 1943 did reach Weihsien. The one informing him of his mother's, ten months later, did not.

The most poignant of Florence's letters is painful to read even now because hindsight allows us to know that the longing contained in it went unfulfilled. The knowledge that her husband read it, and also knew that their separation hadn't diluted what she thought or felt about him, proved to be no consolation for a long while afterwards.

The letter was posted at the end of August 1943. Liddell didn't receive it for another six months. She wrote to him in the way he was obliged to write to her – in capital letters, which always take longer to put on paper than the flow of normal handwriting. It's as though Florence has used them to make certain her hand doesn't rush ahead of her emotions and make them illegible on the page. With capitals, Liddell won't have to stop suddenly or hesitate over a word or a line that is difficult to decipher.

'Dearest Eric,' she begins.

Florence says the children are 'growing like weeds'. She adds that it gave her a 'queer feeling to realise they really belong to me'. She composes pen pictures of them. Patricia's hair is 'short and curly'. She is 'quite the young lady' and has learned to swim. Heather now has pigtails and is so 'inquisitive' as to be 'interested in the whys and wherefore of everything'. A baby no longer, Maureen is still 'a wee thing', who carries herself 'very straight' and has 'such a determined walk'. Of her, Florence also says: 'I wish you could see her trying to make herself heard above the babble of the older children. She is developing quite an auctioneer's voice – and she likes to hear her own voice too.' She tells him: 'The children miss you so and are always asking about when you [will] come home.'

Florence tries to comfort her husband. She is coping. She is 'ever so fit'. She is also 'busy from morning to night' and is grateful for it. 'It is good to be busy,' she insists, intimating that being so is the only way to block out the thought of what her life is like without him. 'I have learnt a great deal in these two years, Eric,' she says, without elaborating on those lessons. 'I guess you have too.'

The closing paragraph is like a sigh, the love and all the sad regret of absence evident. In it there is the promise of a better tomorrow for them – whenever that 'tomorrow' might come. There is the reassurance that he is never out of her thoughts; and also that she and 'the girls' will be waiting for him – however long the waiting takes. There is Florence's belief, implicit in one sentence, that whatever changes the camp has wrought on him, and however different he might find her and the world after Weihsien, nothing will ever mar the relationship between them. All this is compressed into fifty words, which once read demand to be read again because the reader immediately begins to think about the future that was denied to them and what both could have made out of it.

'Oh Eric, my thoughts and prayers are forever with you and I long for the time when we'll be able to live as a family again . . . We will appreciate our life together all the more and in the meantime we have some wonderful memories to live on.'

Love in a letter. Florence writes to her 'dearest Eric' in bold, black capitals.

Florence admits 'Yes, I know I have wild hopes' and also says 'I know I'm crazy', which is designed to both lighten the last paragraph and make him laugh aloud to himself. The final line, however, is a declaration that only someone utterly devoted to another could ever make.

'Yours forever and a day,' she ends.

In early July 1944 Annie Buchan didn't so much walk into Weihsien as march through the gates. Indeed, she tended to march everywhere – head up, shoulders back – and the Japanese guards, as the soldiers in Siaochang had once done, learned not to obstruct her. There'd be a rebuke that crossed the language barrier through tone alone. Her friend, whom she had nursed in the British Embassy in Peking, had died five months earlier. The Japanese reneged on a promise to let Buchan remain there.

She arrived in Weihsien shortly after two seminal moments in the camp's history had occurred.

In early May a new commandant took over, clamping down immediately on what remained of the original, Father Scanlan-inspired black market. A 6-foot-deep trench was dug outside the camp walls to block the Chinese. The digging panicked some of the internees, who mistook the construction of a defensive trench for the preparation of a mass grave. 'I thought: If I'm going to be shot, please let me be one of the first,' a Chefoo teacher admitted to one of her pupils decades afterwards.

In mid-June a pair of internees – Englishman Laurence Tipton and American Arthur Hummel – became the only escapees from Weihsien. Both spoke Chinese. Both had shaved their heads like the Chinese. Both wore long Chinese gowns. And both spent any leisure hour, like sunbathers beside a holiday pool, tanning their skin a pale chestnut brown to more closely resemble the locals. The half-asleep Japanese never suspected an ulterior motive.

The brain behind the brawn was Scanlan's former lieutenant Raymond de Jaegher. His plan, formulated in a toilet near one of the kitchens, proved faultless. 'It took a year of careful working out,' he said. Through his various letter-drops, de Jaegher had made contact with Nationalist guerrillas. Without applying much logic to the idea, one of the guerrilla generals had gone as far as to ambitiously propose attacking Weihsien and freeing the internees in a single swoop. Rescue planes would await them, fuelled and ready to take off from a secret airfield. There was a glitch in his scheme: the airfield had yet to be built. De Jaegher saw the prospect as a sure-fire disaster in the making and dissuaded him from taking it further. Instead Tipton and Hummel, dressed in black, got away on the night of a full moon. The two of them calculated the exact hour when that full moon would cast a shadow across both a watchtower and an expanse of the wall. During the change-over of guards, Tipton and Hummel cleared it, plus the electrified barbed wire and the trench. The men met the guerrillas at a nearby cemetery and were taken to the safety of the mountains. The Mauser-carrying guerrillas, treating this first meeting like a home-coming party, unfurled white triangular banners that read 'Welcome the British and American representatives! Hurrah! Hurrah! Hurrah!'

Next morning the obstacle of camp roll call was cleared without much bother. The Japanese guards were unaware that disguised voices had called out Tipton and Hummel's numbers. Reprisals followed as soon as the escape became known. The new commandant raged over the break-out, seeing it as an ignominious stain on his competence and a traitorous response from the internees, who in his view were 'luckier than you think' and 'better off than the citizens of our home islands' and given 'more to eat than our soldiers in the field'. The roll calls became horrendously long, the guards afraid of missing another Tipton and another Hummel. Rations were slashed. There was even a reduction in horse and donkey meat. Those in the same dormitory as Tipton and Hummel were detained and questioned endlessly. The men without families, including Liddell, were whisked out of the hospital overlooking the wall and placed in the bell tower to prevent them from signalling to the Chinese.

This was Weihsien as Buchan found it – struggling on reduced rations and under the beady observation of guards who were on-edge, mistrusting the internees more than ever. Buchan maintained she was sent there as punishment for Tipton and Hummel's escapade – a hardly creditable claim. By that stage of the war the Japanese were neither sufficiently well organized nor immersed in the necessary fine details to allow them to strategically plot the dispatch of a middle-aged nurse for the purposes of retribution. The Japanese in Peking merely wanted rid of her – much in the same way a family wants rid of a nuisance relative.

Buchan never forgot watching two boys fighting 'in earnest' over a single crust of bread in Weihsien. The position there was now so serious that camp leaders arranged for six severely undernourished internees to parade in front of the commandant. One of those chosen remembered the sight of the 'corrugated ribcages [and] our jutting cheekbones'. The commandant was unimpressed and unmoved, and Langdon Gilkey became convinced he had dismantled the old black market simply to create a new one. 'He wanted to get this lucrative business into his own – or at least into Japanese – hands.' Gilkey saw one guard thump another with a wooden club in a quarrel about stealing his customers.

Buchan had barely got to know the camp's roads and buildings when the profit-making Japanese spivs were made temporarily redundant.

A mule train arrived in Weihsien, lugging two hundred Red Cross parcels. The contents 'surpassed all belief', said Gilkey. The boxes seemed 'gigantic' to him – 3 feet long, a foot wide and 18 inches high. Contained within them were 'a seemingly inexhaustible supply of unbelievably wonderful things'. Here was coffee, tea, sugar, chocolate and Spam. Here was cheese-spread, powdered milk, butter and liver pâté. Here were dried prunes, raisins, jam and salmon. Here were cigarettes. Here was toothpaste and a toothbrush. And here were clothes too – shoes, an overcoat, shirts, a sweater, a cap, a pair of socks and gloves (though, oddly, no trousers). Gilkey said he 'grasped the idea' that his parcel meant 'security', which he characterized as 'safety from hunger for an amazingly long period'. He explained, 'No amount of stocks or bonds, no Cadillacs or country estates could possibly equal the actual wealth represented by this pile of food.' Stencilled on the side of each box were the words GIFT OF THE AMERICAN RED CROSS. The Americans magnanimously shared the bounty. In an act of breath-taking hypocrisy some of the priests and missionaries who had got into moralistic hissy fits about smoking exchanged food for fags.

Buchan was fortunate to be in Weihsien when it briefly became the corner grocery shop and the shelves were full. But, during those early weeks, as she slept during the day and worked at night in the hospital, tending to patients over a shaded candle, what shocked her was the sight of her old friend.

As a realist rather than a romantic, she had never expected to find Eric Liddell exactly as she'd last seen him; she knew he wouldn't be pink-cheeked and sparkly-eyed. But the difference between the Liddell she discovered and the picture of Liddell she held, like a photograph, in her mind was so stark as to disconcert her immediately. The fact that he wore a shirt made from a curtain – and also that his shorts were frayed – was a minor point to Buchan. She saw that Weihsien had significantly altered the man within those clothes. Not only did Liddell look tired, he also appeared ever so slightly slower in his movements. There was no swing in his walk and no spring to his step. Buchan saw that his cheekbones and his chest were sunken. His eyes were further back in their sockets. His back was slightly bent. His legs, once slim pillars of muscle around the calf and thighs, looked especially stringy and frail now. His skin was pallid, a certain greyness showing through despite the summer sunburn. And, whenever Liddell spoke to her, his speech was ponderous, as if he couldn't find the words he wanted to use and was then struggling to shape them into a quick sentence.

Buchan anxiously began to ask the other internees, as though searching for the definitive answer that was eluding her, 'What is wrong with Eric?' The internees looked at her with incomprehension. As they saw it, there was nothing wrong with Eric at all.

Knowing him so well, she was the first to understand – long before anyone else – that Liddell was physically ailing. She observed him around the camp. From what she saw, Buchan concluded that the 'heavy responsibility' he'd assumed was 'more than he should have had'. She told things straight. 'People depended on him too much,' she said. She watched him carrying buckets and running errands, pumping water and shifting sacks. She observed him taking Bible classes and Sunday school, weekend and evening sport and the usual science lessons in class. When a couple wanted to talk about their relationship, Liddell was there. When someone wanted individual tuition on his book *Discipleship*, Liddell was there. And when a teenager was electrocuted on the camp's barbed wire fence – he'd reached out to try to touch the topmost strand as a challenge – it was Liddell who comforted his grieving mother, teaching her his favourite hymn 'Be Still, My Soul' just as he had taught an incalculable number of others beforehand. Buchan knew Liddell's diligence wasn't helping his health. But, unlike him, she still had a sad hunch that neither lack of food nor excessive work was necessarily the cause of his condition.

Confirmation of her diagnosis came quickly.

The top sportsman's greatest moment is a coronation. It takes place in a theatrical fever, the crowd at fiesta-pitch, the roaring, throaty sound of it shaking the bleachers, the steep banks or the high tiers of the stadium. The frenzy is integral to the spectacle. In a few tick-tock seconds the athlete, whatever sport he plays, becomes unforgettable to his audience because what he does – a shot, a pass, a run – is acclaimed in the instant it occurs as transformative, thus making his reputation. The feat is everlasting; age does not diminish the power of seeing or analysing it. The moment survives, intact and imperishable, and defines the man who made it, gaining him sporting immortality.

Bobby Thomson, the darling of New York in 1951, will always be swinging his bat and sending The Shot Heard Round the World skyward at the Polo Grounds in Upper Manhattan, and then circling the bases to the accompaniment of the commentator's breathless five-time repetition of that one shouted phrase: 'The Giants win the Pennant!' Long jumper Bob Beamon will always be suspended in the rarefied air of Mexico City during the 1968 Olympics, his splash into the sand marking the Leap of the Century. Joe Montana, displaying a meditative calm amid the confusion around him, will always be sending the San Francisco 49ers on that 92-yard, eleven-play drive that wins them Super Bowl XXII with only thirty-four seconds to spare, the big clock in Miami freezing Time in bright, Broadway-like lights.

This is how sport ought to be: tens of thousands inside the stadium, incalculable millions watching from an armchair or listening to a radio broadcast.

It was different for Eric Liddell.

The Olympics made him a household name. In Paris he'd had the Hall of Fame hour that would come long afterwards for Thomson and Beamon and Montana. The crowd, emptying from the Colombes Stadium, had talked about him on the tram-ride home and then again next morning when the newspapers came fresh and inky, the smell of the printing presses still on them. But what he did, and the way in which he inspired whoever watched him, doesn't rank as his number one achievement.

Surpassing it, and saying more about Liddell than any gold medal ever can, is a race he ran in – and for – Weihsien. A race barely 1,500 people saw, making it almost a private event. A race he ought never to have attempted. A race no one registered as significant until much later.

This was the last race of Eric Liddell's life.

He'd gone into the big events of his heyday, from the AAA Championships to the Olympics, as the underdog. The students of Edinburgh University were expected to put him in his place on the grass of Craiglockhart in 1921, ending a career before it began. Harold Abrahams was supposed to thrash him at Stamford Bridge in 1923. The Americans were sure Liddell would be overwhelmed and outclassed in Paris. But Weihsien always expected the star among them to win – and to win well too. None of the amateur bookmakers in the camp, who calculated the odds for the inveterate gamblers, ever gave the punters a decent price on him. He was as much the favourite as Man o' War had been on the racetracks of the United States; Liddell was *Big Red*.

There had been a number of races in Weihsien since he'd beaten Aubrey Grandon in the first of them. Liddell lost only the odd relay, his team sometimes unable to exploit the enormous advantage he gave them. No one had ever bested him in an individual contest, however. The old master had always been too fast for any pretender. 'He'd even find a way to beat us boys in the casual races we held,' said an internee. 'He didn't want one boy to crow over another about beating him in case the boasting turned nasty.'

Competition was postponed during most of the late spring and summer of 1944. 'We didn't have much strength for athletics,' explained Steve Metcalf. 'All the strength we did have was saved for chores rather than for running.' The hiatus led to a quiet eagerness in Weihsien for the return of its 'Sports Days'. A month or so after the Red Cross parcels arrived, galvanizing the camp again, the internees packed the course to watch another of them. The competitors were fortified by the liver pâté, the cheese-spread and all that caffeine. Had coloured bunting been available, it would have been strung between the buildings in celebration.

Liddell was sicker than ever. He was perpetually exhausted. He was losing weight at a shocking rate. His belt had so many fresh notches on it that the thin leather was about to disintegrate. But he continued to do his work around the camp and he saw it as his obligation to be a crowd-pleaser too. He participated in the race because he didn't want to let anyone down. The internees, still ignorant of his condition, supposed he would canter through the event without difficulty or drama.

The race followed the same irregular route as before, starting at the softball field, turning into Main Street, crossing the Market Square and down Tin Pan Alley. Also as before, the pathways were scuffed and dusty and the acacia trees, thicker and denser now, formed a leafy tunnel. The shade was welcome on a hot afternoon.

This time the distance covered would be shorter than usual – only two circuits rather than four – as a concession to the athletes, none of them exactly sure how much the awfulness of the year so far had taken out of them. Nor did Liddell give anyone a head start now. He stood on the same line as everyone else, the starter once more atop a packing crate and ready to wave his white handkerchief. Grandon was beside Liddell and comparatively robust in the circumstances. Even throughout the food shortages he had done the drill of his daily exercises, a testament to his youth and his vigour, and the sun had given his skin a healthy burnish.

There was respectful, anticipatory silence before the starter's voice shouted that familiar instruction – 'Ready, set, go!' – and then a whoop and a holler when it broke the air and the dozen or so runners shot off, the dust as ever lifting in small, gritty clouds around them.

Liddell began predictably, striding clear because he was aware of the need to establish an early lead. On the opening lap, the chasing pack – Grandon jostling near the front of it – were like hounds after a hare. You could hear the stampede of thumping feet against the hard earth. You could see the short shadow each man cast and also the strain on their faces and in their eyes, the desperation of some who were already being left far behind.

Liddell was still ahead of them all at the halfway point of the second lap. This was the Olympian everyone knew – the frantic whirl of the arms, the high knee lift, the head back. The spectators, given another exhibition of it, waited for the climactic rush he always demonstrated. He'd slip into a gear no one else could match. He'd glide further away. He'd triumph again easily. Only Grandon clung on, close enough to Liddell to give the appearance of a contest; though no one really believed Liddell was beatable.

That assumption was wrong.

With a muscled power, his arms pumping across his chest, Grandon gradually began to claim back the yards taken from him at the beginning. When he and Liddell reached Market Square for the last time, Grandon made his move. Worn down after his long months of illness, Liddell lacked the breath to resist or respond. With Tin Pan Alley in sight, his legs let him down; he couldn't find any 'kick' in them. For once, throwing his head further back wasn't enough to give him that late spurt. There was no spark, no extra burst of energy in him. His heart was willing. His body was not. Grandon, surprise in his eyes, came on to Liddell's shoulder and then moved past him, overtaking on the widest part of the course. Liddell saw what his opponents normally did: a figure hurtling away, uncatchable. The broad-backed Grandon surged on, the lowered sweep of the white handkerchief signalling that the honour belonged to him. Liddell came second, several yards adrift.

His response was generous and instinctive. An internee standing near the finish said Liddell gave Grandon a broadly beaming smile and then 'warmly wrapped his arms around him'. One man tried to grab Liddell's wrist and raise his arm anyway, as if he were a boxer in a ring at the end of a fight. He shook his head, pushing aside the gesture.

His defeat surprised the camp. But, according to Steve Metcalf, the internees assumed Liddell had experienced nothing more than a rare 'off-day'.

No one timed that race. No one wrote a paean to it. And no one, as the war progressed through the first half of the winter, dwelt on the meaning beneath the result. The placings were simply stuck on the notice board until another, more topical item replaced them.

The passing years slowly assign context to things and place them in order of importance; we appreciate that only from the distance hindsight allows us. So it is with this race, a couple of minutes in a faraway corner of a faraway country that show the quintessential Liddell, a stricken man running because he felt it was the right thing to do. A man, moreover, who made no excuses for his defeat and got involved in no histrionics about it afterwards. As the party-like atmosphere continued that day, he merely went back to his normal duties, still pretending there was nothing wrong with him.

But seen in the terrible light of what awaited him, this race is Liddell's best and unquestionably his bravest. Where his initial speed came from, and how he managed to sustain it for so long, is unfathomable. The courage he summoned to run at all is extraordinary, a testament to his will.

Liddell never competed again, and those privileged to see his farewell to athletics appreciated only retrospectively the absolute miracle he performed in front of them.

The dying man had lost; but to them he was still the champion.

In a normal environment Eric Liddell's illness would have been identified months earlier; perhaps at least eight months earlier. In Weihsien, where almost everyone was unwell to one degree or another, his early symptoms were hard to pin directly on a specific cause. Only the later symptoms made his disease more obvious. It was nevertheless still difficult to diagnose categorically because conditions in the camp meant the doctors could never eliminate other possibilities, some of them fairly innocent. The hospital lacked the electronic facilities to test Liddell properly. There was no X-ray machine. The hospital was even short of medicine until four crates were eventually obtained through a cunning subterfuge.

The escapees Tipton and Hummel were able to organize an American Air Force drop, which the guerrillas picked up and surreptitiously deposited with the Swiss consul. The real success was getting its contents inside Weihsien. The medicines weren't available in that region of China. Unless the consul could think of a way of either hiding or disguising

A view of the watchtowers in the Weihsien camp and the rough track that carried internees there.

them, the Japanese would realize immediately that he was the final pair of hands in a long line of smugglers. The consul's solution, a light bulb moment, was audaciously clever, deserving of applause for the child-like simplicity of the idea and the nerveless execution. He got his secretary to type out a list of medicines that were easily obtainable, telling her to leave quadruple spaces between each of them. He presented the document to his local Japanese official who, suspecting nothing was amiss, stamped and signed the bottom of it. The consul's secretary then added the names of the medicines inside the crate, typing them into the gaps she had previously left on the paper. The document fooled the Weihsien commandant too.

Nothing in those crates could have saved Liddell. The jumble of memories the internees shared of him between late autumn of 1944 and late winter of 1945 show a man in gradual but irrevocable decline; someone slipping away even as he attempted to grab and hold on to something. The Liddell who comes across is pained and puzzled, frustrated and irritable – though with no one but himself. He can't conceive what is happening to him. He doesn't understand his various infirmities. He seems to think he can get over them the way he might throw off a cold.

First, the stench of cooking began to annoy him. 'We'd be frying something in the dorm and he'd ask, "What's that? It smells awful,"' said Joe Cotterill. Second, the day's harshest light began to burn his eyes. 'He preferred the semi-darkness and candles,' added Cotterill. Third came the thumping, hammering headaches, excruciating to bear. The pain, stopping thought as well as conversation, was worse than a migraine and he could only wait for it to pass. He thought his head was on fire. Liddell lay listlessly beneath the coarse blankets on his bed, seldom able to speak. His friends lightly soaked a cloth, which Liddell hung across his brow like a bandage, also shielding his eyes.

Next his memory, previously excellent, began to drift. He tested it regularly, attempting to measure its deterioration. He read a cloth-bound edition of Charles Dickens's *Tale of Two Cities*, the pages tattered through constant use, and tried to recite the soliloquy of Sydney Carton, who demonstrates devotion to the woman he loves by taking her husband's place at the guillotine: 'I see the lives for which I lay down my life, peaceful, useful, prosperous and happy . . . I see that I hold a sanctuary in their hearts, and in the hearts of their descendants, generations hence . . . It is a far, far better thing that I do, than I have ever done; it is far, far better rest that I go to than I have ever known.' Carton's speech had resonated with Liddell ever since he'd first read it as a boy. Once he had been able to remember every line, faultlessly. Now Dickens's composition began to slide away from him. Only odd phrases stuck. 'I don't know what's going on with my head,' he said. 'But it's frightening.' He'd tried to memorize the passage as he pumped water. He'd put the book on the ground and would pick out a sentence on every downward stroke of the pump's handle. But, as his appetite waned and the weight began to drop off him, Liddell became too weak for manual labour. He was even too weak to deliver Christmas cards and messages. His body was wasting away incrementally, draining him of vitality. The headaches brought dizzy spells, which sent his balance awry. Sometimes Liddell would tilt and stagger, a sideways sway of a step or two before standing upright again. He looked like someone aboard a small ship, suddenly listed by the toss and roll of the waves beneath it.

The camp underwent more turmoil and tumult, the most spiteful and divisive incident since the first prisoner stepped inside it. Food was to blame. Early on in Weihsien, Langdon Gilkey took a mental note of the fact that nationalities soon became irrelevant. No one cared where someone came from. His sentiments echoed Mary Scott's. 'A man's excellence was revealed through his willingness to work,' he said. 'People became to us personalities, pleasant or unpleasant, hard working or lazy . . .' In January 1945, however, the question of nationality did become an issue. The mule train returned, bringing more Red Cross parcels than before. 'Everyone was laughing and crying at once,' said Gilkey. Not everyone, though, thought these parcels – sent again from the American branch of the Red Cross – should be divided equally among the other internees. Some slippery manoeuvring ensued. The parcels were placed in the church, awaiting a decision on distribution from the commandant. Gilkey remembered: 'Every row of rooms and every dorm where Americans lived with other nationals began to stew in bitter disputes.' When the commandant stipulated that every American ought to receive one and a half parcels and every non-American should get one parcel, a group of seven Americans opposed him, their stance vehement and venomous. Finally the commandant asked for arbitration from Tokyo, which took a week and a half to come. The hiatus, said Gilkey, swelled 'hostility, jealousy and national pride' among the hungry. He quoted Bertolt Brecht's couplet: 'For even saintly folk will act like sinners, unless they have their customary dinners.' The lack of them led to fist-fights, the camp degenerating in front of Gilkey into a 'brawling, bitterly divided collection of hostile national groups'. Eventually Tokyo decreed that every internee should get one parcel.

Amid that sordid and unedifying tussle, the desperately sick Liddell made a quiet, private gesture, the exact opposite of the selfishness going on around him. He had seen Steve Metcalf wearing only socks or pieces of cloth that were tied and glued to the old sole of a boot. Liddell fished out the athletics shoes he'd won in the camp races and cleaned them up, scrubbing the fabric and then binding and strengthening it with wound string. 'Here,' he said to Metcalf. 'You could get some use out of these. They might stay together until the spring.' Metcalf held out his hands, like Oliver presenting his bowl, and Liddell placed the shoes in them. 'To give away an old pair of shoes may not seem like much,' said Metcalf. 'But it was a wonderful and generous thing to do in the camp, where *every* possession was valued – especially footwear in winter.' Metcalf finally understood that Liddell was unwell. He still supposed the cause was extreme weariness. 'You could see he wasn't himself. You could tell it from his face and his eyes. We simply weren't aware of the agony he was going through. He kept that to himself and tried to act as normally as possible.'

The cheery masquerade Liddell perpetuated in front of Metcalf fell away whenever he saw Annie Buchan. He and Buchan would sit against the trunk of a tree. He'd produce a pocket-book and glance through snap-shots of his children. 'He didn't have to pretend with me,' she said. He confided in Buchan, telling her what she described as his 'one big regret': he hadn't spent enough time with Florence. The decision to go to Siaochang in 1937, leaving her in Tientsin, bothered him enormously now, as if he ought to have opposed the London Missionary Society's decision to ban the family from travelling. As his headaches persisted, he slipped into a dark mood and became uncharacteristically pessimistic and doubtful. Liddell the eternal optimist became Liddell the depressive. 'One day he told me he couldn't see the future. Everything seemed black,' said Buchan. 'This wasn't like him. He'd always been full of hope.'

He had begun to look over and across his life, as if striving to make sense of it. In the evening especially, shortly before lights out in his room, the melancholy threatened to drown him. This wasn't unusual among the men in his dorm as the war dragged on. What became noticeable, however, was that Liddell couldn't shake himself out of it next morning. His depression wouldn't go away. He remained distressed, dwelling again on his separation from Florence and also discussing the baby he'd never seen. He was missing them all 'very much', said Cotterill. 'The letters he got from home made him more depressed after the initial pleasure of reading them went away because each made him think even more about his family.'

Already fragile, Liddell was weakened still further when influenza with sinusitis struck him. The usual treatment brought no respite. The man who once did everything could now do almost nothing except lie in bed and take short, plodding walks. He looked like someone slogging across sand. He was determined nonetheless to preach in church, writing out short lessons in a shaky hand and speaking them slowly, his voice like a record played at slightly the wrong speed. At the end of January 1945, arriving at the hospital to ask for another check-up, he fainted near the entrance. The internee who discovered Liddell gathered him up, as if lifting a child from its cradle. He summoned friends, who commandeered a door and used it as a stretcher to carry his limp frame into the

The camp hospital where Eric Liddell died in 1945.

whitewashed ward. Liddell had never been a bed-ridden patient before. He'd only ever gone into the ward as a visitor, once tending to a nun who had typhoid. The winter of 1944/45 was far colder than the previous one and the thirty-bed wards were regularly full. The doctors, anxious to discharge everyone but the desperately sick as soon as possible, treated him as a bed-blocking malingerer. Buchan had to force them to accept him. Liddell, she insisted, wouldn't have come in for treatment unless he urgently needed it.

In the beginning Liddell was advised that his condition was purely 'psychological'. The cause was linked to 'over-work', which only rest and recuperation would remedy. The doctors mentioned the possibility of a 'nervous breakdown'. Liddell told Cotterill that he didn't believe 'a Christian should have a nervous breakdown' because his faith ought to sustain him through whatever traumas he faced. In the coming week he showed no signs of deterioration or improvement. He also confessed to Cotterill's fiancée, 'The doctors think I'm spinning this out,' an opinion that upset him.

The seriousness of his illness became apparent on the second Sunday in February. Liddell went into a coughing and vomiting fit before suffering a slight stroke. There was damage to his left leg, which left him with a limp, and also to his left eye. The lid drooped over the pupil, blurring his vision. 'He was so courageous,' said Buchan. The doctors, she added, still had a 'he'll get over it' attitude towards him, assuming Liddell would be back in the bell tower within a week or two. The 'nervous breakdown' was categorically diagnosed now. For a while, the doctors suggested, Liddell should give up teaching and sport and work in the bakery instead. That verdict and also the planned change of Liddell's duties came as a relief to his friends, convinced he'd make a full recovery.

By now his body had become wasted to the extent that his limbs and his neck were like stalks; but no one in Weihsien, including the medical staff, expected him to die.

The following Sunday the Salvation Army band, stationed below Liddell's window, was asked to play a request for the patient. With chapped, frozen fingers and cracked lips, the wind blowing in gusts around them, the band fulfilled it. Liddell heard his favourite hymn, the notes of 'Be Still, My Soul' gliding across the cold air. He then took tea with a missionary and his wife, climbing four flights of stairs to see them. He wore a dressing gown and needed a nurse to support him. The nurse told him the effort of taking those steps was akin to 'reaching for the stars'. When Liddell got to the top, finally sinking into a chair, he was visibly out of breath. 'It was obviously difficult for him to talk,' said his host. Within forty-eight hours Liddell saw the same missionary friends again and once more mentioned his 'nervous breakdown', suggesting he still felt inexplicably guilty about it, repeating to them what he'd told Cotterill. 'There is just one thing that troubles me,' he said. 'I ought to have been able to cast it all on the Lord and not have broken down under it.'

Is your head better? he was asked.

'To answer that question I should require to know what is going on inside my head,' he replied.

That afternoon he began to compose a letter to Florence. He borrowed a hymnal from a friend in the women's ward. He wanted to check the accuracy of a quotation.

On Wednesday, 21 February Liddell was fit enough to go for a stroll around the camp. He wanted to post his Red Cross message to Florence, which had been typed out for him that morning. One Chefoo pupil saw him on the baseball field. 'As usual he was smiling,' he said. And one woman walked with him for a quarter of an hour. She told him he ought to be 'resting more'. He told her, 'No, I must get my walking legs again.'

Early in the evening Liddell received his usual visitor, Joyce Stranks. He'd continued to teach her from his book, *Discipleship*. He was in bed, lying on his left side on a rough grass mattress and a straw-stuffed pillow. His blankets were a dull grey colour, the consequence of constant washing without sufficient soap to scrub them properly. Stranks pulled a chair across the concrete floor and placed it beside him. The two of them were discussing chapter three – the surrender to God's will. Liddell tried to say the word 'surrender', managing only to utter the first syllable three times as his head jerked backwards in a spasm. His whole body stiffened. His eyes widened. His mouth gaped open. He was convulsed with pain. Stranks, completely distraught, rushed to find Buchan. The nurse swept towards the bed and pulled across the screens to shield Liddell from prying eyes. She turned to Stranks, grabbing her shoulders with both hands and shaking them vigorously. 'What did he say to you?' she asked angrily, repeating the terse question before the tearful Stranks could provide an answer. 'You shouldn't have been here,' Buchan went on, as if searching for someone to blame.

His second stroke, which came shortly afterwards, was far more severe than his first had been. For two and a half hours he drifted in and out of consciousness. Buchan was able to ask Liddell whether the medical staff knew what had happened to him. 'They haven't a clue,' he said to her. She stood guard beside his bed, leaving only briefly to seek out his doctor. 'Do you realize Eric is dying?' she asked him, knowing the tide of his life was going out.

'Nonsense,' she was told.

Buchan was the only witness to overhear his last words and preserve them. Looking at her, he said softly, 'It's complete surrender.' Within seconds of that sentence leaving his lips, Liddell suffered a third stroke and fell into a coma. The rest was silence.

At 9.20 p.m. the doctors pronounced him dead.

Nature's timing is sometimes impeccable. The internees awoke next morning to an ice storm that encased the camp in a hard, clear glaze. Ice smothered the ground. Icicles the size of a child's fingers hung from the eaves of the buildings and across the lintels of doors. Every branch of every bare tree was wrapped in ice too. It was as though the whole

The Canadian Red Cross Society

TORONTO BRANCH

50 BLOOR STREET EAST ✚ TELEPHONE MIDWAY 6692

PRISONERS OF WAR AND NEXT-OF-KIN DEPARTMENT

Oct. 16th, 1945.

Mrs. F. J. Liddell,
21 Gloucester Street,
Toronto 5.

Dear Mrs. Liddell,

      We are enclosing three Red Cross
messages which have just been received in
this office.

      We felt sure that you would want
to have these messages in spite of the
distress they would cause you.

      Yours sincerely,

M E Breckenridge.

Miss M. E. Breckenridge

ENCS.3

The letter informing Florence of a backlog of Eric's Red Cross post.

The last words of Eric Liddell: one of the pieces of paper on which he wrote random thoughts shortly before his death in Weihsien's hospital.

of Weihsien had stopped, it and Time frozen in a symbolic act of mourning.

The camp wept for Eric Liddell. Some of the toughest of men openly cried out their grief for him. His roommates stared at his empty bed, gathering like the sad captains of Shakespeare's *Antony and Cleopatra* to find some sort of solace in companionable silence. Each wore the expression of solemn disbelief. How could Liddell be dead at forty-three, taken in midlife? And how could his death have come so suddenly? One of them – he'd later call a son Eric in tribute to Liddell – secretly kept a pocket diary throughout his internment. His account of the camp's response to Liddell's death is wrenching. 'It leaves me shocked and bewildered,' he said, hoping the act of writing about it would enable him to comprehend what had happened. 'His passing stunned us. We could hardly believe it was true.' He encapsulated what Liddell had meant to Weihsien. 'We confided in him, went to him for advice, looked on him as probably the most perfect and honourable Christian friend we had ever known and the whole camp feels that in losing Eric they have lost a real friend. He was loved by everyone . . . It is my prayer that I may live like Eric, a life that is exemplary, lovely, useful [and] full of caring service to others.'

The best tribute he paid was this one: 'For over a year six of us have lived together like brothers and we all looked on Eric as our older brother.'

Without its older brother, the camp felt empty. 'We sat in the quiet of the dormitory thinking about him,' said Joe Cotterill. 'Some of us couldn't speak. There were no words that could make us feel better. His death seemed so unfair. We thought about his wife and his children – especially the child he'd now never see. He'd loved children so much and it seemed so unjust that he'd be denied the company of his own.'

The doctors, who hadn't believed Liddell to be in danger, quickly found the cause of his death. A tumour had grown on the left-hand side of his brain. The medulla was also found to be full of fresh blood. When the result of the post-mortem began to spread, there were those in Weihsien who remembered Liddell's talk about his athletics career and asked themselves whether or not the tumour had developed as a consequence of that on-track collision with the Chinese photographer's camera in Tientsin. Now that story wasn't funny to them.

Annie Buchan had one last duty to perform for her friend. She prepared his body for burial, washing and then wrapping it in a sheet. He was laid in a shed behind the hospital.

There'd been twenty-six previous deaths in Weihsien. None of the funerals was ceremonially as memorable as Liddell's. It was called 'one of the most moving events in the whole of camp life'. A witness to it remembered the pianist playing 'I Know That My Redeemer Liveth', and also the crowds, who crammed into the pews and spilled on to the roads outside and lined the route to the graveyard, where plot 59 awaited him. The ice storm had frozen the topsoil more than an inch deep, which meant a pick axe as well as a spade had had to be used to make the hole. The work was carried out under the inscrutable gaze of the guards, who stood at a respectful and cautious distance from the two grave diggers – one local Chinese, one American internee. The guards tethered German Shepherds on their leads in case the tools were used against them as weapons.

Liddell's rectangular casket – no more than a rough box – was gnarled and elephant-grey. Small splinters, as fine as bristles, stuck out of the wood. The lining of it was made from a freshly laundered bedsheet, which was torn into long, wide strips. The construction was so fragile that some of the pall-bearers – among them Steve Metcalf – feared the nails and glue holding it together might fall apart. It had to be lifted and carried with exaggerated care. The pall-bearers, dressed in coats and hats and gloves, walked in shuffled half-paces. The temperature had risen the day before, bringing a cold rain that left the pathways slushy and muddy. But the morning of the funeral was wind-whipped and shivery, and wispy flakes of snow came from black-angry clouds that smothered out the sun, its light escaping only in slender blades too weak to cast a shadow. The sky seemed abnormally low, as if it were about to sink into the flat farmland beyond the walls. The pall-bearers sometimes glanced down nervously at their own feet to avoid slipping. Metcalf, wearing the running shoes Liddell had given him, was particularly cautious about each pace he took.

Some of the mourners bowed their heads or made the sign of the cross. Others were weeping, their faces streaked with tears. At one point the camp was so still that the only sound to be heard was the rattle and clatter of a faraway train, the faint noise carried on the wind.

Of course, the congregation sang 'Be Still, My Soul'. Of course, there were readings from the Sermon on the Mount. Of course, his friends spoke eulogies to him. 'In his presence I felt it was impossible to speak or do anything less than the best, the purest, the noblest,' said one. Weihsien gave Liddell all the finery it could muster.

It is impossible to think of the service and the funeral procession without thinking also of the opening lines of A. E. Housman's poem 'To an Athlete Dying Young'.

The time you won your town the race
We chaired you through the market-place;
Man and boy stood cheering by,
And home we brought you shoulder-high.

Today, the road all runners come,
Shoulder-high we bring you home . . .

Man and boy had stood to cheer Liddell, watching him run along the same rain-slick roads where the pall-bearers now carried his coffin 'shoulder-high' and then across that part of the camp the internees christened 'Market Square'. Housman's rhyme seemed to have been composed for him.

The internees finally realized that Liddell had run in front of them only six months earlier while suffering from a terminal illness. 'It said everything about his will,' said Metcalf, who was profoundly affected by the funeral. Metcalf knew the details of the day would stay with him for ever. He'd always feel the weight of the coffin on his shoulder and Liddell's shoes on his feet. These would remain, fixed in his mind, because a prince had been buried like a pauper. After the grave had been filled in, Metcalf looked at the wooden cross laid on top of it. The cross was as plain and as makeshift as the coffin. Liddell's name was written across the middle bar in black boot polish. Metcalf stood to consider the man beneath it – an Olympic champion, a missionary, a friend. He looked again at the mound of freshly turned earth, the crude cross with its scrawled name and also the dingy surroundings of the camp; and then he asked himself one question: Is this all that happens to honour such a Great Man? 'He deserves much more than we were able to give him,' he thought.

There was the cruellest of sequels to Liddell's death.

Three weeks later a crate appeared unexpectedly in Weihsien, addressed to the hospital. The X-ray equipment that would have detected his brain tumour – possibly before it became inoperable – had arrived at last.

*

For almost three months, Florence Liddell lived her life without knowing that her husband was dead. She didn't discover the cause of his death for a further five months.

Florence and the children were living in a bay-windowed, brown-bricked Victorian house with gabled peaks. It was spread over three floors on Toronto's Gloucester Street. The house was furnished in Victorian style too. There was heavy, dark wood furniture, a piano, a coat rack in the hall, oriental rugs and glass lamps and photographs on the mantel. The paintings on the wall had ornate frames and gleaming gold-coloured rods fastened the emerald carpet to the stairs.

A month before the shattering news reached her, Florence experienced what she'd later recall as 'the strangest feeling'. Standing beside the stove in the kitchen, she said to herself, 'If you turn around, Eric is

Eric Liddell's wooden cross and overgrown grave in Weihsien. The photograph was taken after the camp's liberation in 1945.

standing there.' Florence said she could 'feel' his presence and swore she heard him speak too. 'Everything is going to be all right,' he'd told her. For three weeks Florence said she was 'conscious of his presence in this way'. She also began to dream 'vividly' about him. In these dreams, she explained, 'we were all terribly happy'. She interpreted them as a sure sign that Liddell would soon be home; though, when Florence attempted to plan for that, she encountered what she described as a 'stone wall'. Later she'd admit: 'I don't know when I have been so conscious of a restraining hand and I simply couldn't understand it. I felt sure there was going to be some change in plans . . . I couldn't see what.' She felt she had 'grown up a lot' since Liddell had last seen her. 'I wanted to show him that,' she explained.

The Red Cross received notification of Liddell's death on 1 May and immediately cabled the news to Florence's local church. The following day two friends arrived on her doorstep. Seeing such stony faces, she instantly thought one of her brothers – in combat overseas – had been killed in action. 'It's one of the boys, is it?' she asked. 'It never crossed my mind that Eric had died,' said Florence, who explained that her first thought after hearing of her husband's death was: 'That is why he has been so near to me lately.'

The house began to fill with family and friends. Patricia, the last home, was used to seeing a crowd: the hospitable Liddells had a wide social circle. But she registered straight away that the mood was sombre and hushed. She asked for her mother and dashed upstairs to find her. That afternoon she'd won a sprint race on the school fields and had wanted to talk about it proudly. In the front bedroom Florence was holding Heather on her knee; both were crying. Patricia refused to believe her father had died. She was convinced either a clerical mistake or a doctor's misidentification had taken place. Every night she and her sister had stared at the big gold moon over the city, knowing the time difference between Canada and China meant he would be watching it rise as the two of them awoke. In this way his daughters had felt close to him. No, he couldn't be dead. A week later Florence received official confirmation, his death certificate containing only date and place.

In a war where death knocks daily on front doors, a single passing can slip by unnoticed among a million others. That week two words dominated the newspaper agenda and appeared on the front pages and advertising boards in gigantic type: HITLER DEAD. Liddell's death was

The Liddell home in Toronto after Eric sent his family back to Canada in 1941.

still reported across the continents. From the *New York Times* to *The Times* of London – and all points in between both eastwards and westwards – the 'reverend in running shoes' who became an Olympic champion was written about, his loss lamented and mourned.

Florence said that even after the shock had left her, she was 'vividly conscious of Eric being happy', seeing only 'his sunny smile and twinkling eyes', which she called 'a strange and wonderful experience'. She went on: 'At times I have been numbed and overwhelmed by a sense of unreality – of pain – [and] of fear for the future, and then there has come welling up from within that power of faith, which has carried me through.'

Florence would always insist that she had not imagined either his presence or his voice in her kitchen that day. 'I am sure that somehow or other he was allowed to come back,' she said.

There is a tightly cropped, upright photograph of the bell tower in Weihsien. The Stars and Stripes is strung between two flag poles like a sheet on a washing line. Above it is the black shape of an aeroplane and nine white-silk parachutes, which are at the mid-point of their descent. The photograph marks a scene from the liberation Eric Liddell never lived to see.

Freedom came to the camp on 17 August – eleven days after the B-29 Superfortress *Enola Gay* dropped 'Little Boy' on Hiroshima and saw the city below it all but vanish after a flash of intense light filled the cockpit. Only seventy-two hours later, 'Fat Man' incinerated Nagasaki. The Japanese surrendered within a week. In Singapore, the general who oversaw those document signatures was Philip Christison – the man behind the Cameron Highlanders' rendition of 'Scotland The Brave' before Liddell's Olympic triumph in Paris.

Throughout the year, the Japanese had been pressurized and pressed back. The Burma Road reopened. Bataan, Iwo Jima, Manila, Mandalay, Okinawa were reclaimed. A 15-square-mile swathe of Tokyo was bombed. Through the usual channels, the internees heard about each incident. Word of the atomic bomb, however, seemed like an invention from science fiction. Weihsien became afraid the Japanese would be ruthless in reply to it, never caring who perished in retribution. Instead what came to them was the distant hum of a plane and then a sweeping roar as it passed low over them. A silver B-24 Liberator glinted like a mirror in a sky of perfect blue. This was Weihsien's 'Flying Angel'. 'I could *feel* the drop of my jaw,' said Langdon Gilkey. There were internees who screamed, who yelped, who leapt upwards, arms outstretched, as if attempting to catch its wings. 'Everyone seemed utterly unconscious of what others were doing,' recalled Mary Scott. 'Some were laughing hysterically. Others were crying like babies.' The plane flew beyond the camp before banking westwards and turning back towards it. En masse the internees rushed for the gate, forcing it open with the press and weight of their bodies. The guards scarcely made a move to stop them before stepping aside, resigned to the pointlessness of the gesture. Gilkey watched one guard raise his rifle and then lower it again. The internees frantically brought out flags – American and British – and spread them across the tall fields of *kao liang* and corn encircling the camp walls.

A confusion of memory slightly mists up the next picture. Some swore the parachutes that came from the plane's underside doors were white. Others saw blue, yellow or red, a kaleidoscopic swirl of colour. No matter. Attached to them were the seven men of Duck Mission – muscled, tanned, fit. 'How immense, how strong, how striking, how alive these American paratroopers looked in comparison to our shrunken shanks and drawn faces,' said Gilkey. The internees saw them as superheroes. Women clipped off locks of the paratroopers' hair as souvenirs. The Salvation Army band had been surreptitiously practising a medley of national anthems and began to play it like party music. The next celebratory tune was 'Happy Days Are Here Again', struck up and repeated so often that the lyrics were finally shouted aloud rather than sung.

No bomb or bullet was needed to liberate Weihsien that summer afternoon. The commandant handed over his sword to the paratroopers, the camp passing peacefully into new ownership. Other planes followed the 'Flying Angel'. B-29s flung out drums containing tinned peaches and pineapple, meat and tomato soup, fruit juices and chocolate. Some of the cans and packages split on impact, scattering or spilling the contents around the countryside. The internees ran into the fields again to find the drums, gorging themselves on the spot. After years of eating next to nothing, the stomach of the average internee was too delicate to take the richness of these foods. Most were retching or vomiting within a few hours.

The camp settled into a fresh routine. The Americans arranged for the song 'Oh What A Beautiful Morning' to be piped through loudspeakers to wake the internees each day. It became as irritating as the clang of an alarm clock. Prisoners no more, but restless for home, the internees now came and went as the mood took them. Steve Metcalf relished the chance to explore the countryside. 'The air seemed so sweet,' he said. 'With every stride you felt the freedom you'd been given. I wanted to know a little of the landscape I'd been confined in.' He did his walking in a pair of sturdy black army boots, traded for Liddell's running shoes.

One anonymous afternoon those boots took him into the cemetery. He paused beside Liddell's grave, finding the cross slightly askew and weeds sprouting in big clumps around it. The question Metcalf had asked himself at the funeral came back to him again; and still he had no answer to it. In that moment the untidiness of the grave made Liddell's story seem more sorrowful than ever to him. He'd given so much and had got back only this – neglect.

The man born in China would always remain in it; and there was no one to tend the soil around him.

It was late October when the envelope, emblazoned with the crest of the Red Cross, arrived without warning on the mat at Gloucester Street. Florence Liddell presumed the contents related to her husband's pension or his insurance policy. Inside she found an accompanying letter, so brief it was barely worth typing. It contained only thirty-eight words, which were spread over six lines.

Dear Mrs. Liddell,

We are enclosing three Red Cross messages which have just been received in this office.

We felt sure that you would want to have these messages in spite of the distress they would cause you.

The letter ended with a 'yours sincerely'. There wasn't even an offer to contact the Red Cross to talk about the 'distress' it had forecast on her behalf.

The organization ought to have hand-delivered these messages. The fact that it didn't suggested those in charge of it were one or a combination of the following: dumb or dumber, insensitive and indifferent or downright cowardly, not wanting to witness a widow grieve all over again. The Toronto office, responsible for mailing the envelope, was only half a mile from her front door.

What the postman delivered were words from Weihsien. For the rest of her life Florence cherished them. The messages, written on familiar Red Cross forms, were among those the Japanese could never be bothered to send on. The American soldiers discovered them – plus hundreds of others from the internees – discarded in a room in the guards' quarters.

Her husband, dead for eight months, spoke to her from the page.

The first message was dated 27 August 1944. 'I have received some of your letters and have news up to January,' wrote Liddell. 'I constantly picture you all. I see Tricia, cycling, swimming and skating and Heather following fast in her footsteps. I wish I could hear them read to me! Maureen – I long to see her . . . I long for you dearest – and the time when we shall start a home together again. May it be soon!'

The second, much shorter and more banal, had been dispatched exactly a year before Florence finally saw it: 'Glorious weather. Winter activities begin. Good start teaching.'

The third was the most precious. It was the one Liddell had composed on the afternoon of his death, dictating the contents to an unknown typist because he was too weak to pen a sentence. Even his 'signature' was typed. The ribbon of the typewriter was short of ink and the vowel keys in particular needed cleaning. Each line was out of kilter – as if the typist wasn't a professional – but nonetheless without mistakes. The contents would only make absolute sense to Florence in the weeks to come when Liddell's fellow internees, now repatriated, wrote to her about the final month of his life. 'Was carrying too much responsibility,' he said. 'Slight nervous breakdown. Am much better after month's rest in hospital.' He then told Florence about the doctors' diagnosis, the suggestion of switching to the bakery – 'a good change', he predicted – and the arrival of one of her letters. He went on about 'comfort parcels', a forthcoming camp wedding – 'wish you could enter into the celebration', he said – as well as the fact that Joyce Stranks had been a 'great help' in passing on news to him. The last sentence sent 'special love' to her and to the children.

There were fresh tears for Florence that day. 'I couldn't believe it, really,' she said, remembering both the upset of reading the messages and the consolation of hearing his voice within them. She put the envelope away, thinking she'd never receive another word her husband had written in camp.

She was wrong.

Late in 1945 Florence was sent a parcel of her husband's belongings which included his Edinburgh University blazer, the colour drained from it. There were also two small slips of plain paper, which Liddell had kept beside his hospital bed during his last hours. Each was torn a little and had once been folded, as if he'd slipped them into a pocket. After reading them in the camp, A. P. Cullen was convinced Liddell had experienced a 'premonition of his death'.

On the first sheet the handwriting, in faint pencil, is neat and fairly orderly. On the second the handwriting is unusually large. The words

COMMUNICATIONS

Approved by the Commandant

FROM
(Name in full) ERIC HENRY LIDDELL
(Nationality) BRITISH   No. 3/88
(Address) BLOCK 23/8 CIVIL ASSEMBLY CENTRE
      WEIHSIEN, SHANTUNG, CHINA

TO
(Name in full) MRS FLORENCE JEAN LIDDELL
(Nationality) BRITISH.
(Address) % REV W. ROULSTON, UNITED CHURCH OF CANADA
      CHUNGKING, CHINA.

MESSAGE

I HAVE RECEIVED SOME OF YOUR LETTERS AND HAVE
NEWS UP TO JANUARY. THE HOT SUMMER IS OVER, WE
ARE ENJOYING THE COOLER AUTUMN ALREADY. I CONSTANTLY
PICTURE YOU ALL. THIS MAY REACH YOU AT OR NEAR THE
ANNIVERSARY OF YOUR FATHER'S DEATH. YOU WILL KNOW THAT
MY THOUGHTS AND PRAYERS WILL BE WITH YOU — AND
ESPECIALLY WITH MOTHER. GIVE HER MY SPECIAL LOVE.
I SEE TRICIA, CYCLING, SWIMMING AND SKATING AND HEATHER
FOLLOWING FAST IN HER FOOTSTEPS. I WISH I COULD HEAR THEM
READ TO ME! MAUREEN, — I LONG TO SEE HER — SHE LOOKS FINE IN
THE SNAPS. I LONG FOR YOU DEAREST — AND THE TIME WHEN WE
SHALL START A HOME TOGETHER AGAIN. MAY IT BE SOON! Love, Eric.
Date AUGUST 27ᵗʰ 1944   Signature ERIC H. LIDDELL

(Message must be typed or plainly written in block letters)

(If message is not legible, it may not be transmitted)

*Too weak to write, Eric Liddell dictated his final
Red Cross messages to a friend.*

tumble across it in a confusion of lines, scarred with false starts and
crossings-out. The difference between these two pieces of paper is so
apparent that you understand Liddell's mind suffered as much as the
body near his end. Florence realized this without needing to be told.
The enormous difficulty Liddell had coordinating his movements and
holding the pencil is clearly evident. The writing on that first sheet is
very faint and almost indecipherable. It contains sketchy prompt notes
for a sermon he is intending to give about confronting and conquering
everyday fears.

The second sheet is essentially a collection of verses from two hymns,
'Abide With Me' and 'Be Still, My Soul'. Liddell's memory is incapable of

recalling either of them faithfully and his hand isn't able to scribble fast or legibly enough the words he wants to leave behind. 'O Lord,' he says, as if knowing death is close, 'the darkness deepens.' The rest is a semi-ramble, seldom coherent or whole, that foreshadows what's to come for him. His mind is shutting down and switching off, no longer brimful of what only recently it could summon at will.

One line nevertheless stands out, as though Liddell forced it on to the page with a last gasp of thought and effort. The short sentence, and the cream-coloured slip of paper on which it was written, is more than seventy years old now. Time has chafed it, making the edges ragged, and exposure to light has faded the once-dark press of pencil-lead. But this simplest of phrases, slanting across the top left-hand corner of the final page, calls out to whoever sees it because the four words Liddell found from somewhere read like a farewell promise to his family and the last expression of his unbreakable faith.

'All will be well,' he says.

And so it proved.

What Will Survive of Us Is Love

Toronto, Ontario, Canada

THE DAUGHTER ERIC LIDDELL never met is sitting on a smoke-grey sofa staring intently at two photographs of her father. Another photograph of him hangs on the wall directly beside the front window of her sixteenth-floor apartment. Beyond it Lake Ontario is a sheet of blue glass, barely rippled. In the way-off distance the sails of boats, like small flakes of white chalk, move slowly across the calm-still water in search of a half-breath of wind that never comes.

This August afternoon is hot and drowsy, the sky cloudless, and Maureen Liddell has arranged an English high tea: cakes and scones, cucumber sandwiches and cups of Earl Grey.

For the past eighteen months I've spent day after day in libraries and archives, straining my roaming eyes over tiny print and dark, smudgy newspaper pictures that look as if the printer rolled too much ink on to the block. I've turned countless pages of faded foolscap documents and also the dusty, ribbon-tied minute-books of long-ago meetings, which were typed on clunking machines or written with a nibbed pen. I've held the gold medal Liddell won in Paris in the well of my hand, astonished at its feathery lightness. I've stood in front of the oil that Eileen Soper painted of him, tucked into the east stairway of Scotland's National Portrait Gallery.

In a journey of over 20,000 miles I've also seen the way in which landscapes so integral to Liddell have changed since his day. Powderhall Stadium, where he sharpened his speed beside the flat-capped Tom McKerchar, is a spread of modern brick housing. The rooftops of George Square are overlooked by the domed tower and the crescent moon of Edinburgh's Central Mosque, emphasizing that city's religious diversity. And, of course, there is Guang-Wen Street, where I found the canvas market stalls and the high-rise offices standing where wooden shanties and mud tracks once stood before them. I've spoken to survivors of the camp – internees, aged between eighty and ninety-nine, for whom Weifang will always be Weihsien. Whatever each has done since liberation – and wherever it carried them as a consequence – those days in the camp have gone with them, a pale shadow ever present across blameless lives.

Everything has led me here, the place where Liddell planned to settle at the end of the war. Home for the daughters he never saw again after 1941 – as well as for the daughter he never saw at all – lies along that section of the Go train-line stretching westwards from Toronto. Only a handful of stops separate Patricia, Heather and Maureen.

Months before, during that warm, smoggy morning in Shandong Province, I'd felt a sense of unreality about being in China. The past seemed more tangible to me than the present because I'd been immersed in it for so long; and, at first, I found it difficult to relate one to the other because the two were so different from each other. In Weifang I mentally dropped a photograph of the *kao liang* fields and the bell tower over the glass, steel and neon around me. In Toronto, experiencing that same feeling again, I think about the colour studio portrait of the Liddell family without its father. Maureen is a baby, wrapped in a white woollen shawl and cradled in Florence's left arm. Patricia and Heather are dressed identically in those Sunday-smart, high-collared frocks. It scarcely seems possible to me that 'the girls', as Florence referred to them in her letters, long ago became mothers and then grandmothers. The baby in her white shawl is now wearing a white shirt and a pair of fawn slacks, her dark hair cut short. She is pouring the Earl Grey. The photo, once fresh from the developing tray, is history.

I tell Maureen what those once in Weihsien had told me: that, after

*The girls: (from the left) Patricia, Maureen and
Heather.*

her father's sudden death, the internees spoke especially of her. About
the fact that she'd never see him or hear his voice. About the fact that
whatever she'd learn about his life would come second-hand from anecdotes, newspaper clippings and pictures stuck into albums. About the fact
that his loss would profoundly affect her when she was old enough to
comprehend it properly. However hazy and indistinct, Patricia and
Heather would at least retain scraps of him – a cycle ride in Tientsin; his
face at their bedside or at the breakfast table; even the last, dim sight of
him during that farewell on the *Nitta Maru*. For Maureen, there would
only ever be blanks where memories should be, each filled with lost possibilities. Weihsien had worried about her.

She nods, acknowledging the perceptiveness of strangers. She will talk
about it in a minute.

First, she shows me the photographs she particularly likes. She hunts out the picture of her father wearing her mother's hat at the wedding of a friend. She then finds the one in which he attempts to tickle her in the garden as she playfully pretends to escape. 'You know,' she says in her Canadian accent, 'I look at these and know how good the relationship was between them; how much each so obviously loved the other. You think of missionaries as serious and stuffy. My parents were never like that. They had a lot of fun and humour in them.' She smiles – the sort of wide smile her parents gave to the camera on those fine days in 1934.

She hasn't always smiled like this. Her childhood, she says, was a struggle to accept her father's absence and a quest to get to know him. She sometimes became angry – 'a huge rage', she says – about the 'monstrous space' he'd left behind. On the edge of her teens, she quarrelled with her mother. 'He can't have loved you,' she'd said to her. 'He made you leave China without him. He made you come here with us.' She admits now, 'I made it difficult for her because I was growing up without him and I couldn't understand it. I wanted him to be there.'

Liddell's status as an Olympic champion and his career as an athlete were always less important to her than discovering the sort of man he'd been. 'I used to ask myself, Was he a deluded Christian? Was he as good as everyone said? Then I'd think: how *could* he have been? He'd let us leave China. I was so confused.'

There were times when Maureen didn't want to discuss him. 'It was like opening a wound,' she says. Questions that had occupied the camp internees in 1945 still occupied her nonetheless. Why hadn't he been spared and come home? 'It seemed especially cruel,' she says. 'I couldn't understand *why* he had to die. I was furious with God.'

She isn't furious any more.

All of us live incomplete lives. At our end something is always left unsaid, undone, unseen. But Liddell's life seems scarcely half-finished. You can't avoid thinking of the birthdays he never celebrated, the weddings he never attended, the grandchildren he never held. The world awaiting him after Weihsien would have been one of endless choice.

But Maureen grew to accept his passing. She believes it was 'meant to be'; that somehow his premature death had a wider purpose, which the years have gradually revealed. After reaching that conclusion, everything about him became clear to her. 'I saw the big plan for my father's life,' she says.

She remembers a drizzly morning in 2008. Alongside Patricia and Heather, she'd stood in front of his rose granite monument in Weifang. Each of them laid flowers and held one another in what her mother used to call the 'magic circle' of family. 'I felt so close to him and, more than ever, I realised what his life had been *for*. It all made sense. What happened allowed him to touch so many lives as a consequence.'

First Patricia and then Heather say the same thing to me. His death will always be a part of his children's lives; but each sees a reason for it now.

'The number of people he's influenced . . . well, things seem to add up, don't they?' says Patricia. 'You only appreciate it when you look at each stage of his life and make the connections between them.' She pauses for a moment. 'I used to ask myself: how would things have turned out if the three of us and our mother had been in the camp with him? Then I understood my father would have spent less time with the other youngsters, which would have deprived them of so much. That didn't seem fair to them. He was needed there. The stories we heard after his death prove that.' Beside her sit big black boards made of strong card on to which she has pasted photographs of him as a missionary as well as an athlete. She uses them to illustrate the talks she gives about him.

'My father was meant to be in that camp,' agrees Heather. 'His whole life was designed to either care for or to inspire people. That was hard for us to accept as children and we shed tears over it.' On a polished table she has laid out the family's archive for me: her mother's letters to him; her father's Red Cross letters in return; the full drafts of commemorative radio programmes and memorial speeches; the messages of sympathy sent to the family from friends and strangers alike; the photograph of his grave in Weihsien; and, finally, those two scraps of paper, preserved in a transparent plastic bag, on which he wrote his last words so faintly with a stubby pencil as his strength ebbed away. 'The response to who he was and what he did goes far beyond anything we ever have imagined,' she adds, glancing across at the accumulation of paper. 'Slowly I began to appreciate how much he had meant to others – and how much others relied on him. That was his purpose. He belonged to everyone else in the world as well as to us. I understood we were meant to share him.'

His daughters will go on sharing him, for his story has no full stop.

That written promise 'All will be well', which Liddell left beside his deathbed, has come true because of the sort of man he was; and also because of the example he set. His character constitutes the basis of his legacy, which is a gift that keeps on giving to whoever discovers both it and him. You see it in those who now quote his daily devotions and philosophies on Twitter. You see it in the references made about him in newspapers, in chat rooms and on blogs across the world. You see it in the stories of men and women, born decade upon decade after Liddell's death, who labour on behalf of others because he inspired them. You see it, too, in the bricks and mortar of Edinburgh's Eric Liddell Centre, formerly Morningside Church on 'Holy Corner'. In its devotion to the community, the centre does today what Liddell began almost a century ago – caring, supporting, educating, inspiring. And so the ideas and ideals he espoused go on. We owe him a debt for that; though we also know Liddell would blanch at the very presumption of it and disown the credit.

Eric Liddell changed the lives of those who were close to him.

D. P. Thomson, who had described his own life in the ordained ministry as 'a lie' until Liddell became a part of it, continued to write, preach and teach until his death in 1974. He organized Liddell's memorial fund, which preoccupied him so completely that his sister fretted over his exhausted state. Thomson remembered a 'long argument' over supper during which she'd rebuked him about his commitment to Liddell. 'Was I making too much of Eric?' was how Thomson recorded the exchange in his diary, also noting that he 'failed to convince' her of the merit behind his devotion. Thomson never doubted that Liddell was worth his all-consuming efforts. He called him a 'friend and a brother' and spoke of his 'transparent sincerity' and 'deep humility' and his 'considerateness and self-forgetfulness'.

Annie Buchan was among those missionaries determined to see China again. Having returned from Weihsien both weary and sick at Christmas 1945, she was back there again in less than two years. She returned to Scotland in 1950 and died there in 1987. Whenever she was asked to describe Liddell's final hours, she did so only after stressing he had been 'the finest' and the 'most remarkable' of men. She didn't want the tragic manner of his death to obscure the achievements of his life.

Aubrey Grandon died in 1990. He was always proud – but never boastfully so – of beating Liddell in Weihsien. At a camp reunion, held after *Chariots of Fire* had brought Liddell alive again as an athlete, Grandon heard one of the internees, only a young child in 1944, claim that his hero 'had never lost a race'. Grandon's wife urged him to speak and correct the mistake. 'No,' he said. 'It doesn't matter.' Whenever Grandon talked about running against Liddell in that last Sports Day, he'd always concede, 'Eric wasn't well then.'

Even Harold Abrahams dwelt on his rival, despite the fact that he neither saw nor spoke to him again after 1925. He died in 1978, well before filming on *Chariots of Fire* began. His preoccupation with Liddell was based on that unanswerable question from history: What if? This troubled him. He'd known, as if memorizing them, Liddell's times over 100 yards, sometimes on appreciably slower tracks than Colombes's in Paris, and so said aloud what others were thinking. 'I have often wondered whether I owe my Olympic success, at least in part, to Eric's religious beliefs. Had he run [in the 100 metres], would he have defeated me and won that Olympic title?' Abrahams was anxious to provide evidence that would dissuade his listener from saying yes – though yes remains the logical conclusion. Liddell was the superior runner, however much Abrahams protested otherwise. As an old man, he was still protesting about it. His language was baroque, as if he thought piling up words in front of an argument would hide the cracks in its structure. 'At this long distance from the actual event I can perhaps say, without seeming self-centred, that I believe I was, in fact, better than Eric over 100 metres – though it is equally fair to say that on the only two occasions on which I ran against him [over 220 yards and 200 metres] he defeated me.' You can read that sentence until the next Olympics comes around without knowing why Abrahams regarded himself as 'better' – apart from hubris or gut instinct – since the only cold data he provides points the other way. The fact that anyone might assume Liddell would have taken gold from him, invalidating the medal he won, clearly concerned Abrahams, suggesting a complex that only a session or two on the psychiatrist's couch might have resolved.

Liddell was the mentor forever at Steve Metcalf's shoulder. What he heard Liddell say in the camp – 'love your enemies' – never left him. During Liddell's funeral, carrying the coffin and listening to the orations, Metcalf decided to become a missionary in Japan. He later learned the language at a rate of twenty words per day. He joined the Overseas Missionary Fellowship and worked for them from 1952 until 1990, believing it to be his destiny. The boat taking him to what had once been an enemy country also took three hundred British soldiers to fight in the Korean War. 'On our first Sunday at sea the officer in charge asked me to speak to them,' he said. 'I'd only recently turned twenty-five. I was still older than some of those who were in uniform. I told them about Eric. What he'd said about praying for those who despitefully use you. How he'd forgiven everyone.' Metcalf referred to 'the baton of forgiveness', which he believed Liddell had passed on to him.

In August 2005 he did so again, giving the keynote speech when internees gathered at the site of the camp to commemorate its liberation. Metcalf looked around him – at the faces he knew, which were as old as or even older than his own, and at the stone bulk of the buildings. His friend was there too – exactly as he had first seen him. His face was unmarked. His eyes were the brightest blue. He was still dressed in khaki shorts and that shirt made from a curtain. He was running in races on roads that didn't exist. He was walking pathways that were no longer there. He was preaching beneath a tree that had been cut down an age ago. He was wearing the athletics spikes given away sixty years earlier. Liddell seemed so alive to Metcalf again that the question he had asked at his graveside – 'Is this all that happens to honour such a Great Man?' – had at last been answered to his satisfaction.

'Oh no,' he said. 'This Great Man lives on.'

In 'An Arundel Tomb', Philip Larkin wrote one of the most memorable lines of his – or anybody else's – collected poetry. It is the last sentence of the last verse. 'What will survive of us is love'.

Eric Liddell is proof of that.

Eileen Soper remained a spinster. The evidence suggests she never found – and never wanted either – anyone else to share with her the sound of that 'lonely peewit crying'. Near the end of her life arthritis confined her to Wildings, where her precious garden gradually became an unruly tangle of unpruned trees, untrimmed hedges, unmown grass and flowers that were left to wilt or grow tall and wild. The house deteriorated around her too, becoming dilapidated and also infested with mice, which lived in her slippers and in chests of drawers. Soper had thrown nothing away. There were over three thousand empty glass jars. There were stacks of cardboard boxes and wooden pallets, which had once contained apples. There were magazines and newspapers, most of them decades old. After her death in 1990, aged eighty-five, a friend, walking into her studio, described every part of it as 'silted up with paper, boxes, mounts'. In this impossibly cluttered but private space, only one of Soper's possessions stood out prominently, making it impossible to ignore. It sat on her mahogany easel. Her friend thought it dominated the room 'like some tutelary deity'. This was Liddell's face. Of all the pictures Soper had painted and still owned – hundreds of etchings, drawings, prints and watercolours – she'd chosen to display his portrait, as though longing for those high summers in the 1920s when both of them still had a life to come and she'd watched Liddell carve E and L on that beech tree with his silver key. This is how he remained in Soper's mind – always blond, always grey-suited, always handsomely serious. The portrait, it was later discovered, had stood on the easel 'for several years'.

Florence Liddell didn't need a painting, or even a photograph, to summon him. She had what she called scores of 'beautiful memories' to sustain her. 'We had as much happiness in our few short years together as many couples have had in a whole lifetime,' she said, thanking God 'for the privilege of being his wife'. He had been 'everything to me', she added.

Florence once confessed: 'I'd always felt that if anything happened to Eric my world would collapse completely – and my faith and everything else.' But she knew dwelling overmuch on her sadness would only multiply it, so she put it aside and pressed on for the sake of Patricia, Heather and Maureen. Thinking of it, 'the girls' remember a mother who never raised her voice and never raised her hand; who educated them with planned visits to galleries, museums and exhibitions; and who would tell them 'your father would be so proud of you'. They can still hear her playing the piano, especially Beethoven's Moonlight Sonata, her favourite, and 'The Sweet By-and-By'. They still see her making clothes or mending them, saving cents to accrue dollars that paid for dancing lessons, piano lessons and summer camp.

The words each uses to describe their mother – 'optimistic, caringly compassionate, faithful, selfless, resilient' – could be used to describe their father too. And the qualities that had attracted him to her so long ago and in another country were apparent more than ever after his death. She became all her husband had known her to be – and more besides. Florence was a woman made of tough fibres, remarkably and resourcefully strong in heart and head. She subsequently tried to live 'more like he lived', she said.

In the days after Liddell's death, her own mother had remarked disconsolately, 'Well Florence, I guess we're just two old widows together now.' Florence disagreed. She wasn't old; her thirty-fourth birthday was six months away. She didn't want to be shut for ever in the same house as her mother either. The bereaved are sick with many griefs, which fill up rooms, and there is a commonality about the process of clearing them. Florence went through each of these – denial and anger, which were brief; depression and loneliness, which lingered; reflection and acceptance and then reconstruction, which led her into a future far different from the one she had envisaged. She disguised the worst of her agonizing behind a front of fortitude and grace and she busied herself with those practicalities that the dead always leave the living to sort and tidy. There was a £10,000 insurance policy to settle. There was a lost will to locate. There was copious correspondence to be answered. There was a memorial service to attend in Toronto and others to read about in Edinburgh and Glasgow, which were conducted in her absence. While her trauma was fresh, Florence admitted, 'My brain still feels rather fuzzy and numbed when it comes to thinking about business matters.' She forced herself to think about them nonetheless. She set and fixed her household budget. She found herself a nursing post at Toronto General Hospital to earn a wage and went back to university to gain more qualifications. Eventually she found an apartment – three rooms and a shared kitchen only a couple of miles from her former home. 'You might as well have the plague as three children when it comes to house hunting,' she had said, remembering the difficulty of securing a tenancy.

Three months of the summer immediately following Liddell's death were spent in a rented cabin cottage at Port Albert on Lake Huron. The cottage was of Thoreau-like simplicity and proved restorative. This was her Walden Pond. She settled on the land the way Thoreau had settled on his own for the purpose of finding 'only the essential facts of life'. With her daughters she found a necessary solitude there – no telephone, no newspaper, no demands, no well-meaning callers. She could think and plan and prepare. At Port Albert, Florence started again. She would still talk about him. She would still drape his university blazer over her shoulders like a cape to be closer to him. Sometimes she would still feel his presence around her too, always believing she'd see him 'right there – if only I could turn my head a fraction quicker'.

In every end there are the threads of a new beginning.

In 1951 she married again. Murray Hall was a cousin. His wife, stricken with terminal cancer, asked Florence to support her at home and also look after him and their three children, aged between twelve and seventeen. Looking back on it, 'the girls' are convinced the request was about more than practical nursing. It was also a piece of match-making from a patient who, aware of her mortality, wanted to be sure that her husband and her family would be cared for after her death. For the sake of this second marriage, Florence put away her first. The photographs and small treasures from it were placed in a trunk and carried into the basement. She became Mrs Hall of the 300-acre Jersey Farm and had a fourth child, christened Jeannie, in 1955. She was widowed for the second time in 1969.

In the second half of her life the woman who'd faced so much with such equanimity was confronted with another misery. She was diagnosed with Cushing Syndrome, a rare hormonal disorder that occurs when the body secretes too much cortisol into the bloodstream. It causes obesity, high blood pressure and extreme fatigue. The skin can bruise easily. Florence suffered each of these complaints, coping with the condition as phlegmatically as she had everything else.

She'd assumed the only landmarks to come in her life would be more grandchildren, never thinking the past would be recreated in front of her.

She lived long enough to hear Allan Wells' response to reporters' questions after becoming the first British runner since Harold Abrahams to win the 100 metres Olympic title at Moscow's 1980 Games. Wells was born in Liddell's Edinburgh and raised 4 miles from Morningside Church.

'Did you win for Harold Abrahams?' he was asked afterwards.

'No,' he replied. 'For Eric Liddell.'

Then came *Chariots of Fire*. The anonymous, silver-haired Florence found herself nearly famous. There was a screening to attend. She 'wept all the way through it', she said. There were letters requiring replies. These were composed entirely in her own hand. There were television and newspaper interviews to be done. The questions were nearly all the same, her answers to them well rehearsed. Yes, she found the interest around the film 'kinda fun'. Yes, she thought Ian Charleson's portrayal caught the 'spirit' of Liddell's personality. No, the script hadn't quite captured him completely. The cinema version was 'a bit too solemn' and 'a little too preachy', she explained.

One evening Florence sat on the couch at her daughter Heather's home and watched a reel of celluloid she'd never seen before. It was Pathé's black and white film of Liddell's 400 metres win in Paris. She saw then what anyone can view now on YouTube. The focus on his twenty-two-year-old face. Those long fingers resting on his hips. That number – 451 – on his shirt-front. The crowd massed steeply behind him. That stare down the line and the curve of the Colombes track before the gun releases him on the race of a lifetime. His fleet feet pounding along the cinder. The spray of that cinder as he runs. His head thrown back. The snap of the tape.

'She couldn't believe what she was seeing,' remembers Heather. Florence leaned forward on the very lip of her seat, oblivious for more than a full minute to absolutely everything except the scene played out in front of her on a 21-inch television. 'It was as if she was there with him, sitting in the stand,' Heather adds. As the race began, Florence was lost in the brightness of it. She even yelled, 'Come on, honey. You can beat him. You can do it.'

The last frame of that film shows Liddell after his triumph. He is accepting a congratulatory handshake. The image lingers, freezing him in that pose for a while – the splendour of the man he'd once been so apparent. Florence stood up and looked at it as though in that moment she was remembering every one of the yesterdays she had spent beside him. She bowed her head, raised her hands to her face and began to weep.

In the years left to her she would reminisce about him and also re-live their courtship and marriage. She was living with Patricia, who one afternoon had to comfort her after a dream.

In it, the *Nitta Maru* was slipping across the Yellow Sea again. Her husband was leaving the ship and she was attempting to chase after him. Somehow – for there were no shackles and no rope to tether her – she found her feet were rooted to the spot on which she stood. Attempting to move towards the gangway, she was unable to take a step. She was sobbing and shouting in panic, pleading with him not to leave her. 'Don't go,' she was saying over and again before an abrupt, confused awakening in her own bed. 'You were having a dream,' said Patricia, placing her hand on her mother's brow. 'Don't worry. Everything is all right now.'

Florence died in June 1984. She had never stopped loving him.

*

Shortly before the Beijing Olympics in 2008, the Chinese claimed that Eric Liddell had refused repatriation from Weihsien, giving away his place instead to a pregnant woman. The Chinese further insisted that Winston Churchill was directly responsible for persuading the Japanese to offer him his freedom. None of his friends gave the story any credence; those who had lived so closely with him in the camp were adamant that a 'secret' of that magnitude could never have been hidden there. They saw the notion of it as a nice but idealized fantasy, designed to enhance his reputation still further. 'He was so good anyway that no one ever has to overstate it,' said Joe Cotterill. 'The basic facts alone tell you everything about him.'

You can only nod your head at that assessment.

He was some man; and he lived some life, however briefly. Most of us don't leave much of a mark and we disappear almost completely when the last person who remembers us dies also. But the mark he left is ineradicable. *The Disciplines of the Christian Life* – that collection of thoughts and quotations he wrote on his blackwood desk in Tientsin – has sold tens of thousands of copies. It sells still.

Valorous lives like his, which must be calculated in terms of value rather than length, encourage us to make our own lives better somehow. In his case that's because everything he did was selfless, each kind act bespoke for someone else's benefit. He believed entirely that those to whom 'much is given' are obliged to give 'much in return' – and should do so without complaining about it. In adhering to this, he never demanded grand happiness or great comfort for himself. He grasped only for the things that mattered to him: worthwhile work and the care of his family. He'd once – on that hot July evening in Paris – grasped for an Olympic title as well, knowing nonetheless even as he won it that the glory of gold was nothing in his world compared to the glory of God.

It isn't fair to say that becoming an Olympic champion counts as his least significant act; but that's only because the feat brought him a wider audience for preaching than he would otherwise have achieved. It is fair to say, however, that the consequences of taking the medal were of far more value to him than the glint of the medal itself. He knew that whatever else he would surely have achieved as an athlete was trivial beside what he went on to achieve as a missionary, forever combining public service and private sacrifice.

It is said that every movement and speech reveals us. What revealed him – especially his attitude towards athletic prowess versus missionary duty – was his response to a specific, long-winded question at a particularly apt moment. It came in 1932. He was in Toronto, coincidentally a stop-over for the Great Britain team which was then on its way to the Los Angeles Olympics. He could have been competing there too instead of watching his countrymen like a kerbside spectator observing a passing parade. Button-holed by a pushy interviewer, he faced a series of questions rolled colourfully into one. The way each of them was framed suggests the newspaperman regarded him as slightly out of his mind for choosing a career in China ahead of a career in athletics.

'Are you glad you gave your life to missionary work?' he was asked. 'Don't you miss the limelight, the rush, the frenzy, the cheers, the rich red wine of victory?'

The part of Liddell's reply that really matters is humble; and it firmly ranks his missionary responsibilities well ahead of his running. He told his inquisitor: 'A fellow's life counts for far more at *this* than *the other*.'

So true, so true.

But only Eric Henry Liddell – that stillest of souls – could have said it with such sincerity.

Acknowledgements

Thoughts about the Chinese philosopher Lazoi rattled around my head as soon as I thought of writing this book. You'll know his most celebrated quotation because repetition has (almost) turned it into a cliché. The line, from chapter 64 of the *Tao Te Ching*, reads: 'A journey of a thousand miles begins with a single step.'

That seemed especially poignant to me at the start of *For the Glory*. It seems even more poignant now.

I knew well in advance about the long roads Eric Liddell had travelled during his relatively short life. I also knew I'd have to travel them too. A journey of a thousand miles? I have one thing to say to Lazoi. You don't know the half of it, old sport. On Eric's trail, I went to China, the United States and Canada. I've also covered every compass point in England and Scotland, which was a stroll to the village post office in comparison to totting up all those overseas hours in the air, on a train and also on a boat.

But I've been lucky – terribly lucky, in fact. Biography not only obliges you to get out of the house, it is also a lovely way to meet people. The company I've kept is proof of that; for those who were once strangers to me have since become acquaintances or, better still, friends, which has made me feel a little less guilty about constantly pestering them – for memories, photographs and documents – during the process of researching and writing and then checking and rechecking.

I list them here, hoping no one has been missed out.

Whoever writes about the past piles up personal debts during the accumulation of the sort of detail necessary to bring it alive again.

Not surprisingly, the biggest I owe is to Eric and Florence's 'girls': Patricia, Heather and Maureen. Each was instantly receptive to the idea of the book. Each was a tremendous supporter of the aims I expressed for it. Each showed me unfailing courtesy, kindness and a wonderful sharing spirit. I'd also like to pay tribute to Patricia's husband Mervyn (despite his allegiance to a certain football team which I can't bring myself to mention), and to Heather's husband Gerry (one day I hope we'll share a baseball diamond).

Other family members deserve more than honourable mentions too: Finlay (Florence's brother), who speaks so intelligently on art as well as China; Louise (Florence's sister), who knits faster than Usain Bolt can run; Sue, the daughter of Eric's brother Ernest, and Joan, the daughter of Eric's sister Jenny, who both so willingly talked to me about their parents.

I regard – and I sense 'the girls' do too – Bob Rendell as an honorary member of the Liddell-MacKenzie clan. Bob is now the former 'CEO' of the Eric Liddell Centre in Edinburgh. When I first spoke to him – a 'cold call' on the telephone – I suspect he thought I was ever so slightly crazy in wanting to trek across the globe. If so, it didn't deter him from doing whatever he could to make it easier. Bob is a star, an all-round nice guy.

My friend Simon McGee, who no doubt one day I'll be compelled to call 'Sir', made diplomatic introductions for me in regard to China.

Once there, no organizations could have been more accommodating than the British Embassy in Beijing and the officials in Weifang. To be the recipient of two banquets in China made me feel VIP-like. I am tremendously grateful to Wang Hoa, Director of Weifang Foreign and Overseas Chinese Affairs; Song Yuelin, the Deputy Director; Qi Yanling (the lovely Emily); and C. U. I. Xvexian, party secretary of the Middle School. Baoshu Xia, who has intently studied both Eric's life and the history of the Weihsien camp, was inexhaustible in his help both on the day and afterwards.

Nick Douse, the First Secretary (Regional City Engagement) of the British Embassy, shepherded me to Weifang and, on occasions, acted as my interpreter too. His company was not only integral to the success of the visit, but also a pleasure. I can no longer look at the results of AFC Wimbledon without remembering his passion for that club.

Through various sources, I was able to track down the descendants of those who played integral parts in Eric's story. Harry and Brian McKerchar, grandsons of Tom McKerchar; Doreen Grandon, wife of Aubrey Grandon; Margaret Buchan, Annie Buchan's niece; Joanna Cullen-Brown, daughter of A. P. Cullen; Sir Arthur Marshall, who shares his father's name; Ian Stone, related to Alec Nelson; Susan Liberta, the daughter of Horatio Fitch.

Our view of something always depends on the perspective from which we observe it. Sometimes that is simply geographical (where we are standing in the room, for example). Sometimes it is because we think/judge/recall a certain person or specific happening in a particular way. As I stress in the main text, memory can also be a very fickle beast. For each of these reasons, no one account of an action or a speech is normally identical to another. It can differ in tiny or even big ways. We are only human. We recollect things differently. That became more apparent than ever to me as I read eyewitness accounts of Weihsien. So I must pay particular tribute to those who experienced the camp and contributed towards the picture I have drawn of it. Desmond Power was fabulous in every way. Estelle Horne proved so generous in providing her own, pitch-perfect recollections. Peter Bazire acted as my 'chauffeur' at one stage. Pamela Masters spoke so freely and well about her experiences too. Mary Previte pointed me in many important directions. Margaret Holder was able to tell me about what it was like in one of Eric's classrooms. Ron Bridge was illuminating about the bricks, the mortar and the measurements of the place. Yvonne Finlay, the wife of Donald Finlay, related to me the stories her husband told her. So did Joan Michell, wife of David Michell, one of those who called Eric 'Uncle'; I am also grateful to their son Ken.

I count myself as fortunate to have met three exceptional people. The first was Steve Metcalf, who I interviewed in his London flat and spoke to again subsequently. I imagine that talking to Steve is a bit like talking to Eric would have been. There was such a gentle warmth about him, a point I particularly wanted to make to his son Stephen jnr. Joe and Joyce Cotterill were superb interviewees – two wise heads who put things into perspective for me. I left their home proud to say I'd spent time with both of them.

Others who deserve a salute are: John Keddie, the doyen of Scottish athletics history; Ronald Clements, who worked with Steve Metcalf on his life story; Rev. Jim Cowie of the Scots Kirk in Paris; Robert Gilmor, who knew Eileen Soper; Mark Stickings of Eltham College; Thomas P.

Jabine; Frank Bardgett, the biographer of D. P. Thomson; Rev. James McMillan of the Peterhead Congregational Church; Jill Forest, Clare Button and Denise Abbott of the Edinburgh University Library; Ray Dingwall of the Armadale History Association; Paul Dudman of the British Olympic Association Archive; Neil Fraser of SCRAN; Brian Stanley, Professor of World Christianity and Director for the Study of World Christianity; Lord Jonathan Porritt, son of Arthur Porritt; Joseph Romanos and Graeme Woodfield, the biographers of Arthur Porritt; Dr Alister Bull, of the Church of Scotland; David Wootton of the Chris Beetles Gallery in London; and Chris Beetles himself. Staffs at the following institutions were a credit to their profession: Edinburgh University Library; the London Library; SOAS, the University of London; BBC Written Archives Centre; the Bodleian Library; the Manchester Social Sciences Library; the Imperial War Museum; the National Archives of Scotland; the Library of Congress (particularly Amber Paranick); the National Gallery of Scotland; Archive of the Cambridge Athletics Association; the Philip Noel-Baker Archives; the Sir Winston Churchill Archives; the British Library; Birmingham University Library Cadbury Special Collections (which hold the archives of Joe Binks, Wilf Richards, Gus Tatham and the minutes of the General Olympic Committee); Alton Library, Iowa; the Historical Archives, Iowa; the University of Pennsylvania Library; the British Film Institute.

No author can survive without editors. I've been extremely fortunate to lean on the advice and expertise of Virginia Smith, Giles Elliott and Craig Pyette, each of whom made sage and sensible recommendations and, like the archetypical good coach, were always there for me. They were Tom McKerchar-like during the making of this book. I'd also like to thank Annie Badman, particularly for her stoicism in regard to my total lack of technological savvy, and Vivien Thompson for her patience as well as her assiduous checking.

As ever, my agent Grainne Fox was indispensable, her contribution worthy of a line of gold stars. The very admirable Christy Fletcher, of Fletcher & Company had the inspiration to suggest the book, and Grainne guided me to and through it. I can't praise Grainne enough for her patience, her persuasive powers, her all-round nous and her sense of humour. Most of all, she puts up with me; and for that I'm truly thankful, believe me.

Also at Fletcher and Company, I came to rely a great deal on the marvellously efficient Rachel Crawford, who answers some of the nuts and bolts questions about the publishing industry that still flummox me.

I often wonder how any book of mine would ever get started, let alone finished, without my wife Mandy. I think of each of them as a collaborative effort. So of course she came to China. Of course she came to America and Canada too. And of course she read and re-read drafts and created the good weather that made it possible for me to write them.

We met in an obscure bar (sadly no longer in existence) during an otherwise nondescript Thursday night in Leeds. The bar was around the corner from Dyson's clock in Lower Briggate. That's the landmark, familiar to any Loiner, which Tony Harrison writes about so memorably in the poem 'Under the Clock' – 'where my courting parents used to meet'.

Staying in Weifang, and staring through the early morning smog from the balcony of our hotel room, I reflected quietly on how far we'd travelled together as a consequence of that first meeting. It also reaffirmed this: no step I've taken in the past decade is as important as the one that carried me to her.

Lazoi will know what I'm talking about. He did, after all, believe that 'love is of all passions the strongest'.

A wise man indeed . . .

Timeline of Eric Liddell's Life

1898: James Liddell posted to China as a missionary.

1899: Marriage of James Liddell and Mary Reddin.

1900: Rob Liddell born in Shanghai.

1902: Eric Liddell born in Tientsin.

1903: Jenny Liddell – christened Janet Lillian – born in Siaochang.

1907: Liddell family return to Britain on furlough.

1908: Eric and Rob enrolled in LMS School at Blackheath. The rest of the Liddell family returns to China.

1912: Ernest Liddell born in Peking. Eric and Rob become pupils at Eltham College after LMS School is moved and renamed.

1920: Liddell family is reunited after James Liddell is given furlough.

1921: Eric begins his athletics career as an Edinburgh University student on the grass track of Craiglockhart. Launches his partnership with coach Tom McKerchar and wins two individual Scottish AAA titles that summer.

1922: Makes international rugby debut for Scotland against France in Paris – the first of three appearances that season. Retains his Scottish AAA titles. James and Mary Liddell are posted to Tientsin.

1923: Collects four more international rugby caps for Scotland. Again retains his Scottish AAA titles – and wins the 100 yards and 220 yards titles in the national AAA Championships at Stamford Bridge. Newspapers christen him the 'Flying Scot'. Speaks at Armadale after accepting a personal invitation to do so from D. P. Thomson. Travels to America for the University of Pennsylvania relays. Tells the British Olympic Association that he cannot run in the Olympic 100 metres or either of the relays because of his policy of not competing on a Sunday.

1924: Wins the Olympic 400 metres gold medal in Paris and a 200 metres bronze. Graduates from Edinburgh University.

1925: Agrees to sit for a portrait in oils by Eileen Soper. Wins three Scottish AAA titles. Sets off for China, where he teaches at the Anglo-Chinese College in Tientsin. Meets nurse Annie Buchan.

1928: Says he will not compete in the 1928 Olympics in Amsterdam.

1929: James Liddell is taken ill and returns to Britain. Eric Liddell races against German athlete Dr Otto Peltzer, who encourages him to enter the 1932 Olympics in Los Angeles.

1930: Becomes engaged to Florence MacKenzie. Joins the London Missionary Society.

1931: Returns to Scotland on furlough and takes part in a series of evangelistic meetings across the country.

1932: Ordained into the ministry and then returns to China.

1933: James Liddell dies, aged sixty-three.

1934: Marries Florence in Tientsin's Union Church.

1935: The Liddells' first daughter, Patricia, is born in Tientsin.

1937: The Liddells' second daughter, Heather, is born in Tientsin. The family leave the Anglo-Chinese College and Eric becomes a country missionary in Siaochang, where he works beside his brother Rob and Annie Buchan.

1939: Arrives in Scotland on his second furlough.

1940: His family join him in Scotland for the summer before returning to China. Death of Tom McKerchar.

1941: Forced to abandon Siaochang and return to Tientsin. A pregnant Florence leaves China with Patricia and Heather. The Liddells' third daughter, Maureen, is born in Toronto.

1942: Within a month of Pearl Harbor (at the end of 1941), Eric is held with other missionaries under house arrest in Tientsin. He begins writing a series of books and pamphlets.

1943: Sent to the Civilian Assembly Centre at Weihsien.

1944: Mary Liddell dies in Edinburgh, aged seventy-three.

1945: Eric dies in Weihsien of a brain tumour.

1984: Florence dies, aged seventy-two.

Notes and Sources

Prologue

He is crouching on the start line: Information about Sports Days at Weihsien, and what EL wore, from interviews with Steve Metcalf, Pamela Masters and Desmond Power. Other details from Joe and Joyce Cotterill (formerly Joyce Stranks), specifically on EL's weight; Norman Cliff, *Eric Liddell in Weihsien Camp* (weihsien-paintings.org) and *Courtyard of the Happy Way* (Arthur James Evesham, 1977); Pamela Masters, *The Mushroom Years* (Henderson House, 1998); David Michell, *A Boy's War* (OMF, 1988); *I Remember Eric Liddell* (OMF, undated); *The Spirit of Eric Liddell* (OMF, 1992).

A track of crimson cinder: *Time*, 14 July 1924.

Liddell claimed his gold medal in a snow-white singlet: Pathé News film from 1924 Olympics.

'A speck of glitter': Quotation from David Michell; interview with Joan Michell. Also *I Remember Eric Liddell* and *The Spirit of Eric Liddell*.

Until the Red Cross at last got food parcels: Description of food relief and the condition of the internees before it: Norman Cliff, *Courtyard of the Happy Way*; *Prisoners of the Samurai* (privately printed, 1998); *Memories of China* (undated); Pamela Masters, *The Mushroom Years*; Langdon Gilkey, *Shantung Compound* (Harper, 1966); Myra Scovel with Nelle Keys Bell, *The Chinese Ginger Jars* (Harper, 1961); Mary Scott, *Kept in Safeguard* (Nazarene Publishing, 1977); Steve Metcalf and Ronald Clements, *In Japan the Crickets Cry* (Monarch Books, 2010); Mary Previte, *Hungry Ghosts* (Zondervan, 1995). Also interviews with Steve Metcalf, Joe Cotterill, Joyce Cotterill, Mary Previte, Peter Bazire, Estelle Horne.

Every few weeks he merely slits a new notch-hole: Interview with Joe Cotterill and Joyce Cotterill.

He is waiting for me: I travelled to Weifang in April 2014.

Guang-Wen Street: History and details from interview with Baoshu Zia in Weifang.

The Japanese called it a 'Civilian Assembly Centre': Details of the composition of the camp from both Weifang officials and the camp list (weihsien-paintings.org) compiled by Ron Bridge, who also answered supplementary questions.

The place already had a past: Hilary Spurling, *Burying the Bones: Pearl Buck in China* (Profile, 2010); W. A. Swanberg, *Luce and his Empire* (Scribner, 1972).

With infinite patience: Interview with Joyce Cotterill.

'You came away from his meetings': Elsa Watson, BBC interview, not broadcast.

'Everyone regarded him as a friend': Interview with Estelle Horne.

Someone else saw an enigmatic side: Jeannie Hills, BBC interview, not broadcast.

'You knew you were in the presence': Interview with Steve Metcalf.

'It is rare indeed': Langdon Gilkey, *Shantung Compound*.

There are countless anecdotes of his sportsmanship: Neil Campbell, BBC interview, not broadcast in its entirety. Interviews with EL's daughters, Patricia, Heather and Maureen.

'Seemed to do everything wrong': *New York Times*, 4 June 1946.

The *Daily Mail*'s celebrated caricaturist: The British Cartoon Archive, University of Kent (www.cartoons.ac.uk).

One of my favourite stories: Interviews with EL's daughters.

Chapter One

There was an impish look about him: Photographs supplied by the McKerchar family and the Church of Scotland.

The father of twelve children: Interview with the McKerchar family.

He began there as a paper ruler: Census information (1891, 1901, 1911).

Like most of his working-class generation: Interview with the McKerchar family.

McKerchar studied the physiology and psychology: Details of McKerchar's methods and approach to athletes: EL's own account of his running career in *All Sports Illustrated Weekly*, 5 June to 3 July 1926; R. Hadgraft, *Beer and Brine: The Making of Walter George, Athletics' First Superstar* (Desert Island ebooks, 2006); R. McWhirter, *Get to Your Marks: A Short History of World, Commonwealth and European Athletics* (Kaye, 1951).

Athletics meetings during McKerchar's early days: C. M. Usher, *The Story of Edinburgh University Athletic Club* (Constable, 1966). Climate of athletics in the 1920s and subsequently: G. Butler, *Runners and Running* (Herbert Jenkins, 1929); H. Abrahams and J. Crump, *Athletics* (The Naldrett Press, 1954); F. A. M. Webster, *Great Moments in Athletics* (Country Life, 1947) and *Olympic Cavalcade* (Country Life, 1946); Mark Ryan, *Running with Fire: The True Story of Chariots of Fire Hero Harold Abrahams* (JR Books, 2011). Neil Campbell's memories recalled in John W. Keddie, *Running the Race* (Evangelical Press, 2007).

This attitude and approach: Mark Ryan, *Running with Fire*; interview with Ian

Stone, author of *Alec Nelson, Professional Runner and Athletics Coach*, which was part of the Sporting Lives Symposium at Wychwood Park, Cheshire, 2010; R. L. Quercetani, *A World History of Track and Field Athletics, 1864–1964* (Oxford University Press, 1964).

Always saw them as a trio: EL's own account of his running career in *All Sports Illustrated Weekly*.

Craiglockhart was a spacious expanse of grass: Description of Craiglockhart: C. M. Usher, *The Story of Edinburgh University Athletic Club*; J. W. Keddie, *Scottish Athletics, 1883–1983, The Official Centenary Publication* (Scottish AAA, 1983). Also, my visit to what remains of the facility.

The Americans complained: *Oxford Dictionary of National Biography*; *Glasgow Herald*, 21 July 2008; A. Guttmann, *The Olympics: A History of the Modern Games* (University of Illinois Press, 1992); B. Henry, *An Approved History of the Olympic Games* (Alfred, 1984).

Edinburgh University's reluctant athlete: The account of EL's climbing holiday, his first races and initial instruction with TM are his own and written in the first person. The publication in which these appeared was not attributed. Also, interview with Steve Metcalf. Details on German Max Sick and his book (available as an ebook): R. Tyrell, 'Marvellous Max, the Iron Master', *Physical Culture Journal*, April 2000. When EL first spoke about 'Maxick', the reporter covering the event mistakenly reported that the 'muscle man' was Mussolini.

Only another three years: I am grateful to John Keddie's dedication in researching and listing EL's races in *Running the Race*.

There was no sporting streak: Family details of EL's parents, their background and early days in China come chiefly from interviews with EL's daughters, Sue (daughter of EL's brother Ernest) and Joan (daughter of EL's sister Jenny). Other sources are Jenny's unpublished manuscript *Memories of China Days*.

The Society of Righteous and Harmonious Fists: Accounts of the Boxer Rebellion come from Jonathan Fenby, *The Penguin History of Modern China* (Penguin, 2008) and *Generalissimo: Chiang Kai-shek and the China He Lost* (Free Press, 2005); Theodore H. White, *In Search of History* (Harper & Row, 1978) and, with A. Jacoby, *Thunder out of China* (Da Capo Press, 1980); Edgar Snow, *China* (Random House, 1981); David Silbey, *The Boxer Rebellion and the Great Game in China* (Hill and Wang, 2013); Robert Bickers, *The Scramble for China* (Penguin, 2012); Richard O'Connor, *Boxer Rebellion* (Robert Hale, 1974).

A contemporary eyewitness: W. F. Rowlands, *The Plain and the People* (The Livingston Press, 1937).

To steel herself for the daily adversities: Jenny Liddell, *Memories of China Days*.

She was at 'death's door': Ibid.

She called him 'Yellie': Ibid.

He walked so awkwardly: Ibid.

In the cocoon of childhood: Ibid.

He uttered his first Chinese phrase: Ibid.

On the day she sailed back to China: Ibid.

Augustus Pountney Cullen: Interview with APC's daughter Joanna Cullen-Brown.

The 1918 school championships: Eltham School records.

Later told a friend: Arthur Green, BBC interview, not broadcast.

The dreary commonplace of practice: EL's own account (publication unattributed).

His church was Morningside Congregational: R. G. Davies and A. Pollock, *Morningside Congregational Church, The Story of Fifty Years, 1887–1937* (privately published, 1937).

He was compared to . . .: a **startled deer**, Grantland Rice, *New York Herald Tribune*, 12 July 1924; a **windmill**, Harold Abrahams in M. Ryan, *Running with Fire*; a **terrified ghost**, press agency accounts of his Olympic win, 12 July 1924, reported in the *Evening News*, Harrisburg.

Liddell relied on humour: EL's stories about himself were published in most newspapers after his Olympic success; this comes from the *Hartlepool Mail*, 18 July 1924. He retold them in Weihsien, later telling his friend Steve Metcalf that he'd also done so well before his Paris gold medal.

To force him into change: EL outlined the mechanics of his running, his diet and homilies to a 'Mr Chivers', a fan who received a letter from him dated 19 February 1926.

During the remainder of his first season: EL's own account of his running career in *All Sports Illustrated Weekly*.

The prizes piled up: Jenny Liddell, BBC interview. Also EL's own account (publication unattributed).

Assessing his first phenomenal summer: *Glasgow Herald*, 11 August 1921.

Not everything went so smoothly: EL's own account (publication unattributed).

Chapter Two

Eric Liddell could identify precisely: Date and time from the diary of D. P. Thomson (unpublished).

Armadale was not the sort of place: Details from the Armadale Historical Society.

As Thomson conceded: Account from D. P. Thomson, *Eric Liddell: The Making of an Athlete and the Training of a Missionary* (ELMC, 1946) and *Scotland's Greatest Athlete: The Eric Liddell Story* (The Research Unit, 1970).

C. T. Studd's Heart of Africa Mission: N. Grubb, *C. T. Studd: Cricketer and Pioneer* (Lutterworth Press, 1970).

The number of his digs: *Edinburgh Telephone Book*, 1923.

'He really couldn't tell': D. P. Thomson, *Scotland's Greatest Athlete*.

An unprepossessing town hall: Details from photograph supplied by Armadale Historical Society.

'A secret disciple': D. P. Thomson, *Scotland's Greatest Athlete*.

For the morning after: Russell W. Ramsey, *God's Joyful Runner* (Bridge Publishing, 1987); *Glasgow Herald*, 29 and 30 June and 1 July 1925.

'I was brought up in a Christian home': David McCasland, *Eric Liddell: Pure Gold* (Discovery House Publishers, 2001).

D. P. Thomson had been born: F. Bardgett, *Scotland's Evangelist, D. P. Thomson* (Kindle edition), and an interview with the author.

The American Frank Buchman: Obituary, *The Times*, 9 August 1961.

The light lilt of Scots: Several friends spoke about Liddell's accent, including Marcy Ditmanson (*OMS Outreach Magazine*, November/December 1988) and Joe Cotterill, Joyce Cotterill and Steve Metcalf in interviews I conducted with them.

'In scarcely more than a whisper': *Scotsman*, 5 June 1925; *Sunday Times*, 13 July 1924.

As one correspondent wrote: *Scotsman*, 17 July 1924.

One sermon presented the quintessential Liddell: Interview with Steve Metcalf. EL told him he had learned this story at Eltham.

Time and again Liddell returned to the term 'be perfect': EL's own book *The Disciplines of the Christian Life* (SPCK, 1985).

From Armadale onwards: Ibid.

Liddell didn't write out rigid compositions: Page found in his Bible, which now belongs to his daughters.

He kept a profusion of fountain pens: *Scottish Daily Express*, 5 December 1948.

'If I take a fish': *Peking and Tientsin Times*, 20 January 1926. This was clearly a favourite line of EL's. It appears in other reported sermons.

'Better than I have ever heard him': From D. P. Thomson's diary.

A 'waste of £5': EL's own account of his running career in *All Sports Illustrated Weekly*.

'The week before': Ibid.

He was often asked why championship times: Ibid.

One story – surely apocryphal: M. Watman, *History of British Athletics* (Robert Hale, 1968); *Dictionary of National Biography*; G. Butler, *Runners and Running*; F. A. M. Webster, *Great Moments in Athletics* and *Olympic Cavalcade*.

'The most misplaced direction of energy' (and subsequent Abrahams quotes): M. Ryan, *Running with Fire*.

'It was a grilling, hot day': EL's own account of his running career in *All Sports Illustrated Weekly*.

'I surprised even myself': Ibid.

'When he smother-tackled you': A. A. Thomson (no relation to D. P. Thomson), *Rugger My Pleasure* (SBC, 1967).

'Rugby . . . a blessing and a small curse': EL's own account of his running career in *All Sports Illustrated Weekly*.

'It had exactly the opposite effect': D. P. Thomson, *Scotland's Greatest Athlete*.

The race began on a bend: *Stoke Sentinel*, 14 and 16 July 1923; *The Times*, 16 July 1923.

'No thanks': Letter to D. P. Thomson from an athlete, unnamed, who helped EL to his feet.

As 'Mr Baker': Philip Baker may have added his wife's surname to his own shortly after their marriage in 1915, but newspapers continued to use only Baker until much later. He is now known only as Noel-Baker and I have used it throughout to avoid confusion. Biographical details of his life come from D. J. Whittaker, *Fighter for Peace* (William Sessions Ltd, 1989). Also, EL's recollections of Noel-Baker from Steve Metcalf, and Arthur Marshall, *The Marshall Story* (Patrick Stephens, Ltd, 1994).

'The analogy is similar': EL's own account of his running career in *All Sports Illustrated Weekly*.

Raised in that all-male environment: Interview with EL's daughters.

Liddell the young man had begun to call on the artist: Biographical details from D. Hart-Davis, *Wildings: The Secret Garden of Eileen Soper* (Whiterby, 1991); D. Wootton and F. Pearce, *The Art of George and Eileen Soper* (produced by Chris Beetles Ltd for the Soper estate). The connection between Eileen Soper and EL came about after he stayed with one of her father's friends, Ralph Holder. Wildings was used as a name for the house only after EL knew it. I refer to it as such to avoid confusion and because Wildings is now so firmly established in relation to Eileen Soper's work.

Chapter Three

Comfortably settled in the upholstered leather: Details of the workings and composition of the BOA from the organization's minutes held at the University of East London. Biographical details from *Who's Who* and *Debrett's* throughout the 1920s.

Lavish dinners were held at the Savoy: *The Times*, 11 January 1923.

Funding for the British Olympic team: Details of the British Olympic team from the *Daily Mail*: 14 March and 27–30 June 1923; 9 April, 24 and 31 May, 3, 6 and 20 June 1924.

In spats and a flat-topped silk hat: Newspaper photograph from the BOA archive.

'No one seems to know or care': Minutes in the BOA collection.

There was a debate: Ibid.

The Association hired the London department store: Ibid.

'Ghastly': M. Ryan, *Running with Fire*.

Cadogan called the uniform 'serviceable and neat': Minutes in the BOA collection.

According to Abrahams, it was a 'little miserable': M. Ryan, *Running with Fire*.

The draft timetable for the Games: Ibid.

The BOA didn't understand Olympic history: F. A. M. Webster, *Great Moments in Athletics* and *Olympic Cavalcade*; A. Guttmann, *The Olympics: A History of the Modern Games*; B. Henry, *An Approved History of the Olympic Games*; S. Greenberg and B. Frei, *Olympic Games: The Records* (Guinness, 1987); Geoff Tibballs, *The Olympics' Strangest Games* (Robson, 2004); David Miller, *The*

Official History of the Olympic Games and the IOC: Athens to Beijing (Mainstream, 2008).

He'd already stated his opposition: *Pittsburgh Post Gazette*, 31 March 1924; *Guardian*, 14 July 1924.

He dropped out of an international: *The Times*, 28 and 30 July 1923.

As Britain beat the French: *Dundee Evening Telegraph*, 30 July 1923.

The BOA did none of this: BOA papers.

'My Sabbath lasts all day': Ibid. Also, *Boston Daily Globe*, 12 July 1924.

Liddell liked to recite what he called 'the three sevens': Interview with EL's daughters.

As Peter Fryer points out: In *Mrs Grundy: Studies in English Prudery* (Dobson, 1963).

Signing himself 'Olympian': *Evening Standard*, 28 December 1923.

'They hammered on the door': Greville Young, *Sporting Witness* (BBC World Service) and George Graham-Cumming, BBC interview.

The religious newspaper: *Life of Faith*, 26 July 1924.

Level-headedly lamented: *Daily Mail*, 28 June 1924.

In favour of the local boy: *Edinburgh Evening News*, 4 January 1924.

Alfred George: Biographical details from *The Times*, 20 June 1934.

Walter George: Biographical details from R. Hadcraft, *Beer and Brine* (Desert Island).

In one piece about Paris: *All Sports Illustrated Weekly*, 11 February and 5 July 1924.

A vicar in Aberdeen: *Aberdeen Journal*, 2 July 1924.

He was likened to 'Daniel': *British Weekly*, undated.

In a widely syndicated column: *Motherwell Times*, 4 July 1924.

Chapter Four

As Liddell would later confess: EL's own account of his running career in *All Sports Illustrated Weekly*.

He was 'hurt': Annie Buchan, BBC interview.

He made an ally: Binks's articles about Liddell's preparation for the Games appeared in the *News of the World* on 20 January, 2 and 16 March, 11 May, and 8, 15 and 28 June 1924.

Liddell was invited to guest for the Achilles Club: Interview with Steve Metcalf. Also, *Edinburgh Evening News*, 13 February 1924; *Yorkshire Post*, 19 March 1924; *New York Times*, 24–25 April 1924.

The bare details make the journey seem horrendous: Interviews with EL's daughters.

Liddell was an inadequate fourth: *Athletics News and Cyclists Journal*, 5 May 1924 (see also 18 February, 21 April and 19 May 1924).

Before sailing, Liddell said: EL's own account of his running career in *All Sports Illustrated Weekly*.

On the ship home: Arthur Marshall, *The Marshall Story*.

'My motto': Russell W. Ramsey, *God's Joyful Runner*; *Sunday at Home* (magazine), October 1925; interview with Steve Metcalf.

'He plotted out the vital stages': EL's own account of his running career in *All Sports Illustrated Weekly*.

'Always, when running the quarter': Letter to Mr Chivers.

'Slowness in becoming perfectly fit': Ibid.

McKerchar was 'handling me beautifully': EL's own account of his running career in *All Sports Illustrated Weekly*.

A 'friendly tussle': George Graham-Cumming, BBC interview.

Only in Paris: EL's own account of his running career in *All Sports Illustrated Weekly*. For Paris in the 1920s: D. Franck, *The Bohemians* (Weidenfeld, 2001); A. J. Hanson, *Expatriate Paris* (Arcade, 2012); R. Davenport-Hines, *A Night at the Majestic* (Faber, 2005); D. J. Taylor, *Bright Young Things: The Rise and Fall of a Generation, 1918–1940* (Chatto, 2007).

Once, when pointedly asked *how* he won races: Greville Jones, *The Flying Scotsman* (BBC, 1984).

'Even late as it is': *All Sports Illustrated Weekly*, 11 February 1924.

Philip Noel-Baker was particularly supportive: Interview with Steve Metcalf. Also, biographical detail on Noel-Baker from the Noel-Baker Archive.

Liddell still had to overcome stabs of self-doubt: Philip Christison, *The Flying Scotsman* (BBC), and Christison's unpublished memoir from the Imperial War Museum, London.

'Cherry ripe': EL's own account of his running career in *All Sports Illustrated Weekly*.

The opening ceremony in Paris: Pathé News film and photographs from the IOC archive (olympic.org).

A photographer caught him with his head turned: University of Birmingham archive.

Correspondents christened Abrahams 'The Cambridge Cannonball': BOA archive (news cutting is undated).

In the second he sped up: M. Ryan, *Running with Fire*.

An exchange with Abrahams: From EL's own account of his running career in *All Sports Illustrated Weekly*.

A. B. George had claimed: *All Sports Illustrated Weekly*, 5 July 1924.

'The papers now and then reminded me': Ibid.

Fitch kept an Olympic diary: Published in instalments in the *Alton Democrat* between 11 October 1924 and 17 January 1925.

A typical forecast: *Sunday Chronicle*, 29 June 1924.

Euphoric afterwards: EL's own account of his running career in *All Sports Illustrated Weekly*.

Next morning Liddell read reports: Ibid.

'It surprised me as much as anyone': Interview with Fitch from *National Masters News*, April 1984.

Just one voice among the Americans thought differently: Jack Moakley's warning from David McCasland, *Pure Gold*.

Chapter Five

There were headline performances in Paris: Details of Olympic Games from A. Guttmann, *The Olympics: A History of the Modern Games*; B. Henry, *An Approved History of the Olympic Games*; F. A. M. Webster, *Great Moments in Athletics* and *Olympic Cavalcade*; S. Greenberg and B. Frei, *Olympic Games: The Records*; David Miller, *The Official History of the Olympic Games and the IOC: Athens to Beijing*; F. G. L. Fairlie, *The Official Report of the VIII Olympiad* (BOA, 1924).

'Come quickly, your comrade is dying': EL's own account of his running career in *All Sports Illustrated Weekly*.

'More vividly imprinted on my memory': Ibid.

Liddell still overheard him squabbling: Ibid.

'Curiously enough I was quite cool': Ibid.

He had been handed a folded square of paper: Letter from the unnamed masseur to D. P. Thomson in 1945. Liddell, though referring to the incident on his return from Paris (*Edinburgh Evening News*, 15–18 July 1924), never identified who gave him the note. The BOA papers in Birmingham University show three masseurs were taken to Paris: Argot Johansson of Sheffield, E. G. Horwood of Cambridge, and Wilfred Smith of London. Horwood died in 1941 and I could find no trace of Johansson in Britain after the war. Smith, therefore, is the most likely candidate.

Stagg told Fitch there was 'no need to worry about Liddell': *National Masters News*, April 1984.

'Despite the times the others had put up': EL's own account of his running career in *All Sports Illustrated Weekly*.

When Joe Binks wandered down from the press box: Recollection of Binks from *News of the World*, 21 September 1941.

'Go all out – and don't be behind at the last straight': EL's account from *All Sports Illustrated Weekly*.

'He went off at such a terrific pace': M. Ryan, *Running with Fire*.

Marshall can't believe what he's seeing: Arthur Marshall, *The Marshall Story*.

'Can I last home?': EL's account from *All Sports Illustrated Weekly*.

'Not until I got to the top of the straight': Ibid.

'A comforting thought flashed into my mind': Ibid.

'I had no idea he would win it': *National Masters News*, April 1984, and the *Denver Post*, 13 June 1982.

'I was amazed to find': EL's account from *All Sports Illustrated Weekly*.

He confessed to being 'more amazed' at his time: The International Amateur Athletic Federation initially awarded Liddell the world record. This was later revoked. The record reverted to the American Ted Meredith, whose 47.4 seconds over 440 yards (not metres) was recorded in 1916.

Liddell and Fitch posed together: Description of the aftermath of victory and the Tango Tea Dance: Ibid. Also, interview with Steve Metcalf; Arthur Marshall, *The Marshall Story*; Horatio Fitch's diary.

'If the papers want to call me the Flying Parson': EL's account from *All Sports Illustrated Weekly*.

The news agency Reuters: *Daily Express*, 14 July 1924.

'Very fortunate': EL's account from *All Sports Illustrated Weekly*.

What he got were barbed questions: Details of the aftermath of the Games: *The Times*, 21, 23 and 24 July 1924; *New York Times*, 23, 24 and 25 July 1924; *Guardian*, 24 and 26 July 1924.

Chapter Six

Eric Liddell expected only a handful of well-wishers: *London Evening News*, 15 July 1924.

He now knew what Jim Thorpe felt: *New York Times* obituary, 29 March 1953; K. Buford, *Native American Son: The Life and Sporting Legend of Jim Thorpe* (Random House, 2010).

One of Liddell's housemates: George Graham-Cumming, BBC interview; P. Donovan, *The Radio Companion* (HarperCollins, 1991).

Treasure Island: *Radio Times*, 5–11 July 1924.

Repeated at Waverley: *Edinburgh Evening News*, 16 July 1924; *Scotsman*, 16 July 1924.

Serendipity dictated: Details of the graduation and his subsequent speech from: *Edinburgh Evening News*, 17–18 July 1924; *Guardian*, 17 July 1924; *Scotsman*, 17 July 1924; *Daily Mail*, 18 July 1924; *Dundee Courier*, 18 July 1924.

Pindar: *The Odes of Pindar* (University of Chicago Press, 1947).

Beatrice Webb: The diaries of Beatrice Webb: London School of Economics digital library (digital.library.lse.ac.uk).

A true 'hero' – and subsequent comments by Liddell about Henry Stallard and Olympic competitors in Paris: EL's own account of his running career from *All Sports Illustrated Weekly*.

When Philip Christison had gone to offer his congratulations: *The Flying Scotsman* (BBC).

At Eltham College: *The Glory of the Sons: A History of Eltham College School* (1952).

Liddell is shown reading the passage from Isaiah: The report of his reading in the Paris Kirk comes from the *Davenport Democrat and Leader*, 27 July 1924. The Psalm is taken from the King James version of the Bible.

Jack Hobbs, etc.: Biographical details and salaries taken from: Leo McKinstry, *England's Greatest Cricketer* (Yellow Jersey, 2001); Ric Sissons, *The Players: A Social History of the Professional Cricketer* (Pluto Press, 1988); R. Creamer, *Babe: The Legend Comes to Life* (Simon & Schuster, 1992); T. Clavin, *Sir Walter: Walter Hagen and the Invention of Professional Golf* (Simon & Schuster, 2005); F. Deford, *Big Bill Tilden: The Triumphs and the Tragedy* (Open Road Media, 2011); R. Kahn, *A Flame of Pure Fire: Jack Dempsey and the Roaring '20s* (Harcourt Brace, 1999); Paul Gallico, *Farewell to Sport* (Simon & Schuster, 1988 – reprint).

The makers of Liddell's track-shoes: *Athletic News and Cycling Journal*, 14 July 1924.

'**Runs for Six Days a Week**': *Altoona Tribune*, 22 July 1924.

He could 'preach' as well as he could 'run': *The Bee*, Dansville, 18 July 1924.

'**Muscular school of Christianity**': *Literary Digest*, 30 August 1924.

There was no shortage of offers: Liddell made this clear to Steve Metcalf during his incarceration in the Weihsien camp and also spoke of his friends in Cambridge and the offer to 'pull strings'.

John Betjeman: *On Churches* (Collins, 2011 – new edition).

Liddell told one congregation that 'the greatest danger was victory': *Dundee Courier*, 6 November 1924.

Only D. P. Thomson's intervention: D. P. Thomson, *Eric Liddell: The Making of an Athlete*.

'**Because I believe God made me for China**': Interview with EL's daughters and talk EL gave in the Weihsien camp (interview Steve Metcalf).

Chapter Seven

While the Games were still hot in the memory: *Football Post*, 25 August and 1 September 1924.

As well as Liddell's gold medal: Reports of Stamford Bridge event from the *Sunday Times*, 20 July 1924; *The Times*, 21 July 1924; the *Daily Mail*, 20 July 1924.

In the 4×400 metres: Guy Butler's view on the relay from *Runners and Running*.

Charley Paddock had watched Liddell: Paddock's recollections of the race appeared in the *Charleston Daily Mail*, 24 August 1930 (earlier versions appeared elsewhere).

Liddell estimated that Fitch was 'ten yards' in front: EL's own account of his running career from *All Sports Illustrated Weekly*.

'**I thought I could never close the gap**': Ibid.

'**Probably he was feeling the effects of Paris**': Ibid.

'**No man found it harder to say no**': D. P. Thomson, *Eric Liddell: The Making of an Athlete*.

It was estimated that only fifteen out of every hundred: *Guardian*, 3 May 1922.

The Moderator of the Assemblies of the Scottish Churches: *Guardian*, 28 May 1920.

One minister believed: Ibid.

Weekend motoring had slashed the size of congregations: *Guardian*, 22 May 1923.

'**Live wires**': *Guardian*, 3 May 1922.

'**We reached audiences**', and crowd figures: D. P. Thomson, *Eric Liddell: The Making of an Athlete*.

Liddell introduced himself: Views on drink: Interview with EL's daughters. Also recalled by the *Edinburgh Evening News*, 3 August 1926; *Dundee Courier*, 9 December 1931; diary of D. P. Thomson.

'**The good team sportsman**' / **Always Liddell welded sport to sportsmanship**: Interview with Steve Metcalf and EL's daughters. Also, *Guardian*, 27 April

1925; *Sunday Times*, 19 April 1925; *Hawick News and Border Chronicle*, 15 April 1932; *Edinburgh Evening News*, 14 April 1932; and D. P. Thomson diary and *Eric Liddell: The Making of an Athlete*.

Liddell was also concerned: *Aberdeen Journal*, 21 April 1925.

Liddell's Olympic gold was delayed: Interview with Steve Metcalf, and M. Ryan, *Running with Fire*.

An Olympic memento for his coach: Details about the watch from Harry and Brian McKerchar, Tom's grandsons.

Eileen Soper: D. Hart-Davis, *Wildings*.

The art critic Andrew Graham-Dixon: *Daily Telegraph*, 8 August 2000.

His last athletics season was a long lap of honour: Details of Liddell's last races from J. W. Keddie, *Running the Race*.

D. P. Thomson ambitiously booked: *Glasgow Herald*, 29 June 1925.

His 'impressive send off' from Edinburgh: *Glasgow Herald, Scotsman, Edinburgh Evening News, Aberdeen Journal* – all 30 June 1925.

One of his best-known essays: George Orwell, *Essays* (Everyman Library).

'Earthquake Destroys Town in China': *Guardian*, 21 March 1925.

On the day Liddell left Edinburgh: *The Times*, 29 June 1925.

Chapter Eight

In late May 1925: Reports in *The Times*, 3 to 15 June 1925.

In 1924 he referred to China's 'sad condition': Reports of the London Missionary Society held at Archives and Special Collections centre at School of Oriental and African Studies, University of London.

He boarded the Trans-Siberian Express: EL letters about his journey; Peter Fleming, *One's Company: A Journey to China* (Cape, 1934).

Annie Buchan was on the cusp of her thirtieth birthday: Biographical details of Buchan from two privately printed books: *Adventures in Faith* (1973) and, with William Spiers, *A Scotswoman in China* (1988). The more revealing notes, letters and documents about her life are held by the Centre for the Study of Christianity at the University of Edinburgh.

Liddell often quoted Robert Louis Stevenson's assertion: Interview with Steve Metcalf.

The London Missionary Society: N. Goddall, *A History of the London Missionary Society, 1895–1945* (Oxford University Press, 1954).

Dr Samuel Lavington-Hart: Ibid. Also, S. Lavington-Hart, *Education in China* (1923); *The Times*, 9 March 1951.

Liddell had always clipped out and saved newspaper cuttings: Interview with EL's daughters.

Eric Scarlett: *Citizen*, 4 April 1930; *Guardian*, 4 April 1930.

He'd often be seen playing tennis against himself: William Toop, BBC interview, not broadcast.

Tientsin's 'other face': Accounts of the city from Annie Buchan's papers, the recollections of A. P. Cullen, and EL's own account.

A train and then a springless mule cart: Conditions in Siaochang and her account of them from the Annie Buchan archive, University of Edinburgh.

Liddell once caused a social kerfuffle: Interview with EL's daughters.

Chapter Nine

The photographer from the *Tientsin Times*: Annie Buchan archive, University of Edinburgh.

Another eyewitness confirmed it: Letter to the *Daily Telegraph*, 25 August 2005.

One telegraphed dispatch: Ibid.

Liddell avoided reporters as much as possible: Interview with EL's daughters.

'I fear your correspondent is rather at fault': EL's own account from *All Sports Illustrated Weekly*.

Along with a dozen other sportsmen, and BOA report: *Daily Mail*, 16 February and 12 April 1928.

In its first week Lowe: *Brooklyn Daily Eagle*, 2 May 1928.

The London Missionary Society staff loaded mule carts and escaped: Annie Buchan archive, University of Edinburgh.

According to one dispatch: *Peking and Tientsin Times*, and EL's own account.

There was a bizarre coda: *Peking and Tientsin Times*, 10 October 1928; interview with EL's daughters.

Dr Otto Peltzer: Biographical details from *Observer Sports Monthly*, 20 June 2008. Accounts of the race: *Berwickshire News*, 31 December 1929; *Singapore Free Press and Mercantile Advertiser*, 1 February 1930; interview with EL's daughters.

His hobby of photography: Jenny Liddell, *Memories of China Days*.

At the beginning of 1929: Interviews with EL's daughters.

He could also remember, often verbatim, sections of novels: Interviews with Steve Metcalf, Joe and Joyce Cotterill, EL's daughters.

Missionaries moved through China: Accounts of atrocities from *The Times*, 1, 13 and 24 January 1930; 13, 15 and 22 February 1930; 1, 4, 5, 7, 10 and 31 March 1930; *Nottingham Post*, 4 April 1930.

A. P. Cullen and Eric Scarlett were travelling to Peitaiho: *The Times*, 4 and 7 April 1930; *Guardian*, 4 and 6 April 1930; *Nottingham Post*, 4 April 1930.

In the first nine months: Figures from London Missionary Society and British-American newspapers.

When his train had left Waverley station in 1925: *Edinburgh Evening News*, 29 and 30 June 1925.

Thomson noted that he looked: D. P. Thomson, *Eric Liddell: The Making of an Athlete*.

Liddell now became a convert too: Information about Frank Buchman from *The Times*, 6 August 1961; *Dundee Courier*, 23 June 1932.

China was convinced: *Dundee Courier*, 13 March 1930; 5 and 13 October 1931; *Scotsman*, 1 October 1931.

The feeling was particularly powerful: EL letter.

There was a terrible misprint: *Hartlepool Mail*, 13 November 1933.

Chapter Ten

Tientsin's Union Church Literary and Social Guild: *Peking and Tientsin Times*, 10 January 1926.

He chose Florence Jean MacKenzie: Biographical information from interview with her daughters.

'One of Nature's gentlemen': D. P. Thomson, *Eric Liddell: The Making of an Athlete*.

When his sister Jenny gave Florence advanced piano lessons: Jenny Liddell, *Memories of China Days*.

In the summer of 1929: Interview with Florence's brother, Finlay MacKenzie.

'There's something I want to talk to you about': Florence Liddell, BBC interview, not broadcast.

His fiancée announced herself: Ibid.

'Why is he marrying Flo?': Interview with Finlay MacKenzie.

Liddell bought Florence an engagement ring: Jenny Liddell, *Memories of China Days*.

In the same sentence: BBC interview, not broadcast.

'The mainspring of his life': Ibid.

One of Florence's friends: Ibid.

D. P. Thomson heard about two instances: Letters to D. P. Thomson.

One of the most curious: London Missionary Society archive.

Ink took the place of speech and sight: Letters between EL and Florence.

When Florence finally arrived back in China: Interview with Finlay MacKenzie.

'Incurable romantic': BBC interview, not broadcast.

A home was built nonetheless: Interview with EL's daughters.

'I picked up a cushion and threw it at him': BBC interview.

The LMS became concerned: LMS archive and interviews with EL's daughters.

'It took him a long time to be sure': BBC interview.

That call could not have come at a more dangerous time: Details about the situation in China from Jonathan Fenby, *The Penguin History of Modern China* and *Generalissimo: Chiang Kai-shek and the China He Lost*; Theodore H. White, *In Search of History* and, with A. Jacoby, *Thunder out of China*; Edgar Snow, *China*.

The civil war caused Liddell inconveniences: London Missionary Society archive.

The pop and crack of fireworks: Ibid., and interviews with EL's daughters.

An agency report: Articles about the conditions in Tientsin: *Guardian*, 30 and 31 July and 1 August 1937.

Chapter Eleven

Eric Liddell was precise and clear-eyed: *Hawick News and Border Chronicle*, 25 September 1931.

Liddell publicly announced: *North China Herald*, 8 August 1925.

In August 1937: Jonathan Fenby, *The Penguin History of Modern China* and

Generalissimo: Chiang Kai-shek and the China He Lost.

The Anglo-Chinese College opened: A. P. Cullen, *Lavington-Hart of Tientsin* (The Livingstone Press, 1947).

He and Rob had made two early attempts, and subsequent description of journey to and arrival in Siaochang: London Missionary Society archive.

Stuck in a district: Annie Buchan archive.

On his arrival: London Missionary Society archive.

Buchan gave Liddell a graphic account: Annie Buchan archive.

A sign hung over the gate: F. McAll and K. McAll, *The Moon Looks Down* (Darley Anderson, 1987).

'The floods are only a small part': London Missionary Society archive.

The people in Siaochang were 'burdened': Ibid.

The peasants' homes: Ibid., and Annie Buchan archive.

The guard would hold up a slate: Ibid., and F. McAll and K. McAll, *The Moon Looks Down.*

His fellow missionaries: Ibid., and Annie Buchan archive.

When another missionary wanted to arm himself: Ibid.

The Chinese proverb: Interview with EL's daughters.

Chapter Twelve

Once asked outright: Annie Buchan archive.

Florence Liddell saw the change: Letter to D. P. Thomson.

Liddell considered the Chinese to be 'calm': London Missionary Society archive and Annie Buchan archive.

Buchan would hear someone say: Annie Buchan papers.

As Buchan pointed out: Ibid.

He compiled charts and schedules too: Ibid.

'He never expounded elaborate theories': Ibid.

Liddell liked to teach the Chinese hymns: Ibid.

'The scenes have changed so quickly': London Missionary Society archive.

He discovered babies and children naked and abandoned: Ibid.

'The invaders were trying to convince the people': Ibid.

Nothing betrays the character of a man like his manners: Interview with Steve Metcalf.

'Take it all with a smile': F. McAll and K. McAll, *The Moon Looks Down.*

Out of earshot of his own troops: Ibid.

Turning travel into a trial: Ibid.

For Liddell, the Japanese were 'not to be feared or hated': EL letter.

'I think that I have had nearly every type of experience': London Missionary Society archive.

'People said it couldn't be done': Ibid.

She suggested that Liddell hollow out a baguette-shaped loaf: BBC interview.

The story Liddell told is essentially broken into two parts: London Missionary Society archive.

'It was hard for him,' said Annie Buchan: BBC interview.
Liddell sent an air-mail letter to the London Missionary Society: Interview with EL's daughters.
The LMS rattled on: Ibid.
Thomson found him 'different in many ways': D. P. Thomson, *Eric Liddell: The Making of an Athlete*.
Liddell himself tried to enlist in the Royal Air Force: BBC interview with Jenny Liddell, not broadcast.
He was convinced the missionaries were within sight: *Aberdeen Journal*, 5 February 1940.
The zenith of it: Interviews with EL's daughters.
In early August 1940 the Liddells sailed from Liverpool: EL's account, and interviews with his daughters.
'We were running for our lives': BBC interview, not broadcast.
One theatre of war disappeared behind him: Theodore H. White with A. Jacoby, *Thunder out of China*; Jonathan Fenby, *The Penguin History of China*.
Liddell was also coping with a piece of sad personal news: Death certificate of Tom McKerchar.
It was late autumn: London Missionary Society archive.
There was a solitary spot of colour: Ibid.
Annie Buchan said the soldiers: Annie Buchan archive.
Five months earlier: The Tripartite Pact was also known as the Berlin Pact.

Chapter Thirteen
For a fraught month: Interview with EL's daughters.
'My people': Interview with Steve Metcalf.
During the first months of 1941: *History of the Second World War* (BBC).
'It was like sitting on the edge of a volcano': BBC interview, not broadcast.
He grew increasingly afraid: Interview with EL's daughters.
The LMS was maddeningly inept: London Missionary Society archive.
'I wouldn't have gone': Letter to D. P. Thomson, and BBC interview.
Liddell tried reassuring her: Interviews with EL's daughters.
Liddell told her about another of his ambitions: Ibid.
Liddell's first decision was strategically shrewd: Ibid.
'Some of our friends still thought': BBC interview, not broadcast.
The show-cabinet: Interviews with EL's daughters.
Instead Liddell lifted Patricia: Interview with Patricia Liddell.
When the moment came to part: Interviews with EL's daughters.
'I had to snap out of it': BBC interview, not broadcast.
Cullen liked to listen to the BBC: Interview with Joanna Cullen-Brown.
As summer faded into autumn: A. Beevor, *The Second World War* (Weidenfeld & Nicolson, 2014); M. Hastings, *All Hell Let Loose* (HarperPress, 2012).
The Japanese undermined the missionaries: London Missionary Society archive.
Then dawn rose on Sunday, 7 December: Richard Overy, *War in the Pacific*

(Carlton Books, 2012); D. M. Goldstein and K. V. Dillon, *The Way It Was: Pearl Harbor* (Brassey's US, 1995).

Time **regarded the raid**: December issues of the magazine.

The record was 'Ave Maria': Jonathan Fenby, *The Penguin History of China.*

A. P. Cullen saw Liddell's distress: Interview with Joanna Cullen-Brown.

Other restrictions were so prohibitively harsh: London Missionary Society archive.

She had arranged for a colour studio portrait: Interview with EL's daughters.

The postal system in China was erratic: Ibid.

Liddell managed to contact her through convoluted channels: Ibid.

Cullen said that 'almost every day': Interview with Joanna Cullen-Brown.

Sermon writing was only a sliver: Letters to Florence.

'Persistent study': Interview with Joanna Cullen-Brown.

His advice to everyone: EL, *The Disciplines of the Christian Life.*

Cullen disagreed: Interview with Joanna Cullen-Brown.

He believed Liddell's progress: Ibid.

Cullen observed close up: Ibid.

Liddell took inspiration from diverse sources: EL, *The Disciplines of the Christian Life.*

The Sermon on the Mount: Ibid.

Liddell owned a postcard-sized picture: Interview with Steve Metcalf.

The Christ of the Mount: E. Stanley Jones (The Abingdon Press, originally published 1931).

Late in the summer of 1942: London Missionary Society archive.

By now the Japanese had bombed: Jonathan Fenby, *The Penguin History of China.*

Eric Liddell had never relaxed: Letters to D. P. Thomson.

The LMS enquired: Letter to Florence.

The repatriations turned out to be a sham: Interviews with EL's daughters.

'Half the things we worry about never happen': Interview with Steve Metcalf.

Chapter Fourteen

To be captive in Weihsien: Descriptions of the camp from: Pamela Masters, *The Mushroom Years*; Langdon Gilkey, *Shantung Compound*; Myra Scovel, *The Chinese Ginger Jars*; Mary Scott, *Kept in Safeguard*; Sister Ann Colette Wolf, *Against All Odds: Sisters of Providence Mission to the Chinese* (SoP, 1990); J. Bradbury, *Forgiven but not Forgotten* (self-published, 2000); M. Helsby and C. Helsby, *He Goes Before Them . . . Even into Prison* (OMS, 1993); P. J. Scanlan, *Stars in the Sky* (Trappist Publications, 1984); M. Servatia, *A Cross in China* (Cuchullian Publications, undated); Raymond J. de Jaegher and Irene Corbally Kuhn, *The Enemy Within: An Eyewitness Account of the Communist Conquest of China* (Doubleday, 1952). Also, interview with Joe Cotterill.

Those going to Weihsien wrapped sentimental keepsakes: Ibid.

Internees found the Japanese brazenly stealing: Ibid.

The Japanese made sure photographers: Ibid.

It was 300 miles from Tientsin: Description of train journey: interview with Joe Cotterill.

On that same day: *The Times*, 1 April 1943.

No one put the sight of it better: Langdon Gilkey, *Shantung Compound*.

Ever the bright optimist: EL's Red Cross letters to Florence.

In both outgoing and incoming mail: Norman Cliff, *Courtyard of the Happy Way*.

He was an 'unruffled spirit': Langdon Gilkey, *Shantung Compound*.

Another recalled him as 'always cheerful': Interview with Joe Cotterill.

'He never let anyone see him downcast': Ibid.

Langdon Gilkey remarked: In *Shantung Compound*.

Internees were drawn into the camp: Ibid.

Every stratum of society was locked into it: Weihsien camp lists. The roll call up to 30 June 1944 lists 173 Roman Catholic priests, 176 missionaries, 20 nuns, 67 nurses, 10 Protestant priests, 19 Salvation Army representatives, four bishops (Catholic and Protestant), three monks, one Roman Catholic lay preacher, and three of other orders.

'Queuing for everything': Mary Previte, *Hungry Ghosts*, and interviews with the author, as well as Joe Cotterill and Joyce Cotterill, Estelle Horne, Peter Bazire and Steve Metcalf.

There was no privacy: Ibid.

Territorial quarrels arose: Ibid., and Langdon Gilkey, *Shantung Compound*; Mary Scott, *Kept in Safeguard*; Pamela Masters, *The Mushroom Years*; M. Scovel, *The Chinese Ginger Jars*.

A few went as far as rubbing out the chalk: Langdon Gilkey, *Shantung Compound*.

As one captive said of these crude latrines: Mary Scott, *Kept in Safeguard*, and interview with Mary Previte.

Since the English had always treated him well: Pamela Masters, *The Mushroom Years*, and interview with author; Report of the Recent Developments in the Situation of Americans in the Orient, 14 May 1942 (National Archives); Concentration Camps, Occupied China, 1 May 1943 (National Archives).

Committees were promptly set up: Norman Cliff, *Courtyard of the Happy Way*.

The situation changed when the Japanese became aware: Interviews with Joe Cotterill and Steve Metcalf.

The sisters turned up the long hems: Mary Scott, *Kept in Safeguard*.

A river ran beside the compound: Interview with Joe Cotterill.

The camp, however, did begin to take some sort of rough shape: Ibid., and with Steve Metcalf. Also, Langdon Gilkey, *Shantung Compound*; Mary Scott, *Kept in Safeguard*; Pamela Masters, *The Mushroom Years*, and interview with author; M. Scovel, *The Chinese Ginger Jars*.

A laundry was set up in the basement: Interview with Mary Previte; and Mary Scott, *Kept in Safeguard*.

He put up a row of shelves: Interview with Joe Cotterill; and Norman Cliff, *Courtyard of the Happy Way*.

'He was the man we turned to': Interviews with Mary Previte and Steve Metcalf.

Liddell was always being asked whether he'd be free: Interview with Joe Cotterill.

Liddell rose before it got light: Ibid.

Liddell's advice was always: EL, *The Disciplines of the Christian Life*.

'I once saw him unloading supplies': Interview with Estelle Horne.

These tattered and patched clothes: Ibid.

The internees had brought an eclectic collection of outfits: Interviews with Steve Metcalf and Estelle Horne.

The curtains he'd brought with him: Interview with Steve Metcalf.

The internees were able to shower only once a week: Interviews with Joe Cotterill and Joyce Cotterill, Mary Previte, Peter Bazire and Steve Metcalf.

There was no Pied Piper to combat the rats: Norman Cliff, *Courtyard of the Happy Way*. Also, interviews with Steve Metcalf and Mary Previte.

'Often we had to stand in lines for hours': Ibid.

'A loud grunt and a pointed bayonet': Pamela Masters, *The Mushroom Years*, and interview with author.

One of the guards was known as Gold Tooth: Interviews with Joe Cotterill and Joyce Cotterill. Also, Langdon Gilkey, *Shantung Compound*; Mary Scott, *Kept in Safeguard*; Pamela Masters, *The Mushroom Years*, and interview with author; M. Scovel, *The Chinese Ginger Jars*.

The most unflattering label was pinned on a sergeant: Interviews with Joe Cotterill and Joyce Cotterill.

Those who cooked the meals: Interview with Mary Previte.

A woman found Golden Syrup: Norman Cliff, *Courtyard of the Happy Way*.

In error, one of the cooks: Raymond de Jaegher, *The Enemy Within*.

One family was fortunate: Norman Cliff, *Courtyard of the Happy Way*.

Such a beggarly diet: Interview with Joe Cotterill.

The Japanese allowed the establishment of a White Elephant Shop: Interviews with Joe Cotterill, Joyce Cotterill, Steve Metcalf, Mary Previte, Estelle Horne and Peter Bazire.

Chapter Fifteen

Liddell was asked by a fellow internee: Interview with Joe Cotterill.

'No. At my age I am a little past it'. Ibid.

As late as 1939: Interviews with Patricia and Heather Liddell.

An Australian Cistercian monk called Father Patrick Scanlan: Accounts of the black market and also propaganda from Scanlan's own memoir *Stars in the Sky*; Raymond de Jaegher, *The Enemy Within*; Langdon Gilkey, *Shantung Compound*; Mary Scott, *Kept in Safeguard*; Pamela Masters, *The Mushroom Years*, and interview with author; Norman Cliff, *Courtyard of the Happy Way*, and interview with his sister, Estelle Horne; M. Scovel, *The Chinese Ginger Jars*.

Misinformation about the war was non-stop: P. J. Scanlan, *Stars in the Sky*.

No matter how implausible: Ibid.

One maliciously mischief-making internee: P. J. Scanlan, *Stars in the Sky*; Raymond de Jaegher, *The Enemy Within*; Langdon Gilkey, *Shantung Compound*.

One of Scanlan's colleagues: Raymond de Jaegher, *The Enemy Within*.

De Jaegher managed to get letters: Ibid.

Coolies also brought in information: Ibid.

'We presumed even its sports results weren't true': Interview with Steve Metcalf.

In saying so, the paper dropped place-names: Norman Cliff, *Courtyard of the Happy Way*.

Remarkably slow-witted: Interview with Joe Cotterill.

As a way of communicating it to the camp: Ibid.

'Our forced inactivity': P. J. Scanlan, *Stars in the Sky*.

The camp decided to stage late-afternoon athletics races: Interviews with Joe Cotterill, Pamela Masters and Steve Metcalf (in this instance relating the story he had been told after entering camp).

There was no space to create a track: Interview with Desmond Power.

He had once given Patricia a pep talk: Interview with Patricia Liddell.

He was spindly: Interviews with Joe and Joyce Cotterill.

Now Liddell wore his loose short-sleeved shirt: Interview with Steve Metcalf.

Aubrey Grandon, powerfully built enough to be nicknamed 'Muscles': Interviews with Desmond Power, Pamela Masters, Steve Metcalf and Doreen Grandon.

Winning over even the elderly ladies: Interview with Pamela Masters.

'You didn't pour your own coffee': Interview with Doreen Grandon.

After Weihsien, his father's fortune long gone: Ibid.

Sportingly, Liddell gave his opponents a slight head start: Interview with Steve Metcalf.

The narrowness of the pathways made overtaking difficult: Ibid.

Not every missionary and Churchman: Langdon Gilkey, *Shantung Compound*.

The compulsive smokers: Ibid.

One man was desperate enough: Norman Cliff, *Courtyard of the Happy Way*.

Langdon Gilkey remembered: In *Shantung Compound*.

Another preacher Gilkey recalled: Ibid.

Early on Gilkey was called: Ibid.

The most divisive differences: Ibid., and P. J. Scanlan, *Stars in the Sky*.

Aware of how the internees: Ibid.

Among them was eighty-two-year-old Herbert Hudson Taylor: Interview with Mary Previte, his granddaughter.

'We were not badly treated': P. J. Scanlan, *Stars in the Sky*.

The priest had geography on his side: Ibid.

He was also fortunate: Ibid.

Under the pretext of facing the wall to pray: Ibid.

'At first I made it a rule': Ibid.

Eggs were particularly important: Interviews with Mary Previte and Estelle Horne.

'It tasted like crunchy chalk dust': Interview with Mary Previte.

Tomatoes, apples, corncobs: P. J. Scanlan, *Stars in the Sky* and Raymond de Jaegher, *The Enemy Within.*

One live goose was hurled over the wall: Ibid.

Some of the Chinese grew irresponsibly bold: Ibid., and also interview with Joe Cotterill.

Scanlan, hiding five dozen eggs: P. J. Scanlan, *Stars in the Sky* and Raymond de Jaegher, *The Enemy Within.*

Scanlan was forced to shut down the operation: Ibid.

Scanlan had taken his breviary: Ibid.

Then his luck ran out: Ibid.

Knowing nothing of Scanlan's Trappist religion: Ibid., and also Norman Cliff, *Courtyard of the Happy Way.*

Supposed to serve fourteen days: Ibid.

So his freedom was celebrated: Ibid.

The risk of conducting business became more dangerous: Ibid.

Liddell said cheerfully: Norman Cliff, *Courtyard of the Happy Way.*

The internees began to swap jewellery and trinkets: Interviews with Joe Cotterill and Steve Metcalf.

Others dealt with a hideously vulgar character: Norman Cliff, *Courtyard of the Happy Way*, and interviews with Joe Cotterill and Steve Metcalf.

He began willingly to donate the only valuables: Interview with Steve Metcalf.

The food Liddell got: Ibid.

Much later he also had his gold watch and chain valued: Speech made by A. P. Cullen at Liddell's funeral.

A colleague called it 'a sacrifice': Ibid.

In the late summer and early autumn of 1943: Accounts by Scanlan, et cetera.

Liddell became 'Uncle Eric': Interviews with Joe and Joyce Cotterill, Mary Previte, Peter Bazire and Steve Metcalf.

'If he'd told us the moon was square': Elsa Watson, BBC interview, not broadcast.

Liddell adopted whoever needed him: Interview with Joyce Cotterill.

A contemporary of Stranks's: Interview with Peter Bazire.

One of Liddell's friends in the dormitory: Interview with Joe Cotterill.

He hand-wrote an instructional book: Interview with Joyce Cotterill, who still owns the book.

Outside the classroom Liddell trained anyone: Interview with Steve Metcalf.

'The fallen hurdle left a gap': Ibid.

When Liddell occasionally spoke of his family: Ibid., and also Joe Cotterill and Joyce Cotterill.

Liddell always locked away the sports equipment: Interviews with Steve Metcalf, Joe Cotterill and Joyce Cotterill. Also, Norman Cliff, *Courtyard of the Happy Way*, and Langdon Gilkey, *Shantung Compound.*

In the web of forced associations: Langdon Gilkey, *Shantung Compound*, and interviews with Estelle Horne, Steve Metcalf, Joe Cotterill and Joyce Cotterill.

Gilkey said he regularly saw Liddell: In *Shantung Compound*.

Liddell encouraged a sixteen-year-old Greek: Interviews with Steve Metcalf and Pamela Masters.

God Remained Outside: The original title.

'My God . . . Why hast Thou forsaken me?': Matthew 27.46.

His close friend in camp: Interview with Joe Cotterill.

As Weihsien deteriorated in every way: Ibid.

Dwelt on one passage: Ibid., and interview with Steve Metcalf.

He had told the story of the disciples: Matthew 18.21.

'They had missed the whole point': *Hawick News and Border Chronicle*, 15 April 1932.

There were enough books: Interviews with Pamela Masters, Joe Cotterill and Steve Metcalf.

As well as the professional jazz combo: Interviews with Joyce Cotterill, Desmond Power and Pamela Masters.

The guards were at least mollified: Interview with Pamela Masters.

There were enough would-be thespians: Ibid.

Aside from culture: Interviews with Mary Previte and Steve Metcalf.

The Chefoo pupils: Interviews with Mary Previte, Peter Bazire and Estelle Horne.

Those who weren't sporty: Ibid., and also Steve Metcalf.

In the search for entertaining speakers: Interview with Steve Metcalf.

At Christmas Liddell organized the distribution: Interview with Joyce Cotterill.

One man planted gladioli bulbs: Myra Scovel, *The Chinese Ginger Jars*.

One boy raised four peregrine falcon chicks: Ibid., and interview with Steve Metcalf.

One woman painted: Interview with Peter Bazire (speaking about his mother).

A snowy-coloured kitten: Interview with Mary Previte.

Students sat Oxford Matriculation Exams: Ibid., and also Estelle Horne.

Girl Guides and Brownies: Ibid.

Weihsien's calorie count fell to barely 1,200: Ibid.

There were internees who foraged: Ibid.

One of the Japanese owned a nanny goat: Interview with Joe Cotterill.

A song called 'Weihsien Blues': Norman Cliff, *Courtyard of the Happy Way*.

Some were desperate enough to attempt suicide: Pamela Masters, *The Mushroom Years*, and interview with the author. Also, interviews with Joe Cotterill and Steve Metcalf.

Often overheard singing one of three hymns: Interview with Steve Metcalf.

Chapter Sixteen

Liddell was frequently seen staring at photographs: Annie Buchan, BBC interview.

The most poignant of Florence's letters: Supplied by EL's daughters.

In early July 1944: Annie Buchan archive.

In early May a new commandant took over: Langdon Gilkey, *Shantung Compound*.

'I thought: If I'm going to be shot': Mary Previte's conversation with her teacher.

In mid-June a pair of internees: Details of the escape from Raymond de Jaegher, *The Enemy Within*; Langdon Gilkey, *Shantung Compound*; Norman Cliff, *Courtyard of the Happy Way*. Also, interviews with Joe Cotterill and Steve Metcalf.

Next morning the obstacle of camp roll call was cleared: Ibid.

The new commandant raged: Ibid.

Rations were slashed: Ibid.

The men without families: Interview with Joe Cotterill.

This was Weihsien as Buchan found it: Annie Buchan archive.

Buchan never forgot watching two boys fighting: Ibid.

One of those chosen: Desmond Power, *Little Foreign Devil* (Pangli Imprint, 1996).

A mule train arrived in Weihsien: Langdon Gilkey, *Shantung Compound*, and Norman Cliff, *Courtyard of the Happy Way*. Also, interviews with Joe Cotterill and Steve Metcalf.

Not only did Liddell look tired: Annie Buchan, BBC interview, and her archive.

'What is wrong with Eric?': Ibid.

Buchan concluded that the 'heavy responsibility': BBC interview, not broadcast.

When a teenager was electrocuted on the camp's barbed wire fence: Interviews with Estelle Horne and Joe Cotterill.

'He'd even find a way to beat us boys': Interview with Douglas Sadler.

The Red Cross parcels arrived, galvanizing the camp: Interview with Steve Metcalf. Also, Langdon Gilkey, *Shantung Compound*.

The race followed the same irregular route: Interview with Desmond Power.

Grandon was beside Liddell and comparatively robust: Interview with Steve Metcalf.

Liddell began predictably: Ibid.

An internee standing near the finish: Interview with Desmond Power.

The hospital was even short of medicine: Langdon Gilkey, *Shantung Compound*; Norman Cliff, *Courtyard of the Happy Way*. Also, interview with Joe Cotterill.

The jumble of memories: Interviews with Joe Cotterill, Joyce Cotterill, Steve Metcalf and Estelle Horne.

The stench of cooking began to annoy him: Interview with Joe Cotterill.

Next his memory: Interview with Joyce Cotterill.

He'd tried to memorize the passage: Ibid.

The camp underwent more turmoil: Langdon Gilkey, *Shantung Compound*.

Amid that sordid and unedifying tussle: Interview with Steve Metcalf.

The cheery masquerade: Annie Buchan, BBC interview.

'One day he told me he couldn't see the future': Ibid.

He had begun to look over and across his life: Interview with Joe Cotterill.

Liddell was weakened still further: Ibid.

The internee who discovered Liddell gathered him up: Interview with Desmond Power, and information from Yvonne Finlay, whose husband Douglas carried EL.

In the beginning Liddell was advised: Interview with Joe Cotterill.

He also confessed to Cotterill's fiancée: Jeannie Hills, BBC interview, not broadcast.

The seriousness of his illness: Annie Buchan archive. Also, interviews with Joe Cotterill and Joyce Cotterill.

The following Sunday: Norman Cliff, *Courtyard of the Happy Way*. Also, interview with Peter Bazire.

He then took tea: Interview with Joe Cotterill.

One Chefoo pupil saw him: Recollections of David Michell.

Early in the evening Liddell received his usual visitor: Interview with Joyce Cotterill.

His second stroke: Annie Buchan, BBC interview.

Buchan was the only witness: Ibid., and Annie Buchan archive.

Nature's timing is sometimes impeccable: Interviews with Joyce Cotterill, Joe Cotterill, Steve Metcalf and Estelle Horne.

One of them secretly kept a pocket diary: Marcy Ditmanson (OMS *Outreach Magazine*, November/December 1988); passage read to me by Joyce Cotterill.

Without its older brother: Interview with Joe Cotterill.

The doctors . . . quickly found the cause: Ibid., and Annie Buchan, BBC interview, not broadcast.

Annie Buchan had one last duty: Ibid., and interview with Joyce Cotterill.

It was called 'one of the most moving events': Recollections of A. P. Cullen.

The ice storm had frozen the topsoil: Interview with Steve Metcalf.

Liddell's rectangular casket: Ibid.

The construction was so fragile: Ibid., and also with Estelle Horne.

Metcalf knew the details of the day: Interview with Steve Metcalf.

Three weeks later a crate appeared: Interview with Joe Cotterill.

Florence and the children: Interviews with EL's daughters.

A month before the shattering news reached her: BBC interview, not broadcast.

'It never crossed my mind': Ibid.

The house began to fill with family: Interview with Patricia Liddell.

Florence said that even after the shock had left her: BBC interview, not broadcast.

The internees frantically brought out flags: Interviews with Mary Previte and Steve Metcalf.

The camp settled into a fresh routine: Ibid.

It was late October: Red Cross messages: Interviews with EL's daughters.

After reading them in the camp, A. P. Cullen was convinced: Letter to Florence Liddell.

Epilogue

The daughter Eric Liddell never met: I travelled to Canada to interview Patricia, Heather and Maureen in August 2014.

D. P. Thomson, who had described his own life: Diaries of D. P. Thomson.

Annie Buchan was among those missionaries: BBC interviews, and my interview with Margaret Buchan, Annie's niece.

Aubrey Grandon died in 1990: Interview with Doreen Grandon, Aubrey's widow.

Harold Abrahams dwelt on his rival: M. Ryan, *Running with Fire*.

Liddell was the mentor: Interview with Steve Metcalf.

Eileen Soper remained a spinster: D. Hart Davis, *Wildings*.

Florence Liddell didn't need a painting: Interviews with EL's daughters, and BBC interview, not broadcast.

Button-holed by a pushy interviewer: The interviewer was R. E. Knowles of the *Toronto Star*, 9 July 1932 (see also 5 August 1932).

NEWSPAPERS AND MAGAZINES CONSULTED

Aberdeen Journal (26 July 1924; 3 and 6 September 1939; 13 August 1940; 5 May 1945)

Appleton Post Crescent (11 July 1924)

Atlanta Constitution (12 July 1924)

Athletics News (14 July 1924)

Athletics Weekly (October 1934)

Bakersfield Californian (29 July 1937)

Baptist Times (7 and 14 September 2000)

Boca Raton News (14 January 1983)

Boston Daily Globe (4 March 1924; 22 and 26 April 1924; 7 May 1924; 5 June 1924; 11 July 1924; 5 June 1925; 12 May 1945)

Bridgeport Telegram (19 March 1928)

Brooklyn Daily Eagle (8 May 1928)

Chicago Tribune (5, 11, 12 and 20 July 1924)

Christian Science Monitor (15 April 1922; 29 June 1922; 12 July 1922; 11 July 1923; 2 August 1923; 23 July 1924; 10 January 1925; 19 March 1925; 26 August 1925; 7 December 1927)

Chronicle-Telegram (24 April 2005)

Church Times (11 November 1988)

Collier's Weekly (5 May 1928; 23 April 1932)

Daily Chronicle (7, 22 and 23 July 1924)

Daily Express (22 and 28 July 1924; 11 June 2013)

Daily Graphic (27 May 1924)

Daily Herald (4 July 1923)

Daily Mail (27 December 1921; 5 February 1923; 14 March 1923; 2, 5, 6 and 24 July

1923; 7 August 1923; 27 October 1923; 31 May 1924; 9, 11, 12, 14, 15, 18, 19, 21, 23, 27 and 28 July 1924; 4 and 9 August 1924; 14 January 1926; 16 February 1926; 13 March 1926; 26 July 1928; 21 January 1930; 17 July 1977; 3 February 1981; 31 March 1984; 7 May 1988; 4 June 1988; 15 August 2008)

Daily Mirror (13 August 1924; 7 August 2008)

Daily News (19 and 23 July 1924)

Daily Notes (10 March 1927)

Daily Record (12, 13, 20, 21, 23 and 24 June 1923; 12, 14, 22, 23, 24 and 25 July 1924; 16 September 2008)

Daily Sketch (23 July 1924)

Daily Telegraph (8, 9 and 30 July 1923; 6 and 7 August 1923; 12, 14, 22, 23, 24 and 25 July 1924; 3, 4, 8, 9, 15, 20, 25 and 29 June 1925; 11, 14, 20, 21, 22 and 31 July 1937)

Dorset Life (August 2008)

Dundee Courier (1 June 1925; 17, 18 and 26 July 1924; 21 May 1925; 31 January 1931; 1 and 2 September 1931; 21 December 1939; 11 January 1946; 13 March 1950)

Dunkirk Evening Observer (23 May 1928)

Edinburgh Evening Times (24 July 1924; 29 June 1925)

Evening Citizen (20 January 1924; 7 February 1924; 12 and 14 July 1924)

Evening Dispatch (21 July 1924)

Evening Independent (19 May 1924)

Evening News (27 May 1924; 5 June 1924)

Evening Standard (8, 9, 10, 11, 12, 15, 16 and 22 July 1924)

Evening Telegraph (30 July 1923)

Field (17 July 1924)

Football Post (1, 8 and 22 September 1924)

Game (1989)

Glasgow Herald (12, 14, 22, 23, 24 and 25 July 1924; 3 January 1992; 11 and 15 August 2007; 15 February 2008; 23 November 2009; 24 September 2011)

Gloucester Citizen (23 and 30 July 1923)

Gloucester Journal (4 August 1923)

Good Housekeeping (July 1923)

Guardian (28 May 1920; 22 May 1923; 4 May 1924; 17 July 1924; 3 August 1924; 4 January 1925; 4 and 26 February 1925; 7 April 1925; 7, 29 and 31 May 1925; 25 August 1925; 26, 28 and 29 March 1927; 9 April 1928; 14 May 1928; 16 August 1929; 6 June 1930; 2 December 1930; 4 August 1931; 1 September 1931; 7 October 1931; 27 July 1937; 2, 14 and 17 August 1937; 27 and 29 September 1937; 2 October 1937; 11 May 1945; 13 September 1960; 8 October 1981; 6 October 1990; 8 and 9 June 1991; 9 March 1998; 5 July 1999; 14 October 1999; 9 December 1999; 25 October 2003; 4 January 2012)

Hamilton Evening Journal (25 March 1927)

Hartford Courant (12 July 1924)

Herald Zeitung (1 July 1999)

Hi-Desert Star (2 December 2000)

Illustrated London News (31 May 1924)

Irish Times (12 and 19 July 1924)

Lancashire Evening Post (4 September 1939)

Le Athlétisme (May 1982; March 1983; May 1984)

Le Gaulois (7 January 1924; 25 April 1924; 10, 12 and 15 July 1924; 22 August 1984)

Le Populaince (21 January 1924)

Le Temps (13 July 1924)

Leader Magazine (26 May 1945)

Lebanon Daily News (31 March 1924)

Les Miroirs des Sports (5, 12 and 19 July 1924)

Life (October 1981)

Life of Faith (30 July 1924)

Lincoln Evening Journal (18 May 1928)

Lincoln State Journal (26 July 1924; 18 May 1928)

Literary Digest (26 July 1924; 2 and 30 August 1924)

London Gazette (21 October 1924)

Los Angeles Times (22 March 1924; 10 and 12 July 1924; 13 May 1928; 11 November 1945)

Manchester Evening News (24, 26 and 28 July 1924)

Modern Maturity (April–May 1983)

Modesto Bee (15 June 1934)

Morning Post (24 June 1924; 7, 11, 12 and 14 July 1924)

Motherwell Times (12 and 19 December 1924)

New Castle News (24 April 1924)

New Statesman (26 July 1924)

New York Herald Tribune (25 and 27 April 1924; 5 May 1924; 5, 6, 8, 9, 10, 11, 13 and 14 July 1924)

New York Times (13 July 1924; 20 March 1927; 4, 8, 11, 12 and 13 July 1937; 2 July 2005)

News of the World (13, 20 and 27 July 1924)

North China Marine (May 1946)

North West Arkansas Times (29 July 1937)

Nottingham Evening Post (9 June 1924)

Observer (29 June 2008)

Olean Evening Times (26 April 1924)

Ottawa Journal (30 June 1939)

Outlook (22 July 1925; 14 August 1926)

Peterhead Congregational Church Magazine (Summer 2012; Autumn 2012; Christmas 2012; Summer 2013; Scottish Week Special, 2013; Autumn 2013; Christmas 2013; Easter 2014)

Referee (20, 21 and 28 July 1924)

San Bernardino Daily (12 and 18 July 1924; 24 November 1924)

Scotsman (11 March 1924; 14, 19 and 23 July 1924; 12 December 1925; 7 July 1930;

1 October 1931; 19 May 1945)

South China Morning Post (4 May 2008)

Southern Reporter (2 June 2012)

Sporting Chronicle (4 and 19 June 1924)

Sporting Life (9 and 11 July 1923; 30 May 1924; 23 June 1924; 10, 22 and 30 July 1924)

Sportsman (30 May 1924; 21 and 23 July 1924)

Stage (26 April 1924)

Straits Times (2 November 1931)

Sunday Chronicle (25 May 1924; 18 and 25 July 1924)

Sunday Mail (28 June 1925; 12 August 2007)

Sunday Post (31 May 1925; 28 June 1931)

Sunday Telegraph (27 August 2000)

Sunday Times (13 July 1924; 19 April 1925; 6 September 1925; 8 March 1981; 12 February 1989; 14 June 1992; 23 June 1996; 14 July 1996; 1 August 1999; 4 June 2000)

Time (14, 21 and 29 July 1924)

The Journal (12, 13 and 14 July 1924)

The Times (29 May 1922; 7 January 1923; 25 May 1923; 8 and 9 July 1923; 6 and 7 August 1923; 12, 14, 22 and 25 July 1924; 20 and 25 June 1925; 22 December 1930; 6 May 1931; 10 and 16 July 1931; 17 August 1931; 3, 9, 16, 17, 19, 21, 22 and 29 September 1931; 6 and 17 October 1931; 30 November 1931; 4 May 1932; 5 October 1933; 9, 11, 19 and 20 April 1934; 16 June 1934; 10, 11, 14, 20, 21, 22 and 31 July 1937; 10 and 26 August 1937; 1 April 1943; 7 July 1956; 23 July 1958; 13 September 1960; 20 May 1973; 16 January 1978; 2 and 3 April 1981; 6 March 1982; 13 May 1985; 9 January 1990; 30 October 1992; 4 January 1994; 28 April 2012)

Titusville Herald (19 July 1991)

Toronto Star (7 November 1923; 31 January 1924; 28 April 1924; 23 June 1924; 9, 15 and 28 July 1924; 9, 16 and 18 August 1924; 29 October 1924; 4 and 16 March 1925; 17 July 1925; 9 July 1932; 5 August 1932; 4 May 1945)

Washington Post (29 April 1924)

Western Gazette (21 July 1924)

Western Morning News (31 October 1939)

Winnipeg Evening Tribune (11 and 12 July 1924; 16 December 1924; 6 August 1925; 4 October 1940)

World Sports (January 1961)

Yorkshire Post (5 September 1939)

OTHER BOOKS CONSULTED

Abrahams, H., *Sportsgraph* (Young World, 1972)

Allen, F. L., *Only Yesterday: An Informal History of the 1920s* (Wiley, 1997)

Anon., *The Olympics, From Athens to Athens* (Weidenfeld, 2008)

Anon., *What is the Oxford Group?* (Oxford University Press, 1933)

Auden, W. H. and Isherwood, C., *Journey to a War* (Faber, 1939)

Begbie, H., *Life Changers* (Booksurge Publishing, 2009)

Benge, G. and Benge, J., *Eric Liddell: Something Greater than God* (YAM, 1998)

Broomhall, A. J., *Hudson Taylor and China's Open Century* (Hodder, 1982)

Brown, G., *Wartime Courage* (Bloomsbury, 2008)

Bruce, J. W. G., *Birds in the Fowlers' Net* (privately published, 1985)

Caughey, E., *Eric Liddell: Gold Medal Missionary* (Barbour Publishing, 2000)

Chang, I., *The Rape of Nanking* (Basic Books, 1997)

Chang, J. and Halliday, J., *Mao: The Unknown Story* (Knopf, 2005)

Chapman, J., *Past and Present: National Identity and the British Historical Film* (I. B. Tauris, 2005)

Craigh, W., *The Fall of Japan* (Dial Press, 1967)

Dobbs, B., *Edwardians at Play* (Pelham, 1973)

Dyreson, M., *Making the American Team: Sport, Culture and the Olympic Experience* (University of Illinois Press, 1997)

Feldon, M., *Children of the Camps* (Pen and Sword, 2011)

Fleming, P., *News from Tartary* (Cape, 1936)

Fleming, P., *To Peking* (Tauris Parke, 2009)

Gibson, M. R., *An Intrepid Woman: The Odyssey of Dorothy McLorn* (Matador, 2009)

Gilbert, M., *Churchill: A Life* (Heinemann, 1991)

Goldsmith, E., *God Can Be Trusted* (OM, 1984)

The Guide to Track and Field Literature, 1275–1968 (Athletics Arena, 1969)

Gunther, J., *Inside Asia* (Hamish Hamilton, 1939)

Gunther, J., *Procession* (Harper & Row, 1965)

Hanson, A. J., *Expatriate Paris* (Arcade, 2012)

Hulme, D. C., *Tientsin* (Iumix, 2002)

Jocelyn, E. and McEwan, A., *The Long March* (Constable, 2006)

Jones, E. S., *The Christ of the Mount* (Hodder, 1931)

Kerr, D. and Kuehn, J. (eds), *A Century of Travels in China* (Hong Kong University Press, 2007)

Landon, C., *Classic Moments of Athletes* (Moorland Publishing, 1982)

Lean, G., *Frank Buchman: A Life* (Constable, 1985)

Leck, G., *The Japanese Internment of Allied Civilians in China and Hong Kong, 1941–45* (Shandy Press, 2006)

Lovesey, P., *The Official History of the AAA* (Guinness, 1979)

Lucas, J., *1930s* (Harper Press, 1978)

Magnusson, S., *The Flying Scotsman* (Quartet, 1981)

Malcolm, K. T., *We Signed Away Our Lives* (InterVarsity Press, 1990)

Malies, J., *Sporting Doubles* (Robson, 1998)

Mead, R., *Churchill's Lions* (Spellmount, 1997)

Meyer, H. A., *Athletics by Members of the Achilles Club* (Dent, 1955)

Morgan, T., *FDR: A Biography* (Grafton, 1981)

Nicholson, A., *Among the Bohemians* (Viking, 2002)

Osborne, F., *Lilla's Feast* (Transworld, 2004)

Payton, J. and Spencer, B., *Champions in the Making* (Pelham, 1969)

Philip, R., *Scottish Sporting Legends* (Mainstream, 2012)

Philips, M. and Hadden, M., *Behind Stone Walls and Barbed Wire* (BMA, 1991)

Pugh, M., *We Danced All Night: A Social History of Britain Between the Wars* (Bodley Head, 2008)

Robler, J., *Henry Luce: His Life, Times and Fortune* (Macdonald, 1965)

Shearman, M., *Athletics* (publisher unknown, 1901)

Swift, Catherine, *Men of Faith: Eric Liddell* (Marshall Morgan and Scott, 1990)

Taylor, A. J. P., *The Oxford History of England, 1914–1945* (Oxford University Press, 1965)

Taylor, D. J., *On the Corinthian Spirit* (Yellow Jersey, 2006)

Taylor, H., *Early Years, Vol. 1* (CIM, 1911)

Taylor, J., *The Struggle for Modern China* (Harvard University Press, 2001)

Thompson, E. T. (ed.), *Theodore White at Large* (Pantheon, 1992)

Tuchman, B. W., *Sand Against the Wind: Sitwell and the American Experience in China 1911–45* (Macmillan, 1970)

Tyrer, N., *Stolen Childhoods* (Weidenfeld, 2011)

Walker, C., *A Legacy of Scots* (Mainstream, 1988)

Watkins, P., *Eric Liddell: Born to Run* (JM Books, 1993)

Williamson, D., *Chariots to China* (Goodwill, 1991)

Wilson, J., *Complete Surrender: A Biography of Eric Liddell* (Monarch, 2012)

Witt, R., *A Lifetime of Training for Just Ten Seconds* (Bloomsbury, 2012)

Wotherspoon, I., *The Scots and China* (CreateSpace, 2013)

Wright, G., *Olympic Greats* (Queen Anne Press, 1980)

Ziegler, P., *King Edward VIII* (Collins, 1990)

OTHER RADIO AND TV PROGRAMMES CONSULTED

Sporting Witness (BBC World Service, 2011); *The Real Chariots of Fire* (ITV1, 2012); *The Flying Scotsman* (BBC, 1984); BBC Radio Tweed: *Interview with Jenny Liddell; I Knew Eric Liddell* (drama, BBC, 1954); *Stories from History: Eric Liddell* (BBC, 1956); *The Story of Eric Liddell, Olympic Champion, Man of Courage* (DVD, Day of Discovery, 2011).

Index

Duncan Hamilton is the author of *Provided You Don't Kiss Me: 20 Years with Brian Clough*, which won the William Hill Sports Book of the Year for 2007. In 2009 he was awarded the William Hill again, for *Harold Larwood*, as well as winning the prestigious Wisden Book of the Year for 2009 and Biography of the Year at the 2010 British Sports Book Awards. He lives in the Yorkshire Dales.